To Bob & L,
Congrats on winning the
English championship in Iowa.
Here's wishing you continued success.

Bob Allen
2001 GRAND AMERICAN

MW01128104

"Shooter"

"Shooter"

An Autobiography

The Life and Times of Bob Allen

Additional copies of this book may be obtained directly from the author if desired.

Bob Allen
15229—215th Avenue
Spirit Lake, IA 51360

Voice: 712 336-2264
Fax: 712 336-2878
Email: sbask@lakescable.com

Dedication

It is with great pleasure that I dedicate this book
to the memory of Ruthie, my wife of forty years,
and to my three children and eight grandchildren.

CONTENTS

Introduction

Not everybody has the opportunity and the unique privilege of retrospectively looking at his lifetime after eighty-one years. Following, a serious car accident, I finally came to the realization that I am not immortal, and since I'm not buying any more green bananas, I decided to get cracking and dive into this autobiographical task.

This examination of my life, points out many people and events that helped mold me, in particular a pair of loving parents with high morals and ideals, a tremendous amount of Irish luck that positioned me in the right place at the right time, a loving wife and family who endured my building a business and shooting career along with tolerating the constant travel required, and last but certainly not least, my God who watched over me in war and peace.

In his book "The Greatest Generation," Tom Brokaw is referring to my generation. Experiences during World War II in the Army Air Corps, my tournament shooting career, a supportive family and varied business encounters, creates the framework for my story—a typical young man from Iowa, growing up in the greatest generation of all.

I realize that I am an extremely fortunate man and so very thankful that I am now able to reminisce my many adventures for my friends and especially for my children and grandchildren. My hope is that you will have many laughs and perhaps a few guffaws on my behalf.

Bob Allen

Chapter 1

Shooting Became My Life

It was 1945, I was 25 years old, and had made it through to the signing of the peace of World War II—alive!

Now stationed at our headquarters on Guam, I was the Gunnery Officer for the entire 20th Air Force and my Commanding Officer was General "The Cigar" LeMay. Under my jurisdiction were several skeet ranges, as well as an ammunition dump containing a half-million shotgun shells and a million targets. With the war over all of the munitions were being disposed of by loading them on ships and bulldozing them into the sea. After spending a year on Tinian and Guam, as a gunnery officer, and with aspirations of making my living in the competitive shooting world, I concentrated my last four months overseas practicing my skills with great intensity. The task at hand, I decided, was to shoot up all the ammo before it could be destroyed. With a few of my friends, we began racing against the bulldozing clock by spending the whole day, everyday, at the skeet range. "Practice makes perfect!" we always said and shooting perfect scores became instinctual and an easy standard.

We became so good that we thought nothing of shooting several hundred targets a day—*straight*. It even became boring to shoot so well. To break the monotony we invented a competitive game called, "Monkey Skeet." The lead man would hold his gun in some unorthodox fashion, like behind his back, and then each competing shooter would have to mimic the leader's innovative technique. We invented some really wild monkey-positions, including holding the gun left handed, upside down, on the top of our heads, from the hip, and even between our legs. By virtue of the competitiveness and daily practice some of us could break every target just as well in our *monkey* game as we could in regular competition.

As you can imagine, before leaving for home I was cocky-as-hell about my shooting and ready to *take on the world!* The big shooting money was in the live-pigeon tournaments of Europe, so, I decided to start my post war career by taking on something *small;* like challenging the top shooters of the world in the renowned pigeon ring at Monte Carlo.

After arriving home from my tour in the Pacific, I spent most of the next year building my shooting-clothing business. At that time, there were no special clothes made for shooters other than a shooting-sweater, and nothing was manufactured to wear in hot weather, so I decided to begin with designing the first shooting vest; and I guess it was a pretty good piece of merchandise that retailed for $5.95, because my friend Homer Clark, the great shooting World Champion, wore the first vest he purchased from me from 1947 till 1998 when he passed away. I peddled my wares at a number of trap, skeet and pigeon shoots while I was also shooting competitively to maintain my prowess and make a little money.

Boy, was I pumped up about my skill level, while in the back of my mind, I spent every spare moment planning my first European trip to compete for the big prize money. My self-assurance was heightened further by the peculiar beliefs I held about my competitor's abilities. During the war we had been fed a lot of propaganda about our enemies, so I knew that the Japs couldn't shoot because they all had *bad eyes,* the Italians lacked *ambition and ability,* and the Germans had no *hunting experience;* therefore, the American pioneering background made us superior in all the shooting sports. I was soon to find out the fallacy of my brainwashed mind! Not only were the Europeans great sportsmen, they had a big advantage over Americans because shooting live pigeons was their game. Live pigeon shooting in the United States had been frowned upon for years and was illegal in many states. Most Americans, like myself, only had experience in shooting mild-mannered *clay* pigeons. Believe me, there is a hell-of-a-difference between a wild pigeon having had its tail feathers cut at a 45-degree angle just before being placed in a trap-box and a docile, predictable clay pigeon!

At this point I wasn't too long on finances, so it was quite a challenge to raise enough money for this important European trip. The round-trip airline ticket was quite expensive, plus I needed other travel expense money. The shooting entry fees didn't worry me too much, because I was so cocky, I knew I would begin winning from day one!

It was 1947, and we were a contingency of American shooters, traveling overseas together but competing individually. Our first stop was the renowned Monte Carlo competition where we stayed in the DeParis Hotel, a five star establishment. The shooting club was built-out, on a platform, over looking the Mediterranean, and part of the famed Monte Carlo Casino. To get to the pigeon ring, you went through the casino, over a walkway bridge and then into an elevator tower that took you down into the gun club. On the top floor of this magnificent shooting club was a five star restaurant. The next floor down was reserved for the gamblers, gambling being such a big part of this European shooting sport. The next floor down was for the shooters and the level below it was designated for the armory where all the guns and ammunitions were secured. The club was torn down in the late sixties and the big Loews Hotel is now in its place.

Attending the gun club during the February/March shooting season was the fashionable thing to do in Monte Carlo for both residents and visitors. Most people came for lunch and spent the whole day gambling on the shooting events or as spectators. European pigeon shooting was and to some extent still is a "gentleman's" sport. Shooters were expected to wear a coat and tie, and to act with great dignity and sportsmanship. (A far cry from American shoots where

Monte Carlo Scene. Pigeon Ring is bridge-like structure jutting out over sea.

Gun Club at Monte Carlo with Casino Towers directly behind.

the average shooter is dressed in blue jeans, a T-shirt and sneakers.)

Now allow me to set the scene into which my cocky-self would show the Europeans how it is done. The pigeons used were called "Zuritos," named after the family that became celebrated for breeding pigeons specifically for the sport. Their birds are similar to our barn pigeons except they are all the same slate gray color, approximately the same age, and the same size. At most European Clubs the pigeon handlers have jobs that are handed down through several generations and they are expert at judging the performance of pigeons. Before the pigeons are place in the crates for the day's shoot, they are run through a ring to determine a consistent size. Any bird that is too big for the ring is set aside as is one that slips through it too easily. Birds that appear sick or with ruffled feathers are also set aside. These eliminated birds are used for shooting practice. I learned real early in the game to not feel too cocky about scoring several practice birds. I knew I was just shooting at what are called "scrubs" and that when the real race began the first team birds coming out of the trap would be quite a challenge.

The pigeon ring is a parachute shaped arena surrounded by a fence, thirty inches high. The birds are released from metal trap boxes, about twelve inches square, with spring-loaded hinges. When the front side of the box is electronically released, all four sides of the box literally explode open making a loud "clang" as they flatten out against the metal base. To make sure the bird would fly, an eighteen-inch arm with a small wooden ball on the end extending up from the side of the trap at a 45-degree angle, would fall when the trap opened causing the ball to roll into the trap base frightening the bird to fly if it was just sitting. It really wasn't necessary as birds rarely sat and if they did they were declared a "no bird" by the referee and the shooter would call for a new pigeon.

The shooter stood on a sidewalk, with lines indicating the handicap from 25 to 34 meters. He faced a line of five trap boxes mounted on the ground and arranged in a slight semicircle, about five yards apart. When facing this line of traps, with your gun at your shoulder and your cheek resting against the stock, it was difficult for your peripheral vision to take in all five boxes. The two end boxes, #1 and #5 were just a bit fuzzy. The shooter has two shells in his gun, he calls out to alert the puller of the traps; "trapper ready?" who in turn listens for the shooter to call out "pull" when he wants the bird released. With a push of a button, an electronic device selects one of the five boxes and when the box opens, the shooter must drop the bird inside the boundary fence. A pigeon handler immediately retrieves the dead bird and any bird that can be retrieved inside the fence is considered dead and counts as a score. Many birds are shot inside the fence but the wind or their momentum carries them outside the fence where they are scored as "lost!" It always seemed to me that the referee took a fiendish delight in calling out *lost*.

Each day of the tournament was devoted to a different shooting event. Almost half of the daily events were handicapped. This meant that each shooter was assigned a yardage from which to shoot based on his reputation and ability. In my case, being a new shooter to the European circuit, I was taken into the manager's office of the shooting club to be assigned my handicap. Handicaps ranged from 25 meters to a maximum of 34 meters.

An American friend of mine, Ben Gallagher, (who married a French girl and remained in France after the war) was the interpreter for the American shooters. He accompanied me into the club manager's office. Monsieur Callens looked up from his desk then sat back in his chair, arms crossed over his big fat belly, looked me over very carefully, and then barked out something in French. With a strange look on Ben's face he translated. To my astonishment, Callens had assigned me a *32-meter* handicap! (My cocky attitude must have been showing.) It was unheard of for new and unknown shooters to be given this extremely long handicap. Here I found myself with the somewhat dubious honor of shooting *behind* the top, hotshot shooters of the world. There were only three or four shooters, I could think of, at that moment who held handicaps of 32 to 34 meters.

With great distress and puzzlement, I asked why he gave me this outrageously long handicap. Ben translated Callen's words "I can tell he is a good shooter because he has *dead eyes*." (This coming from a fat, little beady eyed Frenchmen). Apparently, my *new found* fan, Monsieur Callens, had read something about *Dead Eye Dick!* Dead eyes indeed! Through out the competition, I would learn that the French were always rougher on the Americans. Did they forget so soon that we Americans saved their rear-ends in the war?

Not only was I irritated about the long handicap; I also felt insulted because everybody in the past had always admired my *pretty, blue eyes*. In spite of my objections and consternation the handicap stood, but fortunately, not all the events were handicaps. More than half, including the Championship Of The World were shot from a fixed distance of 27 meters.

Enthusiastically, I launched into the first day of shooting with in a 27 meter, *miss-and-out* event. This means that the 400 shooters who entered this race would take turns, each shooting one bird, and if they missed that one bird they were eliminated from the competition. When the referee shouted, "lost!" he was not only referring to your *bird* but also to your entry fee. As you can imagine, there was lots of waiting around between your turns to shoot, a lot of time to become anxious!

This is the toughest part about the shooting game. In golf, you have fewer people to beat and if you make a mistake you can feasibly get back into the game with brilliant after play. Not so in shooting. You make one mistake, miss one bird and you're out! We were competing with 400 or more shooters each day. Today, at the Grand American National Championship Trapshoot in Dayton, Ohio, one shoots against, would you believe, 5,000 other shooters. The "Grand American" is the largest, individual participant, sports event, in the world! In what other sport would you have to beat 5,000 people to win?

They only had one pigeon ring in Monte Carlo which meant there was no opportunity for practice. You walked out to the firing line cold turkey, in front of several hundred spectators and screaming gamblers, without any chance to warm up. My turn came that first day and wow, the adrenaline really started pumping! The ring was built up on a platform about

100 feet above the Mediterranean facing south. The brilliant sun made a glare on the water that was almost blinding. If one had the bad luck to draw a pigeon that flew into this glare it was impossible to see the bird. Of course, I drew such a bird and promptly missed my first shot in the sun's blaze. And, this loss was from 27 meters, not the imposed handicap of 32 meters. I was not alone however; over 50 shooters missed their first bird that day. Still, this did not salve my deflated ego. I was eliminated from the day's race, and I lost my entry fee of *100 dollars,* really big money for me in 1947, the equivalent to about, 500 dollars today.

All I could do was sit around and watch the other shooters. I went back to my hotel resolved to do better the next day. The next day came and I murdered my first bird. Now, I was off and running. But, the second bird eluded me, so I was out once again sitting and watching with another one hundred dollar fee, down the drain. The third day, I missed the first bird again! Now, I was about out of entry fee money, plus my confidence level had been thoroughly eroded. In my egotistical mind, it was unquestionable that by now I'd be winning enough money—surely enough for the entry fees—so, my poor performance was a real blow to my psyche. I had one of two choices; cash in my return airline ticket for new entry fee money, and take the risk of not getting home for a while, or abandon my dreams—tuck my tail between my legs—and push off for home. But then, my good friend and companion, Joe Hiestand; one of America's greatest trap shooters (who was also shooting badly) came along and rationalized that we were both under too much pressure from this new style of shooting pigeons and suggested we take a few days off to cleanse and calm our minds. So after missing-out for three days we went back to the hotel and spent the afternoon playing gin rummy on a verandah overlooking the Mediterranean. We proceeded to get about half smashed, which only took about four drinks in the heat of the sun, and then our poor shooting performance ceased to baffle and torment us.

For the next two days we toured the countryside and played golf. Then, with our confidence renewed, we went back to the gun club. Joe advanced me enough money for that day's entry fees. We didn't win big, that first day back, but we did kill enough birds to be in the money division, and to earn the entry fees necessary for several days of competing. I won a considerable amount of money in the events that followed; enough money that enabled me to return home by *air* instead of a *slow boat,* and enough money to help me finance the start of my Bob Allen Sportswear business. I will always be grateful to Joe Hiestand for his advice and kindness. If it were not for Joe's intervention, who knows where I would be today. We remain good friends and enjoy reminiscing about those good old, Monte Carlo days.

I went back to Europe to shoot in 1949, 1950, and 1951. On February 11th of 1950, while shooting in San Remo, Italy I won an event named the Prix de St. Roman by killing only five pigeons straight. There were about 400 entries so this score gives you an idea of how tough the birds were. There was a thirty-knot wind blowing across the pigeon ring from right to left. Because the ring was built up over the Mediterranean about a hundred feet we were really out in the wind. It blew so hard it almost blew you off your feet when you raised your gun to shoot. Over half of the shooters missed their first bird most of them having been killed but carried outside the fence by the wind. At the end of two birds, there were only about sixty shooters left straight, and by the time we went out to shoot the 5th bird, there were only seven of us. I was the only one of the seven who killed so I won the Championship. It is hard to believe that birds could be that hard but they were. What saved me was that I was an unusually fast shot and usually killed my birds before the wind had a chance to play with them.

The most outstanding year was 1951 when I shot on the American Team, consisting of Joe Hiestand, Homer Clark, Earl Roth and myself. Our group did not have enough funds for the trip until a wealthy Cincinnati sponsor and shooting enthusiast stepped forward, Bill Mashburn, a Coca Cola magnate. As a result of his generosity, we all took off for Monte Carlo and the Championship Of The World in grand style. The Federal Cartridge Company made special ammunition for our team and I designed and manufactured distinctive shooting

U.S. Team in the Match of Nations, Monte Carlo, 1951. L to R: Bob Allen, Homer Clark, Joe Hiestand, Earl Roth.

uniforms. We were, without a doubt, the sharpest looking team at the Championship Of The World.

Unlike the usual miss-and-out events in Europe, the Championship Of The World is a 25 pigeon event. With an entry list of over 600 shooters, the elimination process took three days. Each shooter would shoot three or four birds per day. By the end of the first day many had missed their first three birds and the rule was and still is, three strikes and you're out! By the end of the second day, three quarters of the entry list was eliminated. This meant that if you were still in the race you could finish up your 25 birds on the third day.

When the smoke cleared at the end of the event,
➤Homer Clark tied for 1st place with a 24,
➤Bob Allen tied for 2nd place with a 23 and
➤Joe Hiestand tied for 3rd place with a 22.

I had missed my first bird somewhere in the first ten shots. And, I will never forget, as long as I live, the feeling in my stomach when I missed that 24th bird which knocked me out of the first-place-tie shoot-off. The difference between winning and losing can be very small. With the wind blowing across the ring, I watched shooter after shooter lose birds coming out of the first and second traps, birds that fell outside the fence, even though they had been shot perfectly. As an example, Earl Roth, one of the world's fastest shots, shot both barrels perfectly at his last bird coming out of the number one trap, but the wind carried the dead bird almost horizontally across the ring and bounced it out of the fence; really bad luck for Earl.

Watching this wind, I prepared to enter the shooters' box for my twenty-fourth bird. When I walked out to shoot the noise from the gambling level was resounding because I was one of the favorites to win. I calculated in my mind that instead of holding in the center of the trap line, as normally one would do, I would hold near the downwind #1 trap. Then I'd be in position to get on that bird fast enough to kill it inside the ring. Risking this however meant that my peripheral vision did not clearly take in trap #5 to the right. So, guess what happened? I called pull and the number #5 *trap* opened but at first I didn't see it. I swung the gun from trap #1 to #5 while this bird was almost standing still, bucking the wind above the trap. I said to myself, "I can see it!" By swinging my gun from left to right so fast, I swung by the bird and missed the first shot, the bird then turned with the wind and although I centered it with my second barrel, I watched the wind carry it outside the fence. When they called "lost" there was bedlam in the gamblers gallery; lots of money was lost including mine.

I have always felt that if I had killed this bird and been in the shoot-off with Homer and Luigi, odds are that any *third* shooter would not have also missed *three* birds like Homer and Luigi missed. Homer Clark went on to shoot off with a sixteen year old, Italian boy, Luigi Ongari. To win the Championship Of The World, one must shoot five birds and if the score is still tied, the race moves to a *sudden death,* miss-and-out round.

Shooting off like this was very exciting because the pigeon handlers select and release the most fierce birds. And, on this last day with this tremendous wind blowing, right to left, across the pigeon ring, it sometimes blew shooters off balance. The birds would tip up and out of the trap in a twenty-five-knot cross wind and even if the shooter centered the target with both barrels, the bird would often drift, falling stone dead outside the ring's fence—for a miss!

To everyone's astonishment both finalists missed three birds out of five and were now tied going into the *miss-and-out* phase of the race. Under tremendous pressure and with the gamblers creating bedlam, Luigi missed his second bird. Homer Clark became the very first American winner of the Championship Of The World, and I was thrilled for my friend and happily took second. They ran up the American flag and played our National Anthem. Boy! It was a proud moment for all of us.

The Match Of Nations

The most exciting event during the annual Championship Of The World was and still is the "Match Of Nations." This is an event where teams from over a dozen countries enter. A four-man team representing each country shoots a twelve-bird match to determine the winner. This would be the year we Americans swept this event for the very first time in history.

The event drew a full house of spectators and gamblers, and was considered in the eyes of the Americans, the "Olympics" of shooting. We were not allowed to compete in the world recognized Olympics because of a man by the name of Averill Brundadge who controlled the US Olympic teams during the 1940's. He was a stickler for disqualifying any athlete who had ever touched any competitive prize money. This eliminated our best shooters from the World-wide Olympic games, because all American shooting competition was for prize money. Changes have been made in the Olympic rules over the years and today our Olympic Team is made up of really talented men and women shooters. However, during those times, our greatest shooters were excluded from ever representing our country, and so the Match Of Nations was the closest thing to being an Olympiad for an American shooter.

Our team was outstanding in the Match Of Nations and was favored to win among the gamblers for many reasons. First, our Homer Clark was the new Champion Of The World. Second, Joe Hiestand and myself and Earl Roth had placed second, third, and fourth in the Championship Of The World. And, last, I would like to think, we really attracted the favored attention of the gamblers with the special shooting coats I designed and manufactured for the team. No other country was dressed in a team uniform; we looked really put together.

At the end of the twelve-bird match, our team emerged the winner with a score of forty-five pigeons out of forty-eight; as a team we had missed only three birds. The enthusiasm of the gamblers and crowd made for a thrilling event that took most of the afternoon. When we were declared the winners, we were escorted to the front of the clubhouse for the presentation of our team trophy and individual gold medals. What a thrill it was to see three beautiful American flags raised and our National Anthem played once more! (The first time for Homer winning the Championship Of The World, and now, a day later, for the Match Of Nations.)

Homer Clark won the Championship Of The World, I won second place, Joe Hiestand won third place and now Joe won the Match Of Nations. Afterwards, our team would celebrate by buying champagne for all the contestants, as is the custom in Europe.

Shooting as a team for the first time and representing our country was a deeply emotional experience and totally divergent from the usual dog-eat-dog, fierce competition among this group of Americans. Here, we had to pull together to beat eleven other countries. I've won many other shooting honors but this one will always stand out in my memory as the proudest moment because I was shooting for my team and country - not just for myself.

If you can win "the" shooting event of the year in Europe you are a sports celebrity, much like a bullfighter in Spain. Wherever we went into restaurants, hotels, etc., we were treated royally. Of course, this was wonderful publicity for my fledgling shooting clothing business.

The only down side to our winning was that according to

custom, we were politely informed, the winning team had to buy Champagne for all the other contestants. We should have counted the corks because we were either cheated by the gun club's accounting or the shooters were surely lushes who almost drank up all our winnings.

All told, for six weeks of shooting in Europe, each individual American came home with some pretty exciting cash winnings. Bill Mashburn, our benefactor and team manager, was overjoyed! The team he had made possible greatly exceeded his expectations. As we headed back to the United States we were all on a *high* never experienced before — talk about being on the "Top of the World!"

During the shoot, I had taken several hundred feet of 16MM film. When the film was developed and shown for the first time, people found them so interesting, I decided to hire a film producer to edit them, chose background music, and hired Jim Zabel, Des Moines' leading TV Radio announcer, to do the narration. For a year after the shoot, I traveled around the country showing the film and giving lectures. I have since turned the film into a videotape and it is fun to watch and relive those glorious days.

After my successes in Europe, I knew that shooting, manufacturing sportswear and traveling the competitive circuit would become my life's work. I sensed I was in the right place at the right time. Often, I would think back to all the events and people that created meaningful turning points in my life, turning points that brought me to this place.

Chapter 2

Back to My Beginnings

My Dad ~ Martin James Allen

It all began when my dad, Martin James Allen, born in 1886, came to Canada from Innishannon, County Cork, Ireland. He was a small, young man with brown hair, gray eyes, and one most outstanding feature: his Irish heritage. My dad was so very proud of his roots that he named me in honor of the great Irish patriot, Robert Emmett, who starved himself to death in a British prison rather than submit to British rule.

In the town square of Emmetsburg, Iowa, a predominately Irish and Catholic community, a life-size statue of Robert Emmett proudly stands. Whenever we drive through Emmetsburg, I order my children and grandchildren to get out of the car, stand at attention, and salute the bronze embodiment of Robert Emmett.

Unfortunately, I know very little about my dad's life growing up in Ireland; he didn't talk much about his past. What I do know is that his family was very proud, very religious, and very poor. I wish I knew more to pass on to my grandchildren, about their great-grandfather. This is why I am

My Dad, Martin J. Allen.

writing my story now, so that my children will not be saying the same thing about me years from now.

What I do know about my dad, Martin James Allen, is that in 1906 at the age of 19, he had the courage to sail to Canada on an ocean liner, named the *Lusitania*. Yes! The same ship that became famous when a German submarine sank her at the beginning of World War I. Imagine if you will, the strength and the pioneering courage it took for a very young lad to break all ties and leave for a strange country across the vast Atlantic Ocean about one hundred years ago.

My father was a poor man who traveled to the land of opportunity in steerage, like the rest of the poor Irish. Steerage of course was in the bowels of the ship where there were no individual rooms for people, but where people lived and slept together for over a week, in one great mass. Why dad was prompted to leave Ireland I really never discovered. It's funny how we don't get around to asking our parents the whys and wherefores. I surmised that he had some friends who had immigrated before him and the adventure was too much to resist.

The *Lusitania* docked in Montreal, Canada, and Martin stepped off to immediately begin looking for a job. Back in Ireland, at about fifteen or sixteen years old, Martin James had worked as a counter assistant for a wholesale drug company in the city of Cork. When he decided to immigrate to Canada, his employer wrote what I think is a classic letter of recommendation for Ireland at that time. Notice the phrase: honest, *sober*, and willing—apparently in 1906 Ireland being a sober employee was very important.

The letter of recommendation came from the firm of Baker & Wright located on Patrick Street, City of Cork, dated Feb. 17, 1906.

> *Martin Allen was with us about three and a half years as counter assistant during which time we found him strictly honest, sober and willing. He now leaves at his own request and with our very best wishes for his future success. We shall be very glad to speak for him.*
>
> Signed: *Parker Wright*

As fate would have it, Martin's first job would become his lifetime profession. It was a piano factory in which he very astutely perceived that the highest paid job was in tuning the pianos, not on the assembly line. He learned quickly how to "tune" and shortly thereafter went out on his own, tuning pianos across Canada.

Dad Going West

Dad bought a motorcycle, and for whatever reason that inspired him, took off for Winnipeg. A motorcycle could not have been much of a vehicle at that time, and in 1915 the roads probably were non-existent. Once again, quite courageously, Martin ventured out on his own, determined to tune pianos straight to Winnipeg, and on a motorcycle! I'm not sure if the saying, "Go west young man!" existed then, but something motivated him to go west. All I can think is, "you were really an adventurer Martin James Allen!" What determination! The trip was the equivalent of driving from New York City to Omaha, Nebraska, over 1,400 miles on dirt roads or gravel if he was lucky. Oh! How I wish I knew the details of his journey and all the interesting people and places he must have encountered.

However, his vision was thwarted by the dreadfully cold winters in Winnipeg, so he decided to move south (meaning the United States) first staying in Minneapolis, Minnesota for a short time and then moving on again because the weather was still too bitter. He had friends who immigrated to a town in Northwest Iowa known as Emmetsburg, and decided to join them in this 99% Irish-Catholic town. From Emmetsburg, dad continued to *tune* around the Iowa countryside on his cycle. And, as fate would have it, on a farm near Barnum, Iowa, while *tuning* he met Anna Dwyer, who he soon would ask to be his bride.

Anna Marie Dwyer; Mother

Anna's grandparents immigrated to Iowa from New York State and homesteaded the land that became a 180-acre farm near Barnum, Iowa. Anna's mother's family name was "Moore" and Anna's father's original family name was "O'Dwyer" The family dropped the "O" as many Irish people did when the family moved from New York. The farm was typical for those times with yearly crops alternating between corn and oats. So, half of my ancestors were farmers, who kept chickens for eggs, cows for milk and hogs for market.

My mother, Anna Dwyer, was a very beautiful young woman with dark curly hair when she married Martin James Allen. Martin had plenty of competition in securing Anna's hand, but must have won out because of his very handsome face and his captivating Irish brogue.

Shortly after my parents were married they moved to Fort Dodge, Iowa, where dad opened a piano store, a one-man operation whose earnings were supplemented by his continuing to travel around tuning pianos.

My Mother, Anna.

Mother's Dad; My Granddad—Edward Dwyer

Most of mother's childhood was spent without a father or a mother. On August 29, 1889, her father, Edward Dwyer, came to a tragic death. He was in the town of Barnum with a wagon and a team of horses to pick up a load of lumber. Edward and his son had just finished loading the wagon when the horses became frightened and unmanageable. He ran to the horses' heads to control them. Their frightened rearing and plunging continued and he was dragged from his feet, lost his hold and unable to retain his balance was thrown right into the path of the wheels. The horses, released from restraint, started off in a mad gallop, pulling the wheels of the heavily loaded wagon over him, killing him instantly; before the eyes of his horrified and helpless son. My grandmother never fully recovered from this tragedy and passed away a few years later leaving my mother and her siblings, Josie, Alice and Edward, to be raised by their oldest brother Jim.

So, I never did know my grandparents on either dad or mother's side. Josie passed away before I was born and Edward became a Fort Dodge policeman whose life was lost in the line of duty, also before I was born. Aunt Alice and Uncle Jim were the only relatives I knew growing up. Jim continued to live on the family homestead that was located just seven miles west of Fort Dodge. He and his wife Rose (maiden name Burgfried) never had any children, so I think Uncle Jim really enjoyed having me come out to the farm for seasonal visits and because he was my closest male relative I looked to him as my grandfather.

Uncle Jim Dwyer; My surrogate Granddad

This was back in the days before big tractors, so Jim farmed with eight huge teams of beautiful workhorses, all of whom had names they answered to like Jack, Bill, Charley, George and Jim. I can remember being on the farm in the spring when it was cultivating time for the newly-planted corn. In the 1920's and 1930's they didn't use weed-killing chemicals so cornrows had to be gently cultivated on a regular basis to keep weeds down. Jim's horses were so well trained that they would make the turn at the end of the field and start down the new rows without harming a single hill of corn. It was a real treat to see Uncle Jim and the team come into the barnyard after a morning of cultivating. He would remove all the harnesses and turn the horses loose, and like kids out of school they'd gallop around the yard, roll on their backs and head for the water tank. In the meantime, Jim pushed hay down from the hayloft into their stalls so that when they finished frolicking around they'd find their feast waiting. I could tell he really loved those horses and took good care of them. His example taught me at an early age that having animals is a responsibility that must be met.

Then Jim's routine was to eat his dinner. (Iowa farmers called noon lunch "dinner" and dinner as we know it was "supper") After eating heartily he would lie down on a sofa near the kitchen, light up his pipe; and after enjoying his smoke, take a one-hour siesta. Then, it was out to the barn, harness up a fresh team of workhorses and off to the fields until late afternoon.

Discovering My British Roots

After my dad had passed away I found through some research, I'm sure to my dad's chagrin, some disturbing facts about my ancestry. From a cousin Martin Daly and his wife Peg who lived in England, I discovered that my grandfather was in the British Army and probably met my grandmother, a very Irish Mary Murphy, while stationed in County Cork, Ireland. At that time the British had many troops in Ireland and this is one of the many reasons the Irish have historically hated the British. From my dad's telling, his father was sent to Africa to fight in the Boer War but he never added that grandfather was a British soldier. When he returned to Ireland, grandfather had some sort of fever and died soon after. My grandmother, Mary Murphy Allen, evidently returned to her birthplace, Innishannon, County Cork, Ireland, carrying her children (my dad and his sister) back to her home place. She died soon after returning, leaving my dad to be raised by his older sister, Jennie, and probably others in the Murphy family.

Dad's Claustrophobia

Dad talked very little about his youth, but he did recount to me a story about attending a Catholic school in his hometown of Innishannon that was taught by Monks. The Monks inflicted inhumane punishment on all their students for the slightest infraction of their rules. Dad was punished by being forced to lie down on a shelf in *the dreaded bookcase,* and the doors, which had no windows, were closed; he would be left in this dark and cramped space for an inordinate amount of time. To his dying day, dad suffered from extreme claustrophobia brought on by this cruel childhood experience. Suffering claustrophobia myself, I have deep emotional feelings for my dad's suffering.

Dear and beautiful Ireland and the *good* memories, however, were always on Dad's mind and he talked about wanting to go back for a visit. It was a standing joke in our family that when we gave Dad a nice present of clothing, instead of wearing it, he would put it in a particular dresser drawer where he was saving special items for his trip back to Ireland. As fate would have it he did not make this trip until the 1960's. But this time he traveled first class on the Mauretania.

He stayed about one month and although he enjoyed being with his sister and her children he was shocked at how primitive life remained in Ireland. As an example, only one room in his sister's house had electricity, they burned peat in an open stove for warmth, and most of the rooms in the house had the same dirt floors Dad remembered as a boy. He was happy to return to the comparative life of luxury in Iowa. Dad never talked about going back to Ireland again!

John L. Sullivan

In many ways my dad was a real character! He was just a little guy; according to his naturalization certificate he was 5'5" tall, weighed 150 pounds. Like most Irishmen he was a feisty little fellow and when angered was someone to be reckoned with. I remember one humorous incident that involved a new next-door neighbor in Fort Dodge. The husband in the house next door was a six-foot guy who weighed about two hundred pounds. From the time they moved in he was always complaining about something or other and for some reason I, being seven years old, was always the brunt of the complaint.

This time it had something to do with me running on his lawn to retrieve a ball and he came out and threatened me with disaster if I ever set foot in his yard again. For my Dad, this was the last straw! He came out of our house, strode across the neighbor's yard, banged on the door with his fist, and when this giant man appeared filling the opening, Dad assumed a John L. Sullivan fighting pose (fists up in front of his face, legs apart in a brace) and then, in his best Irish brogue, Dad told this guy that if he wanted to fight someone, to come right ahead! My mother was horrified and I was scared to death for my Dad's life but the next-door-neighbor backed down and from then on we had peace in the neighborhood. Boy! Was I proud of my Dad!

Our Family Moves to California

When I was about six or seven years old, mother started to develop some health problems. It was common for doctors in those days to recommend a warmer climate if they couldn't think of any other way to treat the patient. That was the reason for our move to California.

The house on 13th Street was sold and the whole family was packed into a Nash Ajax 8 Sedan and we headed west. One of the most crushing incidents I remember as a child was an attachment I made to a small valise that I packed very carefully with all my little toys and treasures for the trip. There wasn't much luggage space in the old Nash so at the very last minute my precious little case was taken away from me and left behind. It took me months to get over this loss. I'm sure my folks did not understand the importance of that bag to me or they surely would have made a place for my treasured possessions.

I don't remember too much about the trip except that it was long and tiring all on gravel or dirt roads in clouds of dust, or we found ourselves stuck in mud. I think the trip took three weeks but have no recollection of where we slept at night. I do remember that we had terrible food! We first settled in Burbank, California because we had cousins there by the name of Hyde—my mother's sister Josie, her husband and family.

Uncle Mervin Hyde

My uncle Mervin Hyde had been in the home construction business in the Burbank area for several years and although Dad knew nothing about this business, Mervin talked Dad into learning by helping to build some new houses. It turned out that Dad had a good knack for managing the construction crews and he successfully built several houses. This probably could have launched him on a career that would have been more lucrative than the piano business but he wasn't too fond of working with Uncle Merv and besides, Dad was homesick for Iowa. At that time we lived in one of the new houses on a street that dead-ended against a wash. "Washes" are unique to California and are in a sense a dried up river bed or canal that functions to quickly drain large amounts of water from the mountains to the ocean in periods of heavy rainfall.

Mervin was building a couple of houses at the end of the street near the wash and as a consequence went by our house several times a day. Oh, did I mention that I had an intense dislike for Uncle Mervin? Perhaps he didn't understand children very well for he certainly didn't treat my sister and I well. One day, to get even with him, I placed a row of roofing nails, points up, across the road in front of our house. Please remember I'm only seven at this time. Mervin immediately had four flat tires! By the way, a few other cars got flat tires also; like my dad and several of our neighbors. I was discovered as the culprit and in addition to being paddled, but good, was grounded for a couple of long weeks.

I mentioned the wash earlier as it figured into the life of my sister and me at that time. Every day when we went to school we would walk up to the end of the street, walk down through the dry wash, and then straight to our school, just up on the other side of the wash. This saved a long walk had we gone to the bridge that crossed the wash. On one occasion, as we were walking down the steep side of the wash, we disturbed a very large rattlesnake that coiled up and rattled at us. We were naturally terrified and Anna Marie ran off screaming. And after seeing another rattler a few days later, we decided not to go through the wash anymore. All I could envision was my running home to tell my parents that my sister lay dying from snakebite at the bottom of the wash!

Across the street from our house was a big orange grove. The grove owner had a large water tower (75 feet tall) that provided water for irrigation. One day a little friend and I climbed up on the tower. It was okay going up but the first time we looked down we froze! We were too embarrassed to call for help so had to stay there for a couple of hours until we got used to the height and had courage to climb down. That cured any urges I had to climb for a long time and to this day, remains a vivid memory.

Brush fires were common in the mountains around Burbank. In fire emergencies men were literally conscripted off the streets to go fight the fires. I remember one that was so close and so fierce that burning debris was floating down the gutters in the street in front of our house.

I have a fairly vivid memory of another incident while living in Burbank, The folks took us to the rose bowl parade on New Years Day and we found a grassy place along the curb to watch that colorful event. By parade time I was one really sick little boy. It later turned out that I had the mumps on both sides and probably infected half the people at the parade. I can't remember anything at all about the parade.

The 5 and 10-Cent Store

I also remember shopping with my mother at the Woolworth 5 & 10-cent store in Burbank where I innocently picked up a miniature lead car. When my mother saw it upon our arrival home, she knew *she hadn't paid* for it, and immediately marched me back to the store where she made me give it to the store manager. He went along with her and gave me a stern lecture about stealing, needless to say, one I never forgot. This was about 1927 and I was seven years old. Many years later when my son Matt did the same thing, I smiled inside and immediately knew I would handle the situation just as my Mother had handled me.

Homesick for Iowa

Mother's health improved and because both she and Dad were disenchanted with California, they decided to head back to Iowa. So once again we packed up the Ajax 8 and headed back east. Dad took a different route this time hoping for better roads and time. As it turned out the route he chose was very mountainous and the Ajax 8 constantly heated up and boiled over. I remember we spent a couple of days in Bisbee,

Arizona for repairs. The roads in those days were terrible; you couldn't call them highways! Most were mud or gravel and you lived for days in a dust cloud. There was one stretch of paved road for about thirty miles near Phoenix, Arizona, but it was only paved on one side for one lane. There wasn't much traffic so you could stay on the paved half most of the time. With our Interstate system of today it is hard to imagine roads like those we encountered.

After several days we reached Vinita, Oklahoma and here, for reasons I never really understood, we stopped for about a year. This was the start of the Big Depression and Dad may have run out of money and needed to stop while he earned more by tuning pianos. At any rate we rented a house there and my sister and I were enrolled in a Catholic school, which was also a boarding school for wealthy American Indians. Most of the Indians came by their wealth from oil wells and I remember their parents coming to visit them driving big Cadillacs, LaSalles and Lincolns. The nuns were downright mean to my sister and me, while showing much favoritism to the Indians. The Indians were pretty mean too and during my first couple of weeks in the school I was beaten up a number of times. I remember one Indian who loved to beat me up for pure joy. Fortunately the year went by swiftly and we headed on to Iowa.

When we arrived home in Fort Dodge we moved into a house at 1528 Floral Avenue, which is still located at the north edge of Fort Dodge overlooking a beautiful valley with timber and Soldier Creek. These woods were to become my greatest joy.

The Big Depression

It was 1929, the Big Depression had just started, I was nine years old, and it was winter. An Arcola circulating hot water furnace provided the heat for our Floral Avenue house. The small furnace, which was located in a corner of our kitchen, heated water that was circulated through radiators in each room. It was very similar to a steam heating system except that it utilized hot water. This was before gas or oil heat so the furnace would burn anything from coal, to wood, to trash. Coal was too expensive but we had plenty of wood in the form of old player pianos and pump organs that people had traded in for pianos. My after-school job was to break up these pianos and organs into pieces small enough to go into the Arcola furnace. It was tough work because most of the frames and sounding boards were made of solid oak. You could swing an axe with all your might and it would hardly make a dent in that oak. We had no power saw so it was up to me to muscle the job as best I could. Once broken up, the oak was great fuel and would burn for hours. I'd try to stack up enough wood in the house for a full night and day.

I shudder to think of the thousands of dollars worth of player pianos and old pump organs that became victim to my axe. In today's antique market player pianos and those old pump organs are going for over a thousand dollars apiece. Anyone reading this who loves antiques is probably cringgggging.

During the Big Depression of the late 1920's and early 30's, there weren't too many people who could afford a piano so when we found a new prospect, they really received my parents' full attention. Dad's piano shop was a little twenty-five-foot by fifty-foot building adjacent to our home. He had rigged up a bell so that when a customer came into the shop, the door would trigger the bell to ring in the house. My sister and I were always in hysterics when the bell rang! In the dead of winter, Dad would need a coat, which he could never find and it would become a Chinese fire drill as Dad and Mother tried to get him dressed to trek to the shop which was about one hundred feet from the house. Then we'd all be praying that he was going to make the sale and waited anxiously for him to give us a full report on his return to the house. It was so funny but it was also darn serious, as our livelihood depended upon each and every sale.

Things were pretty rough economically in the late twenties. They really tightened up when Roosevelt became president in 1928. One of his first steps was to temporarily close all the banks and to freeze withdrawals until the government could get a handle on the country's economic problems.

History proved this to be a prudent step but at the time it was catastrophic for most people as the banks stayed closed for about a week—just imagine if that happened today!

At the same time my mother was having some serious health problems again, relating to her goiter. Dr. Kersten said surgery was needed immediately, but when Dad attempted to admit Mother to Mercy Hospital, they would not accept her because he couldn't pay in advance. (I think it is interesting that the hospital's name was Mercy.) With the banks closed Dad was in a bad position. He had money in the bank, owned some real estate, had his store but in spite of all this collateral, "Mercy" would not admit her. In desperation he went to the Monsignor at Corpus Christi Church who interceded and made it possible for mother to be admitted for her surgery. I was a happy little fellow when my mother came home from a successful operation. The most interesting part of this story is how we actually paid her hospital bill.

The Great Depression didn't allow people to purchase a new piano nor the luxury of Dad's professional piano tuning; you might say befittingly these times were—out of tune! However, Dad was very resourceful and if the customer could not pay cash Dad made arrangements to "tune" for chickens or vegetables or anything else the customer might offer. As a consequence, although we were poor in dollars, we ate very well. Dad's horse-trading was supplemented by a large vegetable garden we had in the back yard. Mother was great at canning and by fall each year she had our cyclone cellar full of all kinds of canned goods. Dad's bartering progressed to supply our menu with not only chickens, but also eggs from our own laying hens.

My job was to take care of the chickens Dad brought home. We had a large chicken house with beds for about 25 laying hens. Picture it: laying hens, a special hen house built with roosts and laying nests, and a small boy to clean out the smelly droppings each week. Yes! The most unpleasant job of my life was taking care of the chickens, and the only job I ever rebelled over. A chicken must be the dumbest critter God ever created! You can't teach a chicken, you can't herd them, and they don't have sense enough to come in out of the rain. The stench was absolutely revolting; it made me physically ill, and I was always on the verge of puking. Putting off this chore as long as possible became an art. Mother would badger me to get it done before Dad arrived home from the road. The smell still comes back to me as I visualize shoveling the foul mess into a wheelbarrow and dumping it over the hill, into the woods, behind our house. I've hated chickens ever since!

It was also my job to collect the eggs twice a week, package them up in my bicycle basket and deliver them to the back door of Mercy Hospital. The sister in charge of the kitchen would meet me at the door to receive the eggs, and mark them down in a special ledger so that credit could be applied to my mother's hospital bill. In this fashion her bill was finally paid off. Imagine what would happen today if you tried to pay a hospital in eggs—of course they wouldn't even consider the idea and even if they did our modern health laws would probably prohibit it.

Once when dad came from a bartering trip he carried home a little package for me. He opened the door of my room and with one, surprisingly swift motion placed a wee package on my lap; it was a tiny black puppy. He was just a little black spot that delighted everyone as he ran around the kitchen floor, and then mother laughingly said, "He looks like a little prune!" And, so "Prunes" became his name. He was my faithful dog for all my growing-up years. Prunes was my pal, my hunting buddy, my constant companion. He would lie at the edge of the front lawn until he saw me coming home from school. He would be bouncing on all fours, panting like crazy, but never stepping over the borderline of our property, until I called him to me. Then the dust would fly as he took off in my direction. My dog Prunes and I would head for the woods immediately after school or whenever my chores were done. The memory of Prunes still brings a warm smile to my face and heart—there is nothing quite like the unconditional love that a dog can give a boy. And there is no feeling quite like the pain of losing your boyhood buddy.

There were other ways Dad figured out how to turn his bartered goods into cash during the depression. Fort Dodge only had a few black families and they all lived in an area near the Illinois Central Railroad because most of them worked for the railroad. Dad knew they liked chickens so sometimes when he would come home with a couple crates of young chickens, he and I would take them to the black neighborhood and sell them. As I remember, about all we needed to do was to stop Dad's truck in the area and the people would come out of their houses to buy.

In connection with this I'd like to remark that the word "racism" never existed in Fort Dodge. The black kids were all in school with me and, if anything, were almost more popular than others because they were very bright, fun to be around, and the boys were almost all star athletes. Inter-racial dating was not done but in every other way there was complete equality.

Iowa Gangsters

1933 was the year of the gangsters. Spawned by the depression that had already begun, mobsters like Al Capone, Pretty Boy Floyd, John Dillenger, and Bonnie and Clyde were terrorizing the country and, because in most instances they were better armed than the police, they ran wild. As an example most of the gangsters were armed with the Thompson sub-machine gun while the police relied on pistols, rifles, and sawed-off shotguns—they were certainly outgunned! These desperadoes traveled around the country in big, fast, cars and seemed to be able to rob banks at will. I was thirteen years old and fascinated by the stories in the paper and on the radio. Rumors were flying and I remember one time when Dillenger was reportedly in Iowa and planning a robbery in my home-town of Fort Dodge.

It was almost hysteria as the town took the rumor seri-ously and actually prepared for his visit. The National Guard was called out and they set up checkpoints at all the roads leading into town. My folks' home was a block away from high-way 169 at the north edge of Fort Dodge. I remember riding my bicycle up to the top of the hill on #169 just opposite the Haviland apple orchard where the National Guard had mounted a .30 caliber machine gun on a tripod and there were six guardsmen all armed with .30 caliber rifles. They wouldn't let me hang around but I was suitably impressed. As it turned out, none of the gangsters bothered about Fort Dodge. However Bonnie and Clyde camped out near Dexter, Iowa about that time. Farmers heard a lot of shooting (they were doing target practice) and alerted the Sheriff who in turn called in the FBI. A trap was laid and, in the resulting gunfight, the famous pair and their car were shot up so badly they looked like sieves.

That was the beginning of the end for all the gangsters as the FBI intensified their efforts and gradually captured or killed all of them. John Dillenger was ambushed as he came out of a theater in Chicago and was shot full of holes. It was a colorful era and hearing about the gangster activities was exciting for a young boy growing up.

Mother, My Earliest Recollections

Being cuddled in mother's arms is my earliest recollection; she was always a safe retreat from any problems of my little world. Now that I summon up this memory, I realize that her open arms were always there for me, at any age. Like my dad, mother was a small person, probably about 5' 3". (Where I came from at 6' or my son Matt at 6' 3" and his two teenage daughters topping 5' 11" and still growing—I have no idea.) Mother lived for one purpose and one purpose only, our family! Hobbies or pastimes just were not part of her consciousness. Even her diary entries were short and to the point. Mother spent all her time fulfilling what she thought were her motherly duties for our family.

Growing up in the Great Depression, possessions were repaired not discarded. Evenings would find mother laboriously "darning" stockings by placing them over a wooden knob and meticulously re-weaving them to extend their life. The patched spot sometimes chafed against the inside of my shoe but I would never tell her so, because I thought it would hurt her feelings. Holes or worn out parts of trousers were cut out and carefully patched, matching the fabrics as closely as possible. Shoes were often fixed using glue-on rubber soles bought from the corner general store. Special glue came with the soles, but it never seemed to hold very well and I clearly remember wearing shoes that flopped and flapped at every step; I hated them and was ashamed to be wearing them because I thought everyone knew I had glued on soles.

Mother's specialty was baking! (Can you see me salivating as I write *mother* and *baking* in the same sentence?) Her pies, cakes, cookies, and homemade breads were, as my teenage granddaughters would say, "to die for!" I have fond recollections of coming home from school to a house full of the most incredible aroma from her baking. There was always a little scuffle as mother tried to keep me from eating the cookies as fast as they came out of the oven. One of my favorite addictions was mother's homemade bread. I'd take that hot, nurturing bread and smother it with butter and generous quantities of pure cane sugar. Wow! What a feast! To the delight of my children, I still enjoy this type of dessert, whether I'm in a fast food cafe or at the most posh restaurant. My delicious memories of mother's strawberry short cake have driven me to challenge my daughters to reproduce their grandmother's recipe; however they have been sadly not quite successful. Perhaps that is how it should be—never quite as good as the memory of our mother's.

We had a small garden in our back yard and the whole family worked at raising tomatoes, string beans, peas, carrots, radishes and lettuce. As the produce ripened, mother would begin canning the fruits and vegetables in "Kerr" jars; you know the ones with metal screw lids and rubber gaskets that created a perfect seal. The Kerr jars remain pleasantly in my recollection, as cherished as my Flexible Flyer sled, Bronson Fishing reel, and Hamilton rifle. I have vivid reminiscence of our storm cellar filled with shelf after shelf of Kerr jars that mother had lovingly canned. It was a comforting thought to know we had enough food down there for the winter. Years later, I was to have the pleasure of shooting with Alex Kerr, heir to the Kerr glass fortune and a champion skeet shooter. Alex was tickled when I recounted for him my boyhood happiness over Kerr jars standing like soldiers all over our kitchen and the pleasure of carrying them up from our storm cellar to the supper table. There wasn't much money around our house but we always ate well.

Rarely did I see mother ever sit down to read or to rest; she was always working. If she wasn't repairing something or sewing clothing for my sister, she was cooking or cleaning; I remember a mom in constant motion. The only time I can recall her relaxing was on Tuesday nights when the whole family gathered around our Atwater Kent radio to listen to special shows like, "The Shadow" ~ "Fibber McGee & Molly" ~ "Edgar Bergen & Charlie McCarthy" ~ "Jack Benny & Rochester" ~ "Ed Wynn" or "Grand Central Station." My, how we enjoyed those evenings together!

Mother was as devout a Catholic as could be found and we never missed going to mass or confession. As a young boy, even though I had no sins, mother insisted I go to confession; I figured the priest expected to hear some sins so I made up a few. I felt it was necessary to have different sins each confession and before long I began to run out of sins. If one of us kids did something wrong, she felt as though she had sinned by not raising us properly. Catholicism ruled her life and I must say that she was unhappy many times from worry and fear that my sister and I would not turn out right.

I think mother's education ended about the eighth grade; at that time it was the highest grade taught at most country schools. Despite this limited schooling she was quite knowledgeable and we *never* were allowed to make a grammatical or spelling error; we were always corrected and monitored so we wouldn't make the same mistake twice. In fact, with mother's tutoring, I became the "Spelling Bee Champion" of Webster County, Iowa. Today, if anyone ever doubts my spelling ability, I politely remind the individual of my championship status.

Mother experienced some tough illnesses that were painful and energy draining, however, I never once heard her complain, and we were always cared for with great love and compassion. She never gossiped or said anything bad about anyone. Her motto was, "say nothing, if you can't say something good about someone." I'm sure she didn't understand too much about child psychology but her handling of my sister and me was always right on target. Mother always praised us for a job well done or getting good school grades; she was constantly encouraging us to be the best that we could be. If I did an admirable job of mowing the lawn, she made it a point to praise me at suppertime so that dad and my sister were also aware of my worthy accomplishments.

During these times, I'm sure there were many instances when mother went without for herself so that Anna Marie and I were properly dressed and fed. In fact, mother carried most of the family home-based load, as Dad was a work-a-holic with no hobbies, sports, or other interests to help him relieve his pressures. Mother took on some of his tension also and was always shielding him from any kind of harm. As an example Dad had a little workshop in the garage behind the house, and if Mother didn't stop him, he probably would have worked all night. I'm sure she would remind him of his own saying, "If you don't have it accomplished by midnight, give it up and go to bed, tomorrow is a new day and a new beginning!"

In addition to being a mother and a homemaker, she was also Dad's best piano salesperson and, when Dad was traveling, she was the only sales force left in our little store. She had acquired a good knowledge of the Wurlitzer pianos and had an honesty that people really respected. She closed as many, if not more piano sales than Dad.

She always took good care of Dad and if he was late coming back from a piano tuning trip, no matter what time, day or night, the stove would light up and she'd prepare a full meal for him, always with a big hug and kiss. I cannot remember my parents ever having a fight except possibly a heated discussion over how a lost piano sale should have been handled. I do remember hearing muffled giggling through my bedroom wall; from what I innocently thought was dad tickling mother. "How nice," I smiled to myself, "My dad and mother play with each other!"

My Sister, Anna Marie

We really had a very happy home, full of love and warmth and understanding. The only exception was in my relationship with my sister, Anna Marie, who was two years older. From the age of about twelve until she left home at eighteen, she was a real "pain in the ass!" Anna Marie was filled with false pride and unhappiness over our family's financial condition. My mother, who was an excellent seamstress, had a foot-operated Singer sewing machine and made Anna's clothes utilizing patterns from style magazines and Simplicity pattern books, but Anna Marie was always ashamed and complaining because she thought her classmates knew she was wearing home made clothing. I always thought she was better dressed than most. For the life of me, I couldn't understand her attitude.

Anne, as she liked to be called, was an ambitious and studious type. She was in high school in the depth of the big depression. I remember she had so much pride that she was not about to be seen in Dad's old piano truck and wouldn't accept a ride to school even in terrible weather. Both dad and I thought this was ridiculous and because it hurt Dad's feelings, I stayed angry with my sister practically all the time.

My recollection is that we did not play together much because our interests were totally different. When we were both in our teens I disliked her because she always seemed to be complaining about something. When I was about ten years old, we were roughhousing one day and I accidentally broke her arm. That widened the gap between our getting along, so we grew more and more apart. Her burning ambition was to get out of Fort Dodge and its cliquish social system and be on her own. While working in the office at J. C. Penney she discovered that she had a real affinity for the business world. For sure our folks could not afford to send us to college so Anne saved everything she earned through high school and put herself through a two-year course at Chillicothe Business College in Missouri. She loved it there, had many friends and graduated with honors. My mother's sister, Aunt Alice, lived in Los Angeles so upon graduation Anne took the train to LA. She immediately found a job as secretary to a food broker who represented the Dole Company.

I forgot to mention that Anne had grown up to become a very attractive woman and once she started working she began dressing to the height of fashion. She mowed through several boy friends but didn't become interested in anyone.

The president of Dole came to the office occasionally and Anne learned to know him and he developed a high respect for her and how she handled her job. In 1940 he offered Anne a job as his secretary in Honolulu. Nobody in their right mind would turn down an opportunity like this, so off she sailed on the ocean liner "Matsonia." As I matured, and watched Anne grow, I began to appreciate her point of view and in adulthood, I saw Anna Marie as quite a lovely person—someone to be admired, as well as an astute businesswoman, and we grew to love and respect one another.

My Dad, His Cars and His Idiosyncrasies

Looking back now at my wonderful dad, with all of his idiosyncrasies, I perhaps understand my sister better. For instance: Dad's first car was a Model T Ford. This was Henry Ford's first production car and, as some of you may remember, it was available in any color you wanted as long as that color was *black*. Dad's was a two seater with removable side curtains. There was no electric starter; to start it you put on the parking brake, partially opened the throttle, and then ran around in front of the car and turned the crank that hung just below the radiator. In these old cars, the electricity to fire the spark plugs came from a magneto. Many an arm was broken when the magneto would fire late causing the hand crank to jerk violently. When the engine started, the driver would then have to ungracefully run around the car and jump into the seat behind the wheel. There was no gearshift; and the car was operated with three controls: the hand throttle—foot throttles didn't come until years later— a foot brake, and a foot clutch mounted on the floor beside the brake pedal. To make the car move, you increased the hand throttle while releasing the clutch pedal. The clutch basically consisted of some metal bands that compressed around the drive shaft. There was no way to make a smooth start; releasing the clutch caused the car to start up in a series of jerks. In the winter, forget it! If you could get it started, which was almost impossible, you'd freeze to death. Despite these problems Dad would attempt to travel around the countryside to tune pianos and sometimes would arrive home absolutely frigid.

His next car was a four-door Nash Ajax 8 sedan. This was a far more sophisticated vehicle with gearshift and heater. Dad didn't acclimate too well to new and more technical features and never did learn to shift gears without making it sound like he was tearing out the transmission. He tried to leave it in high gear and then use the clutch and gas feed to make it move. I don't know how many clutches he wore out but I remember that we had to replace a clutch two times on our trip to California.

About 1935 Dad bought a Plymouth coupe that he converted into a piano mover by installing a piano rack over the trunk. He had the same gear-shifting problems with the coupe but it was a better design and lasted him until he finally stopped jerking around town after acquiring a 1950 automatic transmission.

The special rack installed on his Plymouth would crank down to an almost vertical position, the back of the piano would be moved up to it, and then after strapping the piano down, the rack would be cranked up so the piano was being carried on its back. Usually Dad could move a heavy piano around by himself to get it mounted. Once in a while he would call in a moving company to deliver his pianos. It was always amusing to me to watch how those 250 pound moving company men would struggle with the pianos. Dad would always have to pitch in and show these burly guys how to use their own weight for leverage in order to move the piano in place.

He considered himself a very safe driver because he never went over forty miles an hour. When he was out on the highway, I worried that, some day, someone going at the more average speed—sixty or more—would back end him. To his credit, I must admit, he never had an accident and never had any kind of a traffic ticket; not even a parking ticket.

To the family's embarrassment, Dad had absolutely no pride in his cars or how they looked. The car was just a tool or necessity and he couldn't care less if it needed washing or any other cleaning up. His old Plymouth needed new piston rings and burned oil like mad. As he drove down the street he left a smoke screen behind him. It didn't bother him but it sure bothered Mother and my sister. Anna Marie was so ashamed of his Plymouth that she refused to ride in it. She would walk all the way down town in below zero weather rather than be seen in it.

He was such a character that he had many friends. Dad had quite an Irish brogue when he first came over from Ireland. Some of his Irish sayings he used throughout his life and people got a big kick out of talking to him and noting his sayings. If he had been able to join a country club or have some of the advantages that I had in life, I'm sure he would have been one of the most popular men in town. Instead his whole life was dedicated to work and our family. The only vacation our family ever took was to Lake Okoboji, in the northwest corner of Iowa. We stayed for about a week in a cabin at the old Methodist Camp Ground. The only picture left from this trip is one of Dad in his gay nineties swimsuit with legs that came down to just above his knees. He is standing on a diving board extended out over the lake about to dive. It is interesting to note that I have chosen to retire on Lake Okoboji, and found a home located just about a block north of the Methodist Camp Ground. I'm sure the cabin we stayed in is still standing and I have walked through the campgrounds many times trying to remember—trying to recognize it, to no avail.

Saint Patrick's day was always a big event at our house! On that day Dad would act as if he had taken catnip. He'd sing Irish songs and do his rendition of the Irish jig, much to our amusement. And of course we all had to wear something green—a custom that I have followed religiously all my life. We had no TV in those days but on that holiday there would be plenty of radio programs devoted to St. Patrick's Day and playing the Irish music that Dad loved so much.

Dad had never been to a football game in his life but he became an avid Notre Dame football fan just because they were Irish. Without really understanding the game, he listened to all the radio broadcasts of Notre Dame games. Notre Dame could do no wrong and he was always unhappy if they were beaten, which didn't happen too often in those days.

Every year I had season tickets to all the University of Iowa football home games. When Notre Dame came to Iowa I always tried to get Dad to come down to Des Moines and go with us but he would never close his piano store on a Saturday. Finally one weekend after mother had passed away we were able to get him to come down for the weekend of a Notre Dame game. Back in those days we still had a special football train that left the Rock Island station in Des Moines about nine in the morning and pulled into a siding right beside the Iowa stadium. The train ride was almost more fun than the game as there would be bars set up in each car and people prepared elaborate lunches to eat on board. This was all very exciting for Dad and our friends enjoyed seeing how much fun he was having.

When we arrived at the stadium people were crowding their way into the tunnels leading up to the seats. Dad had a claustrophobic attack so we had to wait until the tunnel was almost clear of people before he would enter it. As a consequence when we finally emerged from the tunnel the stadium was packed, the Iowa team was just coming out on the field and the place was erupting with sound. In the bright fall sunshine it was about as colorful a scene as one could imagine. Therefore, Dad's first remark struck me as being both funny but kind of tragic at the same time. His exact words were "Geez, don't any of these people have to work?" He who had never taken a Saturday off in his life simply could not understand sixty thousand people all being in that stadium. Unfortunately Iowa beat Notre Dame that day, one of the few times they had done so. That sort of ruined the game for Dad, as Notre Dame could do no wrong in his eyes.

My Beloved Dad

In November of 1967 I received a phone call from one of Dad's neighbors in Fort Dodge advising me that they hadn't seen him for a few days and when they went to his house they found him sick and thought I should be aware. I immediately drove up to Fort Dodge and took him to see a doctor. He had flu-like symptoms but was pretty weak and run-down so the doctor placed him in the hospital. I went back to Des Moines but drove up to see him every two or three days. On one of my visits I noticed that they were giving him blood and this seemed rather curious. When I mentioned it to the doctor he simply said that Dad was run-down and anemic. After a week Dad was much better so I took him out of the hospital and brought him to our house in Des Moines to recuperate for a few days and have a chance to see the kids at the same time. After a few days he suddenly became ill again and with the same symptoms as before. I took him to see my doctor, Dutch Haines, one of my hunting buddies, who suggested we hospitalize Dad to run some tests. On the third night in Iowa Methodist Hospital I was visiting Dad when Dutch made his rounds. He called me out in the hall and we sat in a lounge area where Dutch really shocked me by telling me "Bob, your Dad is not going to make it!" Tests had revealed that Dad had practically no kidney function and was suffering from uremia. That is why his doctor had been giving him blood and why he didn't tell me the truth I will never understand; he certainly lost my confidence and respect. Dutch said that he could keep Dad alive for a few days with blood transfusions but it would be just putting off the inevitable. In 1967 there was no renal dialysis available in Des Moines and the only such treatment available was in Iowa City and was reserved for young people with kidney injuries. Dutch said he would make Dad as comfortable as possible but doubted if Dad would live more than a few days after being taken off transfusions.

We all spent most of every day in Dad's room and for the first two or three days he was quite cheerful. Somebody had sent him a flower arrangement that had a Playboy magazine in it. A Catholic priest friend of Dad's came up to visit him and Dad made us hide the Playboy. I'll always have a vision of one of Dad's last days when my daughter Kelly (then about 12 years old) was sitting on the edge of Dad's bed and he was playing with her pigtail. It was just a day or two later when I was in my office and my secretary told me my Dad was on the line. When I picked up the phone Dad said, "Come quick, I'm really sick!" I rushed to the hospital and he really was sick. His color was gray, he was very weak, and was so dehydrated his lips were dry and cracked. It was apparent that he wasn't going to be around long. I planned to stay there all night so that he would not be alone at any time. Ruthie and the family were going to spell me if I needed a break. However, just a few hours after I arrived in his room he went into a semi-coma. I was holding his hand when he suddenly opened his eyes really wide, looked right at me, and mumbled something that I could not understand because of his parched lips and mouth. I thought he wanted the nurse so went to the door and called one of the nurses. When I went back to his bed and took his hand, his eyes were shut and he had gone. I was really heartbroken that I hadn't stayed beside him so I would have been there holding his hand at the exact moment of his death. I had told him how much I loved him several times so am sure he realized I was there. He was such a sweet old man that I am really choking up as I write this.

So, at the age of 82 he passed away. We gave him an Irish funeral complete with a green casket liner, green flowers, and a reception at the funeral home and the funeral services at Corpus Christi Catholic Church. He was buried right beside Mother in the Dwyer family plot in a cemetery only a few blocks from our home on Floral Avenue; the same cemetery I had gone sledding in when I was a boy. Dad fervently believed that when he died he was going to be reunited with Mother so he was ready to go at any time.

My Dad—he was the most honest and content man I've ever known. He didn't feel that he needed any more money, loved his home, and thought that he had the best wife and family in the world. I always envied him his peace of mind.

Chapter 3

Boyhood Aspirations

My Favorite Sweater

Well, I decided to put a picture in this book of me at three years old showing off my favorite sweater. As I look at this picture I realize that I was a "dinger!" It's also a word I use to describe my eighth and newest grandchild, Taylor Elizabeth Rice. Every time I see that little monkey face and hear the unbelievable things that come out of her impish mouth, I think to myself what a dinger this little one is, just like I was at three years old.

My folks had bought me this cardigan sweater with long sleeves, a knitted tie belt, and two big pockets. It was a heavy knit in dark brown and soon became my "blankie." I wanted to wear it all the time. I wore it outside to play and to my mother's chagrin, wanted to wear it everywhere including church—we always had a big battle over the church matter. It soon became threadbare and very shabby looking but I still insisted on wearing it. I also had an affinity for wearing hats, as you can see by my sweater picture, a fetish you might say, which has followed me all my life.

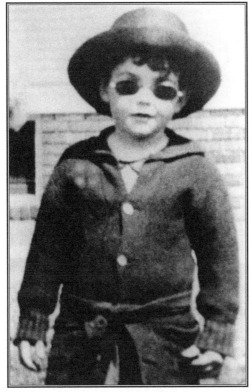

Bob at three years old. My favorite sweater.

My Childhood Sweetheart

From age three till I was about seven years old my childhood sweetheart and best buddy was Mary Virginia Rhodes. She was my next-door neighbor at 818 North 13th Street in Fort Dodge. What wonderful memories I have of the big elm tree in the side yard between our homes and the sand box we played in virtually everyday. Mary Virginia and I were inseparable and thereby constantly in trouble with our parents, and I was usually the instigator of many adventures that got us in hot water. For instance there was the day I decided to give Mary Virginia her very first mud shampoo. We were playing Beauty Shop and I was shampooing her hair in a hole in the ground filled with water and therefore mud. She was kneeling with her head down in the muddy hole when my mother saw us through the kitchen window. Mother came running, thinking that I was trying to drown Mary Virginia. I explained that I would never do that to my bosom buddy.

We had a wooden coaster-wagon and Mary Virginia's house was conveniently located on a hill. I was pushing her in the coaster wagon, and to my horror, it got away from me on the top of the hill. She went screaming down the hill until the wagon finally slowed down on a grassy area. Boy, was I lucky that time!

Mary Virginia and I happily went to the Duncombe School together on our first day of kindergarten. The teacher was trying to explain good manners and instructed the little boys to always hold the chairs for the little girls to sit down. I was holding Mary Virginia's chair and decided, of course, to pull it out from under her so that she would fall. She fell on her butt and began to cry. The teacher made me sit on a stool in the corner of the classroom for fifteen minutes. "I was just having fun with my buddy," I pouted as I looked into the corner. Needless to say, my teacher didn't see it that way.

On another occasion Mary Virginia and I ran away from home together—but only for a few blocks. We were constantly disappearing down the block to the house of a lady who would give us cookies. Mrs. Shenofsky, made oatmeal cookies that were about eight inches in diameter and boy were they good, fresh out of the oven! Upon our deciding to return home we would get punished by being confined to the yard. This punishment never seemed to make any difference to me because I was content to play in the yard with my first love—Mary Virginia Rhodes.

We remained friends all through our primary school days. Mary Virginia went on to take nurse's training and became one of United Air Line's first stewardesses, back in the days when nurse's training was a requirement. She flew Hawaii flights from the west coast. I kept up with her progress in life through her brother who became my friend in our adulthood. Mary Virginia eventually married a west coast doctor. I wonder, in conjuring up these memories of my childhood sweetheart, if she ever thinks about me endearingly after all the trouble I got us into?

An interesting side note—Something I have this moment realized is that the first romance of my life was a girl named Rhodes who became a stewardess for United Airlines, and the main romance of my life was my wife Ruthie, of forty years who was also a Rhoads and a stewardess flying for United also.

My Wooded Valley on Floral Avenue

As I mentioned earlier, when our family returned from our California experience with Uncle Mervin we moved into a house on Floral Avenue that was located on the north edge of town. The town hadn't grown beyond this point because it was on a bluff overlooking a deep, wooded valley with a railroad track and Soldier Creek flowing through it. I fell in love with the woods and spent as much of my time here as possible. My friends and I built a dandy fort on the edge of the bluff. It was just a shack made of boxes and odds and ends of scrap lumber but it was our fortress in the forest. Here we fought off Indian attacks, waged wars, and sallied forth into the woods in search of the enemy.

To make our wars more realistic we even put up barbed wire entanglements on the hill complete with tin cans that contained small rocks so that they would rattle if anyone tried to sneak into our encampment. We made cannons from two-inch pipe, which we'd stick in the ground and fill partially with dirt, so we could insert a Fourth-of-July cherry bomb. We'd light the bomb and jam a green apple in the pipe, and when it went off it would blow the apple almost out of sight. It was miraculous that nobody ever got injured.

Our weapons were slingshots made by cutting off a "Y" shaped crotch of a tree branch. Then we would attach strips of inner tube rubber on each side, and use a swatch of leather from an old shoe to make a pouch for whatever projectile we used. We got pretty good with these slingshots and regularly killed what we considered "bad birds" such as sparrows and black birds. Other weapons were our "rubber" guns. These were made from a piece of wood cut out in the shape of a pistol and with a spring-loaded clothespin attached to the rear of the pistol grip. Projectiles were rubber bands about a half-inch wide cut from automobile inner tubes. The rubber was stretched from the end of the barrel back to the clothespin where it would be secured. To fire, all you had to do was press the clothespin and off went the rubber sometimes as much as twenty-five feet away. To make them better ballistically we sometimes made a knot in the rubber that also made it sting a little when you hit someone. We played rubber gun wars by the hour and the more the merrier! Sometimes there would be eight or ten of us running through the woods playing cowboys and Indians or war. We had all kinds of rules. If a rubber hit you, you had to fall over dead. Anyone who cheated on this honor rule was banned from our games.

Over time our games and weapons became more sophisticated. The rifle construction we came up with was the same as the pistol except for a longer barrel and a stock that you could put up against your shoulder. We finally developed the rifle into a repeating-double-shot-rifle by installing two clothespins at the rear. The rubbers we used for rifles were sometimes two rubbers with knots tied together. Finally I designed a pretty ingenious machine gun. It had a four-foot long barrel made from a 2 X 4 piece of wood. An eighteen-inch diameter wheel was mounted at the rear and it had one-inch wood pegs installed every three-inches around the circumference of the wheel. To load it, you hooked a rubber over the end of the barrel and ran it back to one of the pegs. The wheel was then advanced one peg and another rubber attached, and so on, until all the pegs had rubbers attached. To fire it, you merely let go of the wheel and *WHOOOOOM* ~ all the rubbers went flying! If the enemy was charging it really mowed them down. The kids had a good respect for it because the cloud of rubbers really stung.

Soldier Creek

One of the attractions, down in the woods, was the old swimming hole at Soldier Creek that we named "Round Hole" and another smaller swimming hole named "Horseshoe Bend." My friends and I would rush down after school, strip all our clothes, and then dive into the swimming hole. It was here that I taught myself to swim. Actually, learning to swim was an accident! One early summer the creek was in flood stage and the only way we could get across was on a farmer's wire fence. One time I lost my hold on the fence and fell into the boiling floodwaters. The current was so swift that I could hardly sink and it carried me a couple of hundred yards down stream where I grabbed hold of another fence. I suddenly discovered that I had learned how to swim and enjoyed the experience so much that I ran back to the original fence and tried it again. From that time on I had no fear of the water or any trouble swimming. One of the attractions of horseshoe bend was a mud flat. We took great joy in rolling around in the warm mud in our birthday suits. Unbeknownst to us we were having an erotic experience but all we knew was that it felt good.

My Flexible Flyer

Winters were fun too! As a boy I delighted in Iowa winters. The cold and snow didn't bother me, as I loved to slide on my sled or ice skate. We lived in the midst of some great sliding hills so when the snow was on the ground, much time was spent with our sleds. One run ran from the top of a park road down through the grounds for about four blocks. It was fun but a long walk back up to the top of the hill. We also slid in a graveyard near our house. It had some great hills, however, the gravestones were a real hazard!

The pride of my life was a Flexible Flyer sled the folks gave me for Christmas one year. The Flexible Flyer was the Cadillac of sleds because it was the only one you could steer. Steering was accomplished by turning a cross-pieced handlebar that actually bent the runners on the sled to make it turn. I was the envy of the neighborhood with this sled and survived one adventure on it that I shall never forget. I had just finished a run down the Oleson Park hill. When I got to the bottom I was just lying on the sled resting for a few seconds to catch my breath. To quench my thirst I lapped up some snow from the crossbar of the sled. As you may have guessed, somehow my tongue latched on to the metal portion of the crossbar and instantly froze to it. I was too scared to try to tear it loose. The temperature was around zero degrees and I had to walk up a long hill in the woods and then almost a quarter mile to our house. This distance carrying my Flyer in front of my face was a nightmare but I was afraid to try to pull my tongue loose; the motion of walking was bad enough.

With tears frozen to my cheeks, I reached the house and began to struggle to open the kitchen door. I must have looked a tragic mess when I arrived. My mother was horrified as she came to my aid. God bless my mother as she immediately went to work placing hot towels on the metal part of the sled until it warmed up enough so I could remove my tongue. I'll never forget my dad coming in about this time and he thought it was all quite funny. As it turned out, heating the metal made it easier to get my tongue loose but it didn't keep the skin from peeling off. An inch of tender skin stuck to the sled and now it wasn't funny anymore especially to me. My tongue took several days to heal and both eating and drinking were painful as the dickens.

Another favorite winter sport was ice-skating. When I was only seven or eight I started to skate on a small pond near our house. All the neighbor kids would be there evenings and weekends playing hockey or ice games such as "stink!" To play "stink" you first establish two bases about fifty yards apart. Then in the middle and at the sides you establish prisoner bases. To start the game you choose up sides and make sure that there is the same number of skaters on each team. The game begins when one player skates out of his base and tantalizes someone from the other team to catch him. If he is caught he then goes to the prisoner base and must remain there until one of his team members can skate directly out of home base and can rescue him before a skater from the opposing team catches him. Every time someone leaves his base, he is in danger of being caught by an opposing team member. When you see someone come out of the opposing base, you automatically have "stink" on him and if you can catch him he goes to the prisoner base. The game ends when all of one side is in prison.

The only skates we could afford were the kind that clamped on to our shoe soles, similar to the metal roller-skates of the day that used a key to tighten the clamps around the toes. They were pretty good but as I got older and started playing hockey and other ice games they became a problem. Just as I would be about to score the darn clamps would come loose and I'd take a good tumble. Putting up with my clamp-on skates for several years left me a bit frustrated. I was sure I could be a superior hockey player if I just had skates that would stay on during intense play. Finally, one Christmas, the folks were able to afford a pair of real shoe skates. They revolutionized my skating and I became a really good hockey player and could jump more barrels than any of the other kids. From then on I was a whirling dervish and could out-skate everyone.

As I became a little older I would go down to the Des Moines River where, on weekends, we would have massive hockey games. Our hockey games were something! None of us could afford equipment so our hockey sticks were a crotch cut from a tree with a branch stub for the blade. For a puck we either used a piece of wood or a tin can. We would roll up magazines and put them inside our stockings to protect our shins. My mother made me some sheepskin hip pads that I wore under my pants. The games were pretty rough so this protection was needed.

Our games were massive. I say massive because the north side of town made up one team and the south side another. The game would start in the morning with just a few players on each side and as the day progressed more and more kids would arrive and sometimes there would be over a hundred players on each team. There were two bridges about three blocks apart that were used for goals. If you could get the puck under the bridge it was considered a goal. Sounds easy but as the size of the teams grew, the game would become a flailing mass of hockey sticks and sometimes the puck wouldn't move more than a few feet an hour. There would only be three or four goals scored each day. It was all about brute strength with not too much skill, but I loved it! The city had some warm-up huts built but they didn't get too much use by us, as we didn't have time to get cold.

This was before the day of porto-potties so the city had dug some slit trenches, similar to those used by the Army, that were supposed to serve the purpose. City attendants would periodically scatter lime and dirt into them but most of the time they were a disgusting and smelly mess that made you wish you didn't have to use them. An incident there stands out in my mind as one of the most pitiful sights I've ever seen. A little kid, probably about five, skated up to the edge of the trench and just as he was starting to pee, he lost his balance and skated into the trench. He was absolutely filthy, screaming at the top of his lungs, and nobody was moving to help him climb out of the slippery-sided trench. I couldn't stand to watch so I don't remember how he got out but have often thought about the reception he must have received when he got home.

When I was in high school a promoter put in a hockey rink downtown. He organized some hockey teams that I guess you would call semi-pro. I was on one of the teams and we played games against other towns. It wasn't very sophisticated hockey but we had great fun. Other than this, most of my time in high school was taken up by my work in the Strand Theater and my many other jobs.

My Heroes

When I was eight or nine years old, I had my heroes. I read prodigiously and my favorite authors were the naturalist Ernest Thompson Seton and western writer Zane Grey. When my dog and I went down behind the house into the woods we had adventures that I imagined had happened to these heroes of mine. When I went out hunting, in my mind's eye it was an expedition. Real life stories would dance around in my head about my other heroes, like Admiral Byrd, the African explorers Martin Johnson and Frank Buck, and men of distinguished valor like Charles Lindbergh. For hours and hours I read about explorers' lives and pored over outdoor magazines like *Field & Stream,* and sent away for catalogues like L.L. Bean. My life's ambition was to become an explorer or outdoorsman, and so I felt, at eight years old, that it was very important for me to begin preparing for my idealistic, professional life as a frontiersman.

Fishing Reels and Three Shells For a Dime

Between the ages of eight and twelve, I spent a lot of time hanging out in downtown stores where I would admire guns, fishing tackle, and outdoor equipment fantasizing about when I might be able to buy such wonderful things. The storeowners got to know me and, in retrospect, must have had great patience and empathy for me. To illustrate I must tell the story of a Bronson Fishing Reel.

I had been coveting this reel and had been saving money to buy it for some time. Every time I went into the Thiede Mueller hardware store I would admire this reel. The reels were displayed on a counter and placed inside a little glass cubicle with a price marker clipped to the back of the cubicle as was common in many stores. The particular Bronson Reel I was saving for was a single-action reel with no level wind feature and, at seventy-nine cents was all I could afford. I'd come in a couple times a week to drool over "my" reel and always looked with envy at some of the more expensive reels. In the cubicle right beside my reel was a deluxe Bronson model with level wind but at a whopping $3.95 price that I could not possibly afford. On the day I came into the store to actually buy my reel, lo and behold the deluxe reel was in the 79-cent cubicle and the $3.95 cubicle was empty. I was sure it was a mistake but, being an honest kid, I called Mr. Mueller over and asked him, "Is that reel only 79 cents now?" I'm sure the reel had just been put in the wrong cubicle but an empathetic Mr. Mueller, who had been watching me come in to drool over the reel for weeks, must have decided to let me have the more expensive reel for 79 cents as he answered me with, "It sure is Bobby, do you want to buy it now?" Boy, did I ever want it! I plunked down my 79 cents and went out of there on cloud nine. I'm sure that Mr. Mueller got as much satisfaction out of selling, or should I say, giving it to me it as I did plunking down my big 79 cents. Mr. Mueller showed his generosity in other ways too. Years later I bought my first shotgun from him and he obliged me by breaking up a box of shotgun shells and selling them to me for three for a dime. Try buying three shotgun shells at a time in your local Wal-Mart store today and see what happens!

Many years later, after WWII, I was asked to give a speech to the Rotary Club in Fort Dodge. In the audience I noticed, to my delight, a much older Mr. Mueller. In my speech I related the heart-warming story of the Bronson fishing reel for 79 cents and the three-for-a-dime shotgun shells. The audience loved it and I was happy I had finally found a way to recognize and thank that kindly man who had such great empathy for a small boy enamored with the great outdoors.

My First Real Guns

At this time I also became very interested in guns and shooting. All my buddies had already had BB guns for a couple of years. It was time for me to move forward, I felt, out of the wooden gun phase of my life. My parents were adamantly against me having a real gun. Dad knew nothing about guns, having been born in Ireland, where only wealthy landowners were allowed to possess firearms. Mother, although an Iowa farm girl who had been around guns growing up, had a fear of them because of her brother's near fatal accident involving a rifle.

I read all the books on shooting and hunting I could get my hands on. My pleading to get a BB gun, was to no avail. By the time my folks relented and allowed me to have a BB gun my friends had graduated to .22-caliber rifles and shotguns. I was absolutely ashamed to accompany them into the woods carrying my BB gun, so unbeknownst to my parents, I purchased my first rifle; a single shot .22-caliber Hamilton rifle, at a cost of $2.98. I had saved the money from my many door-to-door sale escapades.

My folks never knew that I hid my Hamilton in a hollow tree, down in the woods, behind our house. When I starting

Bob with his dog "Prunes" and a 16 gauge shotgun.

out on a hunt I would be carrying my BB gun and then I would surreptitiously switch it for the Hamilton hidden in the tree. It was the beginning of the Great Depression, however my mother's supper table always could feature rabbits or squirrels because I had now become an avid hunter. As far as my folks knew, the BB gun remarkably brought down the game I carried home.

A little aside: My Hamilton disappeared from the hollow of the tree after I enlisted in the Air Corps, but I don't know how or why. *Sixty* years later, as I perused a gun show in Des Moines, Iowa, I found *my* .22-caliber

Hamilton. Without a doubt it was mine! I knew *that* gun, as they say, "like the back of my hand!" The markings on the stock were all there exactly as I remembered putting them there. My heart raced as I laid fifty dollars down on the vendor's table trying to contain my excitement. Little did he know that I probably would have paid many hundreds of dollars for all my childhood memories stored up in my first Hamilton rifle. It now is preserved, behind glass, in my gun cabinet, beside my expensive trophy rifles and shotguns.

For months I had been admiring a .16-gauge single-shot shotgun in the Thiede Mueller Hardware store. It had a plain barrel with a hammer and it opened with a lever. It wasn't much of a gun but was all I felt I could afford. I had been admiring it at the regular price of $9.95 for weeks but Mr. Mueller gave it to me at the special price of $6.95. This became another gun that I hid in the hollow tree down in the woods.

Becoming a Trapper

Other heroes of mine were the pioneers, the mountain men, and those who forged forward creating our wild west. Reading about mountain men trapping for a living led me to search through many books about their various techniques. Earning additional money was always a burning desire; I guess because we were so poor, and I thought trapping might be a good means for some additional income. That winter I bought a few traps and began setting them along Soldier Creek in the north woods behind our home.

Trapping muskrats involved getting into where their runs were located and that required getting wet. It was so cold; I soon lost interest in muskrats and focused my attention on trapping mink, skunk, possum, and raccoon. Through my books I learned how to skin animals and treat their hides so they would be marketable. God bless my mother and dad who possessed such amazing patience and constantly encouraged me in my endeavors, because the skinning and treating of hides was a smelly mess. After the skins were prepared it was off to *Clagg Hide & Fur Company* where I sold minks for $8.00, skunks for $3.00 plus possum and raccoon hides for $2.00 each. (The skinning was the part I learned to really hate, and as a result, for my entire life I have never enjoyed cleaning game.)

My interest in trapping lasted only one winter and ended the day I ran my trap line to discover I had caught a skunk that was still alive. Before I could kill it, I was *spraaaayed* ~ but good! Naturally, the smell went home with me and despite everything my dear mother could think of—including bathing me in a mixture of baking soda and lye soap—the smell stayed. After bathing for almost an hour, I doused myself with Dad's after-shave and took off for school. I had become so accustomed to my odor that I didn't realize that I still stank! When I walked into the homeroom my classmates all recoiled and the teacher ordered me to about-face and march home. I spent the entire day bathing in different mixtures from formulas we found in books and volunteered by friends, as well as prescribed by our doctor. My aroma finally faded away however for several months I suffered from my "smelly" reputation, which subjected me to becoming the main object of teasing at school.

The Boy Scouts

About this time, I became very active in the Boy Scouts. A National contest was announced for the one boy who made the most progress toward Eagle Scout. The grand prize (I almost couldn't believe my good fortune) was an opportunity to join an expedition to the South Pole, with none other than, Admiral Byrd. Wow! I really had my heart set on winning this prized opportunity and I worked so hard that I was right up there in the running with Paul Siple from NY State. It turned out that he was selected, to my great, great disappointment. This Admiral Byrd experience certainly changed Paul's life; he became famous writing many books about the South Pole. The way I was taught to look at my losing out was a motto I hold to still today; "Nothing ventured, nothing gained!" In trying to become an Eagle Scout, I received a wealth of knowledge from achieving all my merit badges, an enriching life adventure with knowledge I could not have acquired in any other way. Scouting was one of the most outstanding experiences of my journey into manhood and I feel that Scouting should be mandatory for all boys growing up; I don't think we would be having some of the youth problems we have today if our boys were all Scouts.

Always Looking to Make Money

As I mentioned earlier, from about age eight on, I was always looking for ways to make money. (Mother pointed out one day laughingly that almost every art paper I sketched in grammar school incorporated dollar signs.) A sucker I was for all of the magazine ads that said you could get rich quick by selling their seeds, magazines or household products. If there was no advance deposit required, I would fill out the form and have the information sent to me. Then, with sales kit in hand, I would venture out, knocking on doors with great enthusiasm, to sell my wares. Soon I learned that there were certain houses where I was more successful; possibly because they had more money; or perhaps they had more empathy for little Bobby Allen? One neighbor I remember vividly was Mrs. Woodbury. She would come to the door with a sparkle in her eye and a greeting like, "Well, what are you selling today Bobby?"

For the most part, none of these products made anybody rich except the company. At about age ten, I finally got wise and settled on magazine sales for periodicals like *Liberty* and *The Saturday Evening Post*. Subscriptions by mail were not available in those days so most people bought their periodicals from newsstands or from door-to-door peddlers like me. I developed a number of steady customers and they would see my smiling face delivering their magazines on a weekly basis.

Another store downtown that was one of my favorite hangouts was Kautzkys Sporting Goods. Joe Kautzky became accustomed to seeing me come in regularly to salivate over his displays of guns, hunting and fishing equipment, plus traps and outdoorsmen equipment. I think he recognized that I couldn't afford to buy much then but I was a future good customer and he humored me and did some things that would be unheard of today.

I bought my first bicycle at Kautzky's for eight dollars. I didn't have the eight dollars so Joe allowed me to pay one dollar down and come in to pay twenty-five cents a week. My weekly payment visits whetted my appetite for other things and, as I grew older I was able to reward the store with larger purchases.

In 1939 I bought my first shotgun for trapshooting; a Browning over/under double barrel .12-gauge with single trigger and matted rib. As I began to attend trapshoots, I bought all of my shells there; a case of shells sold for $15.00. When I came home from WWII I bought my first real trap gun, a Winchester Model 12 pump gun with ventilated rib and Monte Carlo stock. This was to become the gun that I won everything with in the forties and fifties and which put me on the All American Trap Team for eleven years straight.

In 1939 the Kautzky's included me in a five-man trapshooting squad that attended shoots all over the state. The squad consisted of Joe Kautzky, his brother Rudy, their sister Marie and Dewey Voss who operated an ice cream shop in town. If one of them couldn't make it, Martin Leitch filled in. We had fun and they taught me much about trapshooting. Marie Kautzky was Iowa's leading woman shooter and in her lifetime won a dozen or more Iowa Championships and Dewey Voss won the Iowa State men's title several times; so I was traveling in good company!

Rudy Kautzky was an outstanding gunsmith and distinguished himself during World War I when he was credited with perfecting machine guns that could fire through an airplane propeller. Prior to his invention, the guns were usually mounted on top of the wing and out of the pilot's reach. Rudy's invention made it possible to mount them on the fuselage directly in front of the pilot so he could reach them and manually load, charge and fire the guns. This gave our pilots a big edge over the Germans until they copied the invention. Rudy became a real hero. Later, in civilian life, he invented one of the first single triggers for double barrel shotguns.

The Des Moines Register

Always looking for my next opportunity, I was successful in securing a paper route for *The Des Moines Register*. (Now I could buy more than three shotgun shells at a time.) Every morning, at five a.m. it was off on my bicycle to the Register's headquarters in downtown Fort Dodge, about a mile and a half away. January mornings are stamped on my memory, when there was so much snow on the ground I couldn't ride my bike. I'd really bundle up with a double layer of pants tucked into my four-buckle, rubber galoshes, a sweater or two and then layered with a heavy sheepskin coat. This outfit was topped off with an earmuff cap and a wool scarf wrapped around my head and face.

I can still hear the snow crunching and squeaking under my feet as only it does when it is twenty below zero. Usually, I'd never see a car or a person until I reached the newspaper office. The absolute quiet and lonely feeling I had while walking alone in the early morning darkness made me feel as if I were the only being in the world; a memory which comes back to me often.

Each paperboy would draw his papers and then stack them on one of the steam radiators that warmed the news office. Then we would go to the bakery next door where the kindly baker gave us special deals on his rolls and doughnuts. He said they were "imperfects" and that is why he could sell them so cheaply. l suspect that he had a great deal of empathy for the paperboys about to brave the elements and was giving us his top quality products. We'd take these delicious, freshly baked rolls back to the paper office and bury them between the radiator-warmed papers in our news bags. Then it was back out into the cold to deliver the paper to my seventy-five customers. My customers were scattered throughout the northeast section of Fort Dodge.

Folding my papers tightly as I walked along, was a significant part of my job. If they were tight, I could make them sail right up onto the customer's porch. If my aim missed the porch, I'd walk up and place the paper by their door. This all was very important to me because I took great pride in doing a good job. I often wonder where I learned to think this way and I always come back to the conclusion that it came from the examples I lived with, my wonderful mother and dad.

My, how delicious those rolls and doughnuts tasted in that cold air, still warm from being nestled between the heated papers! It was difficult, however, to get them into my mouth, past the wool scarf, which by this time was partially stuck to my face. When I finally succeeded it made the warm, sweetness even better.

There were a few really nasty mornings when my dad would insist on driving the route with me in his old Plymouth. My self-respect was shaken if I needed assistance to cover my route; I lost a little "face" in front of the other boys. So, it had to be a really bad storm before I would allow Dad to help me. In the 1930's Dad's cars didn't start too well on frigid mornings so there were times when Dad wanted to help me but couldn't get his old car started.

As you can imagine, the best part of the paper route was finishing up and heading home! Mother would always have a delicious hot breakfast waiting for me. She'd help me unwind the frozen and encrusted scarf from around my face, help me out of my layers and layers of clothing and then she would struggle with my icy galoshes. Finally she would sit me down to her wonderful hot oatmeal and her great home-made-bread toast and gobs of sweet homemade jam. On occasion, there would be time for me to go back to bed for an hour before school. Oh my! How warm and wonderful that bed would feel!

The toughest part of the paper route was collecting from my customers. Usually we were supposed to collect Friday evening and Saturday morning so that we could pay the news company for the papers by noon on Saturday. I had one customer that was a *dead beat* and had gone for about eight weeks without paying. Every week when I came to his door he had some excuse ready. Eight weeks in arrears ate up most of my profit, and I was really worried about my situation and mentioned it to my dad. When he heard the story he was really disturbed and suggested that the two of us call on this questionable customer. (Visions of my dad once again becoming John L. Sullivan came rushing back to me!) When we knocked on the door and the fellow appeared, Dad launched into a good and loud chastising of the man by saying, "You ought to be ashamed of yourself for taking advantage of a kid like this. You'll pay him right now and pay him on time every week or he isn't going to deliver your paper anymore." Dad shamed him into paying right then and there and I didn't have any more trouble with my miserable customer. (Years later, when I became an adult I would find myself in my dad's role as John L Sullivan.)

Getting back to my paper route, I had a much-looked-forward-to Saturday ritual that I followed each week. After collecting, I would go to the paper office and pay my bill. If I had been able to sell a new customer that week (which we called a "start") the manager would give us a pass to a movie at the *Pok-A-Dot Theater.* So with the week's profit in my pocket, feeling like a big shot, I'd go to my favorite hamburger joint called Wimpy's, treat myself to a five cent hamburger and a five cent coke, and then go next door to the Pok-A-Dot for my free movie. The movies were always about cowboys and I had several favorite western actors such as Tim McCoy, Buck Jones, Hoot Gibson, and Hop-a-long Cassidy. I didn't like Roy Rogers or Gene Autry because I thought their singing made them *sissies!* (In my adult life Roy Rogers would become a shooting buddy and he got quite a laugh out of my relating how I felt about him when I was a boy ~ calling him a sissy.)

The theaters always had short subjects before the feature. Usually it was a newsreel, or a comedy, and on Saturdays they'd have a serial of some kind. The serials, which ran about twenty minutes, always ended with the hero in some hair-raising situation; this would make you want to come back the next Saturday to see how it all came out. So I would be looking for a new customer (start) in order to get back into the movies free the following Saturday.

I became the top carrier for the Des Moines Register with seniority. That meant that I graduated to the top paper route;

the three large apartment buildings in downtown Fort Dodge. The route was completely indoors, and if you hustled, you could finish in an hour. It was a far cry from battling below-freezing conditions while cycling or walking a route.

After my episode of trapping and skinning, although I had the paper route now, I was still not content and decided to launch into *another* moneymaking endeavor that was a bit more tranquil. The woods behind our house were full of maple trees, and I became intrigued with articles about making maple syrup by tapping their sap. When I started this project, I had visions of myself selling syrup and maple sugar door to door.

One spring I tapped a dozen trees and embarked on gathering sap. I'd collect the sap every two or three days, accumulating enough for a gallon. Then, with mother's help, we'd boil it down until we had syrup or sugar. What a fabulous smell in mother's kitchen! After trial and error, I soon found out that it took a tremendous amount of sap to produce an infinitesimal amount of syrup and to produce sugar required even more. I soon gave up on the idea of mass-producing maple products. However my family enjoyed the fruits of my labor. Mother, god bless her, was always encouraging about any project I was embarking on.

My First Real Job

Now I was about thirteen years old when I landed my first *real* job working in Mr. Holger Anderson's food store. (Honestly, that was really his name!) It paid a guaranteed salary and that guarantee made it a real job. Mr. Anderson usually had three or four boys for duties like cleaning, stocking, and carrying out groceries for customers. My pay was twenty cents an hour, not bad for those depression years.

Within a few hours of my first day on the job, I discovered *Oreo Cookies!* Cookies didn't come pre-packaged like they do now. Cookies were displayed in fifteen inch, square cases with a glass lid. Customers would place what they wanted in a paper sack and pay for them when they checked out. I got in the habit of lifting the lid and grabbing an Oreo whenever I went by the display. It never occurred to me that I was "stealing" the cookies; they just were such a novelty that I couldn't resist them. The only cookies I had ever tasted up until then were mother's homemade cookies; store-bought were out of the question.

I didn't realize that Mr. Anderson had a little peephole in the wall of his office so he could look down on the store and watch what was going on. He evidently was watching me pretty closely because that night when he paid me for the day, he said, "Bobby, you are a good worker, but I am afraid I can't use you any more ~ I can't afford the Oreo cookies!"

To make a long and sad story short, *I was fired on the first day of my first real job!* I'll never forget how embarrassed I was to go home and tell Mother and Dad. It was a good lesson for me however, and I'm sure Mr. Anderson intended it to be exactly that! He knew my folks well and I found out much later that he and Dad had some good laughs over my Oreo snitching. To this day I'm hooked on Oreo cookies!

The Strand Theater

After losing my job, my Irish luck came into play once again when the Strand Theater called to offer me a job. I was hired as an usher at twenty-five cents an hour. This was considered one of the best jobs in town for a student and I was very pleased that I had been selected. I went to work every afternoon at 3:30 and received special permission to skip my last study hall period in order to arrive at work on time. The movies ran continually from 1:00 p.m. till the last showing at about 11:00 p.m. When the box office closed at 9:30, I could take off and be home by 10:00 p.m., except on "change" nights.

The Strand would change feature films three times a week. On these change nights my job was to replace all the 8 X 10 still pictures, the framed posters in the lobby and outside in front of the theater, plus the "three-sheets" on the side of the theater building. (Three-sheets were approximately a 4' by 10' poster; 1/8 of a billboard.) Next, I would replace burned out light bulbs under the canopy. The canopy was a "V" shaped extension of the building that jutted out over the sidewalk.

Under it were hundreds of light bulbs that were constantly burning out. My toughest job was changing all the letters on the canopy or marquee. Both sides of the canopy were glass, illuminated from behind, and about five feet high, providing three rows of 15" black steel letters that slid into tracks.

When I was finished ushering for the night, I'd go to the basement and change into my old clothes. Planning the layout of the letters on paper was next. Each line of copy had to be centered on the canopy and sometimes it was difficult to get the name of the movie and the cast all on lines that would end up looking even. The next step was to get out the huge fifteen-foot ladder and take down all the old letters from the canopy. I'd then stack up the new letters in the order of my planned installation. All the letters had to be carried up from the basement to the sidewalk in front of the theater. The letters weighed about three pounds each so twelve was just about the maximum armload I could carry. Then with one armload at a time, I'd climb that cumbersome, one story ladder, and finally slide the letters into their proper position. On winter nights the sidewalk was icy and the ladder would slip and slide. I fell off the ladder several times—but luckily, I never hurt myself; there was nothing like workman's compensation then. With practice, I got pretty good at "change" nights. However, it still took a minimum of two hours, (for an extra 50 cents!) which meant that I didn't finish until 11:30 and got home about midnight. Though it was hard work, I took great pride in doing the changes quickly and perfectly.

On summer nights all my friends and their dates would be cruising up and down the main street while I was slaving away on this monstrous ladder. I recall feeling envious of them; however I think maybe they were envious of me too, because I had this good job?

I have some vivid memories of those days and learned a great deal from Mr. Hank Salthun, the theater manager. He was a man who insisted that everything was just right—a perfectionist who was also very quick to compliment us when things were done well. He required all ushers to wear a dark coat and tie. The guy who was doorman wore pancake make up and because I had a shiny nose he suggested that I should use some too. He said I would look better; after all it was permissible because this was "show business!"

The customers could always identify ushers because we stood at attention, and I mean attention, with our flashlights held across our chests. You would greet your customers by asking where they would like to sit, then escort them to the row and point your light down to the floor at the entrance of the aisle. Safety was very important. People waited to be seated, so I'd then hustle back up the aisle to greet the next customer.

Safety lights, for power failures, were unheard of. Everyone in the theater business feared the panic that might ensue if the lights went out. We were trained to meet this emergency by immediately turning on our flashlights (which we *always* carried) and proceeding to the center of the theater where we would become beacons in the dark until the lights came on, or the audience could be evacuated. To this day, I always look to see if there are emergency lights whenever I go to a theater or large public gathering.

To give you a bit of history and to demonstrate how different things were done then, a far cry from our media/communication sophistication of today—the 35-millimeter films were shown using two projectors from a booth behind and high above the audience. Reels ran twenty minutes, so the second projector was always ready to run the next reel. A few seconds before the reel change was due, a bell would warn the projectionist, or in most cases, literally wake him up. He would look out his little projection window and watch for a black dot that soon appeared in the upper right hand corner of the screen for two seconds. This was the first alert that the reel was about to end. He would then watch for a second black dot to signal him to change projectors. The change in reels was accomplished by pulling on a chain that covered the lens of the old projector and uncovered the lens on the new reel.

Part of my job, as head usher, was to stand at the entrance to the right hand aisle. Inside the door was a button that, if pushed, rang a bell in the projection booth. We were trained to watch the screen and if it went brown or white, indicating that the projector needed adjustment, we were to ring the bell. Theater projectors in the 1930's were ponderous things with arc lighting that was always requiring adjustment.

The projectionists had a strong union and considered themselves prima donnas. One of our projection men was an alcoholic who also drank on the job. He was constantly going to sleep and missing the change. I'd ring the bell to wake him but there always would be several minutes of no picture during which time the audience would be yelling and whistling. Our theater manager was constantly fighting with the projectionists and their union. On one occasion he went into the booth to raise hell and the operator physically threw him out. He fell down the stairs hurting his leg and never attempted going back into the booth again!

Cat lovers aren't going to like this next piece of Americana history but it has to be told. There was an old maid who had an apartment upstairs over the theater. She brought in all the stray cats and usually had about a dozen or so. Somehow the cats would get loose and be wandering around in the theater. If we heard some woman in the audience scream, we knew that a cat had probably walked under her seat and its tail was causing the commotion. The manager knew of my interest in shooting and asked me to bring my .22-rifle down to shoot some of the cats that hung out in the basement's coal bin. So you won't think it was so terrible of me to shoot the cats, at that time the Department of Natural Resources was recommending to hunters that any cats found in the wild should be shot because it had been proven that they were the worst predators on the pheasants and quail population so in shooting the cats in the theater I felt I was doing a service for conservation.

One night after the last show, the manager and I went down to the basement and I shot five cats. We placed them in a gunnysack along with coal for weight and he threw them in the river on his way home.

The next day all hell broke loose. Lulu, the cat lady, had placed an ad in the paper and was offering a reward for the return of her cats or information on any foul play. The other ushers and the doorman were all kidding me that they were going to collect the reward. I had a few very nervous days!

Theaters like the Strand advertised that they had "cool-water-washed-air." Air conditioning, as we know it today, didn't exist yet. The front doors of the theater were purposely left open and when you walked by the theater you felt a rush of moist air that usually smelled like a wet dog. The air was literally washed! In back of the screen was a big, box-like, room filled with hundreds of nozzles that sprayed cold water from a deep well under the building. Fans with giant blades gently blew air through this room full of misty water out into the audience. The air was actually cooled and felt good on a hot day. Movies only cost a dime so many people fled to theaters to escape hot weather, even though when they came out their clothes felt damp. Standing at my station at the head of an aisle, that cool air was a gentle breeze that always felt good. I had no doubts, during the summer months that I had a great job.

As a freshman in high school, I had a lot of balls in the air! I was running a paper route in the morning, for a while I was running a trap line or a maple sugar line, going to school, and leaving school at 3:30 each afternoon to work at the theater. Even with a bicycle it was hard to keep up. I was making big money now, twenty-five cents an hour or about fourteen dollars a week from the theater. I decided it was time to buy a car and after shopping around for a few days came upon a 4-cylinder "Willy's Whippet Coupe." I thought it was a good buy at $15.00 but soon learned why the price was so low. It had a flat spot on the crankshaft and kept burning out rods. After a few frustrating weeks I traded it in on a 1930 Model A Ford convertible, with wire wheels and a rumble seat. Wow! With that car I was really something. I hadn't actually discovered girls yet but they were noticing me all right. The car made my busy life easier and I was able to do other activities like hunting. I had this car through most of high school and Junior College.

My Model-A was soon to prove very important to me. You see, my usher job had some other side benefits! All the pretty girls eventually came to the theater and usually there was some way to find out who they were. The second great love in my life, I met after she had been to the theater with a date. As

I remember it, she came out to go to the ladies room and talked to me for a few minutes. I guess I asked her if I could call on her. At any rate, we met and went "steady" for about two years. She was a delightful looking blue-eyed Norwegian blonde; what I called, "a real eyeful!" It was she who took my virginity. I'm sure I took hers also, one full moonlit night, in a cornfield, in my Model A Ford convertible. She came from a large Protestant farming family and they thought they had good reason to forbid her to go out with me because I was a Catholic. So we sneaked around; but that is a whole other story not to be told here. (Its bad enough that my grandchildren will now know exactly when their grandfather lost his innocence).

The Fort Dodge Gun Club

About the same time that I started working at the Strand Theater, I had a Sunday job loading clay targets into the traps at the Fort Dodge Gun Club. This job paid me fifteen cents an hour and was what whetted my interest to become a trap-shooter. I'd sit in that trap house watching those clay birds sailing out, critical of the shooters who were missing easy shots. I vowed that, if I could afford to shoot, I sure wouldn't miss as many targets as those shooters. The negative part of the job was that it was miserably hot with no ventilation in the trap house. The heat combined with the target dust blowing in your face, caused your skin to break out in a rash and itch likes the dickens. The positive part of the job was that I got to know some of the shooters, who encouraged me and gave me my first trap shooting instructions.

Dr. George Clark and President F.D. Roosevelt

I highly prize my association with a kindly dentist named Dr. George Clark. I saw him as a very intelligent and well-educated man. He was seriously involved in politics in 1932 and felt that the youth of the day were not properly educated on our United States' system of government. This view prompted Dr. Clark to found a boy's political club, for which he coined the name, The Ratchet Club. A ratchet, of course, is a wheel, which can only turn forwards because cogs keep it from turning backwards. Recovery was on everybody's mind, during those days, as our country was starting to pull out of the depression. Dr. Clark's philosophy or motto for the club was:

> "The recovery movement with a click—
>   always moving forward with a click
>   at each turn,
>   never will it turn backward."

Dr. Clark chose ten boys from different families and backgrounds, all living in Fort Dodge, and at ages from twelve to fourteen. Why he chose me, I will never know, perhaps, because he knew my parents, and because he had met me at the theater were I worked as an usher. And perhaps my folks had something to do with it because they thought the sun rose and set on Dr. Clark. We were ten boys from completely different walks-of-life and from different political persuasions. Dr. Clark thought of himself as an independent. He bought a bus and had the Ratchet Club insignia printed all over the exterior. He took us around the state to attend political rallies and taught us how to give political speeches.

In addition to the Democratic and Republican Parties, a new party sprang up, started by a Mr. Townsend, who ran for the Presidency on this new Independent Party ticket. His whole platform and solution for the recovery of our nation was the "Townsend Old Age Revolving Pension Plan." Every citizen reaching the age of sixty-five would immediately receive five hundred dollars each month for the rest of his life. His idea was that millions of people having this income at their disposal would "jump-start" the economy of our country after the depression. It was to be a simple program, similar to a flat tax, and that would not require a fat bureaucracy to manage.

At a town meeting in Gowrie, Iowa, with a population of two thousand, I was scheduled to give my first speech and was pretty nervous. On stage with a bunch of dignitaries, I sat in what seemed like a huge auditorium, with my parents proudly and anxiously looking up from the audience at their 13-year-old son. There was the podium, and here with my knees knocking, I bolstered myself by thinking, "I am very well

The Ratchet Club, 1935—Dr. George Clark on the left and his wife on the right. Bob Allen 4th from left. I'm the one with the dark curly hair.

rehearsed." What I remember most is the crowd getting such a kick out of a kid giving a speech about old age pensions and the sound of the resounding applause. Soon, I became more relaxed, confident and quite good at standing up before a crowd.

Dr. Clark and his wife often invited our whole club out to their home in Roelyn, Iowa, to spend the day and have dinner. He would explain what was happening concerning different political issues, we would eat some great home cooked food, play baseball, and have more discussion. My coming home and explaining what I had learned about politics was a new experience for my folks. Before Dr. Clark there was little political talk around my house.

One event that is most significant in my mind is a special trip to Minnesota. Dr. Clark was a friend of the Doctor Mayo that founded the Mayo Clinic. And, President Roosevelt was coming to Rochester to dedicate a new federal dam at Lake City. Dr. Clark arranged for our Ratchet Club to be presented to the President and also to the Mayo Clinic doctors. We got all *spiffed-up* with new ties and coats. Dr. Clark rehearsed each of us to greet the President by saying, "I am pleased to meet you Mr. President."

We fell in behind one another and proceeded through a reception line. President Franklin D. Roosevelt was sitting in a wheel chair with a blanket across his lap. He looked very tired to me; however, he carried a big smile on his face and spoke to each person with great warmth in his voice. His eyes were sharp and unwavering, as he looked straight into my eyes. I was so excited as the President took my hand and said, "How are you young man?" I could tell he was amused at the youth of our group. The President then complimented me on taking an active interest in politics. Mom and Dad were thrilled about my opportunity and experience. As I related my trip's adventures to them, I remember how avidly they listened as I recounted each detail of the day's event.

Some of my peers around town found sport in making fun of our club, but these ribbings were outweighed by the pride we felt. I learned about our political system and that there is more than one side to a story and that no change will come about unless one takes action. This experience was a great help to me later in life when it came to giving sales presentations and other speeches of persuasion. And, I learned something that would serve me well the rest of my life; no matter how far-out an idea, it is worth investigating.

One of my fellow Ratchet Club members became a doctor, another a successful business owner, one a professor who wrote many books about WWII. He was in the navy and our paths crossed again on the Pacific Island of Tinian. Unfortunately I have lost track of most of the members and of course Dr. Clark and his wife are long gone.

Screen Ad Business

While working at the Strand Theater, I got to know many other interesting people who would prove significant to my future. Many of our patrons were regulars who came in at least once a week. I was very impressionable and admired many of these people, especially Jules Stein, a screen advertising man from Omaha. Jules sold merchants the advertising that appeared on our screen between features. He dressed impeccably, had a great extroverted personality and, he drove a big black Cadillac. While I was in Junior College, I got to know him better and asked him how I could get into the screen advertising business. He offered to set me up, train me, give me suggestions on an area in which to work and all he asked in return was that I purchase my 35-MM film through his company. He took a real interest in me, and now that I'm looking back, I realize his influence helped me throughout my life.

At the start of my second year in Junior College, I became ill and spent about two months at home. It was like a virus with high temperatures, chills, sweating and a general feeling of malaise; my illness was never ever really diagnosed. Polio was still around at that time and I might have had a touch of it or it could have been mononucleosis (sometimes called the kissing disease) although at the time I wasn't getting much kissing. At any rate, I missed so much college that it was impossible to catch up. I decided that now would be the time to try the screen ad business. I called Jules Stein and he came to Fort Dodge a few days later and gave me my initial training and set me up with a sales kit.

Jules called upon businesses and theaters in the larger towns and cities. He advised me to concentrate my attention on the smaller towns. I chose Pocahontas, Iowa as my first call and once more my Irish luck was riding on my shoulder. I drove my Model A convertible to Pocahontas one morning, a distance of forty miles from Fort Dodge. Before I could start selling ads I had to contact the theater manager, get his approval for the project, and agree to a price for which he would run my advertising film. I was extremely happy to find that there was no advertising running currently and the manager was very eager to have the added income. I think I agreed to pay him $200.00 a month to run my film twice a night for thirty days. With that deal closed, I began calling on various businesses in Pocahontas to sell them ads. With unbelievable luck I clicked on almost every call and ended up selling ten ads at $250.00 each.

It was with great pride and excitement that I jumped into my Model A and raced home to tell my folks all about my new found prosperity. I arrived in Fort Dodge just before supper and bursting into the house, dumped my earnings of $2,500.00 in cash on the kitchen table. In those days you never saw that much cash, let alone in a pile on our kitchen table. I'm sure that my folks' initial thought was that I had robbed the Pocahontas bank! When they heard my story of success they were so very proud of me. It was a tremendous thrill!

With this victory under my belt, I hit the road calling on other theaters in small towns across northwest Iowa. Some theaters already had screen ads running, so I struck out here and there. However there were enough towns open for my deal to make my trip very successful. In one week I opened up five towns. Inside of a week, I was rolling in cash and bought my first *brand new car*, paying up front, in full, in cash. The car was a 1939 Studebaker Champion Coupe in bright yellow. The price was six hundred and twenty five dollars and included a radio and heater, items that other new cars did not contain. Boy, was I proud of that car! I became such a big shot overnight that I invited Don Hamilton, an unemployed friend, to accompany me on my road trips. He became my *gofer* and ran errands for me so I could devote all my time to selling.

By now, I considered myself quite an entrepreneur and was casting about looking for other money making opportunities. I had ad deals running in theaters located in Spirit Lake and Arnolds Park, Iowa (a resort area taking in many towns surrounding the Great Blue Lakes of Iowa, known generally as Lake Okoboji) so I spent a considerable amount of time there. Lake Okoboji was a pleasurable place I loved, so I combined business and pleasure.

On the north shore of West Okoboji I stayed at The Inn, an old wooden resort hotel owned and operated by two old maids, the Jacquith sisters. It was a four-story firetrap with a veranda running the length of the hotel on each floor. The rooms were somewhat primitive with no bathrooms; you had to trip down the hall for about a hundred yards. However, what it lacked in comfort it made up for in charisma and spectacular views. Speaking of views, there were knotholes in the walls of the rooms so that anybody could spy into the next room!

Several times while staying at The Inn, I heard people

ask the desk clerk if they could rent bicycles. This gave me the idea of setting up a bicycle rental stand for the hotel. I bought six bikes and made a deal with the bell captain to handle the rentals for me on a percentage basis. The rentals went well and although I didn't make a lot of money, I did pay for the bikes in one season and had a little profit left over. I later sold the bike concession to the bell captain. During the war years The Inn burned down so that was the end of that business. Today there is a New Inn, a far cry from the old one but the Lakes of Okoboji are just as beautiful and I have come full circle and retired there. Every time I pass by the Spirit Lake Theater that is now a video store, I remember my first cold call in attempting to sell my screen ad services.

While staying in a hotel in Minneapolis, I ran into the Sales Manager for a division of Johnson & Johnson. We had several visits and he evidently was impressed with what I was doing and offered me a job. I told him that I was not interested but kept his card for future reference. It was a good thing I did because in just a few weeks my bubble and my ad business started to burst.

The screen ads I was selling were like slides; just a still message sometimes with a picture or logo but usually just print. My primary competitor was a large company out of Colorado Springs named Ray Bell. Their ads were like little play-lets in color and much like our modern day TV commercials. Their service normally sold for around $600.00 a month versus my $250.00 and that is why I was so successful. My sales activity and lower prices had shot them down in many theaters in northwest Iowa so they decided to quash me by offering their deluxe play-let ads at my $250.00 price. There was nothing I could do to compete, so I decided that this was the time to bail out. I contacted Johnson & Johnson about the job we had discussed.

Johnson & Johnson

I was nineteen years old and driving to Chicago for a meeting with the J & J Vice-President of Sales, a very nice man by the name of Callahan. He got a kick out of my youth and my story about my defunct screen-ad business. I was hired as a Junior Salesman that day and assigned Nebraska and Kansas as my territory. A few days later I reported to my Sales Manager, Dean Riffe in Kansas City. His first remark upon meeting me was to say, "Callahan has sent me a damn kid!" Needless to say, I wasn't too happy with that reception but later learned to like and respect him. He had a very attractive niece living with him and she helped me to like him more.

I was paid four hundred dollars a month, plus all travel expenses and a car. In those days this was an unbelievably good deal! To say, " I lived high on the hog" would be an understatement! I stayed in the best hotels, had fine meals, and enjoyed spending weekends in various towns in my territory. It was at this time that I took up trapshooting in earnest. Omaha became my headquarters and I stayed at the old Conant Sanford Hotel in downtown Omaha. When I was away, they stored some of my belongings and forwarded my mail. My yellow Studebaker Champion was a little light for the job so I traded it in on a larger, more deluxe, blue Studebaker Commander.

A great fringe benefit to this job was the great hunting in my territory. My weekends were spent where I had acquaintances and over a period of time I developed some great friendships. In Hastings, Nebraska, I became friends with the sheriff, Worthy Woods, a soft drink bottler named Hank Cushing and his wife, and Jim Brule; a man my age with a *very attractive sister*. One of the weekend activities in Hastings was going out to the city dump in the evening and shooting rats with a .22 rifle. We thought it was great target practice while being of service to the community. Their dump had *jillions* of rats. We'd drive up, leave the headlights of the car on, and then locate and shoot the rats when their eyes lit up. We would shoot hundreds of rats each night but their population never seemed to dwindle. The rats acted just like actors playing dead in the movies; they would stand up, stagger, and then finally fall over. We did a little jackrabbit hunting as well as trapshooting.

Getting Serious About Shooting

I have many fond memories of my weekends, especially at the Alliance, Nebraska, Gun club. This was when my interest in trapshooting really became cemented. A really fine shooter came to my attention when I noticed a beautiful young lady. She was a coed at the University of Nebraska in Lincoln and held the title of the Nebraska Ladies Trapshooting Champion. I soon learned that she was Ilene Davidson accompanied by her dad, a local lumber dealer. Of course, I contrived a way to meet her and we hit it off immediately. She and her dad invited me to come to their house that night for dinner. This began a romance that lasted about two years. Lincoln Nebraska became my weekend destination. Ilene and I would shoot locally or she would meet me at other gun clubs where we could match our skills against a new group of competitors. We tried to choose clubs that had good prize money. Ilene had an average of 96%, which means that she broke 96 out of every 100 targets. My average was about 94 and in my efforts to beat her, I really became hooked on trapshooting.

An interesting side story concerned a photo spread of Ilene which appeared in "College Humor Magazine" ~ a forerunner to the Playboy Magazine of today. Their photographer was attracted to her for a feature article when they heard that she had won the Nebraska Ladies Shooting Championship. For one of the pictures they had her sit on a park bench posed with her knees up, her feet on the bench, and her skirt hiked up so that it was about an inch above her knees. She had a great pair of legs and with the spike heels she wore, it was a great picture. To complete the picture she was wearing her shooting sweater and holding her Parker single shotgun. The resulting picture was fantastic; it was so fantastic in fact that the Chi Omega Sorority threw her out. By today's standards, the picture was very conservative but at that time it was considered a little too racy.

Fortunately, Ilene's folks just thought it was funny, so she wasn't in trouble at home. This incident caused her to leave Lincoln and enroll at Colorado University, in Boulder. That was out of my territory so we didn't get to see each other very often and gradually grew apart. I can honestly thank Ilene Davidson for whetting my appetite for shooting and having great fun at the same time. After college Ilene married a doctor in Denver and raised a large family. She came out to watch me shoot in the Colorado State Shoot in Denver one weekend in the fifties and that is the last contact I had with her.

Another friend I had made in Alliance, Nebraska took me coyote hunting in his airplane. It was a small airplane with a pusher engine mounted on the backside of the wing. It had two open cockpits, one for the pilot, and one way out in the nose where I usually rode. It was an excellent position from which to shoot a .12-gauge shotgun loaded with buckshot. Although it was great fun it was also dangerous because we were flying only about fifty or a hundred feet off the ground.

When I was in western Nebraska I occasionally spent weekends with State Senator Art Carmody at his ranch near Trenton, Nebraska where we would do a little trapshooting and prairie dog hunting. We had met at one of the trapshoots where I had the honor and pleasure of shooting with the Senator and we became good friends. He took prairie dog hunting to the nth degree. In an upstairs bedroom with a window facing out towards a big pasture Art had a spotting scope set up and, on a tripod beside it, a .222 high power rifle with scope. One shot from this gun literally vaporized a prairie dog. As you know, ranchers hate prairie dogs because too many horses and cows break legs in the dog's ground holes, and have to be put out of their misery. So, after a few animals have been injured and have to be shot, you can imagine how disliked the prairie dogs became.

I spent Thanksgiving of 1941 with my folks in Fort Dodge and then went to Mexico on a hunting trip with two friends, Don Hamilton of Fort Dodge and Neil Murney, a shooting friend from Wichita, Kansas. We met in El Paso, Texas, drove into Mexico for about two hundred miles on deplorable roads, past the city of Chihuahua, to our hunting ranch; the Hacienda Terrenates. It was a beautiful old home built in a square around a courtyard complete with its charming fountain. We remained overnight and then packed back into the mountains on horses.

We had two guides, a cook, and a couple of horse handlers. My guide's name was "Jesus" and every time I called him, I felt like I was cussing. We were hunting deer, the Mexican wild pig called javelina, and mountain lion. We downed one deer apiece but didn't get shots at anything else. My most outstanding memory of the hunt was of my sore rump from horseback riding. One day I was in so much pain I stayed in camp lying on my stomach all day. Then it was back to the ranch where we had a day or two of duck and dove hunting. These were very happy days for me doing what I loved best.

Two-Day Drive From Mexico to Bedlam in Los Angeles

We drove north out of Mexico to cross the border at El Paso, with a plan to drive to Los Angeles to visit my sister Anna Marie. Don Hamilton had a girl friend, a dancer in the Earl Carroll review, who he was ardently impatient to see. It was 1941, and I was twenty-one years old, and we were three young men, driving to LA and life was full of escapades and pleasures and the potential of new adventures.

As we began our two-day drive out of Mexico to LA we tuned in the radio and the big news about Pearl Harbor was already twelve hours old. It was a broadcast that we could hardly believe. While in Mexico we had no contact with news of any kind from the states. This drive to LA would turn out to be a turning point for three young men and the rest of the world. The radio was full of the details describing the attack on Pearl Harbor. We were shocked! We had thought if we were dragged into the war it would be because of the Nazis, not Japanese! We all knew we would be required to go into the service eventually, with the way the European war was progressing. Now we knew that our plans to go into the service were on the front burner, all the rules had changed.

During the drive to LA, we could not talk about anything except our disbelief and what we were going to do. It was

December 7th, 1941. I was scared of the unknown future but at the same time these were exciting times and we were all caught up in its seduction. As the news developed we began to understand what a tremendous blow our Navy had taken at Pearl. The more we listened the more we knew we were in serious trouble. Wherever we stopped people were asking each other if they had heard any new news. My heart was set on the Air Corps and becoming a pilot. Don Hamilton was considering the Navy because his dad had been a Navy man, but with all the discussion on the best way to go, Neil Murney was uncertain.

When we arrived in LA, my sister had tickets for a popular NBC radio show, Kay Kyser's College of Musical Knowledge, a Saturday night hit parade. We thoroughly enjoyed the show and came out in high spirits to find a near riot going on in the streets of Hollywood. A Jap sub had surfaced off the Santa Barbara shore earlier in the evening and had shelled a refinery setting its gas tanks on fire. The streets were in a state of bedlam!

Rumors were that the Japs were invading and panic spread all over the west coast. The radio stations were asking for a blackout. Most streetlights and store signs were still lit up so the street crowd was throwing anything they could get their hands on; trying to put the lights out. It was pretty scary, I must admit! We finally ended up in a bar that was full of people nervously drinking like mad.

I'm sure sportsmen all over California were getting out their hunting rifles preparing to defend their home and country against the Japanese. It was reassuring to know that we Americans, unlike citizens of other countries, have weapons and are in a position to defend ourselves. Countries like Great Britain, where the civilian population had been disarmed, had to rely on donation of guns from Americans to defend themselves against an imminent Nazi invasion. American sportsmen had been asked to donate high-powered rifles. I personally gave a Winchester, model-70, 30.06-caliber rifle for the cause.

It was time to go home, so we left about mid-December to drive to Iowa. In the fall of 1941 everyone fully expected us to be in the war but as I mentioned earlier most thought it would be in Europe fighting Hitler. Men my age were being drafted and many of my friends were already gone. I wanted to control my destiny, so I had already investigated the Air Corps Aviation Cadet program. The Pearl Harbor attack solidified my plans, so I immediately applied for the Cadet program. I gave notice to Johnson & Johnson that I was resigning but that I would stay on the job until January of 1942 when I expected to receive my orders to report to Fort Riley, Kansas for induction into the Cadets. As was common procedure in those times, J & J promised to hold my job for me until the war was over. These were uncertain and worrisome times for everyone.

Chapter 4

Army Air Corps

Air Corps Enlistment

In January of 1942, I enlisted in the Air Corps Aviation Cadet program, and on February 27th, I was ordered to report to Fort Riley, Kansas for extensive intelligence, psychological, and physical exams. One of the requirements was that applicants had to have two years of college and be able to pass a tough written intelligence test. I had only about a year and a half of college but they said they'd waive that requirement if I passed the written test. I suffered through the test and was astonished to find out that I had done very well. The questions in the test ranged from names of musical bands to mathematics; a general intelligence test. I went back to Fort Dodge to stay with my folks for the last days of civilian life until my induction notice arrived. On April 24th, I gave Johnson & Johnson my resignation, arranged to sell my Studebaker car back to Morton Motors in Omaha, and awaited my orders.

Mom's Diary entry ~ June 10, 1942:
> *Dear Bob got word he had to go into Service. We are all broken hearted.*

Mom's Diary entry ~ June 12, 1942:

*My dear little Bob left for Omaha, then on to Fort Riley
and into the Army Air Corp.*

Fort Riley, Kansas

I received my orders to report back to Fort Riley for
induction. My first ride in a commercial airplane came when I
flew Mid-Continent Airlines from Omaha to Kansas City. It
was one of the first airliners; a Lockheed, eighteen seat, twin-
engine aircraft; and what a big thrill it was for me. Next, it
was on to Fort Riley by train; and then it began!

We were assigned beds in an old barracks, had formations
several times a day, and spent about a week receiving shots
and induction training. How shocked I was the first time I saw
our latrine facilities. It was a big room, approximately 100 feet
square, with toilets and sinks on all walls. There were *no* par-
titions or stalls; just the toilet stools sitting out in the open
side by side! What shocked me most of all, in addition to the
lack of privacy, were the six toilets on one end of the line which
were painted bright red. On the wall behind them was a sign
that read "venereals only!" Welcome to the real world Bobby!

Preflight Training Base, Santa Ana, California

We were there only a few days and then boarded a Union
Pacific troop train for the west coast. Because of my Eagle
Scout training, they put me in charge of the Cadet contingent
(about 90 men) for the trip to Los Angeles. We had not been
issued uniforms yet, so we were all in civilian clothes. The
coaches we were assigned were old and dilapidated; coaches
that probably were called out of the junk yard. It was hot summer weather and our coaches had no cooled air. This was
before air conditioning. The way they normally cooled the
trains was by putting huge cakes of ice in a compartment
under the coach. Air was sucked into these compartments by
fans and the air cooled by passing over the ice, and then it was
blown into the coach. It was rudimentary but it worked! Our
troop train coaches (about three of them) had no such cooled
air. All the other cars had the air cooled coaches; plus we were

hooked on to the back of the "City of Los Angeles," one of the Union Pacific's crack, luxury, steam trains.

To stay cool we had to open all the windows. The train was moving about seventy miles an hour most of the time, so the 98-degree air coming in was like a blowtorch! To make it worse, soot from the coal-driven steam engine ahead of us blew in with the hot air. By the time we had been on the train for a few hours, we all looked like coal miners. Some of us sneaked forward into the air cooled passenger cars, found empty seats, and feigned sleep as we tried to pose as paying passengers. In every case the train conductors found us and shagged us back into our "steerage" cars; and I have disliked train conductors ever since!

A train stop in those days was quite a production! When the train pulled into the station a big crew of workmen descended on it to replenish the ice chests for the air cooling system, water the steam engines; and tidy up the cars; all except ours, of course. One of our stops was during the evening in Cheyenne, Wyoming. Most of the Cadets got off the train to stretch their legs but many of them headed straight for the bars and liquor stores. When the train whistle gave its two toots, signaling instant departure, I was missing about a dozen Cadets. Most of them showed up in California a day or so later and were summarily punished by the Air Corps. To my surprise I was not criticized or penalized for their absence, it seemed like the Air Corps was used to this sort of delinquent thing happening. As it turned out, we also lost a few more Cadets when the train stopped in Las Vegas, Nevada. In those days there was no "strip" as we know it now. All Las Vegas amounted to was the train station, a hotel or two, and a couple of casinos on what is now the main street.

Buses transported us from the Los Angeles train station to our pre-flight training base at Santa Ana, California. This was a new base; we were probably the third or fourth, six-weeks class to attend. The base had been carved out of orange groves and probably covered two hundred acres.

Cadet Training

We were assigned to training squadrons and barracks. Then we were issued our uniforms that made us all feel good. Cadets were given *unofficial*-official officer status so our uniforms were a cut above what the average enlistees received. We soon learned that the life of an Aviation Cadet was to be no fun. The Cadet program was patterned after the West Point system with lower classmen, upper classmen, hazing, and "gigging" for slight infractions of the rules. A "gig" meant walking with a rifle for an hour and 60 gigs could wash you out of the program. We all learned real fast to take things very seriously.

The average day in the six weeks pre-flight program started out about six a.m. with a reveille formation and roll call. Then back to spic-n-span the barracks, make beds, shower and shave in time to be ready for breakfast formation. We marched as a squadron to breakfast and then to classrooms where we had courses in everything from Army regulations to Morse Code. A surprisingly few courses dealt with flying which surprised me. Singing was required as we marched from place to place and one of our guys was assigned the title of song leader. Our day ended about six p.m. when we went to evening mess. The rest of the evening was free for studying, going to the PX (post exchange store) or an occasional movie. Taps were blown at ten p.m. and you'd better be in bed.

Going to the PX or to the base theater was quite a project. There were lines for everything! At the PX there would be a line for the candy department, other lines for drugs, food, or soft drinks. These lines sometimes had a hundred or more cadets. You had to be careful and make sure you got in the right line. One night I thought I was in line to buy some soft drinks but the line ended up at the theater box office; so, I just went to the movie instead. That leads me into a story about the PX.

Although our barracks seemed impeccably clean, somehow they became infested with that Army plague called "crabs." Almost everyone ended up having them so it became almost comical how everyone was itching in the crotch area.

Billy, one of my Squadron friends, had met a pretty girl who worked at the PX and he was in the habit of going there every evening and hanging around her. We were all using Campho Phenique to get rid of the crabs and my friend Billy had just run out and wanted us to get more at the PX; the only hitch was that his girl friend worked in that department and he didn't want to buy from her. He talked me and another Cadet into buying for him. When we asked for the Campho Phenique the girl gave us a knowing smirk but we quickly said "It isn't for us, it's for Billy over there." Billy never forgave us! The base was finally able to get rid of the critters after a mass sterilization of toilets and rest rooms

Learning to march, close order drill, calisthenics, and parades were a big part of Cadet life. Our physical education training was pretty rugged and cruel in some ways! The calisthenics would always end with the whole squadron running a race around a racetrack. To keep us from" dogging" it, they would gig the last ten guys finishing. A few times the whole squadron attempted to slow down a little to let some of the slower guys catch up but the instructor caught on to that and punished us by giving everyone a gig; no way to beat the system! I thought it was cruel because a slow runner, who might have become a terrific pilot, could feasibly be gigged out of the program. But that was what the whole program was about— to winnow out the weakest physically or mentally.

If we were gig-free, we were given a weekend pass, from noon on Saturday to Sunday evening at six. Almost everyone took their pass time in Los Angeles where there were plenty of girls and much to do. The Los Angeles Jr. League sponsored Saturday afternoon dances for the Officer and Cadet's club in the Ambassador Hotel. A big percentage of our guys headed there because you were a mortal cinch to find a great girl, plus most of the Jr. League girls were better looking and came from good families. I sometimes wonder if the parents of those girls knew what they were letting their daughters in for when they let them go to the Ambassador.

I passed all the six weeks of tests. Because there was no place on the schedule open for our class at a flying school, they temporarily transferred the whole squadron to Gardner Field located out in the Taft, California desert. We learned that there was nothing for us to do while we awaited transfer to a flying school. So, to keep us from sitting around, our entire group was given the job of digging a swimming pool for the base. The temperature was about 110 in the shade; and there was no shade! We were instructed to drink a lot of water and take salt tablets. When our sweat-drenched clothes dried there was left a white residue of salt.

Primary Flight Training; The Cream of the Crop

After a few weeks in that hellhole, on August 27th we were transferred to Santa Maria, California for Primary Flight Training. The school was located on an old grass airport. We had brand new barracks, cooler weather, and great food. Now we began aviation training in earnest. Our people were divided into two cadres. One cadre would do ground school in the morning and fly in the afternoon; then each week the cadres would switch. Every morning a dense fog would roll in off the ocean, which was only a few miles away, and the airport would be socked in. Those who were supposed to fly would have other studies substituted. It meant that sometimes you went for days without flying.

Mother's diary ~ September 20th, 1942:
Had a nice letter from Bobby and a picture. He has had only six hours flying instruction.

The six hours I wrote to mom about had taken almost three weeks to complete. This lack of flying time had me anxious and very worried.

The airplane we flew in was a Stearman open-cockpit biplane. Our instructors were civilians, most with very little flying time. My instructor was a guy about forty who seemed like an old man to me. They gave us practically no ground instruction on the theory of flight or what was going to happen when we were airborne. You just got into the front cockpit of the airplane and took off. There was no inter-com so you couldn't talk to the instructor in the rear cockpit. He had a "gosport" tube so he could talk to his student. The gosport tube was simply a three-eighths inch rubber hose with a funnel on one end so the instructor could talk into it. The other end had a "Y" junction with tubes that plugged into little pipes on either side of your helmet, by your ears. The instructor would yell into his funnel and you would pick up his voice (over the sound of the engine) but it was anything but clear. There was no way to tell him that you didn't hear or didn't understand except to shake your head. There was a six inch round mirror mounted on the aft edge of the top wing over your head so the instructor could see your face. It certainly was a difficult way to learn anything!

My instructor was a kind of a wise guy! On my first flight he asked me if I wanted to have him show me what the airplane could do. I was afraid to say no, so I said Yes! He proceeded to do a couple of slow rolls, a spin, and a stall. By the time he finished, I was airsick. He told me to stick my head out, on the right side, so I wouldn't mess up the airplane, fully knowing that the engine exhaust stack was on that side. Inhaling all those exhaust fumes exacerbated my problem and made me doubly airsick. When we landed I could hardly stand but he thought it was funny. Thus ended my first flight which I had really been anticipating with pleasure and on which I learned absolutely nothing.

During my first eight hours I really learned little and therefore had very little confidence. The instructor's way of teaching was to constantly yell at me telling me what a dumb S. O. B. I was, yelling so much that his spit was actually coming through the tube into my ears. The day's flying session began by flying out to a satellite field where I would join several of my classmates. While the rest of us sat on the ground, the instructor would take turns with us. We did stalls to learn the flying characteristics of the airplane, some acrobatics including spins, and of course practice landings and take-offs. For the latter my instructor insisted that I look out the left side of the airplane rather than over the nose. He literally made me turn my head to the left and would be on me the instant I tried to sneak a look over the nose. This was totally wrong as I discovered years later when I learned to fly my own plane for business, and, as any pilot will tell you, you need to look over and around the nose to get proper depth perception and vision to land.

To make a long story shorter, we were coming back to the main field one afternoon and I was to land the airplane. We called this time of the day the "rat race" because about 150 airplanes would all come in from the satellite airfields and arrive at the main field in about a ten-minute period. There were no runways in the grass; you just flew a down wind and base leg, turned final wherever there was room between other planes, and landed. The Stearman had a narrow landing gear and was famous for "ground loops" where the end of one wing would touch the ground causing the airplane to violently turn in that direction. I had planes on either side of me, some only fifty or sixty feet away, when all of a sudden I ground looped to the left. The instructor yelled at me and took over the controls and straightened me out. He yelled at me all the way back to the parking ramp. I told him, I couldn't land the airplane looking out the left side, the way he insisted. With absolutely no empathy or understanding he just told me "Mister you're in the *wash!*"

A few days later I went for a pre-*wash* check ride with an Air Corps pilot. I did everything right until he told me to do "S" turns over a road. I didn't realize it but the road was running east and up into the mountains. As I meticulously made my turns we were progressively getting closer to the ground as we flew toward the mountains on gradually rising terrain. On one turn I looked down and saw a cow flick its tail, which made me notice how low we were. On checking the altimeter I found that I was right on the required altitude, but quickly realized that from that altitude I should not have been able to see a tail flick. Realizing something was wrong, I signaled to the instructor who said, "I wondered when you were going to wake up to the fact that you were flying us into the ground!" Needless to say, he *washed* me out; my Cadet pilot days were over.

It was a crushing defeat for me; the first one in my life, and he knew I was taking it badly. He explained that the Air Corps was in need of pilots that they could train quickly, but that they also needed almost an equal number of bombardiers and navigators. So their philosophy was to advance those pilot cadets who showed an immediate potential and wash out the rest so they could re-train them for those other positions. Washing out was a traumatic experience for everyone! One minute you were the "cream of the crop" and all pumped up about being a pilot, and then you were washed out and on your way to a questionable future. There were several suicides in the Cadet program and it affected all of us deeply. I had a close friend, Steve Burr, who was really depressed about it. Before we were transferred out of Santa Maria we got pretty stinking drunk one night and that seemed to relieve some of the strain. In our minds, there didn't seem to be any rhyme or reason why they washed people out!

One of my classmates was so eager to get in the war that he had enlisted in the Royal Canadian Air Corps in 1940, had graduated as a pilot in their Cadet program, and had considerable flying time. He asked to be transferred into our Air Corps after Pearl Harbor and was told that the only way he could do so, would be to go through our Cadet program. He had already learned to fly so he really breezed through most of primary flying at Santa Maria. One day, on a dare, he flew under a big bridge—admittedly a dumb thing to do. As luck would have it, one of the instructors saw him and threw him in the wash. This guy loved to fly so much that he was absolutely furious. He said if he couldn't fly for us, he'd join the German Luftwaffe! Just goes to show you the degree of embarrassment and even rage that was felt by those who were washed out.

Phil Miller and My Irish Luck

Cadets who were washed out of pilot training were transferred back to Santa Ana for re-classification for Bombardier or Navigator training. Therefore, when I got back to Santa Ana, I was offered the opportunity to attend Bombardier or Navigators school which would also have given me an officer's commission. At this point I was really kicking myself that I hadn't gone into the gunnery program with Phil Miller. While all of this was going on I was in contact with Phil by phone. He said that the only way he could help me would be if I was completely washed out of the Cadet program and said to call him when this was accomplished, so he could arrange a transfer.

The next step was to appear before a Board of Officers who was interviewing washed-out pilots, to determine their new assigned destinies. When my turn came up to appear before the Board, I informed them of my shooting experience, and said that I felt I could be of more value to the Air Corps as a gunnery instructor, utilizing my shooting talent. The Board of Officers were astonished that I was willing to give up the opportunity to be an "Officer!" Navigator or Bombardier held no glory in my mind; Phil Miller and the gunnery program was all I could see for me ~ I convinced them and they eliminated me from the Cadet program. Immediately, I phoned Phil Miller to let him know that I was now free and available for re-assignment, and that I would be located in the Air Corps "unassigned pool" at Minter Field near Bakersfield, California.

The Unassigned Pool

Here all ex-cadets were held until they could be re-classified and assigned to other outfits. All of a sudden, I discovered with great dismay that I was in a precarious position. There was a good possibility of being transferred out to some undesirable situation while I was waiting for Phil to get me reassigned into his program! I watched nervously as many of my friends were transferred into positions like: military police, motor pools, and food service. Ironically, those of us who were once the *cream of the crop,* were suddenly *undesirables* and at the mercy of the system.

Irish luck where are you? After a morning roll call in the Unassigned Pool we had no further duties other than watching the bulletin board to see who was being transferred out. One day while I was just killing time, I heard shotgun shooting. I followed the sound around the airfield until I came upon the base skeet range. Pilot cadets were required to shoot skeet as part of their basic training. My hunger to participate must have shown on my face as I watched. The Lieutenant in charge

Shooting Skeet with my benefactor, Lt. Harold Bates, Minter Field, California, 1942. The man who saved me from the "unassigned pool."

of the range recognized my craving and asked me if I'd like to shoot a round with them; yes, indeed sir! Here again my Irish luck prevailed. Despite the fact that I hadn't picked up a shotgun for a year, and that I was using a borrowed firearm, I somehow broke a 25 straight—something none of the others had done and rare at this range. The Lieutenant was so impressed he wanted to know what I was doing on the base. When I told him about the unassigned pool, and my long range plans to get into the gunnery school program with Phil Miller, this kindly Lieutenant asked if I'd like to temporarily be transferred to his Ordnance Department and become a skeet instructor; this job would be a great way to keep me available for when my gunnery program transfer came through. I call him my *kindly* Lieutenant—a man who saved me—a man who led me in the right direction, at a crossroad of my life.

As it turned out, it took Phil Miller about four months to get me transferred into the gunnery school at Kingman, Arizona. In those four months at Minter Field, my kindly Lieutenant benefactor had me promoted twice; first to a Buck Sergeant and then to Staff Sergeant; a great enlisted rank with more pay and status. He said this added rank would really help me in the gunnery school and boy was he right. Needless to say, I really enjoyed those four months at Minter Field and will always be indebted to Lt. Harold Bates! The man rescued me from the dreaded "unassigned pool."

Mother's Diary ~ May 8, 1943:
> *Bob just phoned me from Omaha. He will be home tomorrow . . . Hurrah!*

Mother's Diary ~ May 17, 1943:
> *It is raining. My dear little Bob left for Kingman at 3:20 this morning.*
> *We are sure lonely for him.*

Aerial Gunnery Training

At Kingman, I was required to go though the Aerial Gunnery Training Program to get my gunner's wings; then I could begin instructing. The six weeks gunnery school included everything from aircraft recognition, radio procedures, and shooting with everything including BB guns, shotguns, hand-held machine guns, and turrets with guns. The culmination of the course was aerial gunnery.

The student rode in the back cockpit of an AT-6 single engine airplane and fired with hand held machine guns. Another aircraft dragged our flag-type tow-targets. Your pilot would dive down alongside the tow-target at a range of about 100 yards. The gunner would commence firing and shoot until he had used up the specified amount of .30 caliber ammunition. You wore a wide leather belt with two straps attached, one on each hip, and fastened to the floor of the cockpit. To fire successfully you had to stand up in the slipstream, straining against those straps, to keep from being thrown out during the violent maneuvers made by the AT-6 pilot. For those of us new to flying, that ride in the back cockpit of the AT-6 was a *terrifying* experience.

The pilots who flew us out on our gunnery missions were just out of Aviation Cadet Flying School and resentful that they had been assigned to such workhorse flying. They had envisioned themselves in a more glamorous role, flying P-51's, and shooting down Germans in the European combat sky. Instead they were flying six to eight missions a day over the Grand Canyon, carrying gunnery students like me. It didn't take much to make these pilots play out their frustrations on the poor gunners, most of who had never been in an airplane before. Ninety percent of the students got violently air sick; and, ignominiously, were required to clean out the airplane after landing. The air was always bumpy and most of the year the temperature in the Kingman desert was over 100 degrees, about as disagreeable flying conditions as possible.

My pilot was one of those wise guys. However, he inadvertently did me a good turn. On our first run at the target my machine gun only fired about three shells and then jammed! When this happened, the procedure was that the pilot would bank sharply around, get in back of the line of attacking airplanes, and then when the gun was ready again, give the gunner another run at the tow target. My gun had jammed because the armorer who prepared it for the mission had mounted the link-shoot too high on the base plate; the links jammed up rather than going down the chute. As my hot-rod fly-boy banked steeply around, I was able to remove the link chute completely; now the gun would fire.

My *hot-rod* was evidently disgusted with me because he had to make another pass at the target, so he was violently banking the plane around and blasting me with plenty of G's making it extremely difficult to stand up against the slipstream. On our second pass, he dove in practically on top of the target, actually as close as twenty-five yards. I opened fire from that close range and was able to put all 200 rounds into the target. When they scored the hits, I had set a "new school record" for aerial gunnery! Thanks to my hot-shot-pilot and his temper, I was a star!

Upon graduation from the Gunnery School, I was permanently assigned to the base and was put in charge of eighteen skeet ranges. I reported to a Major Lyle Pressy, who, before the war, had operated skeet clubs in Palm Springs and Sun Valley. He gave me complete freedom to run the ranges as I saw fit. Skeet shooting was deemed important to the training of gunners because it taught the basics of "leading" a target and following through with your swing much as in golf. As part of his training, each gunner was required to shoot 100 skeet targets spread over several days. My day started at 6:30 a.m. when I met with my eighteen instructors to outline the day's agenda. When the truckloads of students arrived, the first step on the agenda was to have them do a walk-through of the ranges to kill all the rattlesnakes that abounded in the area. When a snake was found, one of my instructors would shoot it. These little devils liked to crawl into the skeet houses; we'd kill a half dozen every morning during the summer months.

Next we'd gather all the students in a group and explain the procedure, the basic principles of shooting, and then spend considerable time on gun safety. A good share of the students were city kids who had never fired a gun before. You'd think that the Air Corps' classification system would have picked out mid-western farm boys to be gunners, kids who had shooting and hunting experience! But no, true to their *SNAFU* (Situation Normal All Fouled Up!) system, they made cooks out of plumbers, plumbers out of carpenters, and city kids (New York City) gunners. As a consequence we had to start out by saying, "This is a shotgun! This is the shell it shoots! The shell goes in here! The shell fires when you pull this!" Most of the kids thought that because it was a shotgun and fired a handful of "bird" shot, it was not too dangerous. To prove to them that a shotgun, at close range, was more lethal than any other weapon, we had a standard demonstration that one of our instructors would put on. This involved taking an empty shell case, a wooden box that normally held 500 shells, and tossing it up in the air. The instructor would then shoot it, taking care to hit it right on one of the corners. The charge of bird shot at this six-yard distance would absolutely disintegrate the wooden box, deconstructing it into toothpick size pieces. We'd then explain that it would decapitate a human, or cut him in two, at close range. Needless to say, this impressed the students and made them more understanding of the need for care and gun safety. We then proceeded to give them individual instruction; starting them out on easy stations with straight away targets, and gradually building them up to the tougher stations that required more lead.

I really had some great instructors. Sometimes, when we were waiting for our students to arrive, we would shoot a round with each other. Most of them could break 25 straight on a regular basis. We'd get bored with regular skeet, so sometimes we'd shoot what we called "monkey skeet" where the lead shooter would hold the gun over his head, behind his back, or any other unorthodox position; the rest of us had to "monkey see—monkey do!" We got pretty good at this; so good in fact, that we had one guy, an Apache Indian, who could break 25 straight from the hip regularly. Sometimes our students would arrive when we were shooting in these strange ways, and needless to say, they would be impressed.

A few months later I was transferred to a .50 caliber machine gun turret range. They wanted instructors to be versatile and cross trained in various programs. On this range we used special trucks each having an electrically operated turret with two .50 caliber guns, identical to the turrets that were on the bombers in which the students would ultimately be flying. A dozen or more of these trucks would be backed up to a triangular shaped track on which ran a jeep that had a large, rectangular, canvas target (about eight feet long and three feet high) mounted on poles. The jeep ran behind a berm of dirt so only the target moving along could be seen above the earth horizon line. As the jeep turned the corner, so the target was broadside to us, I'd give the order to fire and all hell would break loose! The tips of the .50 caliber shells were dipped in paint of a different color for each gunner. The paint marks left on the target as the bullets passed through, made it possible to keep each gunner's score separate.

There were always humorous incidents in the military and one of them occurred while I was running this turret range. A big, black, vulture appeared and was wheeling around over the range about two hundred feet in the air. The students all wanted to shoot at it, but I had to say no! However, I turned my back on the line, gave the order to open fire (on the target supposedly) and of course they all emptied their turrets at the poor vulture. The sky was red, surrounding the bird with tracers. He was diving and turning like mad, but *not one bullet, out of several thousand,* hit him. I thought, "amazing!" and not a very good sign for our intrepid gunners.

Kingman was as horrible a place to be stationed as you can imagine! The town had a population of about 400 people, and nothing to offer. The main line of the Sante Fe Railroad ran through the town (and our base) and I guess that was the only reason for the town's existence. In the summer, the average temperature was well over one hundred degrees, with a lot of wind and dust; plus winters got really cold. It was a difficult place to work. Nobody left the base unless they could get a three-day pass, in order to go to Phoenix or somewhere else that was civilized. Rock fever was setting in on me, and then my Irish luck stepped in.

Officer Training School

Unbeknownst to me, or most others, the giant B-29 bomber was on the drawing board and about to be built. It was to have a very sophisticated new gunnery system and special people were to be trained to use it. As part of this program, a new Air Corps flight rating of "Gunnery Officer" was created with special wings to go along with it. At every gunnery school in the country several top instructors were given an opportunity to take tests to attend Officers Training School in Miami Beach. Those graduating with Commissions would be then sent to a special Gunnery Officer schools. I was fortunate to be selected from Kingman, passed all the tests, and was on my way to Miami Beach! This represented a golden opportunity to become an officer and still stay in my chosen gunnery field. So, here I was, once again, about to subject myself to ninety days of intensive training under the West Point System of discipline.

For the trip to Miami Beach I was put on a Sante Fe passenger train and assigned to a Pullman car with, would you believe, a lower berth for sleeping. It all seemed pretty deluxe to me but, before the trip was over, I was to find out that either the berth or the toilet was infested with those same critters I had encountered in Santa Ana during Aviation Cadets. I got off the train in New Orleans and spent two days in a hotel there while I got out the Campho Phenique again.

Miami Beach was really an experience for a young guy like me. Each Cadet Squadron lived in a commandeered, former resort hotel right on Collins Avenue. I lived in The Carlton Hotel, which today, like all those old hotels; in what they now call "South Beach," has since been renovated to preserve the old *art deco* look; and the Carlton is still standing. Our training course was ninety days; hence the term "90 day wonders!" Classrooms were in the hotels on the beach and we marched in formation from hotel to hotel, boisterously singing such songs as: "It's A Grand Old Flag" ~ etc. If we didn't sing, we got "gigged." In fact, you got gigged for just about any infraction of their rules. The West Point System consisted of lower and upper classmen, hazing, gigging, plus all the other things that were designed to illustrate to you just how much a human being could take. From this, an Officer was supposed to learn, first hand, how much he could push his troops.

You were a lower classman for your first thirty days. On arrival you were given a "butch" haircut and you were made to eat a "square" meal. With eyes on the horizon, you were supposed to lift your fork straight up from the plate to a point even with your eyes, then straight into your mouth. As you can imagine, it is difficult to spear a piece of food with a fork without looking at your plate. But any deviation from this procedure led to a gig. Each gig meant walking with a rifle for an hour. They were serious about these gigs; if you had 36 gigs you were *washed out* of the program. There's that word again!

The upper classmen were always hazing us and could give us gigs if we didn't perform. They would accost you, put you in a "brace" which meant standing at attention with your chest out, your stomach tucked in, and your feet in a precise position. You might be asked to recite Army regulations, sing, or do anything goofy the upper classmen might ask. Some of them let this authority go to their heads and abused the hazing privileges. The real officers who ran the school watched for this abuse and such Cadets could be washed out for sadistic hazing. Some of the upper classmen and their hazing were really unfair. Clark Gable, the movie star, was in my Squadron and he earned his Commission the hard way; the upper classmen took great delight in working him over just because he was a celebrity. As an example, most of us got a "butch" haircut on arrival, but Gable got a shaved baldhead. He was constantly hazed and the only place he could escape to do the studying that was necessary in order to graduate was in the bathroom. The school rule was that no hazing was allowed in the bathroom.

Don Budge, the then famous tennis player, was also in my Squadron and he received similar unfair treatment. If you were on the receiving end of unfair hazing you had an opportunity to get even. After your first thirty days, they had a day that they called "Black Friday." This was one day set aside as a day when lower classmen would be allowed to haze upper classmen. Any upper classman who had abused his position was cut down to size on that day. He could get enough gigs to be washed out. This happened to one guy, who in addition to being washed out, was almost literally killed! He was made to don a raincoat and helmet, put on a full back pack, and then marched up and down the hall, in the middle of a hot Miami day in August, without air-conditioning, and 99% humidity; until he actually dropped from heat prostration. When we took the raincoat off him, he had broken out in a heat rash that was so severe he looked like a lobster. They took him to the hospital, washed him out; and that's all they wrote!

Speaking of heat rash, that was one of the biggest problems at Miami Beach. We had no hot water in our showers and I think this exacerbated the problem. With all the marching, calisthenics, etc., we were always in a sweat, and after about a week, we all broke out in heat rash. Standard procedure for us after a formation was to go to our rooms, remove all clothes, and assume the spread eagle position on the sheets of the bed, while sprinkling liberal quantities of Quinsana powder over our bodies. It was no fun but everyone had it. One of the worst experiences with this heat rash concerned some poison gas training we received. They marched us out to Bayshore Golf Course, where we received a lecture on poison gasses. Then we were issued gas masks, and forced to crawl on our hands and knees through a dirt tunnel about 60 feet long, dug into the golf course. The tunnel had been pumped full of tear gas so it would be a realistic test. We lined up single file, and then almost at a run, we dove into the tunnel and scrambled though it on our hands and knees. I had nightmares about it for days, as did other Cadets. My recollection is of intense claustrophobia, pushing the guy ahead of me to get out sooner, difficulty in breathing with that old fashioned gas mask, and worst of all was the effect of that tear gas on my heat rash. You felt as though you were on fire, and when we all came out of that tunnel we were like mad men! I've often thought that the guy who dreamed up that test should have been court martialled!

Officer Training School was one of the most difficult things I've ever experienced; however graduation day finally came and boy, were we ever proud! We were all given one-week passes prior to assignment to new stations. It was off to a men's store on Lincoln Road, for me, to get completely outfitted in new Officer's uniforms from an allowance we were given of $150.00. What a thrill it was to walk down the street and get my first salutes from enlisted men! I had really worked hard and long for this moment!

Several of us had made reservations to stay in a hotel on Daytona Beach for the rest of our leave. The flight doctors at Miami Beach had told us that the best cure for heat rash was swimming in salt water; that plus the sun would dry it up. I spent a delightful week doing just that; then I felt ready for my next assignment: the Headquarters of the 9th Bombardment Group at AAFTAC, in Orlando, Florida. The letters AAFTAC mean Army Air Force School of Applied Tactics. Bombardment Groups were sent here after their normal training was over for a final course in combat tactics. The 9th Bomb. Group, to which I was now assigned, was responsible for the training of these visiting groups. Most of the 9th personnel had combat experience. As an example we had several men who had flown in the famous Doolittle raid on Japan and many had combat experience in Europe, as well.

Colonel Edward Connally

Our commander, Colonel Ed Connally, was a West Point graduate and a Career Air Corps man. When he found out I was from Iowa, he told me a story about an emergency landing he had to make, while flying the mail for the Air Corps back in the 30's when the civilian air mail system had bogged down. He was on a flight from Chicago to Omaha and ran into a bad blizzard near Carroll, Iowa. The airplane he was flying was a big open cockpit, single engine, and they didn't have much in the way of instruments back in those days. He was able to land in a big cornfield without injury. When he got out of the plane he saw a light through the drifting snow and headed towards it. When he knocked on the door of a farmhouse, the occupants looked out at him through the windows, but were afraid to open the door. He said he must have looked like a man from Mars; he had on bulky sheepskin flying clothes, and was completely covered from head to toe, with his face barely showing. They ultimately let him in and he spent the night there. There was no phone so he had to wait until the next morning to have the farmer drive him into town so he could report that he and the mail were safe.

At the start of WWII, Connally was commander of a B-17 Group that was caught on the ground in the Philippines shortly after Pearl Harbor, and was almost annihilated. Connally and a few aircraft escaped to Australia from where they tried to carry on the war. They were so short of bombs and supplies that they had to make their own bombs. In one instance they filled big gasoline drums with cement, fastened wood fins on them, and rigged them to hang in the bomb bays, along with a few real bombs. With this rudimentary equipment they flew bombing missions in support of landings like Guadalcanal.

Because of his Philippine experience, Connally hated the Japs and had a fervent desire to get back and have another crack at them with the proper equipment; he had to get even. As a result he guided our 9th Group with an iron hand and demanded absolute perfection. He was a tough disciplinarian, but was always very fair. We all liked and respected him. The groups that we trained went out better prepared for combat.

Appointed Group Gunnery Officer

Despite my lack of any combat experience, I was appointed Group Gunnery Officer and put in charge of the training program we had for the bomber gunners. A new system called "position firing" had been developed by the British and had proven to be more effective for bomber gunners to shoot down attacking fighters. The curriculum I set up for the gunners included in-depth training on this new philosophy. This was a rather radical departure from the old "apparent motion lead" system that had been taught in the gunnery schools. This was supplemented with armament refresher courses and some skeet shooting for recreation. As part of my new job, I wrote a skeet-shooting instruction manual specifically for the Air Corps.

Everything pertaining to gunnery was dumped on me. Connally obtained two B-26 bombers, which I converted to tow-target airplanes. I supervised the installation of the sophisticated tow reels, the training of the crews of the B-26's that towed the targets, and wrote all the procedures. There was more to it than I expected, and the only thing that saved me was that nobody else had any knowledge either.

Flying those initial missions to train the B-26 crews was pretty hairy. To release the tow target with its 3000 feet of steel cable, the B-26 had to be slowed down to just above a stalling speed. Once the target was out we would await the arrival of the B-17's that would be training their gunners by firing on our targets. The B-17's cruising speed was about the B-26's stall speed so with the added drag of the cable and target, the B-26 was flying in a very mushy, nose-up, attitude that required the full concentration of the pilots to keep from going into a stall. One of the crew always stood by the tow reel with a big wire cutter, on the ready to cut, should a stall occur. The pilots hated this tow target duty!

We flew our tow missions out over the gulf and when

completed, we flew back to Orlando dragging the target behind us. I had marked a spot in the center of the airport, well away from buildings and runways, where we were supposed to drop the targets for scoring. Dropping them consisted of attaching a "fish" (called this because it was shaped like a fish) to the cable and upon a signal from the pilot, the fish would be released so it could slide back along the 3000 feet of cable and release the target. This whole operation was fraught with danger because it was very difficult for the pilot to know exactly when to signal the crew to release the fish; with all that cable out, it was an educated guess. Then there was a delay while the fish slid down the 3000 feet of cable and finally the release. In the meantime, the airplane was moving along about 160 miles an hour.

I am giving you all of the details so you will understand ~ how easy it was for us to drop one of the targets ~ on top of our Group Headquarters!

It was an event that almost got me court martialled, besides scaring the hell out of Col. Connally.

The target itself was a piece of canvas about thirty feet long and not very heavy; but attached to it was a 2 1/2" pipe five feet in length with a 30-pound weight on the bottom. The weight part made quite a racket when it hit the Headquarters' roof and part of the pipe with the weight attached to it ended up on clerk's desk. That's when the stuff hit the fan and when we landed, there was a reception committee awaiting me.

Crash Boat Base; Tarpon Spring, Florida

In the service we were always told that we should never volunteer for anything. This certainly proved true for me while I was in Orlando. One day during a Staff Meeting, Col. Connally asked if any of us knew anything about boats. Being a young second lieutenant wiseguy, I piped up that I had been a Sea Scout, when I was a boy. Connally immediately said, "You're my man!" He made me commanding officer of a Crash Boat Base that our Group operated, the existence of which, I was totally unaware. So, off I went to Tarpon Springs, Florida

Air Corps crash boat based at Tarpon Springs, Florida.

into a new adventure doing something I knew *absolutely nothing* about.

The crash boat base was located on the banks of the Tarpon River right in the area where all of the sponge boats operated and which has now become a big tourist attraction. Our base consisted of a building about 50 X 150 feet, which housed our office plus the barracks for our crews and staff. We had two 63-foot "P" boats; identical to the torpedo boats made famous by John F. Kennedy in the South Pacific. Ours were equipped with torpedo tubes that we did not use. We did, however, carry racks full of depth charges in the unlikely event that we ran across a German sub in the Gulf. We also had two twin .50 caliber machine gun mounts. Each boat was completely equipped for paramedic duty and our crews were all trained in this work. We also carried complete diving equipment of the old "hard hat" helmet and suit type. We were well equipped to handle just about any situation involving an aircraft crash.

During those war years there were hundreds of aircraft of various types constantly flying around Florida and over the gulf. We kept one boat about 60 miles out in the gulf, with a sea anchor, out doing picket duty. The other boat was kept at our dock or sometimes sent up to Cedar Keys, Florida where we had another small base. At the base we also had two Caterpillar tread "swamp buggies" for going after crashes in the Everglades. My job was as Base commander; we had trained Captains for each of the "P" boats.

One day I asked to go along on a crash call. We left the dock and were slowly creeping down the river. I asked the Captain why we were going so slowly; there was a crash out there with people who needed help. He said, "Do you want to go faster, Sir?" and I said, "Sure, let's get out there and help those people!" With that, he rammed the throttles on the twin 2000-horsepower Kermath high-octane, gasoline engines wide open and we went screaming down the river leaving a wake behind us that put some of the sponge boats up on dry land. Of course we had been in a "no wake" zone, of which I was ignorant. When we came back a few hours later, the havoc we had caused was still obvious. As we sailed by, all the Greek sponge fishermen were shaking their fists at us. The Captain thought it was funny, but he found out it wasn't so funny when I confined him to the base for a week, for being such a wise guy. It took a long time for the Greeks (and *everyone* in Tarpon Springs is Greek) to forgive us.

I got in trouble again in Tarpon Springs because I was so eager to do a good job. In one of our boats, an engine threw a rod and tore itself up pretty badly. We weren't equipped to do major repairs, so a complete new engine was ordered from the Quartermaster in Atlanta. The shipyards in Tampa that did that kind of work were all so busy they couldn't get to us for a couple of months. My crews said they could install it them-selves, if we could find a hoist to lift the ponderous engines. Up the river a few doors from us was a shipyard that worked with the sponge boats. They had a big dock with a hoist mounted on a pair of 18" X 18" wood beams that extended out over the river. After deciding to do the work ourselves, I had the new engine shipped down from Atlanta and deposited on the dock.

Our crews removed all the bolts and wires from the old engine, the boat was moved alongside the dock under the hoist, and we commenced to hoist the 1500 lb. engine out of the boat. Well, as you perhaps have guessed already, the hoist couldn't take the weight, let out one big groan and collapsed about three feet, taking part of the dock with it. So there we were with the engine swinging in the air *over a one-million-dollar boat,* the dock about to fall in the river, and the Greek who owned the dock screaming his head off. My first concern, despite my panic, was to get that boat the hell out of there, before the engine fell THROUGH it. We saved the boat, shored up the dock enough to bring the engine in and put it in a truck, and then we were lucky enough to find a boat-works in St. Petersburg that could do the installation for us.

In the meantime the Greeks started to sue for the damages to their dock and I was called before a board of inquiry in the Adjutant General's Office at Drew Field to explain how things could possibly have arrived at this state. I was able to talk them out of taking any action against me. How I'll never remember. Needless to say, after about six months of Tarpon Springs and adventures like that, I was happy to go back to the 9th Bomb. Hq. and get back to the shooting which I knew something about.

Back To Orlando; Training Gunners

Orlando was a great place to be stationed and I really enjoyed my job. I rented a house on Lake Maitland (at that time, the only house on the lake) and settled into a nice routine. I could have bought that house and the whole lake for fifteen thousand dollars. Now it is completely built up with million dollar homes, but I barely had rent money, so buying wasn't even an option. The 9th Bomb. Group had several bases ~ Brooksville, Montbrook, Pinecastle, and Kississimee. I traveled to them mostly by jeep but once in a while could hitch a ride on a B-17 or B-26.

In addition to my job of training gunners, I was also assigned some design projects, which were very interesting. The first one was to design some kind of a "waist window" for the B-17's and B-24's; one which would allow the gunners to shoot their hand held 50-caliber machine gun, but be out of the blast of cold air they normally encountered. I designed a Plexiglas window with aluminum ribs to give it rigidity. A circular opening with aluminum frame made it possible for the gun to protrude through this opening and still have the range of movement needed to fire at the enemy. The window we created made the waist gunner's job much easier and warmer, because he was now out of that tremendous wind created by the bomber, which was probably flying at 160 miles an hour. An unexpected fringe benefit was a big reduction in noise from the .50-caliber; now the muzzle blast was outside the window. Because the window created less drag than the open waist, the aircraft improved in air speed and fuel economy. Once the window had been well-tested in combat, it was incorporated in all the new bomber production and some existing aircraft were remodeled to accommodate it.

My next project concerned the new "chin" turret that was being installed in all of the new B-17's. In the earlier models the Bombardier (who rode in the nose of the bomber) had two separate .50 caliber machine guns that he tried to fire at enemy fighters. One gun protruded out of an opening on the right side of the nose and the other was on the left. Both were awkward to fire and as a result, the Bombardier's success in shooting down fighters was the poorest of any position on the airplane. So, someone dreamed up the idea of a "chin" turret that mounted on the bottom of the nose just below the Plexiglas. The turret had two .50 caliber guns mounted about 18" apart and operated by a remote control at the Bombardier's station in the nose. The turret turned in azimuth but vertical movement of the guns was provided by a 3" wide slot in which the guns traveled up and down. It worked O. K. but the screaming, shrieking, noise made by the air going through those slots drove the crews crazy. Thus, I was given the job of developing some way of eliminating that noise.

My first thought was to enclose the slot with heavy canvas and a jumbo zipper that would zip or unzip as the gun moved up and down. The idea was great in theory but every time we went up to test it, the zippers would jam and the guns would rip them and the canvas apart. At that time the only zippers available were brass and they didn't run very smoothly. I have a hunch that our modern nylon zippers probably would have worked. At any rate we had to scrap that idea and ended up attaching a piece of material made with a combination of rubber and fiber, to either side of the slot. Above and below the gun the material met and completely closed the slot, so even at high speed, no air went through the slot, thus reducing the noise considerably. As the guns went up, they forced this piece of material open to allow passage; as they went down the material opened again and it was stiff enough that the opening opened and closed smoothly. Now the only problem was that the rubber-fiber material wore with use and had to be replaced periodically. We had to settle for that!

Secret Project; Brooksville, Florida

For a two-month period in the summer of 1943, one of our B-17 squadrons was detached from Orlando and sent to Brooksville, Florida to work on the development of a highly secret project. Most of our headquarters staff went along and for the duration of the project there were no passes or furloughs and we were all confined to the air base. The project was to test a "glide" bomb! Our bomber fleets were being decimated in Europe by flak and fighters encountered enroute to their targets. It was believed that if a glide bomb could be released several miles from its target, many lives and aircraft could be saved. The bomb that was designed for us to test looked like a little P-38. It was a 500 lb. bomb with wings, twin booms extending along the side of the bomb and back to twin tails. One bomb was suspended from special racks under the wings on each side of the B-17. A gyroscope was supposed to keep the bomb flying straight and level. Once our crews had learned how to mount the bombs and had developed a release mechanism we started flying actual test bombing missions.

At first just one or two bombers were used and then later we did testing with eleven-ship formations. The bombing target was a little island in the Tortugas. Our Group Bombardier was Captain James R. Copeland who had the best bombing average in the entire Air Corps. He was a much-decorated hero of the battle of Midway where he was credited with sinking a Jap cruiser; a feat made more remarkable because the B-17 had taken off with only 3 engines operating and just a few bombs. At any rate, if anyone had the credentials to make the glide bombs work, Copeland certainly did.

In the early tests they had a lot of problems with the bombs not releasing properly and the sometimes going into a spin instead of a glide. Finally, after several weeks of testing and many hours of flying time, we put together a typical eleven-ship combat formation and flew a test mission to the bombing island. Out of 22 bombs from the formation, not one hit the island and most spun out of control into the ocean miles from the target. As this was the culmination of the project and was such a failure, the project was dropped.

As with all flying operations there is always an element of danger! Unfortunately, we lost two crews in a spectacular mid-air collision that I had the misfortune of seeing at close range. As one of our eleven-ship formations was returning from a training mission, I was instructing a group of gunners on our skeet range which was located in the center of a triangle formed by the airfield's three runways. As was their custom coming back from a practice mission, the formation would fly over the airfield on their downwind approach to land. Every few seconds, one plane would peel off and turn on base leg; thus the eleven aircraft would be spaced about a minute apart as they made their final approach. This was a spit and polish squadron and they took pride in making the tires squeal as they touched down at precise 60-second intervals—a sign that they were really on the ball! As part of all of this, they flew really tight formations with their wings almost touching. This was a great combat formation as it increased the firepower of the guns in defending against enemy fighters. It also compressed the area the bombs would fall in. I tell you all of this so you will understand how that terrible mid-air collision occurred.

As the big formation approached the airfield at 1000 feet pattern altitude, it was a magnificent and awesome sight. Everyone would drop what they were doing to watch this precision approach and landing. In this instance, as they flew over the skeet range we all stopped shooting and just watched. It was windy and very hot with resulting turbulent air. For this reason the crews probably should have loosened up their formation but they were so intent on being a "crack" outfit that they came over the field in a very tight formation. As we watched, horror-stricken, the turbulent air caused one of the giant B-17's to slide under another and then come up under it cutting the one on top in two. There was a giant explosion and ball of fire over a thousand feet into the air and the remains of the two planes came down in a flaming mass about 200 yards from where we stood. The flames set the forest on fire and we couldn't get near the wreckage for several minutes. It was a foregone conclusion that there were no survivors from the twenty men in the two crews.

Many of our wives were staying in Brooksville a few miles away. The smoke from the crash fires was very evident, so everyone in town knew there had been a crash. The telephone lines suddenly jammed with calls and a big crowd gathered at the front gate. It took a little while to decide who had died and then it was the chaplain's sorrowful duty to pass the news on to relatives and friends who were in town. It was a terrible tragedy and one that bothered all of us for a long time; such a waste of talented men especially now, once we found out that the glide bomb project was a failure.

Testing "Block Buster" Bombs

The 9th Bomb. Group Bombardier, Captain James R. Copeland, befriended me when I first arrived at Orlando. We became such good friends that when he got married, he asked me to be his best man. Copeland was the one who had distinguished himself during the battle of Midway by sinking a Jap cruiser with high-altitude bombs dropped from a B-17. His bombing record was the best in the entire Army Air Corps and that is why he had been assigned to the 9th Bomb. Group. As part of his job he developed bombing tables for new bombs that then were used by all Bombardiers in the entire Air Corps. While I was working on some of my gunnery projects he was working on bombing tables for a new 5000 pound bomb; one so big that it didn't fit inside the bomb bay of a B-17 and was hung from external shackles between the engines. He had dropped several dummy bombs but now was ready to test the real thing. I was intrigued by the project and asked if I could go along on the test-bombing mission to the bombing range near Ocala, Florida. We dropped the two big bombs from ten thousand feet and the explosion was so violent we could feel it at that altitude. On the ground it was even worse! We broke windows in Ocala several miles away and I understand that the bombs each created a circular lake about a hundred yards across and those lakes are still there.

Another officer who I prefer not to name was one of our Officers who elected not to go in the B-29 program so I lost track of him until after the war in 1957. I received a phone call from him advising that he was coming to Des Moines and wanted to get together. Of course I was delighted to hear from him and my wife and I made plans to entertain him. He stayed for three days and we had a lot of fun reminiscing about the days in Orlando. He advised that he was separated from his wife, had been a University Professor, and now was enroute to Colorado Springs where he was to be an instructor at the new Air Force Academy. It all seemed to be on the up and up until the morning when he was leaving town when he came to my office and asked if I would cash a check for him. We didn't keep much cash around but I would have given him whatever he asked for. At any rate, we ended up by cashing a three hundred dollar check and, you have already guessed, it really bounced! I later found out that he had bounced one at the hotel where he stayed and also at Pond's Body Shop where he had ordered a new top for the Packard convertible he was driving. I was really angry at being sucked in by someone that I had considered a friend. Roy Meadows, the head of the FBI office in Des Moines, was a good friend of mine so I phoned him to see what could be done. His investigation revealed that this man had been traveling around all over the country looking up old Army friends and had been bouncing checks everywhere. He didn't even have an account in the bank he wrote the checks on. The information that I gave the FBI instigated a complete investigation and he was finally caught in Alabama and was sentenced to several years in the Federal penitentiary. He was a brilliant man and I can't imagine what turned him from what could have been a great career into being a petty criminal. It was a sad ending to what had been a nice friendship but an interesting side note to relate here.

Bird Dog, Brooksville, Florida

I'd like to tell you about another more pleasant experience while I was stationed at Brooksville. One of our officers had a bird dog, a pointer, which he had brought to the base with him. He wasn't hunting the dog so said I could use it. I'd borrow a gun and shells from the skeet range and just about every day I'd use some of my spare time to go quail hunting. There were a lot of quail within a short distance of the field. I'd bring the quail back to the Officer's Mess and they'd prepare them for dinner. Guess who became very popular with the officers for providing them with this great departure from Army food?

The pointer and I became great friends! He saved my life one day; an experience I shall never forget. This dog normally would hit a classic point when he found birds; tail straight up, one front paw in the air, and his head pointing forward. Generally, I'd walk up beside him and kick the birds out so I could get a shot. One day he hit a point, but his tail was tucked down between his legs, and his head was down very low. I thought it was a strange point but started to walk by him, when suddenly, I saw something in front of him move. He had pointed and hypnotized a giant Florida diamondback rattler! I had my gun off safety, so quickly blasted the coiled snake and killed it. It was the biggest rattler I'd ever seen; about six feet long, four inches in diameter at its thickest point, and had a head the size of my fist. As big as he was, if he had struck, he could have pumped a pint of venom into me. I wasn't properly dressed for snake-country hunting, wearing only light Army chino pants and leather oxford shoes. Now, I wouldn't think of hunting in snake country without snake chaps or boots. At any rate, that pointer with his unusual point alerted me and saved me from walking into that snake. In following weeks we found other snakes and I learned to be very watchful of the pointer's tail.

B-29 Group; Dalhart, Texas

A few weeks after being transferred back to 9th Bomb. Group Hq. in Orlando, Col. Connally called a staff meeting. Although we had heard a little about the new B-29, we were totally unprepared for Connally's announcement. We had been selected to become one of the first operational B-29 groups. We had many combat veterans in our group, including several Doolittle raiders. The surviving Doolittle Raiders had been promised that if they survived that raid on Japan, they would not be required to fly in combat again. So, Connally gave all of us the choice of going with him or remaining in Orlando. All but the Doolittle raiders unanimously wanted to go with him to Dalhart, Texas where our new B-29 Group would be organized. And so, in December of 1943 I was transferred to Dalhart to begin the biggest adventure of them all.

Army people have always said that they should receive overseas pay for serving in Texas. Dalhart, located in the extreme northwest corner of the Texas Panhandle, close to both the Oklahoma and New Mexico borders was often described by those of us who were stationed there as "the A__hole of Creation"! It was also laughingly said that Texas was the only place in the world where you could stand in mud up to your ankles and have dust blowing in your face! Dalhart certainly lived up to all these descriptions. It was a very small town, probably about 2000 then, with one little theater and not much else to do. To add to our misery, while we were there the weather was horrible! One day it would be in the seventies and a few days later a northern would blow in and it would go below zero. At this point we were not doing any flying so weather didn't make much difference. I never did know why they chose to send us to Dalhart but guess it was because they had space for us, for the few weeks we'd need to put our Group together.

Chapter 5

Training For Combat

Fairmont, Nebraska

At another Staff Meeting in January, Col. Connally announced that Fairmont, Nebraska would be our B-29 training base. He ordered a Master Sergeant by the name of LaViolette and me to immediately transfer to Fairmont and begin to gather together the personnel who would make up the Group. Why he chose me I'll never know, as I was still a second Lieutenant; possibly it was because I was such an "Eager Beaver." He advised me that I would be the acting Group Commander and represent him in all matters. I was proud at being selected but really overwhelmed with the task ahead. Here I was once more being assigned to a task of which I knew very little; but wise Connally knew that an old timer in the Air Corps, like Sergeant LaViolette, would know most of the answers and could guide a new Officer like me.

LaViolette and I arrived in Fairmont, Nebraska in January of 1944. It was about 20 below zero and the wind was blowing like hell. LaViolette, a Cajun from Louisiana whose blood had been thinned out by duty in the Philippines,

112

thought he was going to die. I had been a salesman in Nebraska prior to the war, so I knew what to expect. Fairmont was an even smaller town than Dalhart; I'd guess a population of about two hundred. It was on the main line of the Burlington Railroad and U. S. Highway #6. The air base was pretty new and had been training B-17 crews for the last year. It had three runways arranged in a triangle. There were several large hangars on the flight line and very comfortable wood buildings had been erected for barracks and offices.

My first duty there was to pay Col. Connally's respects to the Base Commander, a Col. Marsalis. In the Air Corps hierarchy there is always a Base Commander who is in charge of the permanent personnel. Each Group that would come through for training would have its own Commander such as our Connally. Marsalis was shocked that only a 2nd Lieutenant would represent Connally and immediately rubbed me the wrong way. Marsalis and I would have many conflicts down the road.

Before I left Dalhart, Connally briefed us very carefully on our procedures. Our primary job would be to process all the new men transferred in to make up the three squadrons that would form our Group. He advised us to watch the 2nd Air Force very carefully as they were in the habit of assigning inferior personnel to Groups that were not watching them carefully. We were not to allow the "dregs" of the Air Corps to be transferred into our group. (The 2nd Air Force was the Headquarters in Colorado Springs responsible for all unassigned personnel in the Air Corps.) We were not to accept any men who had a court martial on their record or whose IQ, according to the AGCT (Army General Classification Test) was below 60. A soldier's Service Record accompanies him and contains just about all information from whether drafted or enlisted, enlistment date, AGCT scores, health records, court martial records, etc. A study of the Service Records gave the LaViolette/Allen team all the information we needed to decide if the men were fit to be in the kind of a crack outfit Connally envisioned. And here is where my first big conflict began with Marsalis, the Base Commander.

Just as Connally had expected, 2nd Air Force had transferred in some really inferior people. It didn't take us long to segregate their records but when we tried to refuse them, I was called to Marsalis' office. In our meeting I explained to him the instructions I had received from Connally. I then asked him if he had ever met Connally, to which he answered, "No!" It then was my duty to advise Marasalis that Connally wasn't given the name, "Jungle Jim" for nothing and that I would not disobey him no matter what! Marsalis didn't like it, but began, begrudgingly, to accept our refusals.

Many months later I learned that Connally's wisdom about carefully choosing the personnel really paid off. Three months into training in Fairmont, the 393rd Squadron, which was one of the three Squadrons in our Group, was suddenly transferred out. They subsequently served as the nucleus for the 509th Atomic Bomb. Group. Paul Tibbets, the Commander of the 509th Atom Bomb. Group (who was also the pilot of the Enola Gay, the first B-29 to drop an atom bomb) has stated many times that the reason the 509th Group was so successful was because their men had been "hand picked." Sgt. LaViolette and I were responsible for hand picking all of the enlisted men, so we felt we could share in their success.

Parade-Happy Col. Marsalis; Fairmont

Marsalis was what the GI's called "Parade Happy!" Every Saturday morning there was a parade of all the outfits on the base. Marsalis got an ego trip out of having all those formations pass in review and salute him. The parades were a contest of sorts with special recognition being given to the formation that was judged the best. Generally one of his Base outfits won because they were permanent personnel and accustomed to marching together. Because the Groups coming in for training were made up of men who had only been together a few weeks, they were at a disadvantage compared to the permanent personnel Base outfits. Marsalis knew he had this advantage and maybe that is why he wanted the competition; so he could show up the visiting Groups. At any rate, I had been organizing our formations for the Saturday parades and

I used this as one way of getting even with Marsalis for the way he treated me.

In Miami Beach I had been a Cadet Officer and as such, had led our Squadron in parades that were very competitive. If I learned nothing else out of Miami Beach, it was how to teach troops to march and win. So, when Marsalis ordered us to participate in our first parade, I really dug in to devise a way to win the weekly competition. I took our men into one of the big hangars where Base personnel couldn't see us and arranged them by height. Now when they passed in review there would not be the irregularity of a short guy next to a tall one. After I had them sized, I walked them around inside the hangar and taught them how to march. In every formation there are always a few men who lurch, bob, or jerk and thus stand out in the formation. We were allowed to keep a few men out of the parades as barracks fireguards so those who couldn't march well were assigned this duty.

To rally the men behind me I told them that if we could win the Saturday parades, the Base Commander would probably lose interest and we'd have a good chance of not having to compete any more. I prompted them to razz the Base troops when possible: as an example, when our formations were in the street next to the parade grounds, awaiting their position in the line of formations, they would be at "parade rest." From this position, when some of the Base outfits marched by, our guys would call out things like "sick call" or would boo and laugh. This improved our morale and livened up the competition, but really didn't change our relationship with the base enlisted men because they hated the parades as much as we did.

Col. Connally Arrives

Thus, using the expertise I had just gained in Miami Beach, we won not only the first parade but all of them. When Connally arrived in Fairmont to take over active command of our Group, he immediately advised Marsalis that his troops were not going to participate in the "chicken shit" parades, that we were Air Corps men, not infantry, and the parades

HQ Staff of 504th at Fairmont, Nebraska, 1943. L to R: Col. James T. Connally; Group Commander, Col. Marsalis; Base Commander, Lt. Col. Huglin, Captain Ash, Lt. Bob Allen.

were a waste of everyone's time. Our troops loved him for doing this.

The B-29: A Magnificent Bird

I'll never forget that day in April when Col. Connally called the staff together and advised us that we were all going to fly down to Topeka, Kansas to get our first look at a B-29. We used a B-17 for the trip and Connally flew in the left seat as pilot with Bill Quinlan as co-pilot. Because there were not a lot of seats, I chose to ride in the nose of the aircraft in the bombardier's position. It was a short trip so we flew at about five thousand feet and it was fun to look down from that big glass nose at an earth that was just beginning to turn green after the winter.

Connally's landing in Topeka gave me a real scare! From my vantage point in the nose I could see the Bombardier's air speed indicator and, as we approached the runway, it seemed to me that the air speed was getting a little low and we had better put on some power if we were going to make the runway. Sure enough, we under-shot the runway and set down about fifty feet short of the cement runway lip. The main landing gear wheels dug a pair of small trenches leading up to the runway and there was quite a jolt as the wheels struck the lip of concrete. When we pulled up in front of Base Operations and climbed out of the airplane, the underside of the wings above the wheels was plastered with mud. Of course nobody dared say anything but I could tell from Connally's look that he was not too proud of the landing. To me, with my limited ability at that time, any landing you could walk away from was a good one!

I was totally unprepared for the size of the B-29! It towered over our B-17 and you could almost park a B-17 under each wing. Of great interest to me was the gunnery equipment, which was totally different from any other airplane. All fifty-caliber machine guns were enclosed in rounded turrets and were operated by gunners from remote positions located in Plexiglas domes. Unlike the B-17 and all other former bombers, the gunners did not sit inside the turret or operate any of the guns from an open window. I had gone to a General Electric computer turret school so was not totally unaware of this radical new gunnery system. We spent the rest of the day going through the airplane with each of us studying the part of the aircraft that was our responsibility. When we left to fly home that evening I was really pumped up with the B-29 and couldn't wait to get our first deliveries so I could begin my gunnery training program.

About a month later we received delivery on our first B-29's. I hitched a ride on one at the first opportunity and that first flight was a real experience! I was amazed at how quiet it was inside compared to B-17's and all other bombers I had flown in. The B-29 was the world's first pressurized aircraft and, as a result, the entire cabin was insulated with cloth padding which greatly muffled the engine and air noise. In all older aircraft there was just the bare aluminum with windows and gun openings that shrieked and added to the rattling and engine noise. In fact the B-29 was so quiet that when we broke ground on our take-off, I thought that all four engines had quit. The insulation also made it possible for the heaters to do a better job of keeping the crew warm so it was no longer necessary to wear the bulky sheepskin outfits worn in other aircraft.

Knowing that we would be going overseas in about eight months I wanted to see more of my parents but could not get leave to go. So, I invited them to come to Fairmont to visit me. Our air base and what we were doing was so foreign to my folks that they were literally astounded at every turn. They were very proud that I was an Officer and were tickled to eat at our Officer's Club and meet my friends and the people with whom I worked. One night I took them to the Base Theater to see a movie. As was common then, prior to the feature film they had a musical short subject with a bouncing ball so that the audience could sing along. At one point only women were supposed to sing and since there were generally only a few women in the audience, the troops always sang those parts in a falsetto voice which my mother really thought was funny.

One day I got permission to take Dad out to the flight line and go on board a B-29. I think that what he expected inside that big aluminum fuselage was just a big open space. He couldn't believe how much equipment was crammed into the cabin of the aircraft. The operation of the airplane and all of its equipment completely boggled his mind. He was always prone to claustrophobia and I think he was secretly glad to get out of the airplane after our tour.

I think my folks' visit to Fairmont eased their worries about me. Totally impressed with the size of everything and the efficiency of our people, I'm sure that they went home thinking that their little Bobby was in good hands. We were all sad however when they left, as I wasn't sure when, or if, I'd ever see them again. And I'm sure it was much worse for them! Luckily, I saw them one more time before we went overseas but this time it was from the air. Through a friendship with one of our airplane commanders I arranged for him to fly me to Fort Dodge, Iowa on one of his B-17 training flights. By phoning my folks ahead of time to tell them that I was coming and to be on the lookout for a big airplane about noon that day I knew they would be there and ready. My friend really handled it well! We approached from the southwest and flew over my house at about two thousand feet. From my position in the nose, I could clearly see my house as we passed over. We flew on east of town where we did a big one hundred eighty degree turn and then made another pass over my home. This time he really did a buzz job, dropping down to about five hundred feet and running all four engines at full power. The first pass over the house had alerted the folks and the entire neighborhood so that on the second pass they were all out in the street waving towels. I could clearly see my dad and mother and some of the neighbors. It was a heck-of-a-thrill for me and even more thrilling for them, because that giant airplane made a tremendous noise at that altitude and none of them had ever seen such a plane that low before. After passing over the house we did an immediate turn away from town and climbed back to five thousand feet and got the hell out of there before some kill-joy could get our tail number and report us for buzzing. Unfortunately during the war there were many instances of people getting killed doing buzz jobs when they were not experienced at that kind of flying. I'm sure that our buzz job was the leading topic of conversation in that neighborhood for a long time.

The training in Fairmont began as soon as we had a full complement of personnel, which was about April of 1944. At first we had no B-29's and the crews trained with B-17's. Our first B-29's started arriving in late April of 1944. The initial B-29's had many bugs in them! Engines overheating on take-off were our primary problem. As summer arrived, the problem became intense. Standard procedure was to get off the ground, get gear and flaps up, and then throttle back as much as possible and fly low until the engines cooled down. On take-off the heat gauges would run way over the redline. We had a couple of planes that couldn't climb after take-off and *mushed* into wheat fields near our base. The problem was partially solved by having "cuffs" installed on the propeller hubs; this sucked more air into the engine.

The Notorious "Cook-Offs"

Another bug, which was in my department, was a gun that would "cook-off" after having been fired. The B-29 turrets were all remotely controlled; the gunner did not sit inside the turret as on B-17's, and the guns were rather closely covered by the turret enclosure. Thus, after extended firing they would be so hot that after the firing switch had been released, the .50 caliber shell in the gun chamber would actually bake until it fired, thus acquiring the name "cook-off." This in itself was not a great problem except that in most instances when this happened, the gun was aiming at an important part of the B-29, such as an engine! We set a couple of airplanes on fire and almost shot ourselves down several times. It was my responsibility as gunnery officer to develop procedures to prevent "cook-offs" and then re-train the gunners.

The self-inflicted damage was partially caused by how the turrets were controlled. When operating the turret, the gunner would depress a switch called the "action" switch. As long as he kept this switch depressed, the turret with its guns would swivel around and move up and down according to how the gunner moved his control. To fire the guns there was a separate switch, which served like a trigger. The normal stow position for the turrets was with the guns pointing back and level. Releasing the action switch would cause the guns to come up to level but they would remain pointed in whatever direction the gunner had been firing. Thus, after firing the gunner would release the action switch, the guns would come up to level but then trouble began because the guns might be pointed at an engine, the wing tip, or a gas tank in the wings. The solution to the problem was to have the gunner keep the action switch depressed after firing, point the guns on the belly of the airplane straight down, those on top pointed straight up, and to hold them in that position for a full minute. Thus the air passing through the turrets could cool the guns down so that the action switch could then be released and the guns brought into proper stow position.

The procedure worked but now the problem was to train the gunners to follow it. A few days after starting the procedure, one of our Bombardiers (who sometimes operated the front turrets) let one cook-off into an engine, set it on fire, and the crew almost had to bail out. That afternoon I was called into Connally's office where I stood in a brace as he bellowed

out, "The next time one of your gunners shoots one of my airplanes, your ass is going to be grass!" I immediately issued an
edict that the next time someone allowed a gun to cook-off into
an airplane, they were going to be confined to the base for a
month. Weekend passes were the most valued commodity to
the men, so this really got everybody's attention. But as you
might expect, it happened again, this time to another
Bombardier. I had the unhappy job of advising him that he was
confined to base for a month. He had a girl friend in Omaha so
was really angry with me and threatened me with dire
destruction. However, making an example of a soldier in the
Army way really worked and, as a result, we had no more
cook-off damage.

Maggie's Drawers

As part of our preparation to go overseas, all of our personnel were required to qualify with the M1 .30 caliber carbine. A regulation Army rifle range had been built a few miles
from the airbase and part of my responsibility as Gunnery
Officer was the scheduling and conducting of this qualification
shooting. The 200-yard rifle range had about a dozen targets
with a pit behind an earthen berm. The targets were about six
foot square and mounted on wood frames that were brought
down into the pit for scoring and then raised for firing. If a
shooter missed the whole target, a red flag was waved back
and forth in front of the target. Years ago the Army used the
term "Maggie's drawers" when the red flag was waved. To
show the shooter where his shot had struck, an eight-inch
black "pan" on the end of a pole would be held up in front of
the bullet hole on the target. Each shooter shot from a prone,
sitting, and standing position and was scored on each position.

One day Col. Connally came out to be qualified and I
thought this would be a good opportunity to test his sense of
humor. Being a Texan and an old timer in the Army, I thought
probably he was a good shot and didn't need to qualify; he was
only doing so to impress the troops. When he lay down to shoot
his prone shots, by telephone I told the pit workers to wave
"Maggie's drawers" no matter where his bullet hole appeared

on the target. He very carefully fired his first shot and a few seconds later up came "Maggie's drawers." He took more time on the second shot with the same result. Meantime there is a deathly silence behind the firing line, as the troops waiting their turn to shoot, share in the Colonel's embarrassment. Only the pitmen and I knew of the trick that was being played.

When time for his third shot came, he wiggled around on the ground, and took more time for the shot. Watching through the binoculars, I saw his shot kick up a little cloud of dust on the berm just below and to the right of the target. Almost before "Maggie's drawers" could come up, he fired two more quick shots at the same spot on the berm, kicking up the dust in the same spot each time. What he was doing was shrewdly "shooting for group" to determine just where the rifle was firing. From the three shots into the berm he knew it was shooting where he was sighting. Of course he got the "Maggie's drawers" treatment on all three shots. At this point he rolled over, sat up, and said, "Allen, what in the hell is going on?" When I explained it all to him, everyone, including Connally had a good laugh. He then proceeded to shoot the course without any harassment and easily qualified in the highest division called "Expert" rifleman. It was things like this that endeared him to all his men.

Jack Warner Always a Practical Joke

Another amusing incident happened at the rifle ranges. My friend Captain Jack Warner, our Personal Equipment Officer, found a five-foot black snake on the range. He evidently knew something about snakes, as he was able to calm it and carried it around with him for an hour or so before we headed back to the base. I rode back in his car and along the way he stopped for gas. In those days there was no self-service; someone always came out to pump the gas for you. Jack had the snake wrapped around his neck when the lady in the gas station approached the driver's side of the car. When Jack rolled down the window to talk to her, the snake poked its head out and she let out a scream and almost fainted. Jack thought it was really funny. Since I hate snakes, I shared her feeling.

The snake story didn't end here. Jack took it back to his office at Group Headquarters and, when the day ended, he put it in his civilian secretary's desk drawer. The next morning, I was busy at my desk when all of a sudden I heard a blood-curdling scream. Running into the office I saw Jack's secretary standing up on top of her desk stamping her feet and screaming bloody murder as the snake slithered out of the drawer and on to the floor. Connally also came out of his office and when he saw the snake (which he had seen at the range the day before) he knew immediately what had happened. He bellowed out "Warner" and Jack went into his office where we saw him standing in a brace as Connally reamed him out.

Warner was really a character, always doing something funny which made him very popular with everybody. He and his wife lived in Geneva next door to me, and often we would share rides to the air base. One morning we saw a ring neck pheasant in the ditch and Warner insisted on stopping to shoot at it with his Army .45 automatic pistol. I told him he'd never hit it but he wanted to try anyway. The minute the car door opened, the bird flew, Warner carefully aimed, and at a range of about 100 feet, fired one shot. The bird dropped like a rock and when Warner picked it up and brought it back to the car, we found he had shot it in the head; a lucky and almost impossible shot! His comment was, "I was aiming at its eye!" The pheasant made a nice dinner for us a couple of nights later.

Bivouac Training

Another training requirement for the Group, before we went overseas, was to have a practice march and an overnight bivouac. A wooded area beside a small river about fifteen miles from the airbase was selected as the camping area. The whole Group participated and on the given day the troops, complete with backpacks and rifles, started the fifteen-mile trek. Supplies, food, and cooking equipment were moved to the site by truck.

This exercise was to be as close to a combat operation as possible. To make the march more realistic the airbase at Bruning, Nebraska was contacted to have small L5 single-engine, reconnaissance planes harass us on the march pretending to strafe and bomb our troops. For bombs they used paper sacks of flour and if the sack hit within 50 feet of our people, they were presumed to be casualties. The pilots of the L5s had a hay day; they just loved performing this low altitude flying. They must have flown two-dozen sorties against us while we were on the march. I had coordinated their efforts with their operations officer and assumed that the attacks would end once we reached our camp. I was wrong!

About seven in the evening we had our camp set up, the mess crew had a chow line established, and the troops were queued up in the mess line, which was located along the riverbank under some giant cottonwood trees. I was in the line waiting to get my food and happened to glance out over a wheat field that adjoined our camp. I was astonished to see one of the L5's approaching over the wheat so low that his wheels were almost in the wheat. He caught us completely by surprise and nobody had a chance to take cover before he swooped up over the chow line. I distinctly saw someone in the back seat of the plane drop a couple of flour sacks which hit right in the middle of the, now surprised, line of men. Then, with horror, I saw that the L5 was not going to clear the tall cottonwoods; it flew right into the top of one just past where we stood. The engine screamed as the prop was broken off and then we heard a crunching noise as the aircraft fell through the trees. The wings were torn off and the fuselage, with two figures in it, came to rest with the tail on the ground and the nose leaning up against a tree. Then came a "whoomp" and it burst into flames; flames that went up into the air for fifty feet. Simultaneously, we heard screaming coming from the wreckage.

Grabbing fire extinguishers from our vehicles and bringing pots of water, soup, or anything liquid, we all ran to the scene and vainly attempted to put out the fire. The pilot was slumped over and not moving. The screaming was coming from a girl in the back seat who was enveloped in flames. Four or five of our men heroically ran up to the flaming wreck and tried to release her seat belt to get her out. The first two or three men were terribly burned and had to stagger back from the inferno. Two more took their place and despite being engulfed in flames, they got her out and laid her on the ground away from the fire. All were horribly burned. (Later, they would receive the Army's highest decoration for their bravery.)

By this time the girl had stopped screaming and I helped our flight surgeon and his medics put her on a stretcher and into an ambulance. She was burned so badly that almost all of her clothes were burned off; all that was left was the elastic around her panties and bra. Her flesh was so burned, it looked like bacon rind; charred flesh had curled up and pink flesh showed in the cracks. She made it to the hospital but died about thirty minutes later. We later found out that she was an Army nurse and had been dating the pilot who had invited her along for the "joy" ride. We couldn't get the pilot out; by the time the fire was extinguished his body was just a black hulk.

The smell of burned flesh permeated the campgrounds and not many of our people slept that night. It was a sad and useless way for people to die. It took several days for the effect of the tragedy to wear off. I wish I could remember the names of those who heroically tried to save her; they certainly deserve recognition beyond the decorations they received. Each of them spent many months in the hospital and they did recover in time to accompany us overseas. I had nightmares about the scene for months on end.

Fairmont overall was good duty and the time there just flew. Most of the married Officers lived in the nearby town of Geneva. The government had built some inexpensive housing in a development on the east side of town for us. We all became friends and gathered regularly to commiserate. We were to learn only too soon how happy we all had become there. Married couples knew they only had a few months more to be together.

The 393rd and Mysterious Orders

About July of 1944, strange orders came in from the 2nd Air Force Headquarters in Colorado Springs. Our 393rd Squadron was to be transferred out on the following Friday.

No destination was given but the orders were very explicit that no dependents were to accompany. On Thursday night, a troop train was backed into our rail siding and the next morning all of the 393rd men left; we never heard from them again until July of 1945. We had many close friends in the 393rd and couldn't understand why we did not hear from them. My next-door neighbor in Geneva was a Lt. Buddy Williams from Texas who was the Squadron Adjutant. We had been such close friends I was sure we'd hear from him and his wife, but not one word. It was all gravely mysterious. Later, we would learn the whole story that they had become the nucleus for the top secret 509th Atomic Bomb Group—the group that dropped the first atomic bombs.

Receiving Our New B-29s

Prior to going overseas we began to receive new aircraft to replace the dogs we had trained in. The new aircraft had improved engines that did not heat up as much. They came from three different factories: Boeing of Wichita, Martin of Omaha, and Bell of Marietta, Georgia. We sent crews to each factory to test fly the aircraft after the factory pilots had approved them. I was on the test crew that flew the Omaha aircraft. On test flights, my job was to turn on all of the gunnery equipment and test it to make certain that the turrets and computer sights were operative. The test crew Bombardier checked out the bombsight, bomb racks, and bomb bay doors. In the meantime the pilots and engineers were checking out all the engines and other equipment. They also ran "stall" series with each aircraft to determine its stall speed. Stalling a large aircraft like a B-29 is a pretty spooky operation; as it approaches stall speed (the speed at which it stops flying and starts to fall like a rock) the plane starts to shudder and shake. At this point the pilots would drop the nose while giving it full throttle on all four engines until it regained flying speed. I was glad to get this job completed before an accident occurred.

Bombardment Groups like ours were transferred to staging areas. We went to an air base at Herington, Kansas, where

Bob Allen with "Lucky Lady!" She was lucky for me.

all of the aircraft, crews, and some ground-crew personnel, were sent in December of 1944. There, for about two weeks, we were given shots, issued warm-weather uniforms and flight clothing, and attended various kinds of briefings. We were all given one last three-day pass just before Christmas and most of us headed for Kansas City. The weather was cold, around zero, and it seemed incongruous to see all our guys running around downtown Kansas City in suntan uniforms. Wives and girl friends from all over the country converged on Kansas City for one last get together. Can you imagine what a sight we made?

Lucky Lady—My First leg to The Pacific

Then orders came for the aircrews to fly out. Staff Officers like me were assigned to a crew and flew as passengers. I drew an old friend of mine by the name of Dave Cole and his aircraft named the "Lucky Lady!" Wood platforms had been installed in the bomb bays and attached to bomb shackles the same way the bombs were attached. In the front bay each plane carried an extra engine while the platform in the aft bay was loaded with luggage and personal effects of the crew. This weight, plus enough gas to get us to California, was quite a load. One crew had engine problems on take-off and to save weight and stay in the air, they salvoed the two platforms and returned to Herington, where they spent the next day walking through corn and wheat fields looking for their underwear and other personal effects.

Lucky Lady and I had an uneventful trip and landed at Sacramento, California, where we spent the night prior to the next leg of the trip, which was Honolulu. Our Group almost got in trouble there. One crew stole a jukebox out of the Officers Club and loaded it into their bomb bay. Another crew got caught trying to steal a jeep and load it into their aft bomb bay instead of the platform. We all flew out of Sacramento just ahead of the Military Police!

Honolulu—Second Leg to Pacific Theater

Early the next morning we took off for Honolulu. I'll never forget the emotion I felt as we flew over the Golden Gate Bridge of San Francisco and saw the coastline gradually disappear behind us. The question in my mind and heart was, "Will I ever see it again?"

It took about fourteen hours to fly to Honolulu where we landed at John Rogers field, now the site of the International airport. To maintain the secrecy of our mission, we were confined to the base until our departure the next day. My sister Anne was living at the Halekulani Hotel right on Waikiki Beach while she worked as the secretary to the president of Dole Pineapple. I asked Col. Connally if I could have a few hours pass because I had a sister on the island. He said something like "sure, everyone has a sister here!" I was able to convince him, however, and I think I was the only one in the outfit allowed a pass.

My sister Anne shared a suite with two other girls at the

Halekulani Hotel. It was rebuilt in 1982 and is now a high-rise. In l944, it was a two-story central building with a lot of cottages surrounding it. Anne's suite overlooked the beach and gave her a fantastic view. After phoning her about my luck in getting a pass, I arrived at the hotel about seven in the evening. Her two girl friends both had dates that were there to pick them up when I arrived. One was an Admiral in the Navy and the other was a Marine Corps General, enough brass to practically scare me to death.

They were very curious about our outfit and tried to pump me for information. I couldn't tell them anything and explained why. The girls all made fun of my secrecy and said that from their office window at Dole (near the famous Dole pineapple water tower) they had been watching B-29's land and take off for a couple of weeks. They had even been writing down the tail numbers so they knew that over a hundred B-29's had passed through Honolulu. So much for the big secrecy! If they knew, you could be sure that the Japs were getting the same information from someone on the island.

Anne and I had a nice dinner together and then I was off to the field not knowing when, or if, I'd ever see her again. We took off the next morning singularly (no formation) and our first gas stop was to be Kwajalein, where we would open our sealed orders revealing to us our final destination. We arrived after dark and it was raining cats and dogs. When we opened our sealed orders, we learned that our final destination was to be the island of Tinian and that from Kwajalein on, we would be in a combat zone and should have our guns all loaded and ready. While we were being gassed up, I joined my men to load all the turrets and guns. It was here that I almost became our Group's first fatality.

Kwajalein—Third Leg to Pacific: Destination Tinian

I was on top of the aircraft helping to prepare the upper forward four-gun turret. It was still raining and the top of the airplane was slick. Despite being careful, I lost my balance and started to fall. I made a grab for one of the guns but missed it

Aerial Shot of North Field, Tinian, 1945.

and knew I was going down. Twisting around, I managed to slide down the side of the aircraft on the seat of my pants, thinking that it would be better to land on my feet than fall on my head. My fingernail scratches are probably still on the skin of that aircraft as I frantically scratched the surface to slow my fall. The impact really hurt my spine as I landed on my feet. I had fallen a good twenty-five feet, the distance of jumping off a two-story building. I couldn't get up for a while and my crew thought I was down for the rest of the trip. My back ached for a couple of weeks after and in retrospect, I think the back problems I've had all my life are probably directly related to this one mishap.

The flight from Kwajalein to Tinian was uneventful. The sight of the airfields on Tinian from above was amazing. With four, 10,000 foot runways, it was, and still is, one of the biggest airfields in the world. Built in just a few months by the Sea Bees—a nickname for the Navy's Construction Battalions—it was really an engineering marvel. A small mountain of coral just south of the airfield was systematically dynamited to provide the crushed live rock to make the runways, the miles of taxiways, and hard stands for the B-29's. When we arrived about January 1st of 1945, only one runway was operational and it had not yet been blacktopped. The coral was kept alive by watering trucks that sprayed salt water on it every few hours. (Coral needs to be kept alive or it will turn to dust and blow away.) A big asphalt plant had been built and ultimately all the runways, taxiways and roads on Tinian were black-topped.

Arriving on the Island of Tinian

Having made the trip on ships earlier, most of our ground support troops were already on Tinian. We were greeted like heroes and then transported about three miles away to the 504th camp. The word "camp" definitely describes our accom-modations because at this point the only military buildings on Tinian were for Group Headquarters and the Briefing Hall. That night we pitched pup tents in a cane field and slept in the open for about a week until pyramidal tents, with wooden floors and screened sides, could be erected.

Chapter 6

Combat in the Pacific

Jap Betty Bomber

After everybody had settled down for the evening, around midnight, a lone Jap "Betty" bomber came over at about 20,000 feet. Every searchlight and flak gun, on both Tinian and Saipan, three miles to the north, opened up on the Betty. Hundreds of searchlights coned the bomber and thousands of rounds of ammunition were spent. Finally, she was brought down into the ocean with immense cheering throughout the islands. The *Betty* never dropped a bomb and was probably only a reconnaissance plane. However, for the new guys on the island, *Betty* was the first attack we experienced and she sure had our adrenalin pumping. This first night on Tinian marked the Japs' last attempt at an air raid or any type of reconnaissance. We found out that there had been many attacks during the month before we arrived, and that an earlier raid had damaged the B-29 base on Saipan, burning up numerous aircraft and causing several fatalities.

Mourning First Group Crew Lost

On Tinian we didn't need enemy attacks to lose valuable men. Our first Group crew was lost, not as the result of combat, but because of pilot error. The crew had been out *slow-timing* new engines, breaking them in at low speeds. Upon their return to Tinian, they somehow undershot the runway, crashed on its lip, disintegrated and burned. Remember, these were very inexperienced flyers—young men of 19 to 21 years old who were expected to pilot the huge and sophisticated B-29, the Superfortress! They probably had only two or three hundred hours of flying time before being sent to *hell* in the Pacific.

Someone planned a rather elaborate funeral, including a formation fly-by of several B-29s. Then we all attended a solemn religious service. Grief over the loss was dominating everyone's thoughts, like a black cloud hanging over the base. Soon after, at a staff meeting, Colonel Connally gave an order that later proved to be a very wise decision. "From this point on, we will no longer mourn for people lost in combat or by mishap," he commanded. "We're going to lose a lot of people and if we stop to grieve for each and every one of them, we won't be able to win this war! Effective immediately, when a crew is lost, we will treat the situation as if they have gone home. Their airplane number will be scrubbed off the operations board, the crew's belongings will be gathered up and sent stateside, and despite friendships, you will *not* discuss their fate!" His advice proved to be clear-sighted because, once we started bombing Japan, we lost many crews, many fine men and dear, dear friends.

The Jap Island of Rota

We soon settled into the work routine of our new base. Practice missions were flown over the Jap island of Rota, about fifty miles away; an island that had been bypassed by our invading forces. Approximately five hundred Japs on Rota were totally cut off, with no hope of ever getting rescued or seeing any supplies for the duration. They must have thought we really hated them because thousands of sorties were flown over this little, two-mile-long island, by not only our Air Corps' B-29s, but also by the Navy and the Marines. There were so many bomb craters gouged out of its landscape that it

Bomb Pocked Island of Rota, our bombing target.

looked like the surface of the moon. The Japs only had small arms left and they soon learned that it was not wise to attract attention by shooting at us; it only resulted in additional bombings and strafing by the Navy fighters, who just loved having an excuse for additional practice runs.

First Semi-Dangerous Missions

Our first semi-dangerous mission was against the Jap Navy stronghold on the island of Truk. It was a Japanese Naval Base located about eight hundred miles southeast of Tinian, part of the Caroline Islands. We received a little flak but no damage. Then, our next few missions were to Iwo Jima as part of a softening-up process to prepare for the impending invasion that was planned for late spring. We endured plenty of flak at Iwo, so we flew at high altitudes to escape damage. There were no Jap fighters encountered on any of these missions, so my gunners had little opportunity to use their training. For each mission, of course, all guns were loaded and all procedures were followed plus the guns were test-fired just before reaching the target area. So, by the time we flew our first mission to Japan's mainland, we felt we were ready.

Iwo Jima Invasion Fleet

It was February when we woke one morning to witness the ocean full of massive cruisers and battle ships, majestically steaming north. There were so many ships that it took two days for the fleet to pass. What an awesome sight! We watched the almost endless armada of ships steaming past and the realization of what a formidable task was ahead for those brave Marines began to sink in. I had no idea there were so many ships in the world! We all learned later in the morning that this was our Iwo Jima invasion fleet, on its way to what would become one of the most bloody and devastating battles in the Pacific War.

When the invasion began, we were briefed to stay away from the island and the invasion fleet around it. Once the airfield on the south end, near Mt. Suribachi, had been captured and repaired, many of our B-29s made emergency landings on Iwo. The island was seized with a high cost of Marine lives; however there were 2,400 B-29 emergency landings and thereby several thousand crew members' lives were saved, as well as my own life, which was saved on two different occasions by Iwo.

Kobe, Japan—Our "Baptism Of Fire!"

The 73rd Wing on Saipan had been bombing Japan during January of '45, but we didn't fly our first mission until February 4th when we bombed Kobe, one of Japan's largest cities and a strategic seaport. My B-29 was "The Life Of Riley" with Major Riley as the Airplane Commander. Colonel Connally flew as copilot on the lead crew and I flew with him as CFC (Central Fire Control) gunner. The CFC gunner is located in a blister at the top of the plane, about two-thirds of the way back towards the tail. From this position, six guns were controlled from a revolving seat; the upper-forward-four-gun-turret, located on the nose above the pilots and bombardier, plus the upper-aft-two-gun-turret, located behind the CFC position.

We had developed a very sophisticated system for shooting down Jap fighters. Our nine-ship-formation amassed awesome firepower. As an example, an attack from twelve o'clock high would have fifty-four guns bearing down on the enemy. Fighters attacking from this direction were either shot down or so badly damaged that they no longer posed any threat. It was sort of a shotgun effect; no one gun might be responsible for extensive damage, but that massed firepower from fifty-plus guns could hardly miss. As it turned out, the Kobe mission was our "baptism of fire" as we encountered several hundred fighter attacks. Most were by a small single engine fighter called a "Zeke." This was their best fighter, armed with twenty-millimeter cannons, which could cause extensive damage because of their explosive shells.

We reached the bombing altitude of 29,000 feet and started our approach into Kobe. Immediately, we were under enemy fighter attack and dangerous flak. At the "IP" (Initial Point—the point at which the bomb run begins) it was the bombardier's job to take over flying the airplane, and with the controls of the bombsight he opens the bomb bay doors, which signals the bombing run to begin. After what seemed like a prolonged period of time, we realized we were not making any headway towards the target. The lead crew navigator took a drift reading and, to his amazement, found out that we were only flying the equivalent of about forty-five miles per hour on the ground. The B-29 normally cruised at 225 miles per hour but we were encountering a head wind of about 180 miles per hour, resulting in our low ground speed. Of course this low ground speed subjected us to the enemy flak and fighter attacks for a longer period of time. This went on for over an hour because of a heretofore unknown head wind; a head wind that remarkably could be as high as 200 miles per hour. The B-29 was the first aircraft that could go to 29,000 feet and as high as 40,000 feet; as a result, we were encountering the "jet-

Bob Allen with B-29, "The Life of Riley" on Kobe raid—Feb. 1945.

stream" which was as yet undiscovered and unnamed. And now the fun really began!

Normal procedure in a bombing formation is for only the Lead Crew and the Deputy Lead Crew to have their bomb-sights operative. These two Bombardiers have demonstrated, through their past averages, that they are the most accurate Bombardiers in the formation. Thus, when the Lead Crew Bombardier opens his bomb bay doors, all eight remaining air-craft follow his lead. When he drops his bombs, the other Bombardiers toggle their bombs the instant they see his bombs fall. In the event that the Lead Crew Bombardier has problems, the Deputy Lead Crew Bombardier takes over (the number two plane in the formation) and everyone bombs on the Deputy's drop. This procedure set up a peculiar chain of events that made our Kobe mission a complete disaster. Let me outline the sequences of the bomb run to illustrate how one decision led to another erroneous decision resulting in a major cost in lives.

➢Our formation was plowing along enroute to Kobe Bay, under heavy fighter attacks, when we reached the IP.

➢The Lead Crew Bombardier opened his bomb bay doors to start the bomb run.

➢The rest of the formation followed his lead and opened their doors.

➢Not making much headway towards the target, the Lead Crew Navigator took a drift reading and discovered that the ground speed was only 45 mph! Something was radically wrong but at this point in history we were not aware of the *jet stream* holding us back.

➢The Lead Crew Navigator then advised the Bombardier to *close* the bomb bay doors, in order to pick up more airspeed, and then to re-open them when we got closer to the target.

  • (The first erroneous decision)

➢The *Deputy* Lead Crew Bombardier (remember in the second plane of the formation) also serves as a gunner and at this moment he was shooting at Jap fighter planes. Out of the corner of his eye, he was startled to see the *Lead Plane's bomb bay doors closing!* He thinks that somehow he has missed "Bombs Away," and immediately toggled all his bombs.

  • (The second erroneous decision)

➢Now, all of the other seven aircraft saw his bombs dropping, and of course they knew that this was their signal to toggle all of their bombs.

  • (The third erroneous decision)

➢As a result of this chain-reaction, eight of the nine aircraft dumped their bombs into Kobe Bay, a good 25 miles from the target—*the shipping docks of Kobe.*

  • (And, it didn't end here!)

➢For a mission this long, about 18 hours, we had installed extra bomb bay gas-tanks, which were hung from the bomb racks. They were supposed to be *wired off so that they could not drop with the bombs.*

➢At "Bombs Away" more than half of the aircraft in the formation dumped their bombs *along with their bomb bay gas-tanks.* As I was firing at in-coming fighters, I saw

some elephantine objects tumbling out of the bomb bays
and at first didn't understand what I was seeing.

➤Some of the Flight Engineers had used up the bomb bay gas
tank first ~ those who had not done this we knew would
not make it back to Tinian.

➤Several crews in the Wing had to ditch and some of their people were never picked up by the picket submarines—subs
stationed for this purpose, at intervals of five hundred
miles between Japan and Tinian.

All of this effort and lost lives only to miss the target!
Needless to say, morale was pretty low after the Kobe mission.
The only bright spot for me, besides living through it, was that
I shot down the first "Zeke" enemy fighter that attacked us. It
approached from 12 o'clock high. I was the only one who fired;
my gunners froze and thought they were watching a movie.
With the upper-forward-turret and the upper-aft-turret under
my control, I bore down on this fighter with all six guns.
Opening fire at about six hundred yards, I blew his canopy off
at three hundred yards, and saw black smoke come out of the
engine as he passed over, missing us by only a few yards.
Colonel Connally personally credited me for the kill but was
very critical of how slowly the gunners, under my command,
had reacted on this first attack.

Boeing—A Major B-29 Shakedown!

We ended up shooting down several Jap fighters and,
because of their poor marksmanship, we had little damage to
our formation except what was self-inflicted. As I mentioned
before, our guns had fire interrupters, which would prevent
the guns from firing if they were aimed at an engine or any
other part of the aircraft. However in designing the interrupters, Boeing somehow overlooked the fact that guns would
be firing when the bomb bay doors were open! Thus, on this
mission to Kobe, some of our aircraft shot up *their own bomb
bay doors*. About the same time that I saw gas tanks tumbling
out of our planes, I saw chunks of aluminum ripping off the
bomb bay doors as a result of guns mowing through them

while shooting at the enemy fighters. Open bomb bay doors also create a tremendous drag and reduce airspeed by about 35 mph. Those who had shot up their doors couldn't get them completely closed and in many cases this was another reason why they didn't make it back to Tinian. Before our next mission our armament people corrected this dangerous lack of design in the interrupters.

We also learned that our aircraft needed to keep their position in the formation while guns were firing. If one plane drifted under and in back of another, all of the empty shells and links could cause major damage to Plexiglas noses, blisters and the airplane's skin. Thus, our Kobe raid became a major "shake down." We called this winning the war through "trial and error!" It was also a way to squander many precious lives. This certainly was not my idea of the "Life of Riley!"

> As an aside: On a subsequent and secret mission the "Life of Riley" was lost with all on board. Ken Moore, a nephew of the co-pilot, has made it his life's venture to find out what happened to his uncle and crew. Ken came to one of our 504th Bomb. Group Reunions and briefed everyone on an exciting expedition he put together to locate the lost "Life of Riley." He chartered a boat and crew complete with divers and went to the island of Pagan where the aircraft had last reported. He was successful in finding the aircraft but the expedition had to be called off and the boat and crew returned to Saipan when one of his divers was attacked and seriously injured by a giant Moray eel. He plans to go back and in the meantime is working on his book that will be of tremendous interest to all B-29 flyers.

Harmonizing

Our computerized guns proved to be a good system but it required frequent harmonization of the guns to the sights. This involved moving the B-29 into a "harmonization yard" where it was jacked up, making it perfectly level. The sight was then focused on a point in infinity (actually a mountaintop over on Saipan) and then the guns were adjusted to point at that same mark. Inserting a mirrored device into the barrel so that you could look directly through the barrel served this purpose. When the gunnery system was not harmonized you would generally have a ridiculous situation where the guns were pointed in one direction and the sight a different one. The only problem I encountered was in convincing everyone that this harmonization was critically important and then getting a B-29 released from combat for a half day to perform the harmonization. When we went overseas none of our aircraft had been harmonized. By the time we flew our first mission to Kobe only half of the harmonization had been accomplished and, as a result, our gunnery accuracy proved to be poor. All of a sudden, because people were getting shot at, I had no problem scheduling aircraft for the harmonization yard. In just a few weeks we had all the aircraft harmonized.

Beating the Odds

Our crews' lives were at risk and playing the odds with each additional mission. Can you imagine the odds at completing more than thirty missions? I only flew eleven missions compared to heroes like Art Tomes and his crew who carried out thirty-five missions and came home as testimony for beating-the-odds. During my eleven missions, I experienced my airplane getting shot up and seeing crew buddies wounded on board, but I myself never received a scratch. At times the combat missions didn't seem real to me! The excitement and pressure created a mind-set that was more like I was watching a movie! I sweated out the impending missions, but once we were in battle, I seemed to become detached from it all. The only injury I sustained, as I mentioned earlier, was falling off the top of a B-29, on Kwajalein, while loading the forward gun turret.

It has been my experience that those who fought the toughest war are the ones who are least willing to talk about their experiences. I was luckier than most! I don't consider myself a hero in any way, shape or form. The real heroes in our outfit were those who were killed, wounded, or shot down and imprisoned in the infamous Japanese camps. The heroes in this war were also the men who captured and held places like our island of Tinian and Iwo Jima. Six thousand, eight hundred (6,800) Marines died and over twenty thousand (20,000) were wounded in the horrific battle to capture Iwo. They were and still are the real heroes! For the sacrifices of these Americans, I will always be grateful and have only admiration and affection for each and every one of them.

Father Switzer

Our Catholic chaplain, Father Switzer, endeared himself to us through some events over which he had no control. He was very conscientious about experiencing what our combat crews went through on their missions and was constantly asking to be allowed to go on a mission. Finally the Colonel relented and told "Chappie" that he could go on a weather mission. Before each mission, a weather plane accumulated information. We named her "the porcupine." This specially equipped B-29 would fly to Japan and circle around for eight to ten hours in the target area at high altitudes gathering information through its multiple radio and radar antennas. These were comparatively safe missions because they flew so high that Jap flak and fighters were ineffective. It was on one of these missions that Chappie was approved to fly.

Because he was not a regular crewmember, Chappie was told to sit on the jump seat located between the pilot and the co-pilot in the nose of the airplane. The take-off was uneventful but about an hour out they had an induction fire in one engine and had to return to Tinian. On final approach when the landing gear is put down, it is standard procedure on the B-29 to have the gunners on each side report if the landing gear is down and locked. Just before touchdown one of the gunners reported that the gear was not locked. There was no time to re-cycle the gear and on three engines they could not do a go-around so the airplane commander told everyone to brace for a crash landing.

On touchdown the landing gears collapsed and the nose gear came up through the floor practically between Chappie's legs. When the airplane finally skidded to a halt the crew hurriedly crawled out and ran up the runway to get away from a possible fire or explosion. When they looked at Chappie he looked as though he was drenched in blood and they immediately had him lay down on the runway while they waved to one of the ambulances to come to help. Chappie was blessing and praying for himself and they were all seriously worried until they discovered that the red "blood" he was drenched in was *tomato juice*. When the nose gear came up through the floor it had punctured a half-gallon can of tomato juice that had been stored there with the crew's box lunches. It now became funny and poor Chappie was really razzed for praying for himself. Needless to say it was a miracle that nobody was injured.

Chappie inadvertently became famous on another occasion. It was his custom to drive his jeep down to the flight line and hear the confessions of the Catholic crewmembers just before take-off. He had the Catholic crews paint a small crucifix just below the pilot's window so he could identify them. Then, once take-offs had started, he would park his jeep beside the runway, stand on the hood, and when an airplane marked with a crucifix took off, he would bless it. One night the wind shifted during take-offs and three B-29's never got off the ground and crashed at the end of the runways. The next day at a critique of the mission held at Wing Headquarters, General Davies the Wing Commanders, prefaced the critique by saying, "On future missions, if I'm flying, I'd just as soon have you keep Chappie Switzer back at camp." This story spread rapidly and once again everyone had the occasion to make fun of poor Chappie.

Chappie's tent was right next door to mine and I'm sure the noise and the language used at some of our parties was hard for him to take. One night he came over, knocked at the screen door, and when we let him in he beseeched us to stop using the Lord's name in vain—he said the foul language was bad enough but the swearing was too much. Chappie wasn't too fond of Jack Warner, one of my tent mates. Jack wasn't a religious man—I don't think he was an atheist—perhaps just agnostic. Nevertheless, I talked him into going to Mass with me one Sunday morning. Our Group chapel was a tent with an altar at one end and the rest of the tent lined with rows of sand bags. Jack and my other tent-mates sat in the front row. At one point in the service Chappie turned around for a blessing and, when he saw Jack in the front row, he almost dropped his chalice. He was so shaken he could hardly deliver his sermon later.

We did not have a Protestant or Jewish Chaplain so many of the men of these faiths attended Chappie's services. The popular saying during WWII about no atheists in foxholes seemed true when I realized that a majority of the men attended church services. Chappie was very popular with everyone and did a great job of comforting those who had loved ones at home or who were grieving about friends lost in combat. I've often wished that I could have kept in contact with Chappie after the war. I hope he is still around and, somehow, gets to read this so he will know how much we loved and appreciated him—even if he was the subject of our laughter at times.

Survival Parties

On a contrasting note, Tinian was a beautiful island, at the same latitude as Hawaii, having the same vegetation and climate, plus beaches of equal beauty. It was really great duty and if it weren't for having to fly missions, Tinian would have been an idyllic vacation spot.

Before going overseas, all the officers chipped in some money to form a liquor pool. It was set up so that, once overseas, we could draw a fifth of liquor every week from a repository that was set up by the pool. Choice of brands was limited and one week a month you had to accept a forced issue: that meant you took whatever they wanted to get rid of, which usually meant some under-aged (green) scotch. I haven't been able to look scotch in the eye since!

This liquor became a very important part of our "survival" parties. Upon returning from a mission, crews were transported to the Group Briefing Hall to be interrogated by Intelligence Officers. As you entered the hall the Group Flight Surgeon issued each man a large shot of whiskey. The Red

Cross had a table set up and they'd hand each guy a Coke and a cookie. We'd mix the whiskey (which was usually pretty strong) with the Coke and this routine would really loosen up our tongues for the interrogation. Depending upon the time of day we'd then head for the beach to have a survival party; celebrating the fact that Lady Luck must be on our side since we returned from the mission, once more, alive. It was an ideal way to relax after the pressure and strain of eighteen hours in the air and being shot at by a ruthless enemy.

The survival parties at the beach were most enjoyable. Our officer's beach was in a beautiful cove, nestled between coral caves. A lifeguard tower had been built, complete with loudspeakers. Popular music from home was played; so the whole scene, for a fleeting few hours, was about as far from a war as you could get. The coral caves were cool, and with the sound of the surf, were ideal for naps or sleeping off excesses. A coral reef about sixty yards offshore kept sharks away and provided an excellent place for swimming and snorkeling. Generally, we all brought to the beach any booze that we had stashed away, as this was a perfect spot to enjoy it.

One day in July, the lifeguard in the tower played Bing Crosby's "White Christmas." As it began playing, guys were throwing Frisbees, playing catch, and diving in the surf. Gradually, all activity on the beach began to slow and finally stopped. We all became caught up in the nostalgia that the music aroused. By the time the record ended everyone was perfectly silent, homesick and tearful. One of the guys brought us back to reality by standing up, shaking his fist at the disc jockey in the tower and shouting, "You S.O.B.! If you ever play that song again, I'll kill you!" It was amazing how that music from home affected us all so deeply.

If the crews returned in the evening, then our survival party was held in the living quarters area. Steel, half moon shaped, Quonset huts had been built for the crews. Officers like myself were housed four to a tent. The parties would flow in and out and over this entire area. One (Yes! We Are Still Alive) party, I remember quite vividly. Several truckloads of coral had been dumped in the middle of the area for the future purpose of making sidewalks. The pile looked like a volcano which prompted our Group Communications Officer, Shorty Stallings, to climb to the top with a shovel in his hand and shout to everyone, "I'm Hirohito and this is Mount Suribachi, come up and get me if you can, you Yankee B____s!"

Everybody was smashed by this time, so that was all it took to start an assault on our coral Mount Suribachi. Shorty looked very much like Hirohito; besides being short, he wore horn-rimmed glasses, and had a few gold front teeth. He started taking the defense of his mountain seriously and if anybody got too close to him, he'd hit him over the head or any other place he could reach with his shovel. Taking the mountain became so important that a few men seriously considered shooting him down. Fortunately, the men all ran out of "gas" and the whole incident ended peaceably with nobody seriously injured.

The Matsonia

Speaking of survival parties, it was about June of 1945, when one of our crews flew back to Hawaii for supplies and while there heard a rumor that the old cruise ship "Matsonia" was headed toward an island in the western Pacific. The rumor went on to reveal that the entire ship was loaded with Army Nurses and Red Cross girls ~ eight hundred of them! At this point there were absolutely no women on Tinian, so you can imagine this news was quite exhilarating. A few days later we heard that the Matsonia was headed directly toward us and that they were coming to staff an enormous hospital that was being built on Tinian to back up the planned invasion of Japan. One of our crews was out slow timing engines and did a little scouting to find the lovely Matsonia. Finding the ship, they buzzed it and as they swooped down past her decks, to their complete surprise and delight, they gazed upon hundreds upon hundreds of women sunning themselves!

The ship docked in the Tinian harbor that night and virtually every man (there were 30,000 men on the island) came to greet the Matsonia; it was a real mob scene! They came walking, running, driving, crawling, converging on the dock, crowding and pushing each other, in order to get a look at the nurses as they disembarked. The ladies, in their dress uniforms, walked down the gangplank like it was a New York fashion runway and then boarded transport trucks that whisked them away to the new hospital. As a good-looking gal walked the gangplank, the guys would cheer and the girl would smile and wave back. Even the ugly ones got robust applause. It was an exciting and festive occasion. In the back of everyone's mind was the thought of how they could latch on to one of the girls. For the officers this was solved easily when truckloads of these beautiful women showed up at our beach for the next few days. Life at the beach, as I'm sure you can imagine, changed radically. For that matter, life on Tinian was never to be the same again!

Officer's Club Party for 800 Nurses

All of us had been working a few hours a day for several months building an officer's club. When the Matsonia docked it was almost completed. By this time, Lt. Col. Glen Martin was our Group Commander. He met with the Commanding Officer of the new hospital, and invited him and his 800 officer-nurses to attend our new club's grand opening. They eagerly accepted and this set the stage for one of the wildest parties anyone could imagine. Having been locked up on board the ship for about two months, the girls were as "horny" as the guys who had been on the island for over six months without a female in sight. This, plus the booze we had hoarded for the opening of the officer's club was one-hell-of an explosive mixture.

All the vehicles from our motor pool were sent to pick up the girls from the hospital. They arrived as our Group Big Band was playing the Glenn Miller sound and our dance floor immediately became "back-to-back and belly-to-belly!" Our MPs directed traffic and enforced island rules, which stated that two couples must be together at all times. One couple could not wander off alone because Jap snipers were still hiding out in caves on the island. Despite attempts to keep everyone in the club, couples were wandering all over the surrounding cane fields. The next morning the brand new officers club was surprisingly still standing, however, the surrounding cane fields were absolutely flat! But, I can't imagine how or why!

Unfortunately, a jeep had an accident on its way back to the hospital and several people were injured. All roads on the island were made of coral and were watered down with salt water, which made them extremely slippery. This condition induced skids, which, unlike those on ice, could not be controlled or stopped by turning into them. Once your vehicle was out of control, you skidded until you came to a—whatever fate had in store for you—stop. Another road hazard on Tinian was created by the millions upon millions of giant snails that came out at night and migrated over the entire road system. Vehicles smashed them into a sticky-goo that caused even worse accidents. And, the snails remained a menace even after the roads were blacktopped.

Entertainment before the Matsonia

For entertainment we had our outdoor movie theater. Our theater consisted of a large elevated stage complete with lights and curtains; all built by our people with "scrounged" materials. Seats were sandbags and the roof was the starry sky. Movies were projected from the back end of a truck with a 16MM projector and a speaker mounted on the stage. When you went to the theater you always took along your helmet liner and poncho. It almost always rained at night and although the rain only lasted a few minutes it was heavy. When it started to rain, nobody left; you just put on your helmet liner and poncho and stuck it out. Sometimes it rained so hard you could hardly see the screen. Looking back, it shows just how hard up we were for entertainment.

Waiting for the movie to start, you teamed up with someone and played "dodge" using your flashlight. Dodge was played by shining your light on the movie screen making a dot that your friend could chase around the screen with his dot. Sometimes there were so many dots chasing each other around the screen you couldn't concentrate on your own!

Seems ridiculous for full-grown men, doesn't it? But, then again we were not full-grown—we really were just boys!

What really amused us was while watching a movie, if a girl was shown dressing or undressing, the troops would whistle and applaud, the projectionist would run the picture backwards and forwards several times, and we would try to memorize that vision for future dreaming. Unfortunately, there wasn't much nudity in the movies of that era, so some simple scene of a girl in a bra or panties got big play.

Once or twice a month, a USO show would come through. The performers ranged from violinist Yasha Heifitz, and the Ziegfeld Girls, to western star Gene Autry. Gene's act included a beautifully well-endowed girl as his accordion accompanist. Gene did a great job but everyone, of course, paid more attention to the girl. The guys kept yelling "take it off!" referring to her accordion, which covered up her most outstanding assets. The Ziegfeld Girls' show consisted of ten knockout chorus girls that just about tore the place up. Some claimed that the Army used to put saltpeter in the food to lower our libido; if they did, they sure didn't use enough! Anything with a girl in it was a big hit!

My Red Cross Girl

One day I was coming out of the Quonset that administered our liquor pool with a fifth of booze in my hand and couldn't help but notice two outstanding looking Red Cross girls sitting in a jeep next to mine. They had just arrived on the Matsonia. One of them asked me, "How can we get some of that liquor?" My reply was quick and on target. "You just have to know me!" I explained how the pool worked and told them I'd help them by sharing some of mine and trying to find a few other Officers in our Group who would do likewise. All the while I was talking to them my mind was racing around trying to figure out how I might latch on to the one driving the jeep ~ a ravishing blue-eyed blonde with a knock-out figure and a southern accent that was very sexy. After introductions, I found out her name and that she was the Special Activities Director, and her assignment on Tinian was to catalog all of the entertainment talent we had on the island. Her job was to demonstrate to each outfit how to organize and put on a performance for the troops. Once these shows were planned, they not only entertained their own people but also toured the island performing for other outfits. Some of the shows were pretty darned good. We had a particularly good band because Jack Teagarden Jr. was in our outfit and with his musical background, was able to assemble a praiseworthy band. Plus I found out that she had been a singer with a big name band back in the States. (Little did I know at that moment that a torrid romance would soon begin. And, for the record, I hesitate to tell this story for fear you will think we were fighting a "country club" war on Tinian.) My lead-in was to ask these two beauties if they had been to the beach yet. I then proceeded to tell them about the beautiful Officer's beach we had on the east side of the island. This seemed to excite them so it was easy to make a date to meet them there the next day; I told them I'd bring the booze and mix.

Remember, it had been about six months since I had seen a woman let alone one as gorgeous as this Red Cross girl. I could hardly sleep that night thinking about the next day and the war suddenly became the last thing on my mind. My tent mates Al Kohl and Steve Mesnyak were almost as excited as I was and planned to come along so they could meet my new gal and her roommate. They showed up right on time and when those two gals peeled down to their swimsuits we just about exploded! We spent a delightful afternoon at the beach getting acquainted.

I made a date to bring my new girl to our Officer's Club that night. She had me follow her and her roommate back to the Compound, where they lived, so I would know where to pick them up. They invited me in for coffee and to meet the lady who was their superior. She turned out to be a tough-old-gal who laid down the house rules, for anyone dating one of her girls, in no uncertain terms. Rules included a hard and fast curfew each night at 10:00 pm, that there must always be two girls with two Officers, and that we were completely responsible for the girls. The two couple rule was also an island rule that went a bit further and stated that the two

Officers were to be armed. This was required because of an incident on Saipan where two couples walking on the beach were attacked by some of our own soldiers, the girls raped, and the Officers killed.

We had a big time that night at our Officer's Club; however I quickly learned that it was a mistake to take her there because the instant we stepped out on the dance floor, it was open season for other guys to cut in and dance with my Red Cross girl. She felt that dancing was part of her job so always accepted the cut-ins and I would only get a chance to dance a step or two before another officer would cut in again. She'd come back to me exhausted but had made many guys happy.

It was fun to be with her because she attracted so much attention! All of the nurses and the other Red Cross girls were required to have regulation short hair. Somehow, possibly because of her singing entertainment career, my girl had been allowed to keep her blonde hair long. Part of the time she kept it tied up under her cap but at night, or occasionally during the day when she let it down, she was a sensation. When we were driving around the island in my jeep, GI's would see her with that long hair flowing and would come running to line up along the road just to see her at close range and cheer. She could sing like a bird and once there were some bands to accompany her, she'd always sing when we visited various Officers' Clubs.

Her best friend and roommate was an equally attractive girl. I introduced her to Red Boelsen, an old classmate of mine from Officer's Training School in Miami Beach, who was Commanding Officer of an Army Port Battalion located on the side of a mountain overlooking the harbor. The Port Battalion's men were stevedores, responsible for unloading all the cargo ships. So that we could have more time with the girls, we started taking them to Red's Officer's Club; an old farmhouse that he converted. With an excellent chef and, because his outfit had first grab at the food coming off the ships, we always had great meals at his club.

By this time I was really *gone* on my Red Cross girl and spent as much time with her as was possible with her schedule and my job. Red's Club was a refuge to get away from the mobs of men, the hustle bustle of the busy island, and to have complete privacy. Our romance grew with intensity and we became very close. Afternoons at the beach were particularly enjoyable. The only time we were apart was when I had to work or fly a mission.

Earlier in the year, while exploring the mountains on the south end of the island, I had discovered a beautifully land-scaped old Jap Shinto Shrine, which surprisingly had not been damaged by the war. It was an excellent place to take the girls on a picnic. For food Red brought fresh eggs and bacon that we were cooking over an open fire. The shrine was located at the top of a small hill and about one hundred feet behind it was the base of a coral cliff two hundred feet high. The face of the cliff had several cave openings that had been blackened by flame-throwers during the invasion. While our food was cook-ing, I happened to glance up at the top of the cliff and was hor-rified to see the heads and shoulders of four Jap soldiers who were lying at the edge of the cliff watching us. Nonchalantly, I walked closer to Red and the girls and, as calmly as possible, told them not to look alarmed but listen-up as I explained what was going on. I cautioned them not to make any sign that they knew about the Japs. Then I quickly outlined a plan of action so we could escape. Red and I both had Army .45-caliber pistols and I had my .30-caliber carbine. Red had a .45-caliber sub-machine gun, which the troops had nicknamed the "squirt gun." My carbine was leaning against a tree a few feet away but Red's sub-machine gun was in the jeep that was parked down the hill about fifty feet away. My plan was to slowly walk over to the tree, grab my carbine and start shoot-ing at the Japs. Red and the girls were to run like hell to the Jeep, Red would then start spraying the cliff edge with his sub-machine gun covering me while I ran to the Jeep. I then would start the Jeep and drive down the road while Red con-tinued to spray the cliff top with his gun.

The plan worked perfectly! I picked up my carbine and started shooting immediately from the hip. My first two shots kicked up the coral right under one Jap's chin—I may even have hit him—but all four faces disappeared as I continued to shoot while running for the Jeep. Red then started spraying the cliff-top with the sub-machine gun while I started the Jeep (and thank God it started quickly) and drove us down the road. It was all over in just a few minutes and once we were safely away we started laughing. Red jokingly said we should go back and eat our eggs and bacon, which were still on the fire when we fled. The realization of the danger we had been in didn't set in on us until much later in the day and then it didn't seem so funny.

When we had this picnic the island had been secure for several weeks but it was common knowledge that there were several hundred Japs holding out in the coral caves and mountains of southeast Tinian. By this time the Japs were starving and were not causing any trouble unless they were caught trying to steal food from our camps. A few weeks earlier one of our Officers had been up in the same area as the shrine looking for papayas. He looked up and was startled to see twenty Jap soldiers coming out of the brush with their hands up to surrender. He didn't know quite what to do but accepted the Jap Officer's sword and then had the group march behind his Jeep to the island Prisoner of War Compound. He became quite a hero! Despite living in the caves and jungle, these soldiers had on clean uniforms and seemed quite well fed. The reason they had surrendered was because our Army had patrols out every night laying ambushes for them and they could see by the activity all over the island that the war was lost. In our case, the four Japs who had been watching us were probably more interested in looking at the two beautiful girls than anything else. (On my trip back to Tinian fifty years later, I paid a visit to this same shrine and was pleased to see that it is intact.)

One night Red had liberated a few steaks so we took the two girls to a beach where we built a fire for our cook-out. It was a balmy night with a full moon and with a gentle surf washing up on the beach. We had a few drinks and one thing led to another until we lost track of time. About 10:30 we suddenly awakened to the fact that we had kept the girls out past their curfew. We left the beach and raced back to their compound trying to think of a good excuse we could use on their housemother. We finally agreed our story was that we had

taken the distributor rotor out of the jeep engine to keep anyone from stealing it while we were on the beach and then we
lost it. Most of the jeeps did not have keys, just an ignition
switch, so this procedure was fairly common on the island.
When we arrived at the compound the big gal was pacing back
and forth by the gate along with a couple of MPs. She was
really steaming and didn't buy our excuse. Despite our pleas
that we, not the girls, were responsible for being late, she confined the girls to the Compound for two weeks. That meant
they could go outside to do their work but no beach and no
dates. Thankfully we were allowed to visit them in their common areas, where they had a little lounge area, and this took
some of the sting out of the punishment.

Defeat From A New Enemy

Our mess people always tried to provide the best food for
the crews' box lunches. Turkey was a rare delicacy on Tinian
and happily one day the mess people came up with some great
turkey sandwiches for the crews. The lunches were put on the
aircraft and then, because weather over Japan was questionable, the mission takeoff was delayed several times. Finally
the mission was cancelled. So the sandwiches were taken back
to the mess hall to be served with the evening meal. Now mind
you, the turkey was so sought after that when the sandwiches
were placed in the chow line, an attendant had to make sure
that each man took only one sandwich so there would be
enough to go around. Just about everyone in the outfit had a
sandwich including me. About a half hour after dinner, I was
relaxing in my bunk and heard our P. A. system speakers
crackle. This was always an indication that an announcement
was coming. A somber voice made this announcement:

> "Attention all personnel. Turkey sandwiches served at
> evening mess are believed to be poisonous. If you ate one,
> please report to the dispensary immediately."

My stomach was already growling a little and Al Kohl
said he had a bad stomachache. We took off immediately for
the dispensary and what a sight it was. Our medics had mixed

up a washtub full of some kind of an emetic and were passing out paper cups full for everyone to swallow. Guys were rolling on the ground, puking in the ditches and the latrines were jammed. Three minutes after I swallowed my emetic I was in the same shape. A few men were so sick they had to be hospitalized and everyone felt sick for a day or two. It was so bad they had to scrap one of the missions. Everyone was quick to jump on the mess people but they had good intentions when they saved the turkey sandwiches. Goes to show there are many ways to lose a war!

Getting Back to the War

By mid February of 1945, we had become an experienced bomb group and had settled down to a routine of flying two to three missions a week. The logistics of maintenance and supply to back up this many raids was stupendous. Some mighty good planning had occurred which made it all possible. Tinian harbor had a constant procession of ships and tankers bringing in supplies, bombs, and gasoline. A four-lane highway was built from the harbor to the airfield and on to a bomb dump. Considering that each B-29 carried 6000 gallons of gasoline plus 20,000 lbs. of bombs, these supplies alone represented a prodigious effort. Despite the almost impossible supply requirements, only one mission, that I can remember, was delayed because of a shortage of bombs.

Mission over Tokyo

My second mission on February 25th was to a target in Tokyo. Because of cloud cover in the target area it was a comparatively easy mission. We flew up Tokyo Bay in between two cloud layers at about 20,000 feet. A few black, oily-looking, flak bursts came up through the clouds but missed us by quite a distance. On this mission the Navy's Task Force 58 fighters, from a carrier that was stationed a few miles off the Japanese coast, flew top cover for us. At one point we saw a Jap fighter dive vertically down through the cloud cover ahead of us; a second later, a Navy Corsair broke out right on the Jap's tail.

The two of them disappeared in the lower cloud deck but minutes later; the Corsair came back up through the clouds, did a victory roll in front of us, and disappeared back into the clouds above. The whole crew let out a cheer. It was a comforting feeling knowing that someone was looking out for us.

Thankfully, the rest of the mission was uneventful. After the war, I learned that my good friend and classmate from my hometown, Art Brooks, had flown a Navy Corsair covering us that day. I always meant to ask him if that victory roll fighter could have been him. I like to think that it was!

Training my gunners

My days were a mixture of training gunners, mission planning, and coordinating efforts with my squadron gunnery officers. We needed some way to train the gunners on turrets without having to do it on the aircraft. In March of '45 we had a battle-damaged B-29 make a belly landing, which totally destroyed most of the airplane. I talked Colonel Martin into giving me the fuselage from the nose back behind the last turret. I had it moved from the airfield to our skeet range, which was located at the edge of a five hundred foot cliff overlooking a bay in the ocean. With the help of our armament and maintenance people, the fuselage was mounted on a concrete base so that it was parallel to the edge of the cliff.

Now we had the advantages of training in an actual fuselage that we could load up and fire out to sea without endangering anybody. We now had a great place to test gunners on their procedures and accuracy. We used only the turrets on the top of the fuselage; those on the bottom had been destroyed when the B-29 belly-landed. On our first test fire we opened up with the upper-forward, four-gun turrets and the upper-aft two guns. I hadn't reckoned for the tremendous recoil of six guns fired simultaneously. And, because the fuselage's top turrets were above the center of gravity when the guns fired, the entire structure began to roll on its base scaring the living daylight out of me, not to mention the gunners on board. Needless to say, we stopped firing immediately and anchored the fuselage with some cables before we did any more testing.

Bob Allen performing shooting act on 504th skeet range. Note B-29 fuselage in background.

Had the fuselage gone over the cliff, there undoubtedly would have been fatalities, either from the fall, or from drowning. How would you claim a crash of an already crashed aircraft? And, I would probably have been court martialed because it was all my bright idea.

To make our training more realistic, I made a deal with some Navy fighters to fly simulated attacks on the fuselage so our gunners could practice using gun cameras. The Navy fly-boys welcomed this opportunity for some low level practice of their own and really worked us over for about two hours one morning. The operation was so engrossing that I was totally unaware of the tremendous noise the fighters' engines were making over our Group Headquarters, but even worse, over our 313th Wing Headquarters, up on the hill, overlooking our camp. Simultaneously, we were firing *six .50 caliber* guns, creating such a tremendous sound that I received concurrent complaints from both Group and the 313 Wing Headquarters as well as a complaint directly from General Davies, the Wing Commander, via his Adjutant. To the disappointment of the

Navy pilots who loved it and my gunners who thought it was great training (and for me, the one with—once again—the bright idea!), the whole operation came to a screeching halt! From then on we only used the fuselage for procedure training.

The auxiliary engine in the tail (crews called it the "putt-putt") was actually a Ford V-8 engine that did a good job of supplying auxiliary power for the B-29's. It normally was used to start up the big engines and supplied power for the starters. Once all four engines were running it was generally turned off. I planned to use it to provide power to operate the gun turrets and the computing gun sights on my fuselage. These computers made by General Electric were the forerunners to the computers we have today. Our gunners fed information into the computer that enabled it to figure out the proper lead and trajectory for firing at Jap fighters. The first thing our gunners were required to do was to identify the type of Jap fighter and then set in his memorized wingspan of that particular plane. The gun sight had a glass screen with a circle of red dots projected on to its surface. The gunner would compress these dots around the wingspan of the attacking fighter by turning a knob. The gunner then would move the sight to keep the dots on the fighter as it continued its attack. This fed the needed information into the computer so that the only thing the gunner had to do was to press the firing switch to activate the guns.

General "THE CIGAR" LeMay

It was at this point that General "the cigar" LeMay was transferred to Guam and made Commanding General of the 20th Air Force. Fresh from success in bombing Germany with B-17s and B-24s, he was about to drastically change our bombing philosophy.

When LeMay held his first briefing, I was on Guam and had the pleasure of being able to attend that briefing. I'll never forget it! It was a hot afternoon in the war room with no air conditioning. The room was packed with leaders from all the groups and squadrons on Tinian, Saipan, and Guam.

Someone called out "ten hut" and everybody stood as LeMay strode down the aisle to the stage. He had his trademark cigar in his mouth, walked up on the stage and sat down on a chair near a table. He and his cigar were the only ones on the stage! Everybody sat down; LeMay paused for an excruciating few moments, and then, in an almost conversational voice, conveyed to us his new bombing philosophy.

He said we had the finest aircraft that had ever been built; the cream of the crop crews; the finest training of any outfit; however . . . it was all wasted because we could not hit the target! He said, "Gentlemen, this is all going to change *tomorrow!*" LeMay proceeded to outline his new plan for night, low altitude, single aircraft raids, using firebombs. He said the guns and armor plate were to be removed to save weight. We were going in at low altitudes of five to ten thousand feet in the darkness of night, because the Japs did not have many night fighters. And, we would go in singly—no bombing formations!

As he proceeded, you could have heard a pin drop in that war room! Most thought he was planning a suicide raid for us. However, our first fire raid on Tokyo a day later, March 9, 1945, proved his philosophy was right on! In one night we burned out 90% of Tokyo including several hundred factories, which were primary targets. In addition over 100,000 people were killed, which created total panic throughout the entire Jap Empire.

The Tokyo raid was followed up by night fire raids on Nagoya, Osaka and Kobe—all within one week—appropriately called "The Blitz!" LeMay was right, we were now successful and our losses were less than the high altitude, daylight formation raids. For me there was only one thing awkward about the situation; this new philosophy put my gunnery program out of business for all the night raids.

Briefing: "Gentlemen, the target for today is Nagoya!"

As a Group Staff Officer, I was required to fly two missions a month. When we first arrived overseas, Connally had established an unofficial policy of having each of his Officers fly those two missions. We were not to be observers but working crewmembers. In my case, I would take the place of a gunner who was ill or for some reason could not fly. I ended up flying just about every gunnery position including tail gunner. Connally's policy was a good one because it gave the Staff Officers combat experience, as well as empathy for their men while gaining their respect.

If I had not fulfilled my two-mission requirement for the month, I'd suit up prepared to fly even though I wasn't sure there would be a vacancy. This had a good fringe benefit because the combat crews always received a special breakfast or meal prior to briefing. For example, the only time I ever ate fresh eggs was prior to a mission; ground personnel usually got powdered eggs.

The briefings were real productions! Our briefing hall was a building approximately 100 x 200 feet with an elevated stage. Crews sat together on wood benches. The wall behind the stage had a huge map of the western Pacific and Japan. Our Intelligence Officers would prepare this map before each mission by stringing a red ribbon from Tinian to Japan; the route we would follow. A theater curtain was kept closed, covering the map until the critical moment at the briefing when the mission location was dramatically announced. Those of us in Group Headquarters knew at least 24 hours ahead the mission targets, but the crews usually didn't find out until the briefing, but of course, there were always rumors.

The Colonel would open the briefing, usually with one sentence; "Gentlemen, the target for today is Nagoya!" And, with that the curtain covering the map would be opened with a flourish. Usually there would be an outburst of remarks but then things would settle down for the briefing. He would then sit down and each of us would brief the crews on our specialty. The Group Bombardier, would explain the target and its importance ~ the Engineer covered fuel requirements and management, our Weatherman explained what he hoped the conditions would be ~ and I'd brief the gunners on expected fighter opposition and ammunition requirements. There were always a few questions and answers and then the crews would file out of the hall to trucks that would carry them to the air-fields. Our company clerk tried to have mail ready to distribute after the briefing, so crews could read letters from home enroute.

I'll never forget one briefing! I knew for sure I was going on this one; flying with Major Carr as tail gunner on his B-29, "Satan's Lady." I went to the mess hall with the crews and gorged myself on those wonderful fresh eggs, several cups of the Army's acid coffee, and plenty of hash browns. During the briefing I sat on the front row awaiting my part in the presentation. When the Colonel made the announcement that the mission was *Gentlemen-Nagoya* as the curtain dramatically opened on the big map, something in my bowels twitched and I knew I had to get out of there NOW! I told one of my Squadron Gunnery Officers to handle the briefing for me and took off at a run for the latrine, which was about two hundred yards down the hill from the briefing hall. I never made it! I've heard of people being so scared they s__ their pants, so I'm not sure whether it was fright or all those eggs and the many cups of coffee. By this time there was no point in continuing on to the latrine, so I went directly to the outdoor showers nearby and stood under the streaming water, with all my clothes on, until I felt clean. Then it was back to my tent to put on all new clothes in time to join my crew at the waiting trucks.

A mission take-off from Tinian was one amazing operation and such a spectacular sight it is difficult to describe well enough to give you an accurate picture. However, let me try by enumerating the facts:

➤ The island of Tinian looked like one gigantic aircraft carrier.
   ○ The island is only 8 miles long by 2 miles wide.
➤ The SeaBees (CBs, Construction Battalions) built out of coral
   ○ Four ~ 10,000-foot runways at the north end of the island
      ▪ Each runway approximately 2 miles long
   ○ Two ~ 10,000-foot runways at the south end of the island

- ○ Plus hardstands adjacent to all the taxi-ways for a Wing of B-29
  - ▪ That equals 400 aircraft waiting to take off!
- ➤A Superfortress is:
  - ○ 141 feet ~ wing tip to wing tip
  - ○ 100 feet ~ nose to tail
  - ○ 28 feet high (or approximately two stories high)
    - ▪On a maximum effort mission,
- ➤ "Six" ~ Superfortresses
  - ○ Took off every *50 seconds*
    - ▪ from each runway
- ➤To support this timing there were aircraft lined up nose to tail on all the adjacent taxiways and hardstands
- ➤Imagine the sound of 1600 engines
  - ○ Plus the distinctive pulsating thunder of the 2500 horsepower engines taking off
  - ○ Plus the constant roar of those awaiting takeoff
    - ▪ The whole island literally vibrated with this adrenaline pounding sound.
- ➤Add to this picture, identical operations from two runways on Saipan about five miles to the north and

B-29's lined up for mission take off.

B-29 Formation enroute to Japan.

➢Then add two more runways on Guam about seventy miles
   south
   ○ Then picture the sky with hundreds upon hundreds of
   B-29 Superfortresses streaming compellingly north
   toward the enemy, Japan.

Our 504th Bomb. Group flew from one of the four runways on the north field of Tinian. And, right in the middle of that runway there was a slight hill, that created a problem for the pilot poised for take off. It was just high enough that he could not see whether the B-29 ahead of him made it off the end of the runway. This presented a collision situation for planes taking off every fifty seconds. To solve the problem we built a small tower about ten feet high beside the center of the runway. During mission takeoffs one of our Staff Officers would man the tower with an Aldis lamp, a powerful light with red and green lenses. The procedure was to listen to the engines of the aircraft taking off and if they were all running at full power when they passed the tower you gave the waiting aircraft a green light because you knew the B-29 that had just passed was going off one way or another. He would either take-off successfully or crash over the cliff at the end of the runway. There was no return! Remember, reversible pitch propellers did not exist in those days; you had only brakes to stop you and if you tried to stop past the center mark of the two-mile long runway the odds were against you.

In the case of an aircraft with reduced power when it passed our tower, we'd give the next plane a red light and hold it until the runway was clear again. This tower duty was really thrilling and I literally shook with the excitement of the sound and the sight of it all. Plus, I was awed with our impressive power about to be unleashed against Japan.

To add to our problems and casualties the size of our bomb loads constantly increased. Sometimes the crews had the feeling that 20th Hq. was trying to see just how much a B-29 could carry. With a full load of bombs and gas, the B-29 was really maxed-out on weight and if one engine even coughed, it was usually a disaster. Another problem and probably our biggest cause of aborted takeoffs were *runaway propellers*. Minneapolis Honeywell made the governors for these propellers and we had a civilian technical representative from the Honeywell factory living with us to work on this problem. Despite all our precautions there were several spectacular crashes. One night there were crash fires burning off the ends of three runways. The sight was unforgettable. The worst crash occurred when our Group was carrying extremely sensitive, RDX parachute mines destined for the Japanese harbors. On the mission take-off, a B-29 loaded with these mines ran off the end of the runway and exploded. There were no survivors and the tremendous blast destroyed several other B-29s nearby.

On another night I drew the tower duty and witnessed a B-29 develop engine trouble just after take-off. They dumped their bombs in the ocean to save weight and then turned back over the island so the crew could bail out over land. The pilot's idea was that the autopilot would take the aircraft on out to sea, where it consequently would crash harmlessly—but something went amiss. From my vantage point in the tower, I saw the plane turn back towards the island and counted the parachutes as they came out. Just as the eleventh chute opened, which presumably was the pilot, the plane suddenly rolled and headed directly for me! I jumped from the tower, and into my jeep to flee. Then, at the last minute, the plane veered downwards at a 45-degree angle and crashed, hitting the ground in the midst of a Marine anti-aircraft battery. When it struck the ground I was within two hundreds yards of the explosion. It created a wall of fire over three hundred feet high which spread for several hundred yards. The heat was so intense that it singed my hair. Six thousand (6000) gallons of gasoline and twenty thousand (20,000) pounds of firebombs make for one-hell-of-a-show! Needless to say take-offs on runways near-by were delayed for a few minutes. It was futile to try to put out a fire like this and it was so intense it burned itself out after a few minutes.

To say that it was a thrill being on a B-29 Superfortress for one of these mission take-offs would certainly be an understatement. My position on take-off was on a jump seat between the pilot and co-pilot ~ behind and above the bombardier in the nose. From where I sat I could see the air speed indicator and it always seemed to get up to about 60 miles an hour and then just hang there until the last few feet of the runway when it would finally reach the 85 miles an hour that it took for the big bird to fly. As the end of the runway approached the interval of time between 60 and 85 miles an hour was a real sweat. Once airborne the procedure was to get the gear up immediately and then either dive a little or hold level until the air speed picked up enough to start retracting flaps. A several hundred-foot cliff at the end of the runway made a slight dive possible if you needed the extra air speed.

To save fuel we flew singly, rather than in formation, to a pre-planned rendezvous point just off the coast of Japan. As we flew north from Tinian looking out the windows you could see B-29's everywhere—all majestically proceeding north and gradually climbing. It was an awesome sight! On our daylight raids, the lead ship in the formation would take off first and fly to the rendezvous point where he would start flying in a big circle waiting for the other eight ships in his formation to form up. The leader identifies his position with a smoke bomb of a particular color. These smoke grenades were dropped out of a special hatch at the bottom of the aircraft. As they fell they would leave a readily identifiable stream of smoke that could be seen for miles. Once all nine ships were in formation, they would turn towards Japan and join the stream of B-29 formations proceeding toward the target.

Dropping a smoke grenade out of a hatch seems like a simple task but for one of our crews it was almost fatal. The normal method was to pull the pin on the grenade and then drop it down the hatch. It would explode a few seconds later and start emitting its colored smoke. On one occasion, the Navigator who was handling the grenade somehow fumbled it inside the airplane just after he had pulled the pin. It rolled on the floor and exploded before he could retrieve it. The cabin immediately filled up with smoke. At 30,000 feet and 260 miles an hour you just don't open a window to achieve some ventilation. In a heroic attempt to get rid of the grenade, the Navigator grabbed it in his bare hands, carried it to the hatch and finally dumped it out. The chemical in these grenades makes them burn at a white-hot temperature of several thousand degrees. The grenade instantly burned his hands to the bone. Imagine the courage it took to endure this dreadful pain and still be able to get the grenade into the hatch. Worse, imagine the unbearable pain this young man experienced on the long nine-hour flight back to Tinian.

On another occasion during a daylight raid on Osaka, one of our gunners had an unbelievable experience. Because the Plexiglas blisters on the B-29's had been known to blow, conceivably sucking the gunner out the opening, this gunner made up a heavy-duty web strap, which he fastened to his parachute harness and then to a bulkhead in the airplane. His idea was sound but he erred in making his strap too long. Sure enough flak caused his blister to blow and he was sucked out! He was left dangling outside the airplane at the end of his 15-foot cord. The aircraft was at 21,000 feet, the temperature had to be at least 20 below zero and the 260-mile per hour air speed made for a punishment that was appalling. It took the rest of the crew several minutes to drag him in because of the force of the slipstream. He had frozen hands, ears, and nose but he was alive. Later he required surgery to repair the damage but he survived. I can't imagine his thoughts as he dangled outside that airplane in the midst of flak and fighter attacks.

Our Bombing Success Was Questionable

Our bombing success, up to this point in the war, had not been anything to brag about. On the first missions we had tried to bomb from extremely high altitudes, such as 40,000 feet, the altitude for which the B-29 was designed. Part of the inaccuracy problem came from the unexpectedly high winds aloft; the jet stream. These sometimes-gusty winds blow from the northwest to the southeast and often reach two hundred miles per hour. Our bombsights were not able to handle these winds, even if the bomb runs were made directly into the wind. The sad part of it was that we were losing crews and missing our important targets. Another factor affecting our bombing accuracy was an idiosyncrasy of the B-29 design. The bombsight was located in the nose of the aircraft and about as far away from the aircraft center of gravity as you could get. This meant increased "yaw" (motion from right to left and back) that confused the bombsight and caused it to spray the bomb pattern to the right or left, whichever way the nose was moving.

The Air Force was well aware of the problem and embarrassed at our results to-date. Their first solution was to lower the bombing altitude. We flew some later missions against Nagoya and Osaka at 21,000 feet with much greater success; however, the danger was also much greater and we lost aircraft and men.

"Gentlemen, the Target is Nagoya!"

Nagoya was a heavily defended target located far enough inland that we were subjected to plenty of flak and fighter attacks. The worst part of a mission was the excruciatingly long eight hours one had to dwell on what the future might hold—"Will I return in one piece or return at all?"

Try to visualize this fantastic sight that I will always have imprinted on my mind. On this Nagoya raid there were over three hundred (300) B-29s, creating approximately thirty-three (33) nine-ship formations. Each formation turned in towards the target in a single file stream; the formations were spaced about a minute apart. Each formation, about two football fields wide, spread out in this fashion to open up fields of fire for the gunners to fight off enemy aircraft. Imagine, all this power converging on Nagoya!

For the first time, on this mission, we encounted the Jap twin-engine fighter called "Nick!" Flying as tail gunner, I didn't get as many opportunities to shoot because the Jap fighters usually attacked head on. However, two of these Nicks attacked from the rear and all of us (me plus tail gunners in the other eight aircraft) opened fire. We shot down one Nick, but the second one was bearing in at close range and was causing damage to some of our planes. Suddenly, our combined firing caused black smoke to pour out of one of his engines. He broke off his attack, and with the black smoke getting denser, he then suddenly swung around and pressed toward us to within fifty yards. He had undoubtedly decided to become a "Kamikaze" pilot; he wanted one more kill before he died. Everyone was shooting like mad and finally we set fire to his second engine and may have killed him as the Nick disappeared in a vertical dive. The plane came so close that I saw the outline of the pilot's head. The flash of his guns is imprinted on my mind's eye. I'm thankful he wasn't a very good shot, as he didn't do much damage to our formation.

A Black Cloud Over Nagoya

As we approached the target, we noticed the big black cloud ahead over the city. The crew rejoiced thinking that we might be able to bomb by radar and escape a direct attack. The rejoicing didn't last very long as we soon discovered that the black cloud was barrage flak, the most feared and deadly kind! And now we were about to experience this type of flak first hand ~ for the first time.

It was a strategically important target because most of Japan's aircraft production was located in Nagoya. To protect an important target like this, the barrage-type of anti-aircraft fire was most effective. Imagine a box in the sky two or three thousand feet high and several thousand feet wide located at an altitude that the bombers must fly in order to hit the target. Guns are not trying to aim at any particular plane or formation but are assigned *one spot* in this box. Their gun crews are to load and fire into that one spot as fast as they can until the bombers have passed. With several hundred guns firing into this same box, you have a concentration of bursting flak that is almost impossible to fly through without damage. And at twenty thousand feet they can shoot the hell out of you!

As we watched the formations ahead of us enter the cloud, crippled B-29s were spinning out and being mobbed by the fighters who were lurking like wolves outside the target area. One of our planes had an engine shot up, couldn't keep his position with the formation and dropped out. We last saw him diving towards the ocean trying to get out to sea where sometimes the Jap fighters would break off their attacks. Our formation sustained a lot of damage but we miraculously only lost that one plane. As we came off the target, I was absolutely drained from these few minutes of fear. Everyone was so exhausted from the eight hours of anxiety enroute to the target and then with the strain of the mission that the relief coming off the target was indescribable. Once we were out to sea and safe from fighters and flak everybody but the pilot conked out. We had another eight hours to fly back to Tinian and for some it was limping back. This was before Iwo Jima became a rescue landing field ~ so we had 1500 miles of ocean to fly over before reaching our base.

As the formation came off the target the lead plane would assign an intact plane to accompany a damaged plane back to base. If they had to ditch we would stay right beside them and radio their position for help and assist in any way possible. A conversation I remember on the way back from Nagoya was one commander saying to another, "Langdale, how many engines do you have?" and the answer was, "I've got three." The reply was, "Hell, you're in *good* shape, you better buddy *me* home."

Buddies and Always Looking for Good Food

Back on Tinian my life was improving. Remember my old classmate from Miami Beach, Red Boelsen, was Commanding Officer of the Port Battalion of stevedores. Well, another classmate of mine from Miami Beach, George Emmit, showed up on Tinian as the Commanding Officer of a Radar detachment. His camp was up on the side of the mountain overlooking the airfield. He and Red were friends so Red kept him well supplied with steaks. It was just like George to acquire a mess sergeant who was a gourmet cook. The meals he prepared were a far cry from what we got in our mess hall at the 504th. Some of the best and most relaxing times on Tinian were with these two guys at George's camp. Usually I'd invite one of my tent mates to come along, Steve Mesnyak, Al Kohl, or Jack Warner. The war would seem pretty far away on these occasions.

Speaking of food; because we were always thinking, dreaming, and wishing for food, we had various ways of scrounging good meals. We learned early on Tinian that the Navy had the best food. An invitation to dine at the Navy base was never passed up. We accidentally discovered another way to get our hands on Navy food. One day I picked up three hitchhiking Navy officers who had just left a big APA troop transport in the harbor. They wanted to see the B-29 airfield, so I gave them a conducted tour in my jeep. While visiting one of our crews on the airfield, the Airplane Commander asked them if they'd like to go for a ride; seems that he was going up for a short training mission. They were overjoyed and thrilled with the experience. Afterwards, to show their gratitude, they invited us to come aboard their ship that night for dinner. Hot dog!

Four of us went to the ship directly from working on the flight line. We were dirty, unshaven, and wearing khakis that we had laundered by hand and not pressed. Because we had not been issued short sleeve shirts and shorts, we had cut off the sleeves and pant-legs and were wearing them without being hemmed, and with the unraveled threads hanging. Additionally, we were not wearing our rank insignia because we had been told that Jap snipers were trained to pick off officers. When we came up the ladder to the ship, we must have been a sight! Here were our new Navy friends and all their fellow officers in freshly laundered AND PRESSED suntans, looking as though they had just showered, turning up their noses because I am sure we even smelled bad. We were so starved we didn't let it bother us one bit. All we wondered about as we devoured the great chow was why the Air Corps didn't plan better food for us. We also let the Navy know that while they were living a deluxe life aboard their ship, we were fighting the war!

Iwo Jima saved my life!

On April 24, 1945, I flew a mission to Tokyo and was to learn the importance of Iwo Jima. The aircraft was the "Ace Of The Base" and I flew as CFC (Central Fire Control) gunner with Lt. Urquhart's crew. Our bombing altitude was 20,000 feet, which subjected us to lots of flak and fighter attacks. Alongside Mt. Fujiyama, we encountered heavy flak and had an engine shot out before we could make the target. Dropping our bombs, we peeled out of the formation and turned down Tokyo bay. Sometimes our Navy would station "picket" submarines along our route. If a crew was in trouble they could home in on one of the subs and either ditch or bail out near the sub and hope that ocean conditions were right for them to be picked up. Fortunately, the Jap fighters left us alone that day so we proceeded south towards Tinian. A couple of hours later a second engine began to leak oil and heat up, so we had to feather that propeller also. It was now apparent that we would never make it back to Tinian; with only two engines we were losing a little altitude every moment. The navigator estimated that we could make Iwo Jima. However, we had been briefed that we should not attempt to land on Iwo because the fighting was still intense. They didn't want us to clutter up the one airfield that was open and being used by P-51s in the battle.

Urquhart said we had several alternatives—ditch in the middle of the invasion fleet, bail out over the invasion fleet, or land on Iwo. We took a vote and it was unanimous to land on Iwo. When you are in trouble like this, survival is the only thing on your mind. We were able to contact the control tower on the south field that our Marines had just captured, and received permission to land. They advised us to beware, the Japs were firing mortars in front of planes on final approach, plus the runway was pretty short. Despite all the negatives we prepared to land by starting up the engine that had been leaking oil in order to add its power to our approach. Urquhart performed a great landing and was able to stop the Fortress at the end of the short runway; an accomplishment two other B-29s had failed to do. Both planes lay off the end of the runway, buried in the soft, black ash that covered Iwo. As soon as we landed, we scrambled away from the plane, in case the Japs had us zeroed in with their mortars.

We ended up spending three days and two nights on Iwo—an experience which proved to me that I had made a good choice in joining the Air Corps. The Marine ground troops had taken a terrible beating on the invasion and heavy fighting was still going on in the mountains at the north end of the island. My tent-mates for the first night were a couple of unstrung P-51 pilots. It seems that two nights before, the Japs had staged a kamikaze attack on the tent area. Several pilots were killed or wounded before the attack was beaten off. When I arrived, I found my tent- mates loaded to the teeth

Our crew makes emergency landing on Iwo Jima.

with sub-machine guns, pistols, and hand grenades. And, several times during the night they jumped out of bed because they heard some kind of an unusual noise. As I tried to sleep, we could hear the fighting on the north end of the island. Trip flares would light up the sky so bright that it showed through the tent canvas. Next, the machine guns would open up and the noise would rise tremendously for a few moments. Then, all would settle down again until the next flare. We didn't get much sleep, but I thanked my lucky stars that I was on this volcano called Iwo instead of in the ocean.

While on the island, I spent time touring around areas reported to be safe. After scaling Mt. Suribachi, I stood on the very spot where the famous photo of four marines raising the American flag was made—the picture that became the inspiration for the Iwo Jima Memorial now standing in Washington DC. The Fighter Group's Briefing Hall was an interesting place I found to watch some of the gun-camera film brought back from their missions over Japan. They had just started using color film, and the films were just spectacular. The P-51s were flying all over the empire at low altitudes strafing anything that moved, from fishing boats, to trains, to people on bicycles. One amusing film was of a Jap train that played hide and seek with a P-51 by racing in and out of tunnels.

Iwo will always be held in my memory with great affection for saving my life however, when the opportunity arose to hitch a ride back to Tinian with another crew, I jumped at it. Our plane was left on Iwo until its engines could be repaired.

Through a strange quirk, the word of our safe landing on Iwo never reached our 504th Group Headquarters. As a consequence, presuming we were lost, the number of our airplane had been scrubbed from the operations board and they had already started packing up the personal belongings of our crew. When I landed on Tinian and returned to my tent, I was greeted by my tent-mates with great astonishment. "What are you doing here, Bob?" In their shocked tones of voice they confessed that they had consumed all of my booze and stashed food while they sadly packed up my belongings to send stateside. My next step was to jump in my jeep and head for the Red Cross Compound to see my girl. However, when I got there she was gone. Her roommate was acting pretty evasive, but finally told me that my girl thought I was dead, was pretty shaken up for a couple of days, and *then met a General and now she was his girl!* I made a few attempts to contact her to no avail and, broken hearted, finally gave up. The General was a tough act to compete with because he had a house on the mountaintop, complete with Filipino houseboys and cooks, and could offer her many luxuries that a lowly Captain, like me, could not. Soon after returning to Tinian I was promoted to Staff Gunnery Officer for the entire 20th Air Force Headquarters and transferred to Guam. It would have been tough to carry on the romance from another island anyway, so I gradually got over my broken heart. Notwithstanding, every time I hear the old Vaughn Monroe rendition of "There I Said It Again" a wave of nostalgia sweeps over me because when I was with my Red Cross girl that was our song.

Himeji, Japan

On July 4th, 1945, I flew on a night mission to Himeji, Japan. By this time in the war, all our missions were either night bombings or night mine-laying. Although the plane was stripped, my gunners served many other necessary duties on board the aircraft. Our Group policy of having all Staff Officers fly two missions a month meant that I needed to go on the night missions even if no gunnery was involved.

Most of the larger cities in Japan had been already destroyed, so by July 4th we were down to bombing smaller cities with fewer aircraft. Himeji had a population of about 250,000 and was located along the coast at the foot of a mountain range about one hundred miles west of Kobe. Two hundred B-29's participated in the raid. I flew with a crew whose airplane Commander was a Lt. Binney and when we arrived at the target, the city was a huge mass of flames. There were no fighter attacks, as the Japs generally did not have night fighters. I saw no flak. The mission was uneventful and I was thankful to see Tinian again. (Fifty years later, I went back to visit Himeji under uniquely different circumstances.)

Rashin Harbor, Near Vladivostok, Siberia

My next night mission was a mine-laying in the Rashin harbor, in what is now North Korea, just few miles from Vladivostok, Siberia. My crew commander was Lt. Stacy, on the "Lucky Lady," the same plane that carried me overseas from Kansas. Because of the tremendous distance, we stopped for fuel on Iwo Jima. It was a tricky landing with a big load of mines on board! Iwo was completely secure by this time. We refueled, took a fast walk around the infamous island and then took off. We flew completely over Japan at about ten thousand feet. There was no flak, no fighters, the Japanese Empire was completely blacked out!

Three planes from our Group were to mine Rashin that night. We approached the harbor from the southeast at about one thousand feet, in single file, a mile apart. My crew was number two in line. Intelligence didn't have much information about the flak we might encounter and what they did give us was completely wrong. We watched the plane ahead of us approach the target in complete darkness; all we could see was his four engines' exhaust flames. When he flew over the harbor the entire sky lit up with searchlights that didn't wander around but zeroed in on him so that he lit up like a bright star in a "cone" of light. (We later learned that these lights were radar-controlled so they could automatically focus on their target.) At the same time flak, which looked like a fireworks display, started. It seemed like the Japs were shooting at us with everything from rifles to cannons. When our first plane had passed over the harbor, the lights winked out as one, and the flak stopped just as fast as it had begun. And now, it was our turn!

Airplane Commander Stacy yelled back to me to open up the camera hatch in the aft compartment of the aircraft and start throwing out "chaff" to disrupt the Japs' radar. Chaff consisted of a roll of aluminum tape 3/8 inches wide and about 200 feet long, tightly rolled, with a cardboard tab at one end. When dropped, the tab would allow the aluminum to unroll to its full length. The theory was that the radar would be confused by the chaff and zero in on it instead of us. About the time we got the camera hatch open the lights had *coned* us and it was so bright inside the airplane, it was difficult to see. I was throwing out handfuls of chaff as fast as I could with the help of one of my gunners, but we were too late, it didn't do any good. The flak started and was so heavy and close you could hear the explosions of the shells nearby and shrapnel hitting the fuselage like hail. As we discovered later, we had about a hundred holes and dents on the surface of the airplane; however, miraculously all four engines kept running, not a wire had been cut, and none of us were wounded. What a relief it was to leave that harbor. At a time like this your adrenaline keeps you moving but later the relief is so great you are left absolutely wrung out and weak.

As we made our climbing turn out of the harbor we were able to watch our third plane get it, the same flak and searchlight treatment. Amazingly, they also came through it all okay. I had chosen this mission in order to satisfy my required two missions that month. On paper it looked like a "milk run!" The war was just about over, so in retrospect, it would have been crazy to be killed on a raid like this, particularly when I had a choice not to go at all.

The Importance of Our Mining Campaign

Not enough has been said or written about the mining campaign we waged against Japan. When most people think of the 20th Air Force and the B-29's they think in the context of the mass fire-bombings we did over Japan or the Atom Bomb. What was not publicized was the *tremendous effect* our mines had in winning the war.

Starting in May of 1945, two different Bomb Groups had been taken off regular bombing and assigned the task of mining all of the harbors around Japan, plus those facing it on the China coast. The mines weighed a thousand pounds and were packed with an extremely unstable explosive called RDX. When dropped from about 1000 feet, a parachute opened to gently deposit the mine in the water. Some were magnetic, some sonic, and some were set to allow a number of ships to pass by before exploding under another. This was indeed, a fiendish, successfully planned campaign that completely sealed up all the harbors for the rest of the war and sank more commercial Jap shipping than all other Naval actions combined.

Our aerial photoreconnaissance planes were over the empire every day and recorded how all types of ships, including fishing boats, were destroyed if they tried to leave their harbors. To a country like Japan, completely dependent upon imports for oil, rubber, petroleum, and many other necessities, these mines were the final blow. For our Group, there was a great price to pay, as we lost several crews to the anti-aircraft fire, which was so intense at the low altitudes necessary to do the job; we were clearly sitting ducks. One of my friends, Fiske Hanley, who was the engineer on Lt. Brown's crew, was shot down on a mining mission in the Shimonoseki straits and spent the rest of the war in the Jap's notoriously cruel prison camp in Tokyo. Eight of his crewmates were killed. He has written a book, <u>Accused American War Criminal</u> that really exposes what animals the Jap captors were.

Our Missing 393rd Squadron Shows Up

One day in July 1945, I was down on the line at the air-field and looked up to see a strangely marked B-29 in the traf-fic pattern about to land. All our aircraft had a large circle on the tail with a big E in the center; all of the 313th Wing air-craft had this same circle. The plane I saw had an arrowhead on the tail and I quickly noted that it had no gun turrets except in the tail. Inasmuch as gunnery was my business, this really got my attention. I jumped in my jeep intending to look this new airplane over as soon as it landed. When I arrived at the runway, I was stopped by the MPs. That day about two dozen of these strangely marked planes arrived. Soon we learned that they were the 509th Group whose nucleus was our old 393rd Squadron, separated from us in Fairmont, Nebraska, in July of 1944.

The 509th was the Group commanded by Col. Paul Tibbets specially formed and trained to drop the Atom Bombs. Even on Tinian they were surrounded with complete secrecy; we were not allowed in their area even though we had good friends among their ranks. The 509th joined us on a few fire-bomb raids over Japan, but we really didn't learn what they were all about until August 6th, 1945, when the first Atom Bomb was dropped on Hiroshima.

While the decision was being made to use the Atom Bomb, some consideration was given to the idea of demon-strating the Bomb to the Japanese prior to using it against them. There are small islands off the coast of Japan not far from Tokyo and the idea was to first drop leaflets revealing what would happen if we dropped this horrific Atomic Bomb, and to demonstrate its power, one would be dropped on an island so that everybody could observe the results. They were accustomed to the idea of leaflet warnings because we had used them before on firebomb raids. The thought was that the explosion would be so tremendous that it would scare the Japs into surrendering. The only hitch was that the Atom Bomb had never been dropped from an aircraft and if it turned out to be a dud, we'd have egg on our face. So the "demonstration of strength" idea was scrapped.

Japan's cities and industry had been destroyed, their harbors were all mined, and they were out of oil and other necessities for life and war. The last few missions we flew didn't draw one shot from the ground. There was one school of thought at that time that felt we should just keep Japan bottled up until they capitulated. Peace feelers had been out for some time and it was felt by some that if we just kept them captive and waited, they'd eventually surrender. The P-51's from Iwo were flying all over the empire shooting anything that moved, our Navy task forces had them bottled up, but from bitter experience everyone knew that they would fight to the last man for the defense of their country. We had already been making preparations for an invasion of Japan and casualties were expected to be colossal. The big hospital that had been built on Tinian was just one of many erected to support the invasion when it came. The Atom Bomb decided it all in a big hurry. I sometimes question why we used it and whether it was really necessary at that point in the war but if we were planning an invasion, the Bomb then saved thousands of lives on both sides.

When the second bomb was dropped on Nagasaki on August 9th, we knew it was all over! Although there is absolutely no doubt in my mind that these two bombs ended the war, a lot of us felt that the war was already over and the two bombs just sped up the process.

The many American prisoners of war incarcerated in deplorable Jap prison camps were also a big factor in our decisions. The Japs had always stated that if there were an invasion, our prisoners would be immediately executed. If we blockaded Japan until they capitulated, this might take years and our POWs wouldn't last long the way they were being treated.

I feel no guilt about the Atomic Bombs and know of nobody in the 20th Air Force who does. My only regret is that we, the good guys, the ones who wear the white hats, had to use this dreadful tool of destruction. Our firebombs actually killed more people and destroyed more property than the Atomic Bombs. If nothing else, the dropping of the Bomb demonstrated to the world what a devastating force it is ~ and once demonstrated, one would pray that it would never have to be used again. What's scary to me is the fact that if Harry Truman and our leaders used the bomb, you know darn well that Hitler would have used it and so will terrorists like Sadaam Hussein unless it is controlled.

Chapter 7

Signing of the Peace

Peace at Last

In late August of 1945 there were several rumors that the Japs had capitulated and each rumor triggered spontaneous celebrations in our Group. When the official word of the surrender reached us it was almost anti-climactic. On September 2nd every B-29 that could fly was sent to Japan as part of a "show of strength" over Tokyo during the signing of the peace documents on board the USS Missouri. I wasn't able to get on a crew for this mission but did have an exciting experience a few days later on September 4th when I flew with Captain Charles Kammer's crew on a mercy mission to parachute supplies into the Prisoner of War camp located near Sendai. The following is directly from a diary I carried with me on missions:

My Last Mission

Diary Entry ~ 10:00

It is now 10:00 on 4 September 1945 and we are just passing the island of Sofugan enroute to Sendai, Japan, to drop supplies to a Prisoner of War Camp. We passed Iowa

Jima about two hours ago and except for an oil leak in number three engine our trip has been uneventful. They woke me at 0:300 this morning had some fried eggs at the mess, went to the field at 04:00 and we were airborne at 05:00. We have passed through several storms and the air has been quite rough at times. I was able to get in about two hours of sack time after take-off. Had a wonderful dream about something but can't remember what it was. The air is sure rough right now! I am riding back in the CFC compartment and this is the best spot in the airplane both for thinking and sightseeing. Back here one is utterly alone and seemingly there is no connection with the aircraft. You just seem to float along without any visible means of support! This morning the sun is shining brightly, the sky is partially covered by fleecy white cumulus clouds that look like soft cotton. Actually, I guess a man is just about as near to heaven as possible at a time like this—I really feel wonderful! Sitting here basking in the morning sun I feel as contented and happy as I possibly could be. My crew spot on this flight is as tail gunner so before we make landfall, I need to get back into the tail gunner compartment.

Diary Entry ~ 12:30

We made landfall at Choshi about noon and got a good look at the town from about 1500 feet. We have been over land now for about a half hour but have been socked in for the last 20 minutes. Choshi sure was a mess—burned to the ground, literally.

Diary Entry ~ 13:40

Sendai was socked in with clouds up to six thousand feet. The only way we could find the POW camp was to fly out to sea, let down to a thousand feet and then follow a river up a valley where the camp was supposed to be located. When we finally came upon it, we were going so fast we didn't have time to open the bomb bay doors and drop our parachute supplies. Not knowing how far ahead the valley might narrow down Kammer immediately put on climb power and we pulled up into the soup to do a go-around. As we passed the camp I had the best opportunity of anyone on the crew to see from my tail compartment. The prisoners were all out waving sheets at us and I'm sure they were disappointed that we didn't drop something. We climbed back up to six thousand, flew out to sea, let down again, and this time we slowed down as we went up the valley. By putting down our flaps and opening the bomb bay doors we were slowed down enough that when the camp came into view we had plenty of time to make our drop. The view from in back was fantastic! The chutes lit (landed) right in their midst ~ in fact we later heard that some of the heavy boxes actually caused injuries as the prisoners were madly scrambling for the supplies. I only had a short look as we immediately banked around again and pulled up into the clouds. We didn't have enough gas to make another pass so Kammer set a course for Tokyo so we might all get a good look at it from a low altitude.

Diary Entry ~ 14:00

The oil leak in number three has stopped and with reduced power we may not have to feather the propeller. I can hear Kammer and the engineer on the interphone now and they have decided to go into Iwo Jima for gas on our return. That will give us about two hours of cruising around sightseeing over Tokyo. The mountains around Tokyo are now in View. Mount Fujiyama can just barely be seen—with its snowcap it sure is beautiful!

Diary Entry ~ 15:30

We're just leaving Tokyo. I was so busy looking and taking pictures over the city that I didn't have time to write anything so I am catching up now. There is no way in which I can adequately describe what we have seen! The city is utterly devastated and seeing it today is the supreme thrill of my life. Makes me feel that we have evened things up since Pearl Harbor. At times we flew as low as two hundred feet and had an excellent view of everything there. We saw block upon block of charred ruins, gutted brick walls, demolished tanks, twisted and rusted steel structures. White flags were flying everywhere but there was not much activity on the streets. The

Emperor's Palace seems to be intact, as do some of the
finer residential areas. But the urban and industrial area
is completely gone in Tokyo, Yokahama and Yokasuka. We
buzzed the American and British fleets in Tokyo bay on
our way out and hundreds of sailors waved to us as we
went by about 200 feet over their heads. We also saw a
POW camp in Tokyo proper and it had a big white sign
painted on the roof that said, "GONE." We also saw many
trains stopping in crowded stations and thousands of
faces turned up to look us over. I bet those little b_____
are really sorry about the war now. Very few vehicles were
in sight but literally hundreds of bicycles could be seen
and there were a few horses too. Out in the country people were working in their gardens and they looked to be
beautifully kept with every available piece of ground
under cultivation. All in all, Japan seems to be a very picturesque and beautiful country but I have seen all of it I
care to for awhile. We also flew over hundreds of flak gun
installations and I can understand now how we caught so
much hell here on our missions. The Navigator just
advised us on the intercom that our ETA at Iowa Jima is
18:00. Looks like we will be a little late getting home to
Tinian. Interesting how a place you have hung your hat
becomes "home" after a while, isn't it?

Diary Entry ~ 19:05

Have just landed on Iwo Jima. This island has really been
cleaned up since the last time I landed here. Airstrips are
now covered with asphalt and the invasion mess has been
pretty well cleared except for the stunted and shell-
shocked trees. There are still a lot of battle-damaged B-
29's parked on the ramp awaiting repairs before they can
be flown back. This island still depresses me! It is built on
black, volcanic, ash and the air is permeated with a sulphur odor. The weather here always seems to be cloudy
and rainy with a sullen, gray, sky. An island of tragedy—
that's Iwo Jima!

Waiting To Go Home

After the signing of the peace treaty in Tokyo most flying activity ceased and time seemed to stand still as everybody waited to be sent home. The combat crew Officers spent most of their time on the beach. During the war, the aircrew enlisted men (and this included all of my gunners) were exempt from duties like guard or KP (Kitchen Police). However, after the signing some bright guy in Wing Headquarters got the brilliant idea that these combat aircrew members should start drawing guard and KP like the rest of the enlisted men. All of a sudden what the gunners and other combat crew enlisted men had done for us all in battle was forgotten. I was amazed that anyone would come out with an order this stupid. Upon confronting Wing, I was told that they would rescind the order, but that I should find something for the men to do to "keep them out of sight!"

Western Pacific Skeet Shooting Championship

I thought the best way to keep the gunners occupied would be to organize a Western Pacific Skeet Shooting Championship. Our 504th Bombardment Group gunners spent a couple of weeks practicing on the skeet range and then the competition began. Starting at the Group level, we had elimination shoots so that each Bomb Group ended up with a champion five-man team. Then these teams competed to make up a Wing championship team. The four Wing teams then came down to Guam to shoot in the final elimination to determine the 20th Air Force Championship Team. At this level it became competition between individuals and the top five shooters from the four Wings competing would make up the Championship Team.

About the same time I was dreaming up this tournament I was promoted to Air Force Gunnery Officer and transferred to 20th Air Force Headquarters on Guam where I served on General LeMay's staff. At the same time I was promoted to the rank of Captain and given my "railroad track" twin bars to wear. This new authority made it easier for me to organize and

20th Air Force Championship Skeet Team, L to R: Lt. Sciaroni, CPL. Wood, Lt. Horton, and Sgt. Covert and Capt. Bob Allen.

Shooting skeet match on the Iwo Jima invasion beach. Note Mt. Suribachi in background.

20th Air Force Skeet Champions Shoot Match on Saipan. L to R: Lt. Bobby Horton, Lt. Lloyd Sciaroni, General Parker, Sgt. Bill Covert, Cpl. Wood, and Capt. Bob Allen.

conduct the skeet tournament as well as procuring a B-29 and crew to fly the winning team all over the Western Pacific. We competed in exhibition matches I arranged against skeet teams from the Navy, Air Force, and Marines. We started our exhibition tour with matches on Guam, Tinian, Saipan, Iwo Jima, and at two bases in Okinawa ~ Kadena and Naha. (On Iwo Jima the skeet fields had been built right on the invasion beach directly below the infamous Mt. Suribachi.)

Our team was royally entertained wherever we went. We partied so much our shooting suffered and we lost several matches, one of which was against a Navy team ~ that one really made us angry and injured our pride.

It was pretty fantastic having a big four-engine B-29 as your private plane. I was working on scheduling some new exhibition matches in the Philippines and possibly in Japan when some of the team members accumulated enough points to be sent home. Trying to sell them on the idea that our team's continued experiences would create the opportunity of a lifetime didn't convince them—they just wanted to get home. So, with regrets, we ended the tour after the last match on Okinawa and flew back to Guam.

Monkey Skeet

My only duty on Guam was to write a report on the success of the B-29 gunnery program. I accumulated statistics on the number of Jap planes shot down, ammunition used, the performance of the Central Fire Control system, and the role our gunners played. When I wasn't working on this report I spent all of the rest of my time on the 20th's skeet range. At the war's end I had about a half-million shotgun shells and a million clay targets in the ammunition dump. The Army was loading all unused munitions on ships and then taking it out to sea to dump into the ocean. I issued an order that the shotgun shells and targets be left until last and then my friends at 20th Hq. and I did our best to "shoot it all up." We would go to the skeet range right after breakfast and spend most of the day there. We became bored with shooting regulation skeet so started shooting what we called "monkey" skeet. The lead off man would hold his gun between his legs to shoot and then everyone in the squad had to shoot this same way. We became quite proficient at shooting with the gun behind our backs, between our legs, over our heads, left handed, from the hip, and with the gun upside down.

In an attempt to beautify and landscape the skeet range, I arranged for a detail of about twenty-five Jap prisoners to come out each day and, under the watchful eyes of a couple of MP guards, build walks and stone walls, and plant trees. One day we were shooting our *monkey skeet* and I noticed that all activity had ceased among the Japs and they were all squatting (their favorite position) and watching us intently. One of the guards spoke Japanese so I told him to tell them that all of the American soldiers coming overseas now could shoot like us. That brought a big laugh but you could tell they believed it. However, the prisoners would not believe the war was over! Through their guard interpreter I explained that Japan had been decimated by our B-29's. I drew a circle on the ground with my foot, telling them that was Tokyo. I then brushed out the circle with my foot to show them that Tokyo was completely destroyed and that made them laugh nervously in disbelief. The fact that the B-29's were no longer taking off each day didn't seem to prove anything to them.

Guam is a jungle island and it was very easy for Japs who survived our invasion to escape and live in the jungle. The Army had patrols out every day trying to mop up by-passed Jap soldiers. They didn't cause much trouble unless they were caught when stealing food at night; then there were fatalities on both sides. On Christmas day of 1945 some Marines were taking an outdoor shower. Two Jap soldiers stepped out of the jungle, set up a machine gun on a tripod, and killed five of the Marines. As late as 1995 Jap soldiers who did not believe the war was over were being apprehended on Guam. It was hard to believe how fanatic they were.

Bombing Survey Group

I had enough points so that I could have been sent home but they were trying to keep the 20th Air Force Headquarters staff intact until such time as all records for the war had been brought up to date. I was really getting bored with shooting skeet and going to the beach every day so when a friend of mine at 20th Hqs. asked me if I'd like to accompany him with a Bombing Survey group to Japan, I jumped at the opportunity. Another friend, Johnny Euchner, was an Air Transport Command pilot and flew us all from Guam to Tachikawa airport just outside of Tokyo. The day before we left he asked me if I could get some cigarettes for horse-trading in Japan. I said "how many do we want?" and John suggested that we bring as many as we could get. John and I each bought a full case of cigarettes at the base PX.

Trucks met us at the Tachikawa airport (a city I had bombed once) and took us into Tokyo. I'll never forget that ride for many reasons but one reason stands out. For centuries the Japanese people have fertilized their gardens with human excrement. Ox drawn carts, called "honey carts" containing giant wood barrels with lids, make the rounds of homes each day collecting this stuff and in the evening return to the country with their smelly loads. On the way in from the airport we met a mile long caravan of these carts and the stench was so overpowering we almost vomited. The driver put on a gas mask but said that didn't help any. It was a relief to get to the city and away from that overpowering stench.

Johnny had lived in Japan and gone to school there in his teens. His dad had been with American President Steamship Lines so his family lived in Japan for about eight years. Because Johnny spoke the language so well, and knew his way around, despite the complete devastation caused by our bombing in Tokyo, Johnny located an old friend. We drove through miles of makeshift shanties constructed from bits of tin, wood, cardboard, or whatever else could be salvaged from the fire raids. It was cold (temperature about 40) so people needed shelter. We drove up a narrow little alley-like street lined with those pitiful shanties until we located Johnny's friend who was operating a small store, resembling a poor flea market. After much jabbering in Japanese, Johnny had us dump all of our cigarettes into a big box in the store. At that point his Jap friend handed each of us a stack of Japanese yen bills in various denominations. I stuffed mine into the knee pocket of my flying suit and we took off for the Marinouchi Hotel where the 20th had reserved rooms for us. We brushed up a little and then the four of us went over to the Imperial Hotel for dinner. The Imperial Hotel and many of the newer and more modern concrete buildings were still standing and had little damage from our firebombs. (I'm telling this story because the reality and the gravity of the cigarette exchange didn't sink in until I magnanimously offered to pay the dinner check for the four of us.) We had plenty of drinks, deluxe meals, and had been there for a long time. I gave the waiter one of the larger denomination bills. When he came back with the change, he had a big stack of bills and it took two or three minutes for him to count them out to me. I suddenly realized how much that stack of bills in my knee pocket was worth and what a stupid risk I had taken by bringing the cigarettes in to Japan. Johnny knew better and I never forgave him for exploiting me. The money paid for all my trip expenses for a month, for some new uniforms at the PX, and for several strings of real pearls.

The Bomb Survey Group's duty was to study the results of our bombing in all the cities in that part of Japan and then prepare a report. It was pretty easy to survey as the devastation was 100%. Each day a staff car with driver would pick us up at the Maranouchi Hotel right after breakfast. We'd then spend the day driving to various towns and cities. A few times we stayed overnight but the accommodations were so grim that we tried to get back to Tokyo each night. There were some smaller towns that had not been bombed but most of them had experienced light bombing and strafing by Navy Fleet fighters or P-51s from Iwo Jima.

The Town Surrenders

An interesting and amusing thing happened at one town we drove into. It had a population of about two thousand and had hardly been touched by the war. Evidently we were the first American military people they had seen because the Police Chief came to us and with great pomp and ceremony indicated that he wanted to surrender his town and its armament to us. He led us to the Police Station and into a back room. Here, to our amazement, were stacked hundreds of rifles, pistols, and swords—all the weapons collected from the town's people. Jap swords were bringing big money at that time and had we some way of transporting them, we could have made enough money to retire on. As it was, we each selected a sword, a pistol, and an Arisaki rifle. I still have my sword, which is on display in my office. We thanked the Police Chief and advised him that someone would come by to pick up the rest of the arms. We reported them to the Military Police back in Tokyo but will never know what happened to them.

The Haircut That Could Have Cost Me My life

In the Tokyo YMCA located near our hotel, the Army had set up a barbershop for Americans. I hadn't had a professional haircut for over a year so decided I'd get a haircut and then treat myself to the luxury of a shave by the barber. The barbers turned out to be Japanese girls and they were very good at their profession. My barber cut my hair and then prepared to give me my shave. As she tilted the chair back, the towel she had thrown over my shoulder shifted and my 20th Air Force shoulder emblem came into view. When she saw it she excitedly exclaimed, "B-29, B-29, you burn down my house!" Just a few seconds later she had my face and neck lathered up and I must say I was a little apprehensive as she started to use the straight edge razor to shave my throat!

Johnny Knew Some Very Interesting People

When I wasn't with the survey group, I was with Johnny Euchner. We visited several of his friends. Jimmy Nockabashi had gone to the University of Washington with Johnny. He was the Chevrolet dealer in Yokahama and our bombs had bombed out his business, his home, and killed his wife and one of his children. I don't know how he escaped military service because he was in good health. He said he knew after Pearl Harbor that his countrymen had bitten off more than they could chew. Another friend of Johnny's was Baron Ichijo, a member of the Japanese royal family. He had gone to school in both England and the United States, spoke perfect English, as well as some other languages, and was a delightful person to be around. The Japanese ostracized him however, because his wife Tess was from England. During the war the Japanese women terrorized her, and the personal attacks escalated to the point that her husband finally took her to the north coast of Japan where he had a summer estate. We had dinner with them several times and I remember vividly some of Ichijo's remarks concerning the war.

When Japan attacked Pearl Harbor he thought it was a terrible mistake because he had seen the might of England and the U. S. in his travels. However, when his countrymen over-ran China, Singapore, and the Philippines he said he suddenly started to become proud and thought maybe the military heads of Japan knew something he didn't. However, he was in Tokyo the day the Doolittle B-25s did their low level attack and he said for him that was the writing on the wall ~ Japan was in real trouble!

Johnny, Jimmy, the Baron, and I spent several great days touring around Japan. We visited the famous spas of Atami, stayed in the Fujiian Inn on the slopes of Mt. Fujiami, and saw

In Japan on Bomb Survey trip, Nov. 1945. L to R: Jimmy Nockabashi, Capt. Bob Allen, Lt. John Euchner, and Col. Winburn.

some beautiful mountain scenery. The weather had turned cold in December and a little snow was on the ground most of the time. The bombed-out people of Tokyo were in terrible shape and despite the Army's attempts to bring in food, blankets, and shelter, the people were miserable. We felt particularly sorry for the thousands of homeless little children. One cold morning we noticed a half-naked five-year-old shivering and shaking against a wall outside the railroad station trying to get warm in a narrow shaft of early morning sunlight. His nose was running, he was badly scratched up—the poor little thing was just in terrible shape. We carried him to a Military Police station a few blocks away and took him through their mess line. They tried to stop us but one of our survey groups was a full Colonel. They said there was no way they could begin to feed the thousands of kids like this little one. We left him there and the MPs said they'd let him stay that night so he could warm up and get a good night's rest. I don't know what happened to the little fellow after that and, to this day, I have very emotional thoughts about him and all the other children like him.

In late December I flew back to Guam on an ATC, C-54.

It was a night flight and most of the passengers were Army nurses being sent home. The cabin heaters weren't working very well and to stay warm and ease some of the boredom of a ten-hour flight we all decided to play a little game on the pilots. They had their cockpit door closed to keep their cabin warm. One person called out the commands, and the rest of us stood up and commenced to perform close order drills in the cabin. We marched clear to the rear of the plane, stood there for a few moments and then marched clear up to the front of the cabin and stopped again. If you know anything about airplanes, I'm sure you are getting the picture. The trim tab wheel must have been whirling around while the autopilot tried to keep the plane level. After about two of these marches to the rear and back to the front of the cabin, the cockpit door abruptly swung open with two confused pilots peering into the cabin. Immediately they recognized what was going on; however they failed to share in our humor.

Chapter 8

Going Home

Waiting to Go Home

By the time I was able to leave Guam, everyone was trying to find transportation ~ thousands of GI's were waiting.
An LST ship was my first opportunity to go home. I refused,
saying that if I was good enough to fly overseas, by God, I
wanted to fly home. So, I waited for a seat to open up on an
ATC (Air Transport Command) flight. There were a few war-
weary B-29s flying home; however, the maintenance at that
time was so poor, I didn't feel they were safe; as a matter of
fact, several crashed at places like Eniwetok or Kwajalein,
enroute to Hawaii. Finally, on Christmas Eve, a seat came
available on an ATC, C-54 (the same as the airlines' DC-4) so
I took off for Honolulu. I was chasing the International date-
line, that meant two Christmas dinners—an appropriate way
to celebrate going home!

My sister had already left Hawaii with her husband Jack,
however through her friends at the Halekulani Hotel, I was
able to get a great beach front room. Ships and planes were
backed up for several weeks with GIs like me trying to get
home from Honolulu. I was told that it might take a month or

195

so if I insisted on waiting for a plane ride. Irish luck worked in my favor when I found a little female Corporal in the ATC office who fell in love with a string of pearls I had purchased in Tokyo with my cigarette money. I told her I wasn't in any burning rush but if she could get me a seat within two weeks, the pearls were hers. The beach in front of the Halekulani was wonderful for R&R for about a week, and then one afternoon I received a phone call from my little Corporal advising me that she had a seat on a flight to San Francisco the next day. I said I'd be there with the pearls.

The flight from Honolulu to California turned out to be quite an experience. We had been scheduled to fly to San Francisco but weather forced us to divert to some almost deserted airfield out in the desert. Trucks came out to pick us up ~ about fifty military men. We were taken to an Army Base for breakfast where Italian prisoners of war were interned. In fact, we had breakfast with several hundred of the prisoners. As the weather cleared, we gassed up and flew to San Francisco.

Evidently we were the first GIs to arrive in San Francisco in 1946, so the newspapers and radio people were out in force to greet us. I had been sitting next to a GI from Arkansas, a real hillbilly Private. He was clutching a souvenir Jap Arisaki rifle when he left the plane. He got to the door first and I was right behind him. As he stepped out the media crowd greeted him and a gorgeous girl stepped up and hugged him for the cameras. He was being recognized for being the first service man to arrive in 1946. The girl turned out to be actress/dancer Cyd Charisse! While I was in San Francisco this guy's picture with this magnificent woman was plastered all over the papers attending all sorts of parties and publicity events. I was dying of envy and kicking myself repeatedly for not moving a little faster and being the first one out the door of that airplane.

Transportation out of San Francisco turned out to be even worse than it had been in Hawaii. The city was jammed with returning service men and all buses, planes, and trains were booked up for weeks. Hotel rooms were in such short supply that I ended up sharing a room in the St. Francis Hotel with a Navy Officer, a former Submarine Commander in the

Pacific. He decided to make up for lost time by trying to drink up all the booze and seduce all the women in San Francisco. He made for a good roommate because he was hardly ever in the room.

I was in San Francisco for about a week and really enjoyed myself because I spent time with my sister Anne and her new husband Jack. However, I was beginning to get anxious to go home and trying every way possible to get out of California. My Irish luck came through for me one night when Anne and I had dinner at the "Top Of The Mark" in the Mark Hopkins Hotel. We were having an after-dinner drink and there just happened to be a very pretty girl sitting next to me at the bar. She was telling the bartender that she had to leave because she had to catch a plane. This really got my attention and made me a little angry at the same time. Being a little high on drinks, I turned around and said, "How do you rate getting a reservation when this town is full of service men like me trying to get home?" She listened to me carefully and then said, "Do you need a plane reservation?" I guess I nodded looking a bit dumbfounded. She proceeded to write down a man's name and a phone number on a cocktail napkin and told me to call United Air Lines the next morning and maybe this man could help me.

Next morning, after breakfast, I found the napkin in my pocket. My hotel was just across the street from the United Air Lines ticket office so I walked over. When I asked the reservation clerk for the man on the napkin, she promptly picked up the phone and talked to someone. Then she gave me the man's office number upstairs and told me to go right up. I introduced myself to him and explained in detail how I had received his name. He asked, "Did she promise you that she could get you a seat?" When I said yes, he got on the phone and then asked me if I could go on short notice. He told me that he would put me on stand-by for what he called a "mail" seat. Sometimes if their mail load was lighter than expected, they could board more passengers. He said to stay close to my phone in the hotel and he'd call me soon. When I asked him how this girl could be so influential he told me that she was the daughter of United's President, Patterson, and that she didn't ask for favors very often but when she did, they helped her out. Somehow I must have impressed her. A few years later, when I was doing some business with United, I ran into her husband. He got a big kick out of my story, as I related it to him.

The next morning I left on a United DC-3. The first stop was Elko, Nevada where there was about a foot of new snow on the ground. All the passengers were GI's who had been in the Pacific and hadn't seen snow in a long time. We all got off and had a snowball fight and pelted the stewardess with snowballs too.

The next stop was Cheyenne, Wyoming where the flight was canceled due to weather. United got us all reservations on the Union Pacific Railroad so we continued on to Omaha where I stayed for a day while I looked for a new car. Back in 1942, when I enlisted in the Air Corps, I had been traveling out of Omaha and had sold my Studebaker Commander back to Morton Motors, from whom I had purchased it. As was common in those days, auto dealers made special arrangements for service men. They bought my car but only paid me about 50% of its price; the other 50% was kept in an escrow account for me to use at the end of the war. Had I been killed in the war, I don't know what would have happened to that 50%; probably would have gone to Morton's bottom line profits. Morton didn't have a very big selection of cars because new cars were still not being produced. He had a pretty good used Studebaker Commander, which I bought and then began driving home to Fort Dodge to see my family.

Remember, it's January when I arrived in Omaha and there was a foot of snow on the ground and the temperature most of the time was running around zero. Believe me, after having been in the Pacific for a year, it was a shock to my system. I left Omaha in my newly acquired car and was very anxious to get home to Fort Dodge to see my folks. I had been phoning them ever since I landed in Hawaii, so they were anxiously awaiting my arrival. As I drove toward Fort Dodge, I made a decision that I would tell my folks very little about the destruction and misery I saw during the war or how many times I almost lost my life. Instead, I would dwell on the funny things that happened.

Mr. Fix-it!

Yes! This would be a great story to tell my folks, I thought, and as I drove it all began to play on my memory screen. The crew Quonset hut quarters and the Officer's tent area were located midway between the Company street and the Pacific Ocean. The only latrine was located about midway between the two areas. For those Officers quartered at either end of the street it was a long walk to the latrine. Some of the guys got lazy and wouldn't walk that far during the night. The area soon started to smell so someone got the idea of installing urinals every one hundred feet between the tents and huts. It was a simple matter to do so; a hole was drilled into the coral ground and a pipe with a metal trough was installed thus solving the problem. Now a problem developed because one of the urinals, about three hundred feet from my tent, got plugged up; however, the men continued to use it. The ground for several feet around was soaked up and the stench was unbearable. During an inspection, the Colonel walked down through the area and discovered the smelly mess. He ordered that it be corrected immediately.

The Colonel assigned a young Second Lieutenant at Group Hq. to correct the problem, whose name I shall not divulge here. This Officer was our general handyman and known as "Mr. Fix-it!" The fact that he had been a Second Lieutenant for years with no hope of promotion, should give you a hint as to his prowess. He had a similar group of miss-fit enlisted men who did the work at his bidding.

As I remember, it was shortly after the noon chow and my tent mates and I were having our usual after lunch siesta when we saw Lt. Fix-It drive up in his jeep followed by a truck carrying several GI experts to solve the problem of the plugged-up urinal. We saw them talking as they gathered around the hole and then the Lieutenant drove off in his jeep, returning a few minutes later. To our horror we watched him tying several blocks of TNT together, attaching a wire and then dropping the explosives down the urinal pipe. Backing away, they unrolled the fuse wire 200 feet and then slipped back between two of the Quonset huts. The next thing we heard was him calling out in a loud voice "fire in the hole" and with that pronouncement he pressed the detonator. Instead of a loud explosion, there was just a tremendous "squash" and a mountain of urine-soaked mud erupted about 25 feet into the air and settled back down all over the area tents and buildings. The explosion was so intense that the stinking mud blew in the screened sides of those tents nearest to the blast. Men came roaring out of their beds covered with the slimy mud and angrily surrounded the Lieutenant who was peering down the ten-foot-deep crater he had just produced. If someone had found a gun I'm sure *Mr. Fix-it* would have been dead! He fled in his jeep and stayed out of sight for several days until tempers subsided. His GI crew filled in the crater with sand and coral but the stench persisted for several days until the sun finally dried things out.

In *Mr. Fix-it's* defense, he probably got the idea of using TNT from watching the SeaBees who used TNT for everything from blasting mountains of coral to cutting down trees. I guess this incident would best be described as one of the many horrors of war! To those who were not directly affected, it was a hilarious incident. I would tell mother and dad that war was definitely hell!

Cheese Sandwiches

Because our missions were fifteen to eighteen hours in length, box lunches were always prepared for the crews. Our mess personnel tried to be as clever as they could but the food supplies made it virtually impossible for them to put together very interesting lunches. Cheese was always available so on a majority of the missions they packed cheese sandwiches that the crews soon learned to despise. On some of our earlier missions to Japan a lot of chatter went on between our aircraft on the radio. Idle conversation interfered with necessary official transmissions plus there was a theory that the Japs might be able to use our radio transmissions to zero in on us with their anti-aircraft or to vector in their fighter planes. Thus, an order came down from Wing Hq. forbidding any radio transmissions except those that were required for the mission.

In order to check to see if these orders were being carried out, a recording device was put on one of the B-29's going on the next mission. I attended a critique that was held at Wing Hq. after the mission. General Davies, Wing Commander, opened the critique by indicating that there was still a lot of unauthorized radio chatter going on and that he would like for us all to hear the recordings they had made.

When the tape first started there was a lot of static noise and then out of the clear came the words, "We're at the IP!" The letters IP were short for "initial point", the place where the bomb run would normally start. Evidently some crewmember on one of the airplanes had his microphone on and thought he was making the announcement to his fellow crewmembers on the aircraft intercom system. Then there was a period of more static and the next thing heard was, "We've got those G___D____ cheese sandwiches again!" Well, when the group heard this they all broke up in laughter. After things had settled down again, General Davies came on and said, "My what an intrepid group of airmen we have! Here we are starting our bomb run and everyone on the crew should be alert, nervous and probably scared and here's this guy who is eating his lunch." This got another big laugh and then Davies went on to say that the radio problem was much improved but we should continue to be vigilant on all trans-missions.

Needless to say, when I finally arrived home it was truly an emotional moment in time! My dad was not one to show too much emotion so I'll never forget how he touched my soul when he greeted me with tears in his eyes.

Mother's Diary ~ My little Bobby is home safe!

In the meantime, I was in contact with my pre-war employer Johnson & Johnson who was holding a job open for me. After resting at home with my folks for a couple of weeks, I journeyed to Chicago to meet with J & J in their Wrigley Building offices.

Chapter 9

Birth of My Business

The Parachute Factory

Without realizing it at the time an idea I developed on Tinian, in 1945, was to be the seed that began my business after the war. Like most new businesses, this one developed because of a need. B-29 crews, especially the pilots and bombardiers, needed some kind of a sun cap. The B-29's entire nose area was made of Plexiglas. At high altitudes the sun shining through the nose of the aircraft literally cooked the crew inside. You would think that someone would have designed some kind of a cap for the crews but instead, we were issued helmets and goggles, which were totally useless! So, I came up with the idea of making my own cap with a large visor.

With the fabric from an old pair of Army pants plus a piece of sailcloth for the visor, I made the first cap using a sewing machine in our parachute shop. The cap had a 5½" square visor that was great for keeping the sun out. I designed it with a shallow crown so it sat on the top of your forehead and had a very rakish appearance. The minute other crewmembers saw it, they wanted one! I made up as many of them as I could in return for a fifth of whiskey. A bottle of whiskey could be sold on Tinian for as much as $40.00, so I could have come home a wealthy guy—instead my friends and I drank up all the profits! The popularity of the visor cap gave me the idea that they could be commercially profitable back in the states.

Holding My Pre-War Job

I delayed doing anything about the caps because Johnson & Johnson had held my job until after the war as did most companies. Upon discharge, in January of 1946, I reported to a sales manager by the name of Riffe. My salary was $400.00 a month plus all travel expenses and a car; a pretty good deal for those times and a slight increase over what they had been paying me as a Junior salesman prior to the war. A plus would be a bonus program based on sales increases.

During my meeting with the sales manager, he seemed a little reticent to give me the bonus history for my territory. Apparently, the man I was replacing was fired for not reaching his quota. And now they were going to give me a larger quota than the fellow who just got fired. I challenged my boss' reasoning but he felt that I was a superior salesman and with the prosperity everyone expected after the war, I should have no problem in making some good money by exceeding the quota. I left the office with misgivings but thankful that I had a good job.

My first trip around the territory revealed that all of our distributors were over-stocked with inventory making it almost impossible for me to write orders for new business. It seemed that they all had liked my predecessor and, when he confided to them that he might be fired for not making his quota, they gave him advance orders to beef up his sales. The way all the distributors were loaded up made it impossible for me to top my quota and make any interesting money. I might even have a tough time making the quota! So, I was off to a bad start and immediately began thinking of alternative ways to make a living.

Flight Kaps

Early in 1946, I had started going to trap, skeet and pigeon shoots and was making a little money. I had the idea that if I could spend most of my time shooting, I could make a living that way. Then it occurred to me that if I had something to sell along the way, it would take some of the risk out of following the shooting tournament circuit and only depending upon my winnings. The cap I had made overseas immediately came to mind. I just knew it could be a good seller!

While I was in Chicago for a meeting I contacted the Commercial Cap Co. and made arrangements for them to make the caps for me. With their professionally made samples I started to make a few test sales calls as I traveled around the territory on my Johnson & Johnson job. Every call I made resulted in an order! I'd sell a dozen or two to a sporting goods store, as many as a gross to a men's store, and so on. With the profit margin I had established I knew I could make as much money from the caps as I was making with J & J. After a couple of weeks of selling the caps, which I had trademarked as "FLIGHT KAPS," I turned in my resignation to J & J.

My parents' home in Fort Dodge served as my office and headquarters while I looked for my own place. My cap orders from the Commercial Cap Co. were shipped to my dad who put them in his garage until I returned on the weekend to take care of re-shipping them to my customers. The caps repeated well in the stores so soon I was receiving fill-in orders by mail. It was apparent I had a going business and would need a larger location soon—I was happily outgrowing Dad's garage.

Now I was able to buy a house on 55th Street in northwest Des Moines. The purchase price was a little over nine thousand dollars, for a two-bedroom, two-bath house with a full basement that would be ideal for my new business. It was time to expand so, noting a need for shooting garments, I designed a vest and coat that were then manufactured for me by a factory in Des Moines. Now I had three items to sell to stores as well as sell at retail, out of the trunk of my car at shooting tournaments. This, supplemented with some shooting winnings, was giving me a livable income. It was at this time that I received some unexpected help from a shooting acquaintance.

A Boxcar Load

Harold Russell was V. P. of Sales for Federal Cartridge Co. of Anoka, Minnesota. He took a liking to me and, recognizing that I was just starting out, made me an offer I couldn't refuse. At that time, right after the war, shotgun ammunition was in extremely short supply. At a time when everyone was clamoring for shotgun shells, Harold arranged for me to get a full boxcar load (635 cases) of 12 gauge trapshooting shells, worth about $25,000.00. And, by having them shipped into a bonded warehouse, I was able to get a bank loan to finance the shipment.

Selling the shells was a cinch. I sold almost the entire shipment on the phone within a few days. All that remained for me to do was ship the shells and collect my money. My profit on the carload was over 10,000.00 dollars; operating capital that my little business dearly needed. And, of course, I continued to do business on Federal Shells for several years. I'll always be indebted to Harold Russell who gave me preferential treatment. He opened the way for me to get my business started. When I shot, Federal shells were always in my pocket. Every championship I won using Federal shells boosted their reputation at a time when their trap and skeet market share of the business was less then ten or fifteen percent.

Court Avenue, Des Moines

At this point in my business career, I wasn't sure whether I was a retailer, wholesaler, or manufacturer. I was just fumbling around trying to make a living. In 1947, I put together a mail order catalog that included all kinds of shooting accessories along with the cap, vest, and coat. In addition I set up displays and sold my merchandise at all the shoots I attended. Thus, the business grew and finally, in 1949, it had outgrown my house basement, so I rented a storefront at 211 Court Avenue in downtown Des Moines. It was a good location for me because the entire building (which covered a quarter block) was empty and whenever we needed additional space, all we had to do was call the landlord, knock a hole in the wall, and occupy the new adjacent space—we called our handy work making a new "mouse hole."

Next, I acquired some sewing machines from a factory that had gone out of business. I moved the machines to the Court Avenue building, hired an experienced supervisor and a few sewing machine operators, and started making my own products. Those were tough times and making payroll was tight every week. Collections from our dealer customers were sometimes slow and we hadn't set up any kind of a credit policy to protect ourselves. I had a small credit line at the bank that extended money on pledged accounts receivable. The business muddled along, growing slowly, but I was constantly scratching around for additional money. If it hadn't been for the cash I received on retail and mail order sales plus my shoot winnings, I couldn't have made it.

(Our Court Avenue building with all its "mouse holes" will always conjure up warm memories. I'll never forget the sweat, and yes, the tears, but most of all the wonderful comraderie and friendship developed with other men just starting out in their businesses around me on Court Avenue.)

First Tent Store

A large part of our sales volume, at this time, was from my traveling tent store that I set up at the larger trapshooting tournaments. This was a "first" in the trapshooting world— we were the first and only tent store at the shoots.

I bought a big Buick Roadmaster station wagon (the old type made of wood) and used it to pull a specially built two-wheel trailer, and a custom-made twenty-foot square tent with all its poles, ropes, and stakes fitted into the bed of the trailer. Display tables, curtains, folding chairs, and display material were also packed into the trailer that had a heavy canvas cover to protect the contents. My inventory of goods to sell was packed in the station wagon. It was a compact and efficient rig but so heavy that the Buick brakes couldn't stop her. So, I had special electric brakes installed on the trailer that were operated by a lever mounted beside the steering column.

Knowing that this rig was difficult to stop, and to make sure vehicles ahead heard me coming before I passed, I had a set of 36" Buell Air Horns installed on the right front fender. The two silver horns looked just like trombones and when I blew them, all the traffic for a mile down the road moved over!

Making the shoots was like being in a circus! I always hired a young man to travel with me to help drive, set up, clerk, sleep in the tent to protect it, and help to tear it all down and go on to the next shoot. We'd set up the store on a Tuesday or Wednesday as those were the starting days of most big shoots. We'd start in the early spring at the Texas State Shoot and then as the season progressed we'd work our way north setting up at State Shoots in Oklahoma, Kansas, Nebraska, Missouri, Illinois, Colorado, Wyoming, Montana and also at the larger tournaments such as the Sun Valley Open, the National Championship Skeet Shoot, and annual Grand American Trapshoot in Vandalia, Ohio. In addition to the profits from the store, I usually made a little prize money from the shoots. It took me away from home almost the entire summer but this was the sacrifice I had to make to get my business started.

We had some remarkable experiences, to say the least! One night, while driving to the Kansas State Shoot, I heard a loud noise and then the car and trailer started to sway. Out the windshield I saw a wheel pass the car on the shoulder, make two or three big bounces and disappear into a cornfield. We stopped on the shoulder to learn that the right wheel on the trailer had somehow come off. We spent most of the night hunting through that cornfield with flashlights. Finally we located the wheel and were able to continue the trip.

Weather was always a worry! We had many close calls with tornado type weather and one year, at the Iowa State Shoot, the tent and all its contents blew down. I arrived at the gun club in the morning to find my employee disconsolately sitting in the middle of a bunch of soggy, wet, shooting cloth-

My tent store set up at the Ohio State Shoot, 1949.

ing and accessories. We spread everything out in the sun so it could dry and then had a "rainy day" sale offering everything at half price. Looking back at it, I'm sure the reason we sold out was because the shooters felt sorry for us and wanted to help out by buying something so the disaster ended happily.

By 1949, the line had grown to a size that precluded using a tent at a big tournament like the Grand American. Using a loan from a Vandalia bank, I constructed a 30' X 50' building with special signs reading "BOB ALLEN SHOOTER'S SUPPLIES ~ Des Moines, Iowa." This greatly improved business and made it possible to display our wares much more attractively. It was also wonderful to go back to the hotel at night and not worry about the place blowing away. We hired local high school and college girls as clerks. We didn't discriminate against girls if they were pretty—we just went ahead and hired them anyway! The shooters loved it and many of them would make it a point to come to see us as soon as they arrived on the grounds, just to see our beautiful girls. l found one good source for girls and that was on the trap line. The operator of the shoot also hired local girls to keep score. As I went down the line shooting, if I saw a particularly beautiful girl with a good personality, I'd offer her job for the following season. We paid more than the gun club did so all the girls would accept. Plus they were all well aware of the attention the "Bob Allen Girls" were getting and felt flattered to be asked to join our crew.

As the size of the annual Grand American grew, the trap line spread west along the south side of the Dayton International Airport. All of a sudden our building, which had been in the center of the line, was at the east end. It then became necessary for us to build a second building. This one was 40' X 60' and much better than the original building. We were pleased to learn that having the second building did not detract from sales in the old building and more than doubled our sales at that event.

A Big Turning Point

A big turning point in my business occurred in 1955 when I met and married Ruth Rhoads, a United Airlines Stewardess. At that time our little factory was always scratching for work to keep it busy. During her flying days she had noted how travelers were always looking for gifts to carry home to their children. From this she dreamed up the idea of making a miniature, zipper top, flight bag that would be marketed filled with candy. We brainstormed the idea and thought that if the little bags could be miniatures of the large airline bags, with their official logo and identifiable colors, they would sell like mad. Realizing that we had to have the airlines' permission to use their logos, we decided to first contact the airlines serving Des Moines—United, Ozark, and Braniff—for their authorization.

My first call was to Ozark at their headquarters in St. Louis. Here again my Irish luck came into play. The first airline executive I contacted, Paul Rodgers, V. P. of Sales and Promotion, was enthusiastic about the idea and gave me the names of the people I should contact at United and Braniff. His help was largely responsible for the establishment of the new bag division of my company, which we named "Airline Textile Mfg. Co." or Air-Tex for short. My attorney, David Belin, drew up a license agreement for the airlines to sign.

Bob Allen girls in front of one of our two stores at the Grand American. My daughter Abby is fifth from Left, Matt's wife Becky is seventh, Sharon Ellis, our Sales manager is tenth, and Bob & Matt Allen, 1980.

This instrument not only gave us the license to use the airline name and logo but gave it to us on an exclusive basis so no other manufacturer could copy our bags. It was so well written that it stood up against several legal actions in later years. Legal departments of airlines accepted our agreement exactly as it was written—something almost unheard of in the business world. (Paul and I became good friends and remained in contact with each other until 1999, when he passed away.)

Armed with these three exclusive agreements, I proceeded to have 48 dozen bags made up divided equally for the three airlines. The little bags were 7 1/2" long by 4" high, had zipper openings, and handles—an exact replica of the large bags most airlines were using for sales promotion. To make them more exciting for kids, we filled them with salt-water taffy and attached a little tag that was a replica of the baggage tags used by the airlines. I contacted the managers of the airport gift shops at Midway airport in Chicago, Des Moines, and Omaha and made arrangements to send them test orders on a guaranteed sale basis. We shipped twenty-four dozen assorted to Chicago and six-dozen each to Omaha and Des Moines. We anxiously waited until we were sure the bags had been received and then phoned to see how they had sold. Chicago had sold out in *one* day, Omaha had sold out in *two* days, and Des Moines was just about sold out in *four* days. We knew we had a winner. We also knew that if we didn't tie up all of the airlines, some manufacturer would copy our bags using other airline names and dilute our market. So, armed with samples I headed out to call on all the other airlines and set them under agreement. Boy, was I pumped up!

I had just bought an airplane and learned how to fly. I began on a whirlwind trip that took me to the headquarters of

Ruthie Allen with her creation the Junior Airline Flight Bag, 1956.

Ruthie Allen as a United Airlines' stewardess. A publicity picture made for "Ground Hog Day."

all the existing airlines. The first trip was about three weeks and I hit Pittsburgh, Boston, Washington National, New York City, Atlanta, and Miami. I was successful in locking up all of the airlines with the exception of American and Air France. Both of these gave me authorization to use their name and logo but not on the exclusive basis I needed. This was later to cause us some problems but was the best we could do under the circumstances. We then published a catalog sheet and commenced our sales program.

Here again luck played an important hand in our success. As I made sales calls on retailers, I would always inquire if they knew of a good sales representative that I could hire to sell our bags. The same name kept coming up—Martin Berman! I contacted him and then flew to New York for a meeting that resulted in Marty becoming our National Sales Representative. Berman's other lines and his expertise was in the candy field. At his recommendation we purchased a booth in the national candy convention in New York. Ruth and I both worked in the booth with Marty and his attractive wife Anita. The little bags were an instant hit and we wrote orders for most of the major department stores for our little "Jr. Flight Bags" to be sold in their candy departments. Woolworth's also placed a sizable order. And, of course, selling them to airport gift shops was like any of the clichés you can think of—*taking candy from a baby, shooting fish in a barrel,* etc. By the year's end we had sold over a million of the little junior bags and had really attracted the airlines' attention. A million of anything is a lot! Marty and I became life-long friends. He was a gentleman and the most honest person I had ever met.

Financing this rapid growth became my next major problem. When I approached Jim Brown (loan officer) of the Iowa Des Moines National Bank, despite our success he turned me down! His comment was that we shouldn't bank on the longevity of a novelty item, "It will come and go like the Davey Crockett Cap and the Hula Hoop," both items which had boomed in sales the year before and then had died. Nothing I could say would influence him to help us. It was the typical story with most banks; they were happy to loan you money if you had money. It pleased me greatly that in a few years he was to eat his words.

Just a few nights later, I ran into a friend, Jack Bryant, manager of the Des Moines office for Morris Plan Loan Co. After hearing my story Jack said that although his company specialized in small personal loans, he'd be happy to work with us on a simple assignment of invoices. He would advance us 80% of the value of our invoices. We had more than 30% profit in the bags so this program would allow us unlimited growth. Each day we would take a stack of invoice copies up to Jack's office and he'd issue a check for 80% of the value. With his great help we were able to sell just over a million of the little bags that first year—with profits that really launched Air-Tex! The only hitch in working with Morris Plan was that we quickly borrowed up to their maximum loan limit of five hundred thousand dollars. It was apparent we had to have another source for money! I went back to Iowa Des Moines bank and with our success story this time was able to convince them to give us a similar arrangement but with a two million dollar loan ceiling and this enabled us to continue growing.

In the meantime, we had grown from a half dozen sewing machines to over sixty operators and had added full-size flight bags to our line. Airport gift shops had become our best customers and we had furnished special metal, revolving, floor racks for the display and sale of our bags. Business was booming and airlines were buying their sales promotion bags from us. United Airlines became our biggest customer and I worked so closely with them that I was at their EXO headquarters in Chicago several times a month. Once again I was lucky and found a life-long friend in Bill O'Donnell, United's Director of Promotions. Between us we developed some ideas that enabled our business to grow further.

R.O.N. Kits

The first one was the result of a gag joke I played on O'Donnell. His office was in Chicago's downtown loop known for its great food. After work we had dinner together and somehow Bill missed the last train for home. I had a twin bed-room at the Palmer House so suggested he spend the night with me. We bought him a toothbrush, toothpaste, and a razor and this scenario stimulated an idea for a gag gift for Bill.

When I got to my factory I had my people make up a lit-tle toilet kit that was just one of our Jr. Flight bags with the handles removed and the zipper placed on one edge rather than in the middle. We silk-screened it with a design that read, "Special R. O. N. Kit for Bill O'Donnell of United Airlines" and made it up in United's logo and colors. The letters R. O. N. are often used in military and airline jargon to stand for "Remain Over Night." I filled the bag with toilet articles plus a few gag items and sent it special delivery to Bill. The next day he phoned me and was absolutely ecstatic about the kit and said he had an exceptional idea for me. He went on to explain that on the occasions when United misplaced someone's baggage and that person needed toilet articles to get through the night, United's policy was to have the customer purchase what they needed from a drug store or gift shop and United would foot the bill! United had just done a survey and learned that the average cost per customer was about $40.00 and most people would buy jumbo sizes of the most expensive shampoo, after-shave, etc. Bill had me quote a price for the same kit I fur-nished him but with only the toilet articles needed. I quoted on a "His" and a "Hers" and the price to United was about $4.00 per kit. Bill's idea was for these kits to be kept in the baggage claim area at each airport and be presented to cus-tomers instead of giving them carte blanche to buy their own articles.

We estimated that our little kit would save United about a half million dollars a year. Bill presented the idea and it was accepted enthusiastically. This would mean about $50,000.00 a year in sales of RON Kits to just United. To sweeten up the situation even more, Bill advised me that in three weeks he was going to a conference of baggage service executives from all airlines being held in San Francisco. At Bill's suggestion, we made up His and Her RON Kits for each of the airlines in their colors and logos and had them sent to Bill at his hotel in San Francisco. He had the sets hand-delivered to his counter-

part in each of the other airlines. Within two weeks of the con-
ference, we had over 30 airlines adopt the RON Kits. The kits
resulted in over one million dollars a year in sales for us. This
continued for many years until the airline industry hit on hard
times and stopped giving the kits away. However, while it
lasted, it was a great little side business. Sometimes a simple
idea can have big results if properly followed through. Moral
of this story is that you never know when a good-natured gag
may turn into millions of dollars of sales.

First Seat Pocket Catalogue

Bill and I concocted another idea a few years later that
resulted in a tremendous sales increase for Air-Tex. Seat
pocket mail order programs didn't exist then. The closest
thing to it was a one-page order envelope that TWA put in
their seat pockets and which featured their flight bags. In
talking about a similar program for United, Bill said we should
feature all our different model United bags—flight bags, golf
bag covers, garment valets, ski covers, and even the RON kits.
He then carried it a bit further to include travel posters, model
airplanes, beach towels, and other travel related items.

We ended up with a small twenty-four page catalog that
became the first complete in-flight, seat pocket, mail order
program; an industry "first." We printed the catalogs at our
cost, United placed them in the seat pockets, and the orders
came to us in Des Moines. We processed and shipped the
orders and paid United a percentage royalty at the end of each
month. We formed a separate division to handle this end of our
business and named it Travel House Inc. Within a couple of
years we had eleven different airlines for which we administrated these programs. The airlines included: Continental,
Western, PSA, Pacific, Aloha, Hawaiian, just to name a few.
The programs were profitable at the beginning however, each
time we re-negotiated our agreement the airlines wanted a
bigger percentage of the gross. Competitors who were jealous
of our business were bombarding the airlines with proposi-
tions offering bigger percentages. For this reason we had
become disenchanted with the programs and were pleased to

have a company named K Promotions approach us to buy our Travel House Division.

Their president Bob Hersch and I had many meetings and finally agreed upon a price, which was contingent on the airlines approving the sale. Fortunately, I was able to sell each of the airlines on the idea and we consummated the sale. This freed up operating capital so that Air-Tex could grow in some new directions. We got out at just the right time because these programs have since fizzled out. Irish luck wins again!

By the time my son Matt graduated from college and joined the business, Air-Tex's market had changed drastically. The airlines had fallen on hard times and were not using bags very much. Airport gift shops had become greedy and were importing cheap bags without airline logos on which they could make more profit. Travel agents and the big travel tour operators had been big business for us but they too were now going direct to the Orient to buy their bags.

Matt did a study and recommended a drastic change in our method of distribution. Instead of selling direct, he suggested that we sell our bags exclusively through the advertising specialty industry. The local advertising specialty jobber would sell our bags to his customers, we'd make them to his specifications, and ship directly to his customer using his labels—the customer would not know who made the bags. This was a radical departure from our present way of doing business and I was scared to death to make the change. I suggested to Matt that we do a test by assigning the eastern half of the United States to the ad specialty industry and see how it worked.

It only took a few months to convince me that this was the way to go and we finally changed all our direct customers over to buying from ad specialty jobbers. We lost a few customers because the jobber had to add his profit to the bags and that made him non-competitive with other manufacturers who would sell direct. New sales more than made up for what we lost and within a year we were 100% ad specialty.

Our sales promotion was simplified because now we had only one big convention to attend. Matt would hold sales meetings with jobber-salesmen to convince them to sell bags instead of other advertising trinkets such as ballpoint pens, jewelry, or calendars, and of course to see to it that they featured our bags instead of some made by a competitor. And, thanks to my son Matt, we soon became the leading bag maker for the industry.

Once our company had hit its stride, we were constantly approached by investors who wanted to buy us out. My stock answer was that we were not for sale and that the family would continue the business after I was gone. Then, almost jokingly I would hasten to add that I was willing to listen to any proposition as everything has its price. Norwood Promotional Products Company of San Antonio and Austin, Texas was the most persistent and approached us several times.

In 1994, there was a little down turn in the economy and this, coupled with some bad loans they had made, caused our bank, Banker's Trust (in rust we trust) to tighten up on their credit lines. They were going through such a rough time that they mowed through several officers to the point where we never knew who was "on first" so every time we needed to talk to someone in the bank our contact person had changed. Several companies they had been loaning money to, they cut off and one of them went bankrupt. Our capital requirements had grown tremendously with the growth of our business and we needed a bank we could depend on. It was time to move on and about this time NPPI was making a strong bid to buy our business.

Our sales were up and I always believed that you sell when you are at the top. Matt and I talked it over and mutually decided that now was the time to listen. Negotiations with NPPI were turned over to my attorney David Belin who was a specialist in sales and mergers.

There were many meetings and much discussion. We received several offers that I thought were acceptable but David had better ideas. Through his efforts we ended up getting almost three times as much for the company as I had expected so it didn't take long to make the decision to sell out in 1995. Belin had done one hell of a good job.

My son Matt ended up with a three-year contract to continue running the company. When this ended in 1998 he left the company to pursue other interests. I'm often asked if I have any regrets about selling. Sure, it was tough to turn loose something it had taken me fifty years to build. I'd have liked nothing better than to be able to retire with Matt running the company until his children might continue the tradition. However, considering everything, we did the right thing by selling when we did.

Chapter 10

Tournament Circuit

Skeet Shooting After the War

In 1946, fresh out of the Air Corps, I started attending shooting tournaments. Because I had shot so much skeet in the Service I naturally gravitated to skeet tournaments where I felt I had the greatest proficiency. It didn't take me long to find out that there was no prize money to be made in skeet. Most skeet shooters shot for trophies and prizes and rarely for cash. Also, from a business standpoint they had much smaller attendance than trap shoots and thus a smaller market for me. Despite the top skill level I had achieved in skeet, from all the shooting on Guam, I didn't exactly sweep the first skeet tournament as I had expected. Even though the first competition was the Skeet Nationals held that year in Las Vegas, Nevada, it didn't worry me. A special skeet range had been built for the event on the ranch of western movie star Hoot Gibson. At that time the hotel "strip" didn't exist and we all stayed in the one big hotel, the "Town and Country." The attendance was only about 200 shooters.

I shot in a fun, five-man, squad that included movie star Andy Devine, Ernie Simmons Sr. and Jr. and myself. Shooting with Andy was like a circus—everything he said came out funny because of his gravel voice. Ernie Simmons was well known among all shotgun shooters as the maker of ventilated ribs, which he had patented, and which could be installed on guns with plain barrels. The installation of one of his ribs converted an ordinary shotgun to a more valuable and more suitable shotgun for shooting skeet or trap and at a much-reduced price. Of course, the purpose of a ventilated rib was to dissipate heat waves from the barrel. Such heat waves distort targets over barrels without these ribs. Because of his business he was well known to sportsmen throughout the country. Ernie and his son were also great fun and good shooters.

I had fully expected to go to the Skeet Nationals, break all of the targets and win all of the Championships. It didn't work out that way because, although I shot decent scores in all the events but the 410 shotgun, I'd break 99 out of 100 but it would take 100 straight to win most events. In the big primary event, the 12 gauge, All-Bore event of 250 targets, I broke 247 but the winner, also an Air Corps veteran broke 248 to win. The first 125 bird portion of the 250 birds was an event called "The Eastern Open Championship" and the second portion was called the "Western Open Championship." I had broken my first 125 targets straight so I found myself in a tie with an ex-Navy shooter, Ben Diorio. We had to shootoff for the trophy and I made a judgment call that cost me the Championship.

I was the leadoff man in the shoot-off (that means I would shoot first at each station). Knowing that there is a lot of psychology in shoot-offs and that sometimes you can win by playing on your opponent's weaknesses, I chose to try to "rush" Ben a little. Ben had struck me as being a slower, more methodical shooter who went through a little preparedness routine before each station. On the contrary I was a "looser" more relaxed shooter who just walked up to the station and yelled "pull!" I thought that by pushing Ben a little I might disturb his concentration enough so that he would miss; it never occurred to me that I might miss! After each shot, I'd quickly move to the next station and stand there staring at Ben while he went through his methodical routine. My plan didn't work! Ben did his own thing and I missed one target probably because I was concentrating more on rushing him than on my own shooting. I ended up as runner-up in the event and thus did not get my name in the record book.

Iowa State Skeet Championships

The first Iowa State Skeet Championship shoot I attended after the war was a different story. The shoot was held at the old Pioneer Gun Club, a two-field layout, located just north of Des Moines, Iowa. There were probably only a hundred registered skeet shooters in the whole state of Iowa and there were only about forty of them who attended the shoot—only forty to beat! At that time, Iowa's top skeet shooter was Dudley Decker, a sporting goods dealer from Mason City, Iowa. Dud had swept most of the pre-war championships in all four of the skeet events; the 410 gauge, 28 gauge, 20 gauge, and the 12 gauge All-Bore. It was no surprise to me to break the 100 targets straight in the 12 gauge event because I had fully expected to do so. It also came as no surprise to me when Dud also broke the hundred. Rather than hang around the gun club all day waiting for the shoot-off that would be held at the end of the day, I went home and mowed my lawn. About four in the afternoon I returned to the gun club and brought a full case of 500 shells fully expecting a long shoot-off with Dud. A big crowd was awaiting the shoot-off and most of them expected Dud to mop up on this "kid" from the Air Corps.

I was the leadoff shooter and we proceeded around the field "straight" (without a miss) until we came to station seven, which is considered to be about the easiest station on the field. I had learned in the Army not to take any station for granted and to always concentrate. Therefore, breaking all four targets from station seven (a single from each house plus a pair of doubles) was easy for me. I fully expected Dud to step up and easily polish off his four targets as well. To my astonishment, he missed the easiest shot on the field—the low house straightaway target! Dud let out an audible "oh shit" as he knew it was almost over and it was, because I went on to break all the rest of the targets for a 25 straight. At this turn of events the crowd went wild! Everyone, including me, had been expecting a long shoot-off of 100 or more targets. Thus, I won my *first* Iowa State Skeet Shooting Championship.

Because there were no other top skeet shooters in Iowa, it was easy for me to win. Although I never considered myself any good with the little 410 shotgun, I won State Championships with poor scores such as 42 out of 50 and 44 out of 50; I wasn't too proud of those scores. One year I won all four Championships and, during the trophy presentation, I got the distinct feeling that I had suddenly become unpopular with the other shooters. I can understand their feeling that, because of my extensive Air Corps practice at the taxpayer's expense, I had an unfair advantage over them. Civilians had difficulty in getting shotgun shells during the war so most shooters had not had much practice. Being afraid that my unpopularity might affect my business, I decided to ease off on skeet and concentrate on trapshooting where prize money made it a much more important sport to me.

One of my shooting records, of which I am very proud, is the fact that I'm the only Iowa shooter who has ever won *State Championships in both Skeet and Trap in the same year, and this record still stands!* That year I shot in the state shoots of Illinois, Missouri, Iowa and Kansas and wound up the trap-shooting season at the Grand American (The National Championship) Shoot in Vandalia, Ohio. I found out very quickly that trapshooting required more intense concentration than skeet shooting. My first good win was the 16-yard Singles Championship at the Iowa State Shoot and the Sports Afield, Ex-Serviceman's Trophy.

Pigeon Shoots

In the fall the live pigeon shoots began. One of the big ones was held at the Elliott Shooting Park in Kansas City and this was to be my initiation into live bird shooting—a totally different ball game, as I quickly learned. The entry fees were expensive, plus you had to pay for each bird. Most pigeon "races" as they are called, were twenty-five birds. And, entry monies were pooled with the club taking a percentage for holding the shoot. In a typical race there would be an entry fee for the total 25-birds, which was divided 50%, 30%, and 20% between the top scoring shooters. As an example, if I were the only one to kill 25-birds, I'd receive 50% of the prize money. When there was more than one shooter with a score of 25, the prize would be split equally, the shooters killing 24 would split 30%, and the shooters killing 23 would split the remaining 20%. If there were no 25s (as the scores are referred to) then the next highest score would split the top 50%. Most pigeon shoots were for money, not trophies. If however, there was a trophy or a championship involved, then those shooters who tied for the top score would divide the money, followed by a sudden-death (*miss and you're out*) shoot-off to decide the champion.

To make it more interesting, in addition to the main entry fee they also had "options" which you could play. As an example most shoots would have options on each of the 5-bird—5s that made up the 25-bird-match, on the first-10, the last-15, and sometimes for the longest run without a miss. To win money on a *5* it generally was necessary to kill *5-straight* and all of the shooters killing *that 5* would divide the prize money that had been paid into *that 5-option*. Of course, these options were expensive to enter and by the time you played all the options it might shape up like this:

Entry fee for 25-bird race	$50.00
Option on 5s—5 X $5.00 per option	25.00
Option on first-l0 @ $5.00	5.00
Option on last-l5 @ $5.00	5.00
Option on long run @ $10.00	10.00
Cost of birds—25 @ $5.00 per bird	125.00
TOTAL	$220.00

As you can see, it becomes pretty expensive to enter and if you weren't winning something back, you better have a good checking account. With inflation you can imagine what these fees would amount to today. There is no other sport that has such a complicated prize system but this system is common at pigeon shoots and has been going on for years. You may be surprised to know that the options gave you an opportunity to win money without winning the shoot. As an example, if the *option* was for the first-10-birds, and you were the only shooter to kill the first-10, you'd receive all the money that had been paid into that option by all the entries. This could be more than the winner of the entire shoot would receive because he might be splitting monies on the various options. You could shoot a lousy total score in the *25* but end up making more money on the options.

In American live pigeon arenas the design is similar to the European rings in shape and size, however the traps are different. In our country we use various types of traps while in Europe the traps are standardized as controlled by the FITASC (Federation Internationale de Tir Aux Armes Sportives de Chasse). In modern shoots the trap to be released is selected electronically, but back in my day, the puller rolled a dice to determine which of the five traps he would open. Pulling on a rope or chain sprang the trap. To illustrate how rudimentary things were then, there was a "flush" rope tied to a stake directly behind the trap box. If the bird failed to fly the puller could jerk on the rope to *flush* the bird out so it would fly. Modern American traps now have compressed air jets and electric stimulation to prompt the bird to fly. Our clubs today have as many as ten traps instead of the five that prevail in Europe.

Toughest Shooting Sport

What makes pigeon shooting the toughest shooting sport in the world is the variation in birds. The birds used in America are pigeons that have been trapped in barns or stockyards. As a consequence they come in all sizes and colors. Drawing a dark bird against a dark background is a serious handicap. By the same token drawing a big, white, slow flying bird is a good break. The age of the birds is a factor also; a younger bird will fly much faster. As I mentioned earlier, the European birds are specifically bred for color and size for the pigeon shooting sport. No such selection of birds occurs at American Gun Clubs. Pigeon handlers take the birds as they come out of the crate. Usually the weak and slower birds are easier to catch in the crate. As a consequence when the handlers get down to the last few birds they are usually much faster and a bad break for the shooter who draws them. You have no idea where the bird is going or what it will do. There are some "soft" shots but generally when the trap opens, the bird boils out twisting and turning as it speeds for the fence. Some fly low, some tower high, and once in a while the bird comes right at you posing a harder shot each second because your shotgun's pattern is getting smaller all the time. These are called "in-comers" and I missed one in Kansas City that took me out of the first place division and made everyone else very happy. When the trap opened, I mistakenly thought the bird was flying away and threw in my first shot, which missed. By the time I realized the bird was coming towards me, it was only a few yards away and flying only a foot off the ground. I fired my second shot just as the bird twisted so I just blew a big hole in the ground. The crowd roared but it wasn't funny to me, as I needed to win—I just couldn't afford to lose, my eating depended on it. Because of things like this, pigeon shooting is a better spectator sport than regular trap or skeet shooting.

Everyone shoots a 12 gauge shotgun, with over-and-under, double barrels being the most popular. Seldom is an automatic or pump gun used because in pigeon shoots they have what is called a "no-balk" rule! That means that if you have a gun malfunction or shell failure, it is your tough luck and you lose the pigeon. Therefore, a shooter would not trust anything except a more dependable double barrel gun.

PETA

It is difficult to defend live pigeon shooting! Such shooting is banned in many states and recently was banned in Italy. The PETA and others have picketed shoots and in many instances the shooters have received bad press. In defense of the sport, many feel that the shoots render a service in helping to get rid of a bird that carries disease and defaces buildings and statues. Even the Pope backed us up. During the Championship Of The World in Rome a few of us were given an audience with the Pope. When he was told what we were doing in Rome he asked if we couldn't come and clean out the pigeons in the Vatican. Anybody who has ever been to the Vatican will instantly remember the thousands of pigeons that live there and menace everybody and every building with their droppings.

Shooting Circuit Wolves

After Kansas City there was a string of shoots to attend before the end of the year. Reno and Las Vegas held big shoots that generally were sponsored by gambling casinos. We also shot in Kentucky, Wisconsin, Illinois, and Pennsylvania. The average shoot had about a hundred entries. Of this hundred there were about a dozen of us who followed the shoots to make a living, a large percentage were shooters who just "hoped" they'd make money, and a smaller but very important percentage were those who could easily afford the sport and came just for the fun of shooting. This latter group was very important because they usually played all the money, didn't shoot too well, and provided more money in the pot for us "wolves!"

Several of us traveled together to save expenses. It was also common for good shooters to provide each other insurance against losing money. One does this by guaranteeing your partners' entry fees or agreeing upon a split of winnings. My friends Homer Clark, Earl Roth, Joe Heistand and I many times traveled together and pooled expenses. The funny part about all this was although we were friends and cooperated with each other, we also were deadly competitors.

Back in the early fifties the four of us had been shooting in Kansas City and decided to pool expenses and winnings at a shoot in Harrisburg, Pennsylvania. It was my turn to drive one night; Homer was sitting in the front seat while Joe Heistand and Earl Roth were asleep in the back seat. Joe hadn't been shooting too well so, in jest, Homer and I were discussing the possibility of excluding him from our money split. Joe was far from asleep and the next thing we knew he had stuck his head over the seat between us and in no uncertain terms, shouted, "I wouldn't split with you two guys if you were the last shooters in the world, and there isn't going to be any-thing for you two to split, because I'm going to win it all!" He had taken us seriously and was really mad. When we got to the shoot he wouldn't split and true to his word, he shot like a-house-a-fire and won all the top spots so there wasn't too much left for the rest of us to split. However, we remained friends and to this day Joe just loves to tell this story.

At Harrisburg we obtained a suite of rooms and stayed together. Homer was a superior bridge and gin rummy player and used these games to expand his income. He often sat in on the big poker games at the gun club as he waited for his turn to shoot. Like most poker players he usually had a pretty good size wad-of-bills in his pocket. This set up a trick we played on him that night in the hotel. He was in the shower and left his money on the dresser. We counted it out and then took $300.00 out of the wad and hid it under a mattress. After Homer came out of the shower we were sitting around talking and one of us asked Homer how he was doing in the big poker game. He counted out his wad of bills and then said, "I think I'm about $200.00 ahead!" The $300.00 we took out wasn't missed and back in those days it was worth about a thousand. Homer had-n't been paying too much attention to his winnings and was pleasantly astonished when we pulled the $300.00 out from under the mattress. As you can see, as we say in Iowa, "we were living pretty high on the hog!" We stayed in good hotels, enjoyed fine food, and had a lot of fun. It was great as long as we were shooting well but believe me, there were plenty of "skinny" times when either our shooting ability was off or the pigeons conspired against us. The splitting was good insur-ance against a "slump" and saved us on many occasions.

Hot Shots

The shoots in Pennsylvania were really competitive and the local shooters who resented us *hot shots* would resort to skullduggery to beat us. As an example, Homer had his shoot-ing jacket draped over a chair as he played poker. Someone took a couple of shotgun shells out of his pocket, substituted small gravel for the lead shot and then replaced the shells in his pocket. Fortunately, Homer detected a slight rattle as he started to load his gun and was able to discard those shells. Another famous trick was for them to put your safety on so that when you went out to shoot the gun wouldn't fire. With the no-balk rules you would lose that bird. For that reason I had the safety on all my pigeon guns removed completely.

Havana, Cuba

After New Year's there was a chain of trap shoots in Florida, which filled up the month of January. Then in February we traveled to Cuba to shoot trap and pigeons. This was before Castro, and live pigeon shooting was a popular sport among the affluent Cubans. Different countries would enter teams so it was known for the national team events as well as individual competitions.

Homer Clark was the top live bird shooter in the world—won the Championship of the World in 1949 and 1951. He and I became very close friends. I considered Homer my mentor. He was shooting perfection, with the fastest reflexes and the most acute vision of any human being and up to his passing at age 78, Homer never wore glasses. He and his wife Mary invited Ruthie and me to fly down to the pigeon shooting competition in Havana aboard his private plane. He had just started flying a new a Beechcraft Bonanza and had 100 hours under his belt. I had complete faith in his ability to fly safely, despite his lack of experience, because everything Homer did, he did well!

We flew from Alton Illinois to Miami but we could not be cleared to fly on to Cuba until we met the requirements for individual life vests. So, we went to the fixed base operator and rented life vests. We flew out of Miami and headed for the beautiful country of Cuba and the magnificent lights and times of Havana. Our flight was pleasantly uneventful. Little did we know that Homer's ability as a pilot was later to be tested.

The shooting competition at the old Cazaderos del Cerro Gun Club in Havana was a combination of clay target trap-shooting and live pigeons. We stayed at the opulent Hotel

Nacional, spent our days at the shoot, and every night experienced Havana's outstanding nightlife. The Tropicana nightclub had a dinner show that was absolutely fantastic.

I drew first blood in the shoot by winning the International Clay Target Championship. And receiving my first really big silver trophy. Homer and I each won enough prize money in the live bird events to pay for the trip. We shot for two weeks in Havana and then decided to vacation for one week on an island about 100 miles from Cuba, the Veradero Beach Resort.

We took off from Havana, but because of construction, several runways were closed. On the only runway open the crosswinds were blowing at 20 knots. Homer, confidently opened the throttle hoping for a lull in the crosswind. A sudden gust of wind caused the plane to leap into the air only after a few feet of runway. As the gust subsided the airplane, which had not reached flying airspeed, dropped down to the runway and commenced to drift sideways. We ran a few more feet and once again we leaped into the air. The air was so turbulent that the stall warning horn kept going off and we were everything but upside down. Our wives, in the back were alternating between praying and screaming. After four or five of these sideways leaps we attained flying speed and began climbing, retracted the landing gear and were finally airborne.

God, I thought, if we have to land in Veradero with cross winds, we are dead! The silence in the Beechcraft was ominous. Homer, however, shrugged it off as being routine. Anyone who has flown for any length of time is bound to have a few exciting adventures.

Verodero is one the world's most beautiful beaches and we had a delightful week there in a fine hotel. The food and the banana daiquiris were outstanding. One day on the beach we decided to test our rented life vests. Tossing them into the water, we watched them fill up and sink like rocks! No other life vests were available so, for the return trip we bought four sets of plastic water wings from the hotel gift shop. It's a lucky thing we didn't have to use them!

Coming back into Miami, Homer scared the girls once again. We arrived over the Miami airport too high. In order to lose altitude quickly, Homer chopped off all the power, which caused the stall horns to blare again. We landed without any problems however, Ruthie had enough and refused to fly any further with Homer. We continued home to Des Moines, Iowa by commercial carrier.

For many years the Casa del Cerro was the gun club in Havana—a picturesque club with a fine restaurant, lounge and spectator facilities. Their pigeon ring was similar to ours but there were no traps visible. When you stood on the walk to shoot, you faced a semi-circle mound or berm of dirt about two feet high. There was a deep pit behind the mound and the traps were rudimentary catapults consisting of a wicker basket on the end of a buggy spring. A pigeon handler stood behind each basket, the bird was placed in it, the spring pulled down and latched, and when the shooter called *Pull* the latch on one of the baskets was released from behind the firing line by a person called a "puller." He would roll a dice to select which of the baskets was to be released. The basket had an open top so the pigeon handler would have to hold his hand loosely over the basket until it was released. This way of releasing the birds made for a totally different type of shooting! You always had a shoot-able bird because the spring threw the bird six feet into the air, even if it didn't open its wings. Some birds were flipped up in the air and were easy to shoot but others would go with the spring and come screaming out of the pit twisting and turning so they were extremely difficult to kill inside the boundary fence. This resulted in the luck-of-the-draw or in our case bird. It also made it possible for some cheating to occur. There were many times when it seemed that only Americans were drawing tough birds while the Cubans drew birds that literally looked like they were standing still in mid air over the mound. This became obvious particularly when there was a shoot-off to decide a tie between an American and a Cuban. One theory we had was that when the pigeon handlers in the pit heard a Cuban voice call "trapper ready" they would either squeeze the bird or damage it in some other way so it wouldn't fly very fast and thereby would be easy to kill. When the puller threw his dice and selected the lever he would pull, it made a click sound down in the pit so the pigeon handler behind that basket was alerted that his basket was about to be pulled. If it was an American voice calling, we theorized that they had time to put in one of the fastest, youngest, birds. However, we were accustomed to shooting fierce birds in the U. S. and so we still beat the Cubans most of the time.

The Cuban shoots were colorful and fun! We stayed in the beautiful Nacional Hotel or the Seville Biltmore. The food and the nightlife in Havana were superb. The Floridita Nite Club had dinner shows that would rival the best Las Vegas extravaganza. In my opinion, Havana was then one of the most exciting cities in the world. There was no middle class in Cuba, only the affluent and the poor. Despite this the people seemed very happy and were always smiling and laughing. I loved to go there until Castro's revolution ended our trips and I was sadly disappointed.

Batista

While in Havana we were constantly hearing about Castro and his revolutionaries holding out in the Camaguey Mountains. Batista was a tough dictator, however most of our Cuban shooting companions were Batista backers. I guess, in those days, you were either a Batista backer or ended up on the dreaded Island Of Pines—a political prison. Batista loved to watch the pigeon shoots and would often come out to the club. He had helped the club to build a beautiful new facility in Havana. The new club had a larger clubhouse, a fancier restaurant and bar, plus three pigeon rings. They also had six combination skeet and trap fields so they could accommodate any kind of a competition. I remember vividly that the new club was beautifully landscaped and had marble sidewalks.

Batista's arrival at the club each day was an event to behold! For several minutes before he pulled up at the club you could hear dozens of police motorcycle sirens. They rode in front and in back of Batista's big, black, armored limousine. Police at the gun club would shoo everyone away from the entrance so that Batista could make his grand entrance. His motorcycle escorts would jump off their cycles and surround the entrance with submachine guns in their hands. Once in the club he fraternized with everyone but you could always feel the presence of his bodyguards. Because I was a winner, Batista actually sought me out as well as other leading shooters like Homer Clark to sit at his table. When he found out that Homer owned the Alcan Co. (an ammunition manufacturer) he approached him regarding the possibility of locating an ammunition plant in Cuba. Homer had many meetings with Batista but the Castro revolution occurred before they could put together any kind of a deal. Actually the dictator was a pretty nice guy to meet socially but like all dictators, you better be in his good graces or his secret police would pick you up in the middle of the night for a trip to his Isle of Pines. We only got to shoot at that new club a couple of years before Castro took over and that was the end of pigeon shooting on the beautiful island of Cuba.

Over a period of years in attending shoots in Cuba I had made many friends. Most of them were Batista sympathizers and when Castro took over, they, like Batista, fled to places like Spain, Portugal and Puerto Rico. One of my friends, Julio Cadenas, was a wealthy sugar producer in the Camaguey Mountains with a large home and a fancy yacht in Havana. He loaded up his family and all the possessions he could on his yacht, and fled to the United States. Julio later was one of the leaders in the Bay of Pigs invasion disaster, and one of the few who didn't get captured. He ended up working as an International Sales Manager for Remington Arms Company.

Another close friend was Jose Artecona who managed an automobile storage ramp in downtown Havana. Unlike most of the Cuban shooters, Jose like myself was trying to make a living from shooting. He was the only Castro sympathizer I knew in the shooting game and I was constantly warning him to keep his political opinions to himself for fear of being arrested. When Batista was overthrown Jose suddenly discovered that Castro was not the "Robin Hood" that many people thought he was originally. Because now there was no pigeon shooting in Cuba, Jose wanted to travel to Mexico and other places to attend shoots. The Castro government would allow him to go but his wife and children had to remain in Havana like hostages. I shot with Jose in Mexico City the year after Castro took over and he was really disillusioned. Ultimately he and his family hid out in one of the Embassies until they could be smuggled out of Cuba. He now resides in Puerto Rico, has become one of the world's greatest shots, and I see him whenever I go to the Championship of the World event.

Ernest Hemingway is remembered as an avid hunter. What few people know is that he was an excellent pigeon shooter as well and had used his winnings from pigeon shoots in Paris to support himself in his early days of writing. Ernest came to the old Casa del Cerro gun club almost every day and we all got to know him quite well. As has been related in some of his books, we all hung out at Sloppy Joe's bar, which was the most popular bar in Havana for the affluent. He became a good mail order customer for my sportswear company and would often call me from his home in Ketchum if he needed something. He was a rugged individualist and a likeable person. When his cancer took over he, characteristically, used one of his favorite shotguns to end his life.

While in Cuba I made a 16 MM movie of the events, which I used to promote my shooting clothing business by loaning it to gun clubs all over the U. S. I now have it on videotape and running it really brings back some great memories.

Jenkins Brothers

In March of each year we generally were back in the U. S. attending shoots. One of my favorite pigeon shoots was held at the Jenkins Brothers Gun Club in Orleans, Indiana. They originated an event called The World's All-Around Shooting Championship. The event consisted of trapshooting events at 16 yards, handicap events at 20 and 26 yards, some trap doubles, and the final event was 25 live pigeons. I considered this event as being one of the most prestigious in the shooting world and am very proud that I won it twice—in 1957 and 1958.

The Jenkins brothers Ralph and Rock were very unusual characters and their gun club reflected their personalities.

Considered very wealthy, neither of the brothers worked after the age of thirty and spent all their time traveling to trap-shoots and running their gun club which held two big tournaments a year. In their youth they had been in the chicken business. They gathered large quantities of chickens, which they shipped to the big cities like Chicago and Detroit. At that time, chickens were put in crates that were loaded into boxcars for transport; however their profits were marginal since half of the chickens would arrive dead. Ralph and Rock then designed a special car with compartments for the chickens that had watering devices and controlled ventilation. The story I heard was that they sold the patent to Pullman Standard (maker of boxcars) for a substantial amount and also collected royalties for many years. Both served as President of the Amateur Trapshooting Association and, at one time, both had the honor of having shot more registered clay targets than any other shooter.

Going to southern Indiana you immediately become aware of the characteristic dialect spoken by these hill country "Hoosiers." Both Ralph and Rock Jenkins spoke in this pleasant dialect and I loved to hear some of their down home expressions; expressions I've never heard anywhere else. Rock, telling me a story one day, described a tall skinny feller with a narrow, skinny face, by saying, ". . . you know, one of them fellers with a face that can drink out of buggy track." Boy, if that doesn't conjure up in my mind a picture of John Carradine in a hurry, I don't know what else could!

At their gun club, Rock ran the shell house where shooters picked up their ammunition. At this point in his life Rock had just about quit shooting but got a big kick out of holding-forth in the shell house where he could visit with all his old friends. He had turned the shell house into a free bar as he always kept several fifths of Early Times or Old Forester under the counter—strictly for medicinal purposes of course! Rock had become an alcoholic, and I think anyone would become one if they drank a fifth of Early Times everyday. The booze loosened his tongue and he sat around telling fabulous stories in that delightful Hoosier dialect. I loved to listen to him and we became good friends.

Ralph was the more serious brother and I think the better shot. I looked the two of them up in the 1961 average book and Ralph had a 94% average but Rock wasn't listed—possibly didn't shoot any that year. The average book listed Rock as having shot 214,000 registered 16-yard targets, while Ralph shot 186,000—a lot of targets for those days.

As I said earlier their gun club was very unusual. Most clubs are built on level ground with a background that is treeless and minus other obstructions. Theirs was built on rolling ground in a forested area that made for a very difficult background for shooting. They had two pigeon rings, one sloped upwards and the other sloped downwards, again adding to the shooting difficulty. On the far side of the pigeon ring was a twenty by twenty foot shed about ten feet tall. The front of the shed and the door facing the shooter were plated with steel so they could not be penetrated by birdshot from the shotguns. The pigeons were stored there and when it came time to reload the traps, the door would open and five pigeon boys would dash out the door, reload the traps with fresh birds, and pick up the dead birds. Because of this shed they had to make a special ground rule to cover the situation when a bird lit on the roof. In most clubs there is a standard rule that if a pigeon lands on the fence it is immediately called a *LOST* bird. The Jenkins club stretched this rule to include the roof of the shed. In one shoot the shed cost me a lot of money! On a dark and gloomy day in March with snow on the ground I drew a little black pigeon that was difficult to see against the black, steel side of the shed. My first barrel hit the bird so hard it rolled on the ground. The bird started to fly again so I poured in my second barrel, which rolled it once more. Then, to my consternation, the bird fluttered up to the top of the shed, landed, and rolled over dead. I couldn't understand how the bird had survived such a beating so during a lull in the shooting I had one of the pigeon boys retrieve the bird and bring it to me. Homer Clark and I picked the bird and found that it had been hit by eighteen pieces of shot, one of which had raked the top of its skull. How that bird survived that long I'll never know but it must have hated me pretty badly to cause me to lose so much prize money!

Side Bets

At pigeon shoots, there was always loads of time sitting around waiting for your turn to shoot. Many stories were told and many bets made. One day my friends, Joe Hiestand and Phil Miller (two of the toughest shots in the country) got into an argument over which of their guns shot the hardest. Phil was shooting a L.C. Smith Crown Grade, side-by-side, 12 gauge shotgun and made the claim that it was the *hardest* shooting gun on the grounds. Joe immediately challenged his claim and said that his Remington, Model 32, over-and-under shot just as hard and added that, as a matter of fact, there was no difference between guns. He stated that the only factor that controlled how hard a gun shot was in the kind of shell used, powder load, etc. By this time a crowd had gathered around them and Phil bet Joe a $100.00 that his Smith shot the hardest. Joe immediately took him up on the bet thinking that this bet was a mortal cinch to win. To prove his point, Phil took a wood shell box and leaned it up against the fence on the far side of the pigeon ring. They both had agreed to shoot the same brand of shell and shot size so that all things would be equal. Phil then fired one shot from his L.C. Smith. The box was brought in and the spots where his shot had hit were circled. (Most of his shot was embedded in the wood.) The box was then placed back against the fence and Joe fired one shot from his Remington Model 32. When the box was brought in again, we gathered around and were all amazed that Joe's shot had just bounced off the wood and none were embedded like Phil's. Joe immediately claimed that it must have been a bad shell and demanded another test. The same test was run three times and in all three instances Phil's gun had penetrated the deepest. Joe sheepishly surrendered his $100.00.

Top Shotgun Ballistician

Homer Clark, who I consider was the world's top shotgun ballistician, had been watching this bet with great interest. He and I huddled afterwards and discussed how it could be possible that one gun shot harder than another. Homer said that he was going to run some tests back at his ammunition factory where he had chronographs and other testing devices. A few days later he phoned me to make me aware that there was definitely a difference in guns and it had to do with the size of the forcing cone. The forcing cone is a six or eight inch area just in front of the shell chamber and it's purpose had originally been designed to prevent the hot gases of the gun powder from getting around the old fashioned wads used in all shells. The theory was that if the forcing cone were too loose, hot gases would blow around the wad and melt some of the shot together. I know this was a fact because in the past I had noticed gobs of shot melted together on the ground in front of the traps at several gun clubs. Of course, the size of the forcing cone also affected the breech pressure, which had some bearing on the velocity of the shot coming out the end of the barrel. To make a long story short, Homer had discovered that you could improve a shotgun's velocity by loosening up the forcing cone. This made the gun shoot harder and a side benefit was some reduction in the recoil (kick) of the gun. We immediately had our guns worked on and it wasn't long before gunsmiths all over the country were doing forcing cone work. The gun companies soon followed by changing their forcing cone specifications on the new guns they were manufacturing.

Most Difficult Sport

The spring shoot in Kansas City was a combination trap and pigeon shoot. One day during the shoot H. R. Peterson of Dillon, Montana and Art Stifal of Casey, Illinois got into an argument with Peterson saying to Stifal "Hell, you couldn't break fifty straight with a hammer." This culminated in Stifal betting Peterson that he could break 50 straight targets with a hammer. A crowd gathered and 50 clay targets were lined up side by side on top of a waist-high stonewall outside the gun club. Stifal began walking along the wall methodically breaking the targets with the hammer, getting cockier and faster all the time until finally, to everyone's amusement, he somehow missed the 49th target and lost the bet. Everyone had a great laugh but it was a good example of how important concentration is in doing something repetitive, especially shooting. If your mind wanders even for an instant, you've lost the bird or pigeon! This points up another reason why the shooting sports are more difficult to win than any other sport. Even in the most important golf tournaments it is feasible that a golfer could make a bad shot but by brilliant after-play get back in the game and win the tournament. Not so in trap, skeet, or pigeon shooting tournaments! You make one mistake and you are dead. If it is a 100-bird race, it takes 100 straight to win; even then you probably end up in a tie and have to shoot off with several others. Absolute perfection is required; there is no room for mistakes. The pressure is horrendous the further you go without a miss. Many shooters can break the first seventy-five straight but go to pieces in the last twenty-five because of the pressure. A psychiatrist once told me that, in times of pressure, your brain plays tricks on you by feeding you excuses to miss in order to take the pressure off the mind. I learned early to concentrate on only the next bird and try to think of nothing else.

Another factor that makes shooting tough is the number of contestants you have to beat. A good example would be at the Grand American, you have to beat approximately 5000 shooters to win; there is no other sport that comes anywhere near this kind of entry numbers or competition.

Another interesting example of how pressure affects different people was my friend Paul Derringer, the famous Cincinnati Reds pitcher. Paul pitched a couple of winning World's Series games so evidently he could sustain that kind of pressure. However, when he took up live pigeon shooting he was famous for being able to score the first twenty kills and then blowing two or three out of the last five. The difference? In baseball he had eight other guys backing him up while in shooting there was nobody to help him.

By May of each year the State Championship Trap Shoots began. I'd start out shooting in Texas, work my way up through Oklahoma into Kansas, and then it was Nebraska, Montana, and Wyoming, Minnesota, Illinois, Iowa, Indiana and Ohio, with a few other major tournaments thrown in. The climax of the trapshooting tournament season is always the Grand American National Championship shoot held in Vandalia, Ohio.

I have some vivid and nostalgic memories of following the State Shoot Tournament Circuit. One summer I had a young student from Iowa working for me. We had just set up my tent store at the Wichita Falls, Texas gun club and because we had chairs and shade, two of my shooting friends, Mercer Tennille, one of our greatest doubles shooters, and Bart Geiger, a top shooter from Florida, were in the habit of hanging around our tent when they weren't shooting. My clerk was very young and as we were to find out, very gullible. Picking up on his fear of sleeping in the tent at night, Mercer and Bart went to work on the kid. When they knew he was listening they'd start to ply him with stories. One morning Mercer said to Bart, "Did you see that big rattler down by the gate this morning?" To which Bart replied, "Yeah, he was a monster but I wonder where his family is—they always travel in families. This place must be running over with rattlers and big ones!" Mercer continued by saying, "We've all got to watch every second for scorpions too. This valley has the biggest, meanest, and most deadly scorpions in Texas and they usually come out at night." Sure enough, a little later the kid approached me about the possibility of sleeping in a hotel in town, but I had to refuse him because we had no way to lock up our tent and someone had to guard it. That night after dinner I went to a movie with Mercer and Bart. While we were in the movie a tremendous Texas thunderstorm struck, complete with high winds, sheets of rain, and thunderous lightning. After the movie a group of us were sitting around in the hotel lobby talking when all of a sudden the swinging doors opened and here came what looked like a wild man but turned out to be my young helper. His clothes were soaked, his shoes covered with mud, and his hair disheveled. Soon as he saw me he blurted out, "I'm gonna go home!" He had his two suitcases in his hands and was really ready to split. I sat him down, had Mercer and Bart explain to him how they had purposely set him up, and got him to get up enough courage so that I could drive him back to my tent store and leave him there. He really was terrified and I was afraid

I'd lose him sooner or later, so after we set up for the Kansas State Shoot in Wichita the following week, I put him on a bus for home. I really didn't chastise him too much because I knew from my own experience how lonesome and frightening it could be way out in the country in a strange place and with nobody to talk to, with the coyotes howling, snakes crawling, the wind and the thunderstorms. I can appreciate how frightened he had become.

Shooting in Pain

During the Texas State Shoot I had developed a boil in my right armpit. By the time we had the tent store set up at Wichita, Kansas it was killing me, so I finally found a doctor to treat me. His method of treating the boil was to surgically "*cooorrrre*" it out, thereby removing the whole boil. This left a hole under my arm 3/8ths of an inch in diameter with a depth of about a half-inch. Into this hole he stuffed a gauze dressing soaked in iodine and taped over it. This little carving in my armpit was performed without any anesthesia and was about as painful as anything I've ever experienced. The whole shoulder and arm were stiff and sore but I had already paid my entry fee for the shoot, so when my squad came up, I grabbed my model 12 Winchester and took off for the trap line. It hurt like fury to mount the gun and the kick felt like I was being stabbed. Despite this I really "smoked" the first 25, then the second 25, and continued on to break the 100 straight. l took a nap after lunch and when it was time to shoot the second hundred, I was feeling more soreness than I had in the morning. I started out the same way—smoking the first 25 and then going on to break the second 100 which gave me the *first* 200 straight score I had ever broken—winning the Kansas State 16 Yard Trophy. I tell you this story because within a few months I came to the realization that I had shot some of my best scores on occasions when I was in pain or sick. Let me share a few examples with you. Later that summer I mashed my trigger finger and two other fingers on the same hand in a car door. This was at the Illinois State Shoot, which was held at Stifal's Gun Club in Casey, Illinois. I was hurting so bad that

I could barely think straight but I had come to shoot (nothing ventured—nothing gained, as my dad always said). Margaret Flewelling, wife of Winchester Pro, Don Flewelling, felt sorry for me and found a small bucket that she filled with ice and water. She had me carry the bucket down the line in order to soak my right hand between shots. This wonderful woman kept the bucket full of fresh ice throughout the shoot. Well, the same thing that happened in Kansas happened here! I was hurting so badly that my concentration was focused only on the targets and I amazed myself and everybody else by breaking my second 200 straight that day. Then on two other occasions I also shot tremendous scores when I was running a temperature. One was the Grand Prix de France in Paris. I had the flu with a temperature of 104 degrees, and won a shoot-off by smashing every bird. A doctor has since told me that with my elevated temperature, my blood pressure was probably up and my visual acuity was at its peak, as were my reflexes. All I know is that the birds looked like they were a slow motion movie and all I had to do was stick the gun in the middle of their backs and blow them away. My friends said they had never seen me shoot so fast. To prove this theory further, I later won a trapshoot when I was down with the flu and had another high temperature. I don't recommend hurting yourself or getting sick just to shoot well, but there is no doubt in my mind that my shooting improved in these situations.

Following the trapshooting tournament circuit with my tent store was exactly like being in a circus. When the shoot was over on Sunday afternoon we'd start to tear down. By Monday noon we'd be packed and ready to start driving to the next shoot. There was generally at least a day of driving so it would be Wednesday by the time we reached our destination. Then it was a full day and evening to get the tent pitched and displays up so that we'd be ready for business on Thursday morning. I must have had tremendous energy back in those days because in addition to all the tent store work, I'd shoot the entire program, which usually entailed shooting about 800 to 1000 targets. It wasn't too bad a way to make a living! I'd sell a thousand dollars or more of merchandise (which was at least half profit) and then I'd make another $300.00 shooting.

In the meantime while I was out on the road, my little store back in Des Moines was gradually growing in the mail order business.

Friends Along the Way

A lot of the same people followed the circuit but at each shoot I made many new friends. In Wichita, Kansas where their State Shoot was held, Harvey and Tiny Blair, owners of the club, became good friends. It was here in 1948 that I lost an important shoot-off to a lady shooter named Iva Pembridge, my first defeat at the hands of a woman! Another shooter J. R. Servis and his wife Nancy became good friends so I always looked forward to coming back to Wichita.

At the peak of my shooting career I'm sure I had a few fans but for the most part I received very few compliments or congratulations on my shooting. One outstanding exception was a Greek shooting friend by the name of Gus Garvis who lived in Des Moines. Gus was a typical immigrant success story. He came to America shortly after WWII barely speaking English. He worked for a while for the railroads then married and, recognizing the need for a place for the railroad workers to have lunch, he and his wife opened a small café near the tracks. It was an immediate success and soon Gus and his wife moved uptown and opened a café he named "The Dixie Barbecue." This too was a success and the rotisserie barbecue roaster Gus had invented attracted so much attention from other restaurant owners that Gus decided to manufacture and sell them to others. I'm sure you recognize the name as his Dixie Barbecues are in use throughout the country. If you see a roaster that is rotating the meat in a restaurant window, chances are it is a Dixie by Gus.

Gus loved to hunt and soon had a pair of pointers and was hunting quail regularly. Because he loved to shoot, he took up skeet shooting at the Pioneer Gun Club and with his competitive nature was soon winning skeet events in the club shoots. It was here that I first met Gus about 1950 and we immediately became friends and hunting companions.

As I traveled around the world shooting I was winning

quite a few events and sometimes there would be coverage in the Des Moines Register. If so I invariably would receive a phone call from Gus congratulating me; the only such phone calls I ever received from anyone! This naturally endeared him to me even more.

Gus had a tremendous amount of pride in everything he did including shooting. I like to tell a story about him that concerns one of our quail hunts together. The dogs hit a classic point but the covey of quail flushed before we could get into position to shoot. We watched as the large covey circled around and landed on a hillside beside a lone pine tree about a half-mile away. We knew we could get them up so we walked over to flush them again. Sure enough, the dogs hit a point right by the pine tree. This time we approached cautiously with our guns off safe and ready. The quail flushed and we each fired three shots from our Remington Model 1100, 20 gauges without drawing a feather. We were both astonished at how we could miss such an easy shot but that is part of the fascination of quail hunting. At any rate, in complete seriousness and with his embarrassment showing, Gus in his broken English said "Bob, we won't tell anyone about this will we." I felt like laughing but restrained myself because I knew Gus was dead serious and taking it badly.

Gus's wife's hobby was entering contests of various kinds. She became ultra-successful and was as close to being a professional contest winner as there is. She won a car, many vacation trips, and all kinds of merchandise. Gus had a son that he wanted to bring into the business with him but the boy was interested only in motorcycles. With the poor reputation bikers had at that time, Gus was sorely disappointed in the boy and didn't think he would amount to anything in life. The Garvis entrepreneurial genes came through though and the son opened a motorcycle shop that is now Garvis Honda and probably the biggest and most successful bike shop in Iowa. Now Gus was justifiably proud of his son.

Gus passed away a few years ago but I shall never forget the encouragement his phone calls gave me. He was a friend to remember!

A Woman, A Child, A One-Armed Man

Then it was usually the Nebraska State Shoot next at Doniphan, Nebraska—a little town halfway between Grand Island and Hastings. I had old friends here from before WWII so it was always fun to return. Here I lost a shoot-off to a one-armed shooter. Having been beaten by a 12-year-old boy a few years earlier I could now state that I had been beaten by all kinds of shooters including women, children, and a guy with one arm! One of Nebraska's top shots was Ralph Kohler of Tekamah, Nebraska. Ralph won many events in his state shoot and at the Grand American, was an All American Trapshooter and an all around great guy. He and his wife and children all shot and were an inspiration to other families. Ralph retired from tournaments and to this day operates a highly regarded duck and goose camp on the Missouri river.

A shoot I always enjoyed was the Sun Valley Open held at the famous Sun Valley Lodge in Ketchum, Idaho. Weather was always perfect and it was a thrill to shoot in that environment. From there we sometimes went on to the Montana State Shoot in Billings or Helena. Zip Eaton, one of Montana's finer shots, came from Helena and we became lifelong friends. I look back with fond memories of a Montana State Shoot where I shot in a squad with Zip, Dan Orlich, and Rudy Etchen; about as tough a bunch as you'd ever find! Another great friend from Montana was Tom Frye who was an exhibition shooter for Remington Arms Co. Tom is in the Guinness Book of Records for having shot over 100,000 wood blocks with a .22 rifle and only seven recorded misses.

Sometimes I would vary from my schedule and go to different shoots. I shot several state shoots in South Dakota, Minnesota, Wisconsin, Missouri, Illinois, Kentucky, Indiana and Ohio. The summers seemed to whiz by and then the National Championship shoot marked the end of the trapshooting season, the "Grand American" held each August in Vandalia, Ohio. As the Grand had grown, so had my business. In 1946, my tent store at the Grand was one of only two stores on the grounds; now there must be over two hundred! The other store was Lawrence Bogert's Gun Store from Sandusky, Ohio.

My tent store at the Grand American, 1947, wearing my first shooting vest design.

Growing

Earlier, I mentioned that in just a few years we had grown to the point where we constructed a 40 x 50 foot building on the firing line for a permanent display. No longer was it necessary for someone to sleep in the tent to guard it; we just locked the door and went to the hotel! As the Grand grew more trap fields were constructed to the west, so we built another larger building to accommodate shooters at that end of the line. For the Grand, we'd bring in a semi load of clothing and accessories, hire fifteen or twenty local beauties for clerks and do exciting business. Here again I generally shot the entire program of some 1200 or more targets. People used to ask me how I could concentrate on my shooting when I'd work in the stores all day long and then run out to shoot when my squad time arrived. I think it may have worked in my favor because I didn't have any time to sit around worrying or anticipating my shooting. I wouldn't even think about shooting until I went out the door to join my squad. On the other side of the coin I can remember several years where I missed the first target out or missed in the first event—pretty good proof that my concentration wasn't working yet.

Grand Prix de France

One of my biggest shooting thrills and honors came in 1950 when I competed in the Grand Prix of France held in Paris. There were about a dozen American shooters and we were all staying in the famed George IV hotel that had been made notorious during WWII because Hitler and Goering had stayed there. The weather should have been glorious—instead, it was rainy and cold. None of us had expected weather this cool, so our clothing was inappropriate. As a result, I immediately caught a bad cold. It was "April in Paris" but not the kind of weather the song indicated.

The gun club was located in a city park called the Bois du Boulogne—a park similar to Central Park in New York City and located a short taxi ride from our hotel. There were several days of preliminary events before the main Grand Prix competition. The prelim day shoots were the typical "miss-and-out" events so common in Europe. Each shooter would shoot one bird at a time and if you missed you were eliminated. It usually took from twelve to eighteen birds straight to win depending upon wind conditions. First money and the day's trophy would go to the shooter who remained after everyone else had missed. Shooters missing just before him would share a smaller percentage of the prize money. I placed well and made a little money in these prelim events but had caught cold and each day my condition worsened until the day of the big event, The Grand Prix of France. I awakened with a temperature, which gradually rose during the two days it took to finish this event.

The Grand Prix was a twelve-bird event and not miss-

and-out; you were allowed to miss two birds, which meant that you were out on the second bird. Although I was feeling lousy I managed to kill the first eight birds straight that first day. Between shots I would lie down in the back seat of Jack Holliday's rental car until he'd call me for my next shot.

On the second day I was one of about a dozen shooters who were still straight. By now I was really sick (103 degree temp) and felt so bad I really didn't care much about anything, but somehow I was really "smoking" those birds. My friends all said they had never seen me shoot so fast or hit the birds so hard, despite the fact that I was shooting from thirty-two meters; a handicap that had me shooting further back than all the other shooters. When the event ended that afternoon there were three of us tied with scores of twelve out of twelve; Horace Tennes an American friend from Chicago, Count Chavenac from Belgium, and me!

The shoot-off to break the tie and declare the Champion was to be a "sudden death" miss-and-out. My chances didn't look too good because I was so sick plus the fact that my opponents both had shorter handicaps. Horace Tennes was a well-known skeet shooter but hadn't shot many pigeons, so he had the shortest handicap—only 26 meters. To give him an even greater advantage he was shooting a skeet gun with open chokes that meant a wide pattern, which *wouldn't* require tremendously accurate gun pointing at that distance. Chavenac was an experienced pigeon shooter who had won many European events, was the favorite of the gambling gallery, and was shooting from 29 meters. As we began, a large crowd of spectators and gamblers assembled. My friend Jack Holliday was carrying my shells and acting as my coach and doctor.

As the shoot-off proceeded I was still murdering my birds and killing them within a few feet of the traps. Horace's open choke barrels resulted in most of his birds going down with broken wings but walking around so they had to be picked up. He looked as though he would lose one at any moment. Chavenac was shooting well but drew a "screecher" of a bird on his third bird and was eliminated, which surprised me and really had the gamblers howling. It was down to Horace and me. After we had shot our 21st bird, I said to Jack Holliday, "With that skeet gun and standing so close to the traps, that guy will never miss!" Jack reassured me by telling me that he had never seen me shoot better and to hang in there because Horace's luck with those open choke barrels was getting him closer to a miss all the time.

My recollection of the shoot-off was like that of watching a movie without sound! My visual acuity and my reflexes were so fast that the traps seemed to open in slow-motion and I could clearly see the pigeon begin to open his wings and lumber out of the trap. Normally, the traps open so fast they are a blur and the pigeon is a second blur streaking for the boundary fence. On this day, all I had to do was put my shotgun's front sight in the middle of the pigeon's back and pull the trigger. Later my friends told me that I was shooting so fast that when the trap opened my first barrel would smother the bird about a foot or two out of the trap leaving a puff of feathers in the air and the second barrel would leave another puff of feathers as the bird was falling so that when I was done shooting there were two puffs of feathers floating away in the wind and the bird would be stone dead near the trap.

Horace's open choke barrels caught up with him on the 23rd bird. (I had just killed my bird and it was his turn.) He grazed the bird with both barrels, but that beautiful pigeon flew over the boundary and was lost. The crowd went crazy, particularly the Americans. Thus, I became the winner of the Grand Prix de France, and as the American Flag was raised, they played our National Anthem through the public address system. My adrenaline had stopped flowing and I felt absolutely drained, plus I always get a little emotional when our anthem is played—this time the combination of feelings was so overcoming that I fainted! I woke up as Jack and some other friends were carrying me into the back seat of his car. Just before we left the club to go back to our hotel, Jack had collected my prize money for me and brought a literal armful of French francs out to the car and ceremonially dumped them all over my body.

A doctor from the American hospital was called and examined me in the hotel. He prescribed one of the early

1936 COMTE DE TEBA
1937 DORA
1938 BARON POWIS DE TENBOSSCHE
1939 CHEVALIER DAVID DE LOSSY
1952 COMTE J. DE TUDERT
1953 R. LAURENTZ
1954 C^{TE} D'OULTREMONT
1955 C^{LE} H. DE GOUVION SAINT-CYR
1956 BOB ALLEN
1957 C^{TE} G. DE GOUVION SAINT-CYR

My daughter Kelly poses by marble plaque at gun club in Paris.

antibiotics and suggested I stay in bed for a few days. A sweet little old French maid took pity on me and brought me ice water and fruit several times a day. After seven or eight days in bed, a weak and washed-out Bob Allen left for a shoot in San Remo, Italy with the rest of the American contingents. I didn't completely recover until several months later and as a consequence didn't shoot well in Italy.

During the Grand Prix I noticed that all the previous year winners back to 1907 had their names and scores engraved on a marble plaque that is mounted on the gun club wall. When I arrived home I received a letter from the gun club asking me if I'd like to have my name in marble also. Of course, I answered *yes!* However, I was shocked to later receive a bill for $300.00 for the honor. I guess it was worth it as my name is still there and each time my children go to Paris they visit the club to take a picture with my name. One year my daughter Abby went to Paris with a student tour and told the chaperones that she wanted to go to the Bois du Boulogne to see my name. She convinced them so the whole group went to the gun club and Abby was quite proud to have them salute my name.

Monte Carlo—Courvoisier

It all happened at one of the shoots in Monte Carlo when I had the good fortune to win a trophy sponsored by the makers of Courvoisier—you guessed it—a two gallon bottle of the elixir in the same distinctive shape as their regular bottle. It was about two feet tall and weighed about 25 pounds. It was so big and heavy that I didn't think I could afford to bring it home. At that time the airlines charged about $8.00 a pound for anything over your 44-pound limit. I was watching expenses carefully so decided that rather than pay $200.00 to get the bottle home—we'd drink it up!

There were about eighteen Americans on the trip that year and we were all staying at the Hermitage Hotel around the corner from the famous Casino. Every afternoon after shooting we'd meet in the hotel lounge for cocktails and discuss the days events. We were all watching expenses so I suggested we drink up my Courvoisier and everyone agreed. However, after a few days we all tired of it and even with eighteen of us drinking from the bottle, when it was time to go home we had hardly made a dent—it was still ¾ full. By this time we were all sick of it—especially me, so to get rid of it, I made a present of it to one of my French shooting buddies. To this day I am unable to look at the distinctive shaped of a Courvoisier cognac bottle and if I get a whiff of the contents I become ill!

Saga of The Hard Rolls

Things are not always what they seem to be—especially in Europe! I learned this from a dining experience at the famous DeParis Hotel in Monte Carlo. Dinner in their formal dining room was a Class A experience. We were required to wear coats and ties while our ladies wore their most exciting duds. Tables were beautifully set with silver and crystal. The waiters were in tails and even the bus boys wore tuxedos. The evening meal was quite a production starting off with one of the waiters bringing around a silver basket of French dinner rolls which he would ceremonially place on your dish using silver tongs—it was all so elegant! The rest of the dinner was just as elegantly served.

One morning I got up early to go down to the pigeon ring and shoot a few practice birds. To save some distance, I walked down the alley behind the hotel. A small pick-up truck full of hard rolls was backed up to the kitchen door and a guy with a scoop shovel was *shoveling* the rolls out on to the kitchen floor. I was shocked to see food handled in this way and even more shocked that night when the waiter with the silver tongs went through his elegant delivery of the rolls. I related the story to all the Americans and it became a big source of amusement every night to watch the silver tong comedy routine.

The Hall of Fame

The Grand American was and is the biggest event of the year for me. From both a business and shooting standpoint, it is the big event of the year. Each year we would try some kind of a special promotion. In 1982 I was to be inducted into the Trapshooting Hall of Fame. As Grand American time approached it suddenly dawned on me that I had shot nearly 100,000 registered targets. By juggling events I arranged it so that on the same day of the induction ceremony, I would shoot my 100,000th target. I put together a squad of close friends and outfitted them all in matching blue shooting vests. With white slacks, shirts, and caps worn with the blue vests we were a handsome group. My squad-mates were four of the great shots of that era: Rudy Etchen, Dan Orlich, Vic Reinders, Bueford Bailey and myself. A photographer took a picture of me breaking the 100,000th bird and despite the growing pressure, I broke it!

All the employees of our two stores came out to congratulate our squad when we finished. They had put up big banners of congratulations in front of the two stores; it was like a big birthday party. That night at the Hall of Fame banquet, I had one of the biggest thrills of my shooting career; being inducted into the Hall of Fame. Other big thrills at the Grand American included winning the National Doubles Champion-

World Record squad scoring 995 x 1000 in 1957. L to R: Fred Waldock, Bob Allen, George Genereux, Bill Waldock, & Marvin Driver.

ship in 1957 after a shoot-off with my friend Bueford Bailey, and in that same year having the honor of shooting in a squad that set a new World's Record on 1000 targets. Members of that squad included Fred and Bill Waldock, Marvin Driver, George Genereux and myself. Our score of 995 X 1000 stood for several years before it was surpassed.

Several different years I put together squads and outfitted them in matching shooting clothing. One year we introduced a shooting version of the leisure cover-alls that were so popular during that era. Just to attract attention I made up the "Shooter-alls" for the squad from a bright turquoise fabric. The result was spectacular and we received a lot of extra publicity.

For many years my sales manager was Sharon Ellis, a really sharp lady who did a great job of shagging our sales force. The first time she came to the Grand American we decided to welcome her with a great practical joke. We roped in the grounds security people who manned the front gate. When we picked her up at the airport we were to alert the guards who would stop our car as we entered the grounds. The

My family at the 1976 Grand American. L to R: Daughters Abby, Kelly, son Matt, wife Ruthie and me.

guards were to tell her that the security people at the airport had alerted them that she might be carrying a controlled substance in her luggage. We were all hiding in the bushes near the gate so we could observe what happened. One of the officers asked her to get out of the car, told her that they had been alerted by the airport police, and asked her to open up her luggage for inspection. It was all going great until the officer said, "Have you ever been arrested before?" At that point I saw that our gag was going a little too far and she was on the verge of tears so we all jumped out of the bushes and said, "Welcome to the Grand American." She was ready to kill us and vowed she'd get even with us but she was really a good sport about it.

One year I conceived the idea of printing a "special edition" of our catalog, one that would have a "Playboy" approach. We hired models to wear our clothing along with spike heels and lots of skin exposed. The first year the catalogs were so popular we decided to put one out each year. We tried to keep them in the hands of shooters only but some found their way to people who found them to be offensive. The shooters and our male dealers were wild about them and, although we haven't printed one for fifteen years we still have people asking for that "special edition." They have become collector's items and are bringing a good price. We finally had to quit printing them because Matt and I were starting to get a lot of heat from women, including our wives, who threatened us with bodily harm.

Jack O' Lantern Lodge

The live pigeon shoots started in September and I have very fond memories of those shoots. One of them was held at a resort on a lake near Eagle River, Wisconsin, Jack O' Lantern Lodge. Walter Warren, a top Wisconsin pigeon shooter who had spent several years living in Europe and following the pigeon shoots, designed the Jack O' Lantern club to be a replica of the Monte Carlo shooting layout. The ring faced east and was on the side of a hill that gently sloped away from the shooter. As in Europe, tags were hung on hooks after each shooter's name to indicate the score, a white tag for a kill and a red tag for a loss. There was always a wind blowing across the ring and some pine trees on the right perimeter of the ring added to the difficulty of shooting.

It was at Jack O' Lantern that I missed one of the most expensive birds of my life! The 25 bird races were shot in 5s. I was twenty straight going into the last 5, most of the shooters had finished the race, and there were no twenty-five straights. If I killed the 25 I'd win the first place money all by myself— about $8,000! In 1950 that was like $25,000! All of the shooters who had killed 24 were praying for me to miss so they would be splitting the first place money. As I walked out to shoot my last five my adrenaline was really pumping. I killed the first four quickly. The fifth bird was a little, black-colored, pigeon that came out of the right hand, number five, end trap. The wind caught it and it streaked for the fence directly towards those pine trees I mentioned earlier. It was practically invisible against the pines but I snapped two shots at it hitting it but not hard enough to keep it in the ring. To the shouts of the other shooters my bird struggled over the fence and dropped dead outside—a *LOST* bird! I was really dejected—my $8,000.00 was now split with seven other shooters who had killed 24. No Irish luck this time!

Up the road from Eagle River in Land O' Lakes, Wisconsin was the King's Gateway Hotel gun club, which held two pigeon shoots a year. They had a beautiful clubhouse and two pigeon rings located at the bottom of a ski hill. These shoots were well attended because it was such a beautiful place. In the fall of the year with the trees turning it was truly spectacular. They had an eighteen-hole golf course and playing was a good relief from the pressure of the shoot. I played many times with a foursome made up with Joe Hiestand, Earl Roth, and Homer Clark. Joe and Homer were serious and good golfers while Earl and I were hackers that really slowed them down. Homer and I would team up and make bets with Joe and Earl. After golf in that invigorating fall weather, dinner in the lodge would be a great treat.

In November it was back to Jenkins Bros. club in Indiana and then to shoots in Pennsylvania in Harrisburg, Reading, Heginstown, and Chalfont. In December generally there were shoots in Reno and Las Vegas. We didn't fly on the airlines much so there was a lot of wear and tear on our cars and tires. My best shooting years were the fifties and sixties. As our business grew the necessity for me to shoot diminished and my time was occupied more and more with business details.

If this sounds like an exciting and great lifestyle, it was! The only problem was if my shooting was off, I had serious financial worries. Fortunately, I had great confidence in those days, trained rigidly, and generally collected good prize money even if I didn't win the shoot.

Chapter 11

Family

The achievement of my lifetime, of which I am most proud, is my family—my three children and eight grandchildren. My original idea in writing this autobiography was for my children to know more about their dad than I did about mine.

A Blind Date

It all began, would you believe, with a blind date, arranged by my best high school friend from Fort Dodge, Gerry Whittemore. I had been divorced from a wartime marriage for several years, was struggling to make my business grow, and constantly traveling to shooting tournaments. Getting married in 1954 was far from my mind. Gerry came down to Des Moines from Fort Dodge on business one day and we had lunch together. During lunch I casually mentioned that I was going to Chicago the next day. Gerry said that I would have to look up a good-looking friend of his who was now flying for United Air Lines. That got my attention immediately because in those days the Stewardesses, or Flight

Attendants, as they are now called, had to be very attractive with great personalities. Gerry went on to describe Ruthie Rhoads and explain that he and his wife met her while she was teaching their grade school child at Fort Dodge's Duncombe Grade School; the same school I had attended in my childhood. I listened to his sales-pitch with enthusiasm, but like everybody else, I was still leery of blind dates. I agreed to contact Ruth *only* after Gerry promised to phone her to prepare her that a Bob Allen would be calling. I was *not* going to just call her out-of-the-blue, and I still wasn't sure I wanted to go on a blind date!

I had driven to Chicago on business and while there I went to the Buell Air-Horn factory to have some specially made air horns installed on my Buick Station Wagon. Their factory was on the south side and not far from the Flamingo Apartments where *Ruthie Rhoads* lived. Figuring that having lunch would be the safest way to spend a blind date, I called her number and she agreed to have lunch with me and said that I should meet her in the lobby of the Flamingo at one thirty that same day.

Nervously, I sat in the lobby of the hotel watching every girl that stepped off the elevators. Oh No, Thank God, and a number of other expletives went through my mind as I watched the door open and close. Finally, the elevator door opened and a shapely little blue-eyed blonde tripped out. I said to myself, "That can't be her, I can't be that lucky!" I was sure that couldn't be *Ruthie Rhoads*. The same thought was going through her mind as she saw me sitting in the lobby, "That can't be Bob Allen!" We were both so pleased and relieved with each other that it got us off to a flying start. She was just as leery about blind dates as I was, I later found out. We had both protected ourselves by creating a story to allow escape in the event we didn't like each other. I fabricated a tale about having to go back to Des Moines that night for business and she fibbed that she had a working flight. At lunch we both regretted our lies but didn't have sense enough to level with each other. I was kicking myself all the way back to Des Moines because nothing would have pleased me more than staying over to have dinner with Ruthie. She confided in me later that most of her blind dates had turned out to be pot-bellied and bald.

Dating

At lunch we had made a date to get together two weeks later in Kenosha, Wisconsin where I was scheduled to attend a pigeon shoot. Our romance flourished and we got together almost every week, often double-dating with one of Ruthie's roommates who was engaged to a corporate pilot from Houston. We went to Notre Dame football games, ate out a lot, and Ruthie joined me at several shoots. By Christmas we were pretty well committed to each other so I took her to Fort Dodge to meet my parents. She immediately captivated my mother and dad.

Ruth Rhoads

Ruth was born in Sac City, Iowa, and in high school, had been an outstanding student, a cheerleader, and actively involved in the choral group. She won a scholarship to Iowa State Teacher's College in Cedar Falls. After graduating, her first teaching job was in Grinnell, Iowa. From there she came to Fort Dodge to teach at Duncombe Grade School, which I had attended. After teaching for a couple of years she felt she needed a change and answered an ad to become a United Airlines Stewardess.

Her *first* airplane ride was when United asked her to fly to Chicago for an interview. She was accepted and then was sent to their stewardess school at Cheyenne, Wyoming. On graduation, Ruth was assigned Chicago as a base—a great city to start off her new career! Commercial airliners in those days were DC-3's, which squatted on their tails, forty-passenger Convairs, and the biggie of the fleet, the four-engine DC-4, which accommodated about sixty passengers. None of them were pressurized!

In Chicago Ruthie shared an apartment with three other United stewardesses. Those four good-looking girls had a lot of fun together in the Flamingo! One story that always amused me was hearing about a pet parakeet, which belonged to one of the girls. She'd turn it loose to fly around the apartment and it was always landing on their toothbrush holder leaving droppings on their brushes. The girls had "had it" with that damn parakeet so one day when its owner was gone on a flight, the girls opened a window, and let it fly out into the twenty below zero night. When their roommate returned she offered a reward for the return of the bird or information about her poor baby. A few evenings later the conspirators were horrified when the doorman knocked on their door with the parakeet in his hand ~ it was frozen solid with its feet up in the air!

The girls never had any food in their refrigerator; however it was always full of booze. Back in those days the airlines didn't use the little miniature bottles of liquor. Instead, liquor was served in small glass cruettes. At the end of the flight, if there were any unused cruettes, the girls would wash out empty milk cartons and fill them up with liquor. So, when you opened their refrigerator you would see stacks of those little milk cartons marked scotch, bourbon, vodka, gin, etc. They also brought home milk, which would be hidden in their luggage as they got off the plane. One time Ruthie was checking in with the crew after a flight and didn't realize it but one of the milk cartons hidden in her bag had sprung a leak and she was leaving a white trail of milk. The Captain called it to her attention so she was able to take steps to keep from being caught.

We tried to get together as often as possible. Whenever she could, Ruth would trade schedules with other girls so she could work a flight to Des Moines. By the same token, whenever I could, I'd try to schedule a business trip into Chicago. Things really started to jell in January of 1955 when I exhibited my sportswear line at the National Sporting Goods Show, which was held in the old Morrison Hotel in Chicago. We had dinner every night and when the show was over I decided to stay in Chicago for a few additional days and checked in at the Flamingo so I could see more of Ruth.

The Flamingo Hotel

The Flamingo Hotel was an interesting place. It was a high-rise (about 18 floors) on the outer drive near Lake Michigan on Chicago's south side. Located directly east of Midway Airport, it was a convenient address for aircrew members. At that time, O'Hare Airport had not been built so Midway was the big airport. The Flamingo's residents were a mixture of airline personnel, FBI men (some kind of a school for them was close by), and believe it or not, the Mafia. There were always parties going on and of course the stewardesses (who always had knock-out good looks back in those days) were welcome guests. Several of the Mafia family members who lived at the Flamingo were involved in a much-publicized racket where horsemeat was mixed in with beef to make hamburger. Sort of a truce existed between the FBI and the Mafia so all could have a good time.

One afternoon during the Sporting Goods Show I ate a hamburger at lunch that evidently was bad because I immediately had an upset stomach and headache. That evening we went out to dinner with one of Ruthie's roommates and my shooting buddy Homer Clark. At dinner in a restaurant a few blocks from the Flamingo, I suddenly became violently ill. I left the group to return to my room and go to bed. Alka Seltzer and Rolaids didn't help and I started to have chills and bouts of vomiting—it was apparent that I had food poisoning! Ruthie was worried about me and left the restaurant to come and see how I was getting along. She was alarmed by my condition, brought extra blankets and a heating pad from her apartment and then called a doctor she knew who prescribed a medication, which she then picked up at a neighboring drug store.

Those Mafia characters in the hotel were great practical jokers. One of them named "Nickie" saw us going in and out of the hotel, assumed that Ruthie was "shacking up" with me and thought this was the opportunity for a good joke. Several Chicago police also hung out at the hotel and were friends of Nickie. He had two of them come up to my room and bang loudly on the door calling out, "Police, open up!" This hap-

pened at the peak of my sickness just as I was having a rough
time with chills and vomiting. When Ruthie answered the
door, the two burly policemen barged in really expecting to
find us in bed together I guess. At any rate it didn't take them
long to realize that this was no time for a joke. Ruthie had recognized them and correctly assumed why they were there. She
gave them hell and they quickly apologized and said that
Nickie had put them up to it thinking it would be funny. They
left quickly and a few days later Nickie called to apologize. So
much for cops and robbers!

On Reserve

At that time she was on a duty that the airline called
"reserve." Reserve meant that she didn't have a regular
schedule but had to keep herself available twenty-four hours a
day, on instant-notice, should United need someone to fill in
on a flight. Sometimes the girls on reserve wouldn't be called
at all but Ruthie got called out almost immediately.

Her first reserve flight was a Denver over-night turn-
around. I bought a ticket to go with her figuring that this
would be a good time to introduce her to my sister Anne and
her family who lived in Denver. Her flight out was a DC-4, all
coach, with only one stewardess for the sixty passengers. She
was worked pretty hard to take care of that many passengers
so I didn't see much of her. In Denver we stayed with my sister and had a wonderful visit. The return flight to Chicago was
a "flight-from-hell" night coach DC-4; flying through terribly
turbulent weather. In those days, they had no radar to steer
around storms, plus the planes were not pressurized, so they
blundered along through the storms at maximum altitudes of
ten or twelve thousand feet. It was a nightmare of a flight with
everyone airsick including Ruthie. She spent the entire flight
carrying burp-bags to the rest rooms. We had additional
reserve flights together to glamorous places like *Omaha,
Dayton, and Newark*. By this time, I had proposed marriage
and Ruthie was ready to quit flying. Being on reserve was the
turning point that convinced her to turn in her resignation.

We planned our wedding for May 7th, 1955. I had no money but I was young and confident.

My business wasn't making much money at that time so I was literally living on winnings from shooting; primarily from the live pigeon shoots, which had good prize money. To get enough money to get married, I scheduled myself to attend a pigeon shoot at the Elliott Gun Club in Kansas City. I had Ruthie fly out so we could drive from Kansas City down to Houston, Texas where our friends, Don and Arlene Utt were arranging a small and quiet wedding for us. Arlene had been one of Ruth's roommates at the Flamingo in Chicago and she had been dating Don Utt when I met Ruthie. We all double-dated many times and became very good friends. When we decided to get married, Don and Arlene had been married for several months and suggested we come to Houston where they would arrange everything.

So, in late April off we went to Kansas City for the four-day shoot at Elliott Shooting Park. Because I so desperately needed money, for insurance against shooting badly, I arranged to split winnings with my shooting buddy, Homer Clark. As it turned out this time, I shot like a house-a-fire, winning three of the four days, plus winning the high over-all event. Homer came down with the flu and didn't shoot as well as usual. When I collected my money—about six thousand dollars—I went to Homer to make the split. By now he and his wife Mary had become well acquainted with Ruthie and they were excited about our upcoming marriage. Homer, who was better off financially, suggested that I would need the money now that we were taking off for our wedding and that I should reimburse him just for his entry fee; about six hundred dollars, and keep the rest until I could pay him back. To top it off, he and Mary insisted that we take their brand new Cadillac convertible to Houston. They would drive my old station wagon back to their home in Alton, Illinois and I could trade cars with them on our return. Wow!

Getting Married

So in early May of 1955, Ruthie and I took off for Houston, Texas with winnings of about five thousand dollars in my pocket; the equivalent of something like fifteen thousand in today's dollars. Here we were, racing down the road in Homer's specially built, beautiful new Cadillac convertible. It was pale green with a dark green convertible top, dark green tires, a Continental tire kit on its rear and, to top it off, a set of 40 inch *Buell air-horns* mounted on the right fender. It was truly spectacular and everywhere we went it attracted jaw-dropping attention. By today's standards I guess you would almost describe it as a "pimp-mobile." For my grandchildren who may never have experienced Buells, picture a pair of chrome plated trumpets one 36" and the other 40", mounted on that beautiful Cadillac and imagine the fun we had with those horns ~ they really got attention! There was much more to the horns than the trumpets. Under the hood there was all kinds of machinery to make the horns work including an air compressor, which worked off the engine fan belt. It pumped compressed air into an air tank also under the hood. The term "blow your horn" must have started with horns of this type because the way you made them blow was to pull on a chain that released air into the horns. You could make them give a gentle hiss by barely pulling the chain or really make them blast by pulling the chain all the way. They made a loud blast similar to a train or a ship but louder. As we drove along, people would recognize the horns and signal for us to blow them by making a pulling gesture with their arms; we, of course, were always willing to oblige by giving them a blast!

Ruthie and I arrived at Don and Arlene's home, where we stayed until our wedding day. They had arranged our wedding ceremony at their Methodist Church, and because Don was in the Air Force active reserve, our reception was held at the Ellington Air Force Base Officer's Club. Don and Arlene stood up for us, many of their friends attended the reception and it was a gala affair complete with cutting the wedding cake with a sword. From there we spent two days at Houston's finest hotel at that time; and an appropriate dwelling for an

Irishman, the Shamrock. When we drove up in front of the Shamrock in that big Cadillac, we really got attention from the doormen and the bellboys. Ruthie had a pretty good head of steam on from all the champagne at the reception and everyone was getting a big kick out of watching her. As we came into the lobby I suggested she sit in chair and wait as I checked us in. She was carrying a big chunk of our wedding cake and I was afraid she'd drop it. As I was signing in, she appeared at my elbow and some rice, which had been thrown at us earlier, fell out of her hair on to the desk. The cat was certainly out of the bag that we were newly-weds! She then happily announced that we had just been married; the clerk was obviously amused. Then, as we turned to go to the elevators, the big chunk of cake got away from her and landed with a big "splat" on the beautiful lobby carpet. We beat a hasty retreat while one of the bellmen said not to worry, that they would clean it up.

Then it was on to Galveston, Texas for a honeymoon on the beach. When the weather turned cold, we returned to Houston and spent a few more days at Don and Arlene's home.

We took a leisurely trip back to Iowa with many stops along the way. Homer and Mary Clark had invited us to stay with them for a couple of days when we returned their Cadillac. Then we were off to Des Moines where I had rented an apartment at Wakonda Village near the airport. Our first home was a very small one-bedroom apartment and, because we didn't have much money for furnishings we improvised. For instance, for drapes we took some material that I made hunting coats out of and dyed it black. Then, using white silkscreen paint, we took off our shoes and made white footprints all over the fabric. The apartment had white carpet so we continued the black and white theme by painting all our furniture black. Our modern, designed drapes became a real conversation piece! It's funny how you remember these early financially rough times that were very happy times.

We were so hard up we couldn't afford to eat out much but we made friends with several couples in Wakonda Village who were in the same financial shape. Dr. Dick Gere and his wife Marge became our closest, life-long friends. Dick was interning at Mercy Hospital and they had a two-year-old baby. We often cooked on an outdoor grill and spent many happy hours together. Marge and Ruthie really hit it off and became very close friends.

Kelly—Our First Baby

Ruthie was a little bored with inactivity, so she started doing some volunteer work at Mercy Hospital. This didn't last long because to our delight we discovered she was pregnant! From then on all attention was focused on the birth of Kelly, who we decided was going to have this name whether Kelly was a boy or a girl.

In the meantime we made many trips to Fort Dodge for Ruthie to get to know my parents and to Sac City to visit her mother, friends and relatives. I was 36 years old and about to have my first baby, and my parents were really excited about becoming grandparents. During this interlude, Ruthie was going to shoots with me and the time just seemed to fly by.

Kelly Kathleen Allen was born on January 12, 1956: the most exciting day of my life! The birth of every baby is a big event but the first one is *uniquely* special. Kelly was an absolutely wonderful baby. Ruthie and I really enjoyed learning to bathe and feed our little bundle. We took turns on the night feedings and some of my fondest recollections are of giving Kelly her bottle in the quiet of the early mornings. She'd suck on the bottle for a few seconds and then would look up at me with those big eyes; we really bonded on those pre-dawn feeding sessions.

Kelly was a joy from the day she was born and through her entire life! She was a happy baby who was easy to raise. We were amazed that she started talking well at age one. Her crib was in our bedroom and I can remember vividly her waking us up early in the morning, standing up in her crib, and with a big smile saying "Hi!" When she was about a year and a half old, she became intrigued with horses and had learned to whinny. We bought her a spring-loaded rocking horse that she loved dearly. She spent so much time on this favorite toy that the poor little thing actually got blisters on her tiny, doll-like hands.

One of the high points of Kelly's life, which I remember most vividly, was at five years old, her first day at school, when my independent little girl insisted on walking to school by herself. In one blink of my eye she was riding her first live horse, becoming a cheerleader and then making the swimming team at Lincoln High School. When time came to go to college, she chose very carefully between Northwestern, Kansas, and Southern Methodist in Dallas, Texas. She chose SMU because of its journalism curriculum, pledged a sorority, and was an outstanding student. In her third year she obtained an intern job with a home furnishings trade magazine and it looked as though she was well on her way to a career in journalism, but then fate intervened. She went to Fort Worth, Texas one day and on her way back to Dallas, she drove past the American Airlines Flight Attendant School. Just on a whim, I guess, she stopped and filled out an application. They were so impressed with Kelly that they immediately tested her and hired her on the spot! I'm sure they recognized an outstanding potential flight attendant and made sure they employed her.

After graduating from SMU and flight attendant school, her first base-of-operation with American was in New York City. Kelly made many friends there and we had several opportunities to visit her in the "Big Apple." I was very proud of my bright and beautiful daughter! On several occasions, when I flew to New York on business, I took Kelly and two of her outstandingly beautiful girl friends out to dinner. It was like escorting "Charlie's Angels" ~ everywhere we went we received extraordinary attention and service. What a big kick this time was for me!

Kelly mowed through several boyfriends before she met Kevin Welsh, a bright young man moving up very rapidly in the business world; and to whom she is now married. In addition to his good looks and great personality, I think she was first attracted to Kevin because he was on *the inside track* at "Studio 54" ~ the *IN* place of big city nightclubs and discos of the 60's. They always got waved to the head of the line. This was a club with a doorman who crushed many an ego by turning people away because they were not *Hip*. I can just imagine these two kids dancing up a storm and the fun they had being the most outstanding dance couple on the floor.

After their marriage they lived in New York City and then, as Kevin moved up in the financial world, they lived in a Chicago suburb, followed by Winnetka, Illinois and then finally made a move to Pacific Palisades, California, where they now reside with their two boys; Kevin Douglas Welsh Jr., nicknamed "Chip" and George Welsh III. Kelly is still flying for American Airlines but on a limited basis. She likes the travel benefits and other fringe benefits.

With all their moving around into new homes, Kelly has become an excellent interior decorator and real estate salesperson. If she needed to change from her flying job I'm sure she could be a success in these fields as well. Every time they move, they buy an older house and Kelly completely rebuilds and decorates. As a consequence, each time they move they are able to resell their house at a profit.

If you were to ask me to describe my Kelly, I'd say that she is beautiful, intelligent, conscientious, very caring, a great wife and mother and is right from the shoulder, just like my mother was. Kelly is very direct and always calls it like it is. I think you can tell that I am very proud of her and love her very deeply.

For my 80th birthday celebration, all my children had a big party for me in California, beginning with staying at the newly refurbished Beverly Hills Hotel. The family had hired a stretch limousine that picked us up and took us everywhere. Kelly arranged a fine dinner at one of Palisades' leading French restaurants and then the limousine took us to Grauman's Theater where she hired a Marilyn Monroe lookalike to greet me and work me over. I ended up with some great photos of myself holding "Marilyn" in her famous white dress from the movie and big red lipstick kisses on my bald-head. There on Grauman's sidewalk, she crooned three little songs to me with my family cheering her on and strangers videotaping. *My Marilyn,* sang a breathy Happy Birthday to me, just like the real Marilyn Monroe sang to President John

Kelly Allen models a Junior Stewardess Cap for our catalog.

F. Kennedy. It was a tremendous surprise and what a fantastic birthday gift. Thanks kids!

Junior Flight Bag

Now, getting back to our early-married life. Our financial condition improved with the beginning of Airline Textile Mfg. Co. and with the sale of the little Jr. Airline Bags that were one of Ruthie's ideas. We now needed something larger than our one room apartment so we bought a new home that had just been built at 1509 Lewis Street. It was a beautiful house in a style that the builder called a "California Trend." It had floor to ceiling glass windows along the entire front of the house. The kitchen, dining room, and living room were literally one

Daughter Kelly's family. L to R: son Chip, husband Kevin Welsh, son George, and Kelly.

big room with a fireplace in the center. It was a very live-able house with four bedrooms and three baths. We were very happy there!

Matt—Our Second Baby

Ruthie was pregnant again and our son Matt was born at 1:14 A.M. on September 29th, 1957. I was hoping for a boy this time, so I was really delighted when Matt was born. With cigars in hand, I took the day off to go around town announcing my son's birth. Raising two kids was a little difficult but Kelly was about a year and a half old, was walking, and now easier to care for. It was a very happy time. Kelly liked to hold Matt and treated him like a doll. We took the kids with us everywhere we went. One of our favorite restaurants was called Wimpy's. We'd put Kelly in a high chair and Matt would be placed on the table in the baby carrier. People would come over to comment on our cute little baby boy.

This was the peak of my shooting career and I was still operating a tent store at the big money tournaments. I was gone a good deal of the time so the job of day-to-day raising of our children was completely in Ruth's hands. Coming home was a joyous occasion for me and we always did family things together. My best friend, Gordon Cobbs, recommended us for membership at the Wakonda Country Club, which was located just a few blocks from our home. Their swimming pool was a wonderful place for Ruthie and the kids to spend their time when I was away. The Saturday night parties became a big part of our social life and Wakonda is where we made many wonderful friends.

When Matt was about three years old I started taking him flying. I had a cushion about six inches thick that I'd put under him on the right seat and then fasten his seat belt. Now he could just about see over the dash. He really liked flying but wasn't much of a co-pilot nor companion as he would fall asleep about five minutes after we took off; the sound of the engine lulled him to sleep. At a real early age he showed an aptitude for flying and even if he couldn't reach the rudder pedals he learned to hold altitude and heading. As an adult, I'm proud to say, Matt has become a really fine pilot with an instrument rating.

My boy showed great signs of intelligence at an early age. As an example, at about age seven, I assigned him the chore of mowing the lawn. Before mowing, I instructed him to go around the yard and pick up all the loose papers, as I had always done. A few minutes later I looked out the window and was a little angry to see Matt driving the mower around in big circles all over the yard. When I went out to reprimand him for what I thought was playing I learned that he was using the rider mower to pick up papers; a much faster and more efficient method than the walk and stoop system I had always used.

Like me, Matt showed a great interest in the out-of-doors. He was involved in Boy Scouts so I bought him the usual Scouting equipment including a camping hand axe. This turned out to be a colossal mistake as he developed a propensity to chop things down starting with some of my splendid trees including a valuable and rare Kentucky Coffee Bean tree. He also had an interest in matches and fire; enough so

Me with son Matt at age three, note BB gun.

that I was afraid he might cause a serious tragedy. To counter-
act these tendencies we started a Saturday routine of going
out in the woods west of Des Moines, where I would have him
chop up firewood, start a fire, and then cook hot dogs and
hamburgers. We'd then go to the Pioneer Gun Club to shoot a
few rounds of skeet. Through this routine I was able to divert
his interest in chopping and fires into a good channel and the
problem corrected itself.

Matt had been taking junior golf lessons at Wakonda and
had developed into a nifty little golfer. He won a Wakonda
Junior Tournament and the Wakonda golf pro, Bill Rose, recommended that we enter him in the State Pee Wee Golf
Tournament at Grinnell, Iowa. Matt began practicing and was
really excited. I'll never forget the cute outfit he wore at
Grinnell, complete with a little straw hat! He looked like a
miniature golf pro. Parents were not allowed to accompany
their children around the course. They played in a foursome

Matt Allen models Junior Airline Captain cap for our catalog.

with a referee accompanying them. From the clubhouse verandah we watched Matt tee off and were shocked to see him top
the ball so that it only rolled down the fairway about one hundred feet and ended up on the edge of a little pond. Matt's body
language told me that he was very angry with himself, so I
called out to him to hang in there and that he could make it
up. He disappeared from our view on the course and we sat on
pins and needles until he came into view again as he
approached the ninth tee. He was the first to tee off for that
ninth hole so we knew he had won at least the last hole. The
ninth was a nine iron shot over a little pond and up to a green
that was about fifty feet higher than the tee. The green was

directly in front of the verandah where we sat sweating him out. Matt stepped up to the ball, made his shot, and we watched the ball sail up into the air toward the green, where we were beside ourselves, as it rolled up and stopped about four feet from the hole. He looked like a real pro as he confidently strolled up and put it in for a "two." It was only then that we found out that his score was way ahead of the field. We anxiously waited out a few other foursomes until finally all the scores were in and Matt had won the Iowa State Pee Wee Golf Tournament. What a thrill! We were tremendously proud of him and probably more excited than he was.

The next winter Matt went skiing at a place called Ted's Ski Hill north of Des Moines. It turned out that the ski slope would have been better with ice skates than skis as thaw and freeze cycles had turned the hill into ice. The operators should have closed it down but they didn't do so until Matt had taken a bad fall resulting in a compound fracture of his right leg. There were no 911 emergency services in those days and no one had sense enough to call an ambulance. Instead, they called Ruthie at home and she went speeding out there; a trip that probably took thirty-five minutes. When she got to Matt he was in shock. Somehow she got him into the back seat of her convertible coupe and took off for Iowa Methodist Hospital. It was a very bad break and caused a lot of pain for some time after being cast. When they took the cast off, we were distraught to hear that his leg was one and one half inches shorter than the left. He was between eleven and twelve years old and growing like a weed. During the time in the cast, his left leg had continued to grow but the cast had retarded the right leg's growth. It was suggested that we take him to Iowa University Hospital to see a specialist. They did some computations and recommended that his left leg be pinned at the knee to slow down its growth until the two legs grew to be equal. We agonized over the decision. The operation and recovery time was again very painful and Matt was laid up for months. Several years later the two legs almost matched but the right was slightly and permanently shorter. This took Matt out of any additional golf tournaments for about two years.

His next adventure was in Junior League Football and once again he played very well. Against my better judgment, he went out for football in his freshman year at Lincoln High School. Here an unexpected attack of migraine headaches ended his football career. He had an opportunity to play well in a couple of games but after every game and every tough practice scrimmage he'd come home with a blinding migraine headache. Our hearts really went out to him as he would literally crawl upstairs to his bedroom where he would pull all the drapes and suffer for hours. Usually the episode would end up with us taking him to the doctor for a shot. I told him that life was too short to put up with this kind of debilitating pain and that football was not all that important. Finally he was convinced and gave up the game.

Every summer our children would spend a week at Bortell's Ranch; a summer camp with emphasis on horseback riding and training. On the last Saturday of camp they had a horse show and all the parents would attend. The Bortel's were aware of my shooting and, because rifle shooting was part of their camp activities, they asked if I'd come down and perform a shooting demonstration. I accepted but told them I needed Matt to assist me. In the few weeks before the show, I had Matt practicing in the backyard shooting a BB gun at tin cans that he would toss up in the air. In a very short time he got really good so when we put on our show at camp, he was the crowd's delight.

I hadn't done any of my trick shooting since coming out of the Air Corps. The popularity of the shooting act with Matt and me together gave me the idea that we might elaborate on it and do some father and son shooting shows as publicity for Bob Allen Sportswear. The first big show we did was at the Nebraska One Box Pheasant Hunt in Broken Bow, Nebraska. They printed posters with pictures of us and had them in store windows all over Broken Bow. Matt did a great job and the crowd loved him. This was the beginning of many such shows that we did all over the country. Over a period of time Matt became the finest aerial shot I have ever seen. With a .22 semi-automatic rifle, he would toss one and a half inch wood blocks in the air and hit them several times, bouncing the blocks around. We also shot washers, fruits, vegetables, and if it was not too windy, we would shoot aspirin tablets. In my lifetime, I have seen most of the great trick shots but Matt was better than any of them when it came to shooting small objects in the air. You can tell I am very proud of my boy!

We continued putting on these shooting shows for many years.' Our act was filmed by the Sports Afield Television show and narrated by Grits Gresham. This film is being re-run to this day and has given us tremendous publicity. Because we were shooting rifles, including the high-power variety, location was a continual limitation; we needed wide open spaces! It was necessary for us to take out liability insurance for the act and it became very expensive. Therefore, about 1992 we decided to hang it up and turned down any new requests to perform.

When Matt was thirteen an event transpired which had a great impact on both our lives. I decided to take Matt on an African Safari with a sportsmen's group known as the African First Shotters. As we made our plans he became more excited every day. First thing I had to do was get him excused from junior high school. At first they were not going to allow it but when I explained what an educational trip it was going to be they finally agreed to excuse him for the four weeks we would be gone.

The group included about sixty people, mostly couples. My friend Dick Griffith, who had founded the African First Shotters and was its president, had invited two astronauts and their sons to accompany us. Deke Slayton, who headed up the astronaut program, brought his son John and Jim Lovell brought his son Jay. Dick Griffith was very wise to invite these astronauts because everywhere we went, we were greeted like celebrities and all kinds of receptions and special events were planned for us. The two astronaut's boys were about the same age as Matt so they soon became friends. John King, the billionaire entrepreneur from Denver, brought his whole family including a daughter about Matt's age.

The group gathered in New York City. One of our members, Fritz Kielman, was the North American manager for KLM airlines and had made special arrangements for us on a KLM flight to Amsterdam, Holland where we spent two days

Trick shooting exhibition by my son Matt and me.

Trick shooting show at Flint Oak ranch in Kansas. This unusual photo caught both objects exploding simultaneously.

sight seeing. Matt and I, along with Jim Lovell and his son, took a canal barge tour and saw the home of Anne Frank and other points of interest. Then we all boarded a KLM DC8 for the long trip to South Africa. We stopped for fuel at Kinshasa in Zaire, formerly the Belgian Congo. As we let down for landing, we picked up the foul smell of the city twenty miles out— it was enough to gag a maggot! Once we landed, we all got off to stretch our legs and were astounded to have to walk between a double line of soldiers with sub-machine guns standing shoulder to shoulder all the way into the terminal. Matt was terrified and I didn't feel too comfortable about it either. I don't know what they thought a planeload of tourists might do in the middle of the night but their show of strength seemed ridiculous. Inside the terminal everyone was hostile so we were happy to re-board for the flight on to Johannesburg, South Africa.

When we landed in Johannesburg, the word was out that we had astronauts in our group so there was a mob waiting to greet us at the airport. The Chamber of Commerce had arranged a special reception for us at the airport complete with cocktails and fancy hors d'oeuvres. We were all tired and wanted to get to our hotel but it was so hospitable of them, we spent an hour at the reception.

Two days of touring Johannesburg followed and then we boarded a South African Airways flight to Beira in neighboring Mozambique. We didn't realize it at the time but there was a full-scale revolution going on in Mozambique between the Portuguese and several guerilla revolutionary factions. Beira was an armed city with Portuguese troops carrying out warlike preparations including the building of sand-bag gun emplacements. Fortunately we did not get caught in any of the conflict. From Beira we took special buses to the Gorongosa Game Preserve about two hours from Beira. They had fine accommodations for us there and the food was excellent. Our folks were divided into two groups; one group was to stay in the game preserve lodge for camera safaris and the other was flown into the interior in small twin-engine airplanes. While we were all together in the lodge, we had one day of special "games" which included archery, water boiling contests, hatchet and boomerang throwing. Prizes were awarded to the winners of these events that evening at dinner. One day Matt and I put on our trick shooting demonstration and it was a big hit.

Just before we were to leave the lodge for our hunting safari, Dick Griffith asked me if I would mind if Henk Guitjens and his wife, who headed up the travel agency that had made all our arrangements, would accompany us. They would not be hunting but wished to come along to take pictures. As it turned out they were a delightful couple and their presence added to the pleasure of the safari.

A twin engine Piper Apache picked us up at the lodge airstrip and flew us an hour and a half back into the interior where we landed on an unmarked grass strip. Just after take-off, the British pilot of the plane asked us if we'd like to fly low enough to see game enroute. We were glad that he did because at any given moment you could look out of the airplane in any direction and see over a thousand animals; everything from elephants to wildebeest, crocodiles and buffalo. It was a real thrill! The only down side was that Matt got a little airsick from the rough ride at that low altitude. As we approached to land I noticed that the runway was full of animals including a herd of wart hogs. The pilot, who had landed there regularly, assured us that they would get out of our way and he was right.

Our Portuguese white hunter met the flight and his blacks loaded our gear into a Land Rover for an hour-long drive to his camp. The camp consisted of several tents pitched on ground that had been swept clean. The forty or more blacks that were to be our trackers and skinners had a special camp close by for their families. Our sleeping quarters were in a nylon tent with a nylon floor and zipper opening. We were glad that it was both snake and insect proof. During several nights we kept hearing a coughing sound that we finally identified as coming from a leopard. For a shower, the blacks heated water over an open fire and put it in a tank that was mounted on posts so it was about seven feet in the air. A pull chain dumped the warm water out of a straight pipe. After a refreshing shower we dressed for dinner. By this time it was dark and getting very cold. They had a small gasoline generator that provided power for one light bulb in our tent and one in the dining tent.

They had built a roaring fire just outside the dining tent and it sure felt good after the sun had gone down. Mozambique is on the other side of the equator and it was their fall season. We had a warming drink and then went into the dining tent where we were astonished to see a table beautifully set with white cloth, candelabra, fine china and silverware. The waiters wore white coats but didn't wear any trousers and were barefoot. The food had been cooked over an open fire and amazingly was absolutely delicious. The evening meal always started out with a fine soup and then a meat course, which we usually didn't recognize because it was wild game. They had freshly baked bread and unbelievable desserts. It was really a shock to find such great food in this camp out in the wilderness.

We visited with our white hunter or, I should say, tried to visit with him, because he spoke very little English. We retired early and just a few minutes after we entered our tent, we heard the gasoline motor that powered the electric generator stop and our one light bulb gradually dimmed out. It seemed like just a few minutes later, but it was actually early in the morning when we heard the generator start up and our light bulb gradually lit up again. About the same time, we heard the zipper on the tent opening and one of the blacks in a white coat came into the tent, squatted between our beds, and offered us hot tea. The tea really hit the spot as the temperature was down around forty degrees. We hadn't been warned about the weather so we didn't have the right kind of clothes. We ended up putting on just about everything we had in order to keep warm. Once again they had a big roaring fire outside the dining tent so we gathered there with our hot tea awaiting breakfast. We were pleasantly surprised once again at the quality of the breakfast which included great toast made from their home baked bread, ham which I'm sure came from a wart hog, and a surprising selection of fruit.

After breakfast the white hunter had us practice shooting the rifles we were going to use on the hunt; we had not brought any of our own guns as we had been advised that they had a fine selection at our camp. I think the white hunter really wanted to find out if we knew what we were doing. At any rate he had us fire a German-made .458-caliber buffalo gun that had a cartridge almost as big as a 50-caliber machine gun. I shot it first and felt like the kick tore my shoulder off. I didn't say anything to Matt and when he fired it the first time, it moved him back about a foot and his face turned white. I know it hurt him but he fired it two more times and hit the target the white hunter had set up.

We then loaded into the Land Rover and took off for our first day of hunting. Even though we were all bundled up we still almost froze to death sitting out in the open in the early morning air. The Land Rover had seats up on top where Matt and I sat with the white hunter. He carried a long stick like a pointer and would use it to direct the driver by tapping on the windshield; to go right, tapping on the right side, left on left side, and holding it still meant to stop. If the driver didn't respond to suit him, he'd reach down inside the vehicle and whack the driver on the side of the head. We later found out that our white hunter had a serious case of stomach ulcers and was in pain all the time. After our safari he retired and went back to Portugal. He was crabby most of the time and Matt and I were shocked at how badly he constantly treated the blacks. After driving for about an hour, we ran across a small herd of hartebeest. Needing camp meat, he indicated that we should shoot one. Once we had shot the animal the skinners descended upon it with knives and machetes, dressing it out in just a few seconds. We then learned that vultures were attracted by gunfire and soon there were a hundred or more of them roosting in the trees around us waiting for us to finish dressing out the kill. The instant the blacks walked away from the carcass, they descended upon it—a shocking and revolting sight! In Africa you get the idea very soon that, as a human, you are just part of the food chain. If you were to become sick or injured and were by yourself, you'd become food for the vultures and hyenas, same as any other animal.

As the sun came up we warmed up swiftly. At this time of the year in Mozambique there isn't a cloud in the sky and the sun really beats down. By noon we were down to our shirts and still too warm. Around noon each day we would stop for a lunch and a siesta. The blacks would put a twenty five-foot-square tarp on the ground and then unload food chests and set up for an outstanding picnic lunch even including wine if you wanted it. After eating, everyone would take about an hour siesta before starting the afternoon hunt.

Although Matt and I each had a license that would entitle us to eighteen different animals, we had decided that we would each like to get a good trophy cape buffalo. As it turned out, we passed up many good trophies in other species not wanting to scare away buffalo with our gunfire. We passed up many shots at non-trophy class buffalo and ended up by not shooting a buffalo. When we came upon the first set of buffalo tracks it was Matt's turn to shoot. We got down off the Land Rover and I was going to accompany Matt but the white hunter indicated that he wanted only "one gun" to be on the stalk. Being the type that always obediently obeys authority, I didn't argue with him when he insisted that I remain with the Land Rover and one of the blacks. I watched Matt, the white hunter, and about six of the trackers and skinners walk off and disappear. The silence was deafening as I waited sitting on the ground with my back against a tree. About two hours later I am really starting to worry and I hear a shot that sounds a long ways off, followed by a second and a third shot a few seconds later; then the deafening silence again. All of a sudden it hit me that I must be some kind of a fool to turn a thirteen-year-old kid loose in Africa with a white hunter who doesn't speak English, to hunt (as we were to learn later) the most dangerous big game animal in the world. I was almost in a panic as I waited for their return. I didn't dare start out to try to find them, as I would most certainly have become lost. Finally, after what seemed an eternity, much to my relief they came walking back. I was never in my life so happy to see my son! They had tracked the small herd of buffalo until they were in gunshot range. Matt fired and they thought he had hit the animal so the white hunter had him take two more shots at it as the herd turned and ran. They couldn't find any blood so had to assume he missed. Had the white hunter been sure that Matt had wounded the animal, he would have been obliged to track it down and finish it off; a procedure which is very dangerous!

I then learned something disturbing from Matt. Normally one of the black gun bearers carried the rifle until you neared the game. He would then hand the gun to the hunter. In this instance the white hunter, thinking that Matt was just a kid and couldn't know too much about guns, would not let him carry the gun until just before time to shoot. The language barrier prevented me from explaining that I wanted Matt to be able to carry the gun, particularly when hunting a dangerous animal. So, when we got back to camp and while it was still light, I had Matt put on a little shooting demonstration for them. I got some small potatoes from the cook and had Matt toss one of them up in the air and shoot it with a .270 caliber rifle. His shot atomized the potato, which really got the attention of the white hunter and particularly the blacks. Just to let them know that his first shot wasn't an accident, I had him shoot several more. By this time the whole camp was watching and each time he hit one of the potatoes the blacks would let out with an "aayeeaa" which I learned was their sign of praise. The white hunter was duly impressed and the next day didn't argue with me when I handed the rifle to Matt and indicated that he was to carry it.

The week passed swiftly and enjoyably. We were both disappointed that we hadn't bagged a cape buffalo but we did shoot hartebeest, wart hogs, and some other smaller animals for camp meat. We took many rolls of pictures and left the camp with great memories. The airplane met us at the airstrip and we rejoined the rest of the group at the lodge. We then stayed there for another week of camera safari, which turned out to be even more fun than the hunt. The Gorongosa Game Preserve contained thousands of animals. Using special Volkswagon buses with sunroofs we were able to get very close to everything from lions to elephants. We took many wonderful pictures.

As it turned out, having Matt with me for this adventure bonded us at a very important age in his life. I've always been thankful that we were able to have this wonderful trip together. Ruthie and the girls were in Hawaii while we were

Matt Allen's family. L to R: Matt, daughter Brooke, wife Becky, sone Chad, and daughter Katie.

gone so we flew out and joined them for a few days of rest and relaxation on the beach at Waikiki. All in all—a wonderful episode in our lives.

About 1962 we moved into a larger house at 3105 Stanton Avenue, still in south Des Moines and once again close to the airport; because of my extensive travel, it was a real convenience being near the airport where I kept my plane. The house sat on an acre of land and I purchased a six-acre pasture beside it and another seven acres right across the street. Kelly had always wanted a horse and with this pasture we were able to give her that first special horse. We remodeled this home to add three bedrooms and two baths to the second floor. One upstairs bedroom with bath was planned for a live-in housekeeper.

Abby—Our Third Baby

Abby Elizabeth Allen was born January 19th, 1964 at 2:15 in the afternoon. Kelly and Matt had been quick births but Abby had her cord wrapped around her neck and it took several hours for Ruthie to deliver her. When Ruthie first became pregnant with Abby, already having one boy and one girl, I was hoping for another girl and my wishes were granted. Abby was a little doll and was a clone of her mother and has been ever since. During the long wait for Abby to be born, I became well acquainted with a young man whose wife was also in delivery. Dallas Vernon was about to graduate from Drake University with a degree in Marketing. When I asked him what he planned to do he surprised me by saying he wanted to be a salesman. I was surprised because most college grads have their sights set on being a doctor, lawyer, or Indian Chief and it was very refreshing to me to hear someone say he wanted to be a salesman. I was so impressed that I told him I would be interested in hiring him for Bob Allen Sportswear but I wanted him to take some other kind of a sales job as an internship before he joined us. I recommended that he apply to a large company with a sales training program, work for them for a year, and then come to me. Dallas did exactly what I suggested and got a job with Goodyear. In just a few months he became one of their top salesmen and after a year he came to Des Moines and said he was ready to go to work. We hired him and he became our sales manager, a job he held for several years. In the meantime his son Todd, who was born the same day as Abby, grew up with Abby.

As I said earlier, Abby was a clone of Ruthie and the two of them attracted a lot of attention because Ruthie usually dressed Abby as if they were twins. I have some happy memories of seeing the two of them together. Ruthie usually put Abby's hair in a ponytail, which involved some brushing. Abby hated the hairbrush and about the only times she wasn't her happy little self were when the hairbrush came out.

Matt became Abby's champion and, although he was constantly playing tricks on her, he really loved her and they had a lot of fun together. Matt loved to have Abby tickle his back. The only way he could get her to do it was to pay her so he rifled her piggy bank and paid her with her own dollars. It was to be a year before she caught on to what he was doing. The bedrooms for the children were upstairs. Sometimes we'd hear

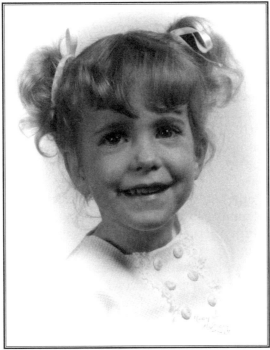

Abby Allen, my happy baby, at age four.

a ruckus going on upstairs and it was usually Matt playing tricks on Abby.

I've never seen anyone have a way with animals like Abby! She loves them and they love her. Her first pet was a big tomcat, which she named Fred. He became a "character" member of our household and was Abby's bosom friend. She would put him in her baby carriage, put lipstick on him, or nail polish on his claws—he put up with all of it! She put together a photo album full of pictures of Freddie and named it "Dead Fred." After Freddie had passed on, we acquired another kitten in an unusual way. We had all been to dinner at a restaurant called the Vets' Club. About ten o'clock as we were leaving, Abby noticed a little kitten that was hanging around the door to the restaurant. It was a below zero January night and the poor little kitten was mewing and looking for a way to get in. Abby wanted to take it home but I talked her out of it by saying it probably belonged to someone in the restaurant and they would take care of it. So we went on home but after we had gone to bed and around mid-night, Abby came into our bedroom crying and worrying about the kitten. She couldn't be talked out of it so I got up, dressed, and the two of us drove back to the Vets' club. It was a good thing we did because the poor little kitten was still there, now curled up by the door and almost frozen to death. Abby picked it up and cuddled it all the way home. Thus we acquired a new cat.

When we decided we wanted to have a dog, Abby suggested a miniature German Schnauzer and accompanied us to a breeder in a neighboring town. Using her intuition we had her pick the one she liked from a litter of four. As a puppy "Josh", as we named him, was pretty ugly. In fact we at first didn't want him in the house and, against Abby's wishes, made him sleep in a box in our garage. Josh finally charmed us and soon became an important part of our family for fifteen years. She had really picked out a winner as he was a very lovable, docile, and faithful pet. I still almost get tears when I think of Josh.

We really didn't intend to get another dog but one of Abby's friends had a female cockapoo puppy that was being abused by her family and she wanted to find a better home for it. Of course Abby's empathy caused her to bring the puppy home and *Buffy* also joined the family. Josh and Buffy became great companions and it was a joy for the whole family to see them play together. In later years when Ruthie's health was failing, the two dogs were her constant support.

I'd like to point out here that I didn't particularly enjoy riding horses and have never been much of a horse fan. My experiences riding while on hunting trips had convinced me that horses were an outmoded form of transportation that I could do without. Thus it was very difficult for me to understand my two daughters' love and devotion to their horses. My son Matt shared my feelings and was never afflicted by the horse fever even though we had horses at home as he was growing up. Matt's dislike was fueled by the fact that he and I shared the disagreeable job of cleaning the manure out of the barn, repairing fences, and caring for the pasture.

Abby had several horses, all which she loved. Her first

Abby Rice's family. L to R: On lap daughter Taylor, Abby, daughter Lizzy, son Trey and husband Austin Rice Jr.

horse Gypsy broke its leg but it wasn't a bad enough break that we had to put her to sleep. We gave her to Living History Farms where she spent her last days as scenery for that tourist attraction. Her next horse Chiquita didn't work out and was sold. The third one she named Sir Freddie II but his ancestry didn't live up to his name. He was sold to one of Abby's girl friends. Her last horse Otis was retired to Abby's husband's farm after they were married.

Getting rid of horses is much more difficult than acquiring them—a fact that I found out the hard way. When Kelly's horse Spats became old and ill it was time to put him to sleep. The simple way would have been to have the veterinarian give him an injection and then call the rendering works to cart away the carcass. This was not to be for Spats; the kids wanted him buried in the pasture that he loved. So instead of collecting approximately $500.00 from the rendering works, I spent several hundred dollars having a big hole dug in the pasture by a backhoe. The vet was hired to do the injection for a couple hundred dollars and, while the kids were in school we led old Spats down into the hole, gave him his injection, and when we were sure he was gone, the backhoe operator filled in the hole. So, in addition to spending a lot of money to dispose of him, I may have violated a city law regarding burying big animals in the city limits. We all missed old Spats, as he had become quite a pet. Abby's horse Otis, who had become Spats' companion, spent several days standing near the hole where he had last seen Spats; it was pretty sad! So much for horses!

We were a happy little family and the years seemed to fly by. We took many family vacations. Sometimes we chose places that we could fly to in my airplane. Flying trips took us to Hilton Head Island in South Carolina and to Sanibel Island in Florida before there was any bridge and the only way to get there was by airplane or boat. Sanibel Island is famous for its seashells, and the kids, except Abby, enjoyed the beach and searching for shells. Matt and Abby were inseparable but Matt was always playing tricks on Abby. Just before the Sanibel trip he had told her that there were sea monsters in the ocean. She wouldn't go in the water and we didn't understand why until we found out about the monster story.

Sometimes when we were traveling either in my airplane or the car, the kids would get pretty boisterous in the back seat. If they didn't quiet down when I asked them to, I'd sometimes reach back and without looking, whack someone. One time Kelly had one of her little girl friends, Janice Glass, with us. When I reached back to do my whacking I hit little Janice and made her cry—I was really the bad guy that day! My philosophy with my children was to give them lots of love but if they needed it, sometimes a light whack was quite effective. As any parent knows, traveling in a car with a bunch of kids can be pretty nerve-wracking. One time I felt a draft and, without looking, hit the switch to raise one of the back windows. I was unaware that I had caught Matt's neck in the window until the rest of the family was screaming at me and I could see Matt's arms flailing about and hear his gurgling.

One of our most memorable family trips was to Las Vegas, San Diego, Disneyland, Los Angeles, and San Francisco. Ruth's mother, Dott Brown, accompanied us and we had a great time. We flew to Las Vegas and then to San Diego.

From there we drove a rental car up the coast and saw all the tourist attractions along the way. We ran into our friends the Geres with their children at Disneyland and that made it even more fun.

One evening in Las Vegas we had dinner in the Tropicana's most formal dining room, which was complete with a group of strolling violinists. They came to our table and were playing beautifully for us when I happened to look at Abby and she had her fingers in her ears; even the violinists thought it was funny!

We had a family Christmas in Hawaii one year. Ed Remington of Sheraton Hotels made special arrangements for us in the new Sheraton Waikiki Hotel. He and his wife even had a Christmas tree and presents awaiting us in our suite when we arrived. We missed the snow but it was a relaxing way to spend the holidays.

Watching your children fumble their way through the dating game is a heart-rending time for parents, as you children and grandchildren will find out. If your child starts to date someone you don't like, you hardly dare say anything as human nature then dictates that they disagree and you've probably made them closer. We were very lucky! Kelly dated nice boys in high school, went with a cowboy for a while in college, and while she was in New York dated a guy who, although very nice, was easily old enough to be her father. She finally settled down to going with Kevin Welsh, a very wise choice that made us happy. Kevin is a real gentleman, a loving husband and father, and a good provider.

My Grandchildren

Kelly and Kevin have two great boys, Chip and George. At this writing Chip is fourteen and George is twelve. Both are good students, good athletes, and fine boys. Because they live so far away, unfortunately I don't get to spend as much time with them as I do the other grandchildren. Fortunately they come to the Lake to be with us every summer so we can spend time together then.

In high school Matt went steady with the cutest girl in

town and we think she did a pretty good job of keeping him in line. When he went away to college at Southern Methodist University in Dallas (same school Kelly attended) he immediately met Becky who is now his wife. He brought her home for Thanksgiving that first fall and we immediately fell in love with Becky. I told Matt that if he goofed that up, I'd shoot him!

Matt and Becky have three children. Their first is Brooke who is now 17 going on 20 and is an absolutely beautiful young lady and super-intelligent as well. She is so striking that she undoubtedly will do some modeling although her present interest for college involves medicine. Katie came along second and is 16 and absolutely beautiful also and has a delightful extrovert personality. Undoubtedly she will end up in show biz because she is very active in local theater and attended a theatrical school in London last year. And then there is Chad who is 10 and is all boy! He's very bright and is a chip off the old block when it comes to sports. When he comes to the Lake he spends fourteen hours a day out on the dock fishing.

Like her sister, Abby attracted and mowed through quite a few boy friends. We were very happy when she finally settled on her husband Austin Rice Jr. Austin is about as dedicated a hunter as you'll ever find, so you can understand that I think he is pretty great. He works with his brother and his dad in the family business, ServiceMaster of Iowa. Austin is one of those people who can do everything. He's a great polo player, good golfer, excellent shooter, water skier, and snow mobiler. Most important of all he is a good husband and a devoted father.

Abby's first child Elizabeth (Lizzy) was born prematurely and only weighed three and a half pounds at birth. She was so little she would fit in the palm of your hand. Of course she spent a couple of months in the hospital in special care. Abby was a devoted mother and spent every day in the hospital with Lizzy so they could bond. Lizzy is 8 now and when you see her climbing a tree or zooming around it is hard to believe she was ever so small. She is very artistic and enjoys the detail of needlepoint. Next came along Austin Rice III (Trey) who is now 6 and about the sharpest little guy you'll ever see. He has eyes that are always snapping and is a very loving child who

Our 2000 family Christmas picture. L to R: Front Row, grandchildren Lizzy Rice, Chad Allen, Trey Rice, & George Welsh. L to R: Sitting, Bob, Daughter Abby Rice, granddaughters Katie Allen, Brooke Allen, grandson Chip Welsh, and my wife Sari. L to R: Back row standing, Son Matt Allen, his wife Becky, my daughter Kelly Welsh, her husband Kevin Welsh, and daughter Abby's husband Austin Rice holding Taylor Rice.

always gives you a big hug. He and his dad are big buddies. And then came along another beautiful little girl named Taylor who is now 3 years old. She's already talking a blue streak and has a delightful, fun-loving personality. Her birth tops off Abby's delightful family and they are all a credit to their mother. You can tell by all of this that after raising three children and having eight grandchildren Ruthie and I felt quite proud of the job we had done.

Tragedy Struck Our Family

Then in 1966 tragedy struck! I had lunch with Ruthie and had just returned to the office after having dropped her off at home. She phoned me and in a wildly erratic voice said, "Come quick, I'm terribly sick" and then she dropped the phone and I could hear her screaming in the background. I immediately phoned our Doctor, Jim Kelsey, advising him what was going on. He said to rush her to the Iowa Methodist Hospital emergency room and he'd meet me there. This was in the days before 911 so I felt it would save time if I brought her to the hospital. I rushed home and when I came in the house she had vomited, was rolling on the floor in agony, and indicated to me that she had a terrible headache. I carried her to the car and rushed to the hospital. Dr. Kelsey had guessed what might have happened and did an immediate spinal tap. I watched the procedure and saw the red color of the liquid that came out so knew immediately that she had a brain hemorrhage. Jim Kelsey advised me that, if it were his wife, he'd rush her to the Mayo Clinic in Rochester immediately. I took his advice and he called to make arrangements to admit her the next day. I called Des Moines Flying Service and reserved a plane for the next morning. They sedated Ruthie and tried to stabilize her in the hospital as best they could that night. She was really suffering but the sedation helped somewhat.

The next morning our housekeeper brought all the kids out to the airport to see Ruthie off. It was about twenty below zero outside so we loaded her in the plane while it was in a heated hangar. The children were in tears and terribly distraught. Ruthie was barely able to say good-bye to them and I'm sure that despite my assurances, the children wondered if they'd ever see their mother again.

The flight to Rochester took a little over an hour. When we landed they directed us to a big hangar whose doors opened as we taxied up. We taxied into the hangar, the doors closed, and the Mayo ambulance was waiting for her inside the heated hangar. She was taken directly to the St. Joseph's Hospital emergency room where a team of neurologists was waiting. After about an hour they came out to tell me that she had what they called "a subarachnoid hemorrhage of unknown origin." Their game plan was to get her into a room and stabilize her for a few hours and then do an angiogram to determine where the bleeding was. In the meantime she was semi-conscious and able to talk but was in excruciating pain. Two angiograms done in the next few days did not find an aneurysm or any specific place where she was bleeding. The doctors explained that she probably had several small blood vessels break in her brain and this was the cause of her pain. Had there been an aneurysm this might have been preferable as then they could have operated and her recovery would have been faster. They said her current condition would require several weeks for the blood to be gradually absorbed and then the headache would subside. She remained in St. Joseph Hospital in Rochester for almost three months and then was moved to Des Moines where she spent another three weeks in the Younker Rehabilitation wing of Iowa Methodist Hospital.

This was a terrible time for the children, and for me as well! I brought them to Rochester several times to see her and we all hoped and prayed for her recovery and return home. It took almost a year for her to recover completely and then, as is common in these cases, she went into a seriously deep depression, which doctors said was caused by a fear of another stroke. Her illness really brought the family together! Abby wasn't in school yet so became Ruthie's constant companion. Ruth gradually got better but this was the start of a series of serious health problems that altered her quality of life. Only our family knew of her problems and suffering. Whenever she left the house she was always impeccably groomed and dressed. She was always smiling and cheerful with tremendous empathy for other people's problems.

She had a long-time bout with stomach ulcers, probably exacerbated by smoking, and finally had two stomach surgeries at the Mayo Clinic. Both caused eating problems and weight loss. In later years she developed a breathing problem called chronic obstructive pulmonary disease, which caused her to be placed in intensive care several times. The list of health problems she endured almost defies imagination. On top of everything else the poor girl had several bouts with kidney stones, which resulted in blockages and the necessity for stents to be installed. She even had a bout with shingles! In March of 1995 we had gone to Florida hoping that the warm weather would improve her breathing. The second week we were there she developed a cold and couldn't breathe. She was admitted to intensive care with a ventilator and all the other terrible things that they do to you in an intensive care unit. For the first time she started to give up and if it hadn't been for Matt, who flew in to be with her, I think she would have passed away. Matt was able to encourage her enough that she pulled through this crisis too.

Later in 1995 our entire family was broken-hearted to lose our two beloved dogs. Josh, a perky miniature schnauzer, had been with us for fifteen years. He became ill and we had to put him to sleep. Then a few months later Buffy, our great little cockapoo, died from pancreatits. These dogs had been Ruthie's constant companions through all her illness—always in bed with her cheering her up. Their loss lessened her will to live some more. The final blow came in February of 1996 when Ruthie was rear-ended while driving her Jaguar. She was badly bruised, injured both knees, and developed back pains. Additionally she was broken-hearted to have the car she loved damaged so badly.

Later that February I flew her out to Palm Springs, California in our Malibu. I had rented a condominium there for the winter hoping that the warm and dry air of that desert resort would solve her breathing problems. We were only there about a week when she came down with a cold. I awakened about two A. M. one morning to see her sitting on the side of the bed gasping to breathe. I rushed her to the hospital emergency room. The doctors came out a few minutes after examining her and advised me that she couldn't make it through the night unless they put her on a ventilator, which would mean going into intensive care again. After her Florida experience in intensive care, she had told me that if she ever had to go on a ventilator again, she'd prefer to be allowed to die. I went in to see her and told her what the doctors had said. My poor Baby asked me if she would recover if she went on the ventilator. I told her that she probably would but that if she did not go on the ventilator, they didn't think she would last until morning. She really wanted to live! So, into intensive care she went again. She made no progress so I called all three of the children and they immediately came to Palm Springs to be with her. It was almost impossible for her to talk with the ventilator and she was so weak by this time she couldn't communicate with us. They tried taking her off the ventilator but she couldn't breathe without it. Watching her was like looking at a burning coal in the fireplace; her eyes just got dimmer and dimmer by the day. The doctors said that about the only way she could live would be with a ventilator and in some kind of an extended care facility. She would have absolutely no quality of life! She had made me promise her many times that I would never allow her to be placed in that kind of a situation. With much sorrow we all came to the conclusion that we should let her slip away as peacefully as possible. Our doctor said that he would sedate her so she'd be in no pain and she should slip away in a few hours.

Our beautiful, courageous, and loving little Ruthie finally gave up on February 29th, 1996—a leap year which none of us will ever be able to forget. We flew her back to Des Moines and planned funeral services at Dunn's. One of her wishes was that she didn't want anyone but our family to see her in the casket; for everyone else it would be closed. I've never seen anything like her reception. More than three hundred people came and there were one hundred and two beautiful flower arrangements. The entire funeral home was filled with her flowers. I was amazed at the number of people who came to pay their respects. It was everyone from relatives and friends to people whom she had come in contact with in her day-to-day life. As an example, several of the check-out girls came from the super market where we shopped, the entire staff of the beauty shop she attended, plus many of our employees who really loved her too.

One of her other wishes was that her funeral service be a happy one. We held the services in St. Paul's Episcopal church and our favorite minister, Father Bill Jacobs, came out of retirement to lead services. Her favorite musical number was "Over The Rainbow" so I arranged for Scott Smith, a friend and well-known local musician and singer, to sing it during the service. Grand daughters Brooke and Katie Allen gave beautiful eulogies as did a good friend Carol Cobbs. I especially wanted to pay tribute to Ruthie myself and gave a special eulogy. I'm sure we did it the way she wanted it. Following the service at the cemetery we invited everyone to come to our home. Life for the Allen family was never to be the same again! I am sure that "somewhere over the rainbow" Ruthie is having an easier life and must be tremendously proud looking down at the wonderful family she was responsible for creating.

Chapter 12

Airplanes and Flying

Air Exploration

As a child I was growing up in the era of air exploration with Lindbergh becoming a hero by flying across the Atlantic. I read the daily headlines about Will Rogers and Wiley Post flying around the world. I experienced the grief of our country when Rogers and Post died in their fatal crash at Point Barrow, Alaska. So, with this exploration of the air in full swing and fancying myself as some kind of an adventurer, it was no wonder that aviation fascinated and excited me. In my hometown of Fort Dodge, Iowa, the Eno family operated the local airport and both Ellis and his wife were pilots. Many times I would go out to the airport just to hang around and watch the activities. It wasn't much of an airport, consisting of the house they lived in and one hangar big enough for their two airplanes; an open cockpit bi-plane and a single engine high-wing monoplane that carried four passengers. There were no runways or paved aprons, just a forty-acre grassy landing field. They didn't have to worry much about crosswind landings on this field, they just lined up, took off and landed into the wind ~ in whatever direction the wind decided to blow!

My First Flight

At about ten years old my first airplane ride opportunity occurred. I was a paperboy for the Des Moines Register and The Register offered a prize for new subscribers which we called "starts." The prize was a ride in their new Autogiro aircraft (named "Good News") for every paper carrier who got six new "starts." Six was quite a challenge back then, but I wanted that ride so bad I really put myself to the task of signing up six new customers, and I was successful. The Autogiro came to town one Saturday morning and the three of us who had won the contest went to the airport for our reward—our first airplane ride and our first flight.

You may never have heard of an Autogiro because not too many of them were made and they were not around too long. They were a cross between an airplane and a helicopter. The aircraft had short, stubby wings, a propeller in front, and whirling helicopter-like blades on top. Unlike a helicopter it could not rise straight up but had to run along the ground for twenty-five yards or so before it could takeoff. It had two open cockpits, one for the pilot in front and the other for the passenger in back. There was no communication between the two cockpits and once the engine was started the noise was horrendous. I was scared to death but wouldn't admit it. They only gave us a ten-minute ride, but for one's first flight it was sensational. We flew over Fort Dodge at about one thousand feet and I had the opportunity of seeing my home and the timber behind it where I spent so much time playing and exploring. The pilot, of cause, became my absolute hero!

This experience stirred me into reading everything I could about airplanes and flying. Pocket books, as we know them today, did not exist then but cheap, pulp paper books were popular and I bought countless stories to read about the Combat Ace Fighters of World War I and the exploits of flyers like Admiral Byrd. Just before talking pictures came out, there were a few movies produced, with great publicity, proclaiming that they had *actual sound*. Remember, up until then the only sound you heard in a movie theater was the audience and the organist; the words of the actors were printed at the bottom of the screen. One of the first sound movies was a World War I flying movie called "Wings." There was no talking but the sound of the aircraft engines and the machine guns was very real and this made "Wings" a movie everyone just had to see. I must have seen this movie three or four times. Within a few months, a similar film called "Hell's Angels"—a picture that made Jean Harlow a star, followed it. It was called a "talkie" because, for the first time in history, it had both sound and talking voices. It is still considered a classic and contains flying sequences never to be equaled, particularly with those vintage World War I aircraft. I probably saw this film six or seven times!

Flying—An Unlikely Possibility

Flying was always in my mind, however it was an unlikely possibility that I would ever learn to fly until the start of World War II. Shortly after Pearl Harbor, I applied for and was accepted for the Army Air Corps Aviation Cadet Program. Earlier, I related that the biggest disappointment in my life was "washing-out" of this program and having my flying career come to a screeching halt after nine hours of flight instruction. I just knew I could fly if I was given half a chance to learn. After the war I was attending shoots all over the country and several friends owned small planes, so I had many opportunities to fly with them. My shooting buddy, Homer Clark, had a new V-tail, Beechcraft Bonanza that flew us in style to many a shoot and this really whetted my appetite to own an airplane.

A quirk of fate got me into aviation about 1955. With the need for a new secretary, I began interviewing candidates for the job and one Margaret (Maggie) Adkins came to apply. Two of her previous jobs had been with flying services. In questioning her about these jobs, I learned that she had not only been their secretary but also a flight instructor and was one of only two licensed female flight instructors in Iowa. The reason she was applying for a secretarial position was because she couldn't find a full time job flying. "Do you mean to tell me," I said excitedly, "that if I hire you as my secretary, you could teach me to fly?" Her reply with an ear-to-ear grin was that she would love to! Needless to say, she got the job and two weeks later, drawing upon her experience, I bought my first airplane, a single engine, four-seater, Cessna 175. Its registration number was N7101M, shortened to "Cessna-Zero-One-Mike" in all radio transmissions.

Every morning, just after daylight, I met Maggie at the airport and we'd fly for an hour or so before returning to the office. I'll never forget the excitement of those morning flights! It was January and the temperature was below zero every day. This made for still air with no bumps of any kind. Steam and smoke came up from homes and buildings below, giving our world an eerie appearance. We'd fly out west of Des Moines to a practice area where I learned to do stalls and figure eights, maintaining a constant altitude, and "S" turns along a road that taught me about wind drift and maintaining altitude. Before returning we'd then head for some out-lying airport where I would *shoot* a few "touch-and-go" landings before returning to Des Moines. *Mike fright* was a command problem for new pilots, however the Des Moines Airport had a control tower so I quickly learned the proper use of the microphone and the radio and from then on radio procedure came easily to me.

I had just started the Airline Textile Manufacturing Company division of my business and was in the midst of setting up licenses with the airlines. Maggie and I flew to Minneapolis, Kansas City, and Chicago on business trips. These flights taught me navigation, an appreciation of weather and the various problems it could create, plus I was gaining confidence that only comes from experience. The Cessna's equipment was pretty primitive by today's standards. The plane was not equipped with an autopilot so I had to hand-fly the airplane all the time. The one radio it had was used for both navigation and communication. It was called a "whistle stop" radio because you tuned it to a station by turning a little crank and listening to a whistling sound. When the whistling sound reached its highest intensity you knew that you were properly tuned into the frequency. The only problem was that in rough air your hand would be jumping around so much it was almost impossible to get a fine tune. This could be very embarrassing in a traffic pattern at a busy airport. Navigation was from one VOR to another. (VOR means Very high frequency—Omni directional—Radio beacon.) The VOR was an instrument with a vertical needle. To navigate you'd tune in the station, center the needle, and fly to the station. If the needle moved you simply turned towards it to keep it centered and this technique would fly you right over the station. Under the needle was a window that showed the words "TO" and "FROM" so you would know your position from the station. It was rudimentary but accurate. (A very handy feature that saved me once. I fell asleep when it said *To* and awoke when it said *From* and missed the landing field. I probably would have kept flying looking for the town I wanted to land in never knowing I had already passed it.) Modern radios have DME (Distance Measuring Equipment), which tells you how far you are from the VOR station, but I wasn't blessed with anything that sophisticated. If I wanted to learn my location along my course towards the VOR, I'd have to tune in a VOR off to the side of my course, get a compass heading from it, and then manually draw a line on the chart to where it crossed my course line. The only thing wrong with this method was that if one was moving along at 130 miles per hour, while one was drawing the line, one's location was always off by a mile or two. However it was good enough that this *one* never got lost.

After I had made several trips and I had accumulated about thirty hours of flying time with Maggie, she decided to solo me. She embarrassed me by making me go through the old fashioned custom of the instructor getting out of the airplane in the middle of the airfield and standing there while her student made three landings. I wasn't the least bit nervous because I knew I could fly the airplane but having her standing out there in the middle of the field, in front of God and everyone, who now knew a student pilot was making a solo flight, embarrassed the hell out of me. After the third landing I picked her up and we taxied back to the hangar where all the flight service employees were lined up to initiate me with the customary ceremonial cutting off of my shirttail, for having successfully soloed.

Just a few days later I took off *alone* on an extended business trip that took me to St. Louis, Washington National, Philadelphia, and would you believe, New York's LaGuardia, Kennedy, and Newark airports. Maggie stayed in Des Moines because I needed her in the office and I was so cocky about my flying, I didn't think I needed her any more. Boy was I wrong! I had hardly begun to learn about flying, and this trip was to be my supreme initiation.

What a wild experience that trip was! The navigation was no problem for me and I was lucky to find good weather for the entire trip. Early on I learned that letting airport tower controllers and VOR radio operators know that I was a student pilot really got their attention and their specialized help. As an example, when I was ready to leave New York's Kennedy Airport, I called ground control for taxi instructions and wondered how I was ever going to get out because the taxi strip had a line-up of about twenty-five, four engine, propeller driven, airliners like DC-6's and Lockheed Constellations. As I sat there in that line-up with all those giant airplanes towering over me, and with my wings rocking like mad from the propellers' "wash," I was feeling pretty insignificant. Finally the ground controller asked me what compass heading I was planning after take-off and then instructed me to switch over to the tower for take-off instructions. The tower advised me to hold my present position and then right after a big TWA Constellation took off, to taxi along the right side of the gigantic line-up of planes and position myself at the head of the line, adjacent to the active runway and to hold! I had already identified myself as a student pilot so I believe the tower controller just wanted me to get the hell out of there. Do you know what it is like to taxi past another airplane that's landing wheels are as big as your entire plane? At any rate, in just a few minutes he cleared me for an immediate take-off and instructed me to make a sharp right turn out just as soon as I was off the ground. I actually did not cause any delays because I was off the ground in about 2000 feet, did my right turn and boy was I out-of-there! This was the typical help and treatment I received everywhere I flew. None of this would happen in today's environment of heavy flying traffic. However, as I shall testify, there really is a guardian angel that specifically looks out for new pilots.

From Kennedy (it was called Idlewild Airport then) I flew out to Amityville on Long Island where I landed at Zahn's Airport to visit my sales manager Marty Berman. Then I flew into LaGuardia Airport to call on the airport gift shops. From there it was into Newark Airport and I remember the tower advising me to proceed to *some* bridge and turn final approach there! Where? Looking out the window I could see about a dozen bridges and not being acquainted with the area I called him back, said I was a stranger and most importantly a student pilot—would he please identify the bridge? He called back and said to just stand by and he'd tell me when to turn which he did and I landed safely. They were very helpful back in those days. Just try something like that at Newark or any other large airport today and you'd be in big trouble!

My visit to Newark was in February and there was a lot of snow on the ground. They hadn't done a very good job of plowing the taxi strips so there were ruts in the snow that had turned to ice. My little Cessna's small wheels would drop into these ruts and literally turn the plane around. It took me quite a while to taxi in and I was embarrassed as I thought all those professional pilots were probably having a good laugh on my behalf.

I finished my business at Newark about three o'clock in the afternoon and I had hoped to fly as far as Youngstown, Ohio on my way back to Iowa. To save time, I bought a box lunch and a carton of milk for my dinner. After an uneventful take-off and climb to my cruise altitude, I opened up my box lunch, set the milk on the instrument panel, and was starting to eat my sandwich when I noticed, out my left side, an Eastern Airlines four-engine Electra climbing steeply beside me. Having been warned about dangerous prop wash from big airplanes, I turned a little to the right so that the Eastern plane passed well above me and to my left. Evidently the winds aloft had changed, because when I turned away from his prop wash, I actually turned right into the full wash. All of a sudden it felt like I had flown into a brick wall, the Cessna bucked violently, turned on its side and almost rolled over. My seat belt had been loosely fastened with about eight inches of slack. I banged my head against the ceiling and then against the side window. My feet came off the rudder pedals and for a few seconds I was weightless like an astronaut in space. I was everything but upside down for about thirty seconds and was absolutely terrified! The milk splattered all over the windshield and inside of the airplane while my sandwiches and chips flew everywhere. I had immediately pulled the throttle back to slow the aircraft and finally the air calmed down so I could proceed in my climb. Of course, immediately I knew what had happened to my little plane but that didn't prevent the momentary panic I experienced. It would have been wonderful to turn the autopilot on while I calmed down and cleaned up my lunch mess, but I had no such luxury. Slowly—ever so slowly—I gathered the remains of my box lunch and continued on.

A couple of hours later it became apparent that I was not going to be able to get as far as Youngstown because of headwinds. I was over the Allegheny Mountains and it was already starting to get dark between the ridges. Night flying instructions were not yet part of my curriculum with Maggie, so I certainly did not want to continue on in the dark. To add to my problems the gauge showed we (the plane and I) were very low on gas. I was navigating on Phillipsburg VOR so I called them, explained my predicament and asked for the nearest airport for a quick landing. They said York, Pennsylvania was very close and sure enough I could see its lights. According to my charts, the airport in York was located just southeast of the town. I let down to pattern altitude but could not locate the airport and the sky was quickly starting to darken. After trying to call Phillipsburg radio with no response I realized that I was down too low in the mountains to reach them. So, I climbed back up into the sunlight and called them again. This time, to my relief, they came in loud and clear! When I told them I couldn't find the airport the controller said that he lived in York and not seeing the airport was understandable because the airport was not lighted and to make it doubly hard to see in the dark, it had runways of grass on soil that was half black coal. The controller said to let down again, fly over the downtown area on a ninety degree east heading following a set of double railroad tracks, and when I came to a river, to turn right, 90 degrees, and turn on my landing lights. I followed his instructions and sure enough, when I turned on my lights, reflectors on both sides of the runway clearly defined its path. With much relief I landed and, from a phone booth off to the side of the strip, I called Phillipsburg radio and thanked them profusely. Incidentally that airport was unattended. This lone phone booth had a sign that read, "Visiting pilots call the police for help." I called the police and a few minutes later a policeman picked me up and took me to a hotel. Once again my guardian angel was working overtime for me!

I was to put a bit of a strain on my guardian angel one more time on this trip. When I had parked the airplane the night before, I had used a tow bar on the front wheel to pull the airplane up close to a building where it would be out of the wind and safer. The next morning when I was ready to leave, I used the same tow bar to pull the airplane away from the building. The tow bar is a "T" shaped bar about forty inches long attached to the front wheel of the airplane to facilitate moving it. You are supposed to take the tow bar off and stow it in the airplane before take-off. Despite my double walk-around inspection before take-off, I missed seeing the tow bar still attached to the nose wheel and lying back over the wheel cover. This is a very dangerous situation because the propeller only missed the tow bar by a few inches and with the bumpy runway, it is a miracle that it didn't flip up and splinter the propeller.

I landed for gas a few hours later at Fort Wayne, Indiana. When I parked the airplane, the wise-guy ramp attendant smirked, "Do you always fly with your tow bar attached?" The luck of the Irish again!

Dad loved to fly with me but it was difficult to get him into the plane for the first time. He had never flown before and was quite fearful. I planned a fishing trip for the two of us at Land O' Lakes, Wisconsin and explained that if he would fly with me we'd have two extra days of fishing. To convince him, I told him that I would fly up to Fort Dodge to pick him up, and if, after he got into the plane, he still didn't want to go, I'd go back to Des Moines and get my car for the trip.

He met me at the airport in Fort Dodge. I was flying a Cessna 175 with a door on each side. While he was sitting in the plane with both doors open, I explained the workings of the airplane, the instruments and how we would proceed. I said that if he was willing, I'd start the engine, we'd taxi out, and if at any time he became frightened I would turn around and we'd go back. He seemed to be willing so I shut the doors, started the engine, and slowly taxied out to the head of the active runway. He was chewing on an unlit cigar and seemed to be okay. Instead of starting out at full throttle, I gradually increased the power so that we slowly picked up speed. That airplane usually broke ground at around fifty miles an hour so it wasn't long before we were actually in the air. I looked over at the old man and he seemed to be enjoying it. I told him "Dad, we're flying now!" His reply was something like "Well is that all there is to it?" We lucked out by having smooth air and nice weather all the way. I think Dad really loved his first flight.

I often flew up to Fort Dodge to pick up my dad and would always fly low so he could identify things on the ground. He had tuned pianos in almost all the little towns in northwest Iowa and knew many farmers. He really got a kick out of recognizing places he knew from the air. I wasn't the greatest pilot in the world but he thought so—I overheard him bragging about me to his friends.

We were doing a lot of business in Chicago so I made frequent trips into the city with the Cessna. Meig's Field, located on Chicago's lakefront adjacent to McCormick Place and between the outer-drive and Lake Michigan, is the most convenient airport in the Chicago area. For a new pilot however it presented many challenges. Meig's had the reputation of being very dangerous primarily because of the prevailing crosswinds. On final approach the tower called off wind speeds so if the crosswind exceeded your aircraft's capacity, you could abort the landing. The first time I flew into Meig's solo was a windy day in April. As I turned final for runway nine zero (heading straight south) the tower was calling off variable crosswinds from the west from 17 to 30 knots. According to the Cessna's manual she was supposed to handle up to a 22 knot crosswind. With some trepidation, I continued my approach to the edge of the runway when it became apparent that the crosswind, gusting up to 28 knots at that moment, was too much for the Cessna or me. I opened the throttle, climbed up to about 5000 feet and made a landing in Gary, Indiana at an airport that had a runway facing into the wind. The North Shore train from Gary, I decided, was a pleasurable and unruffled way for me to get into the city. On my next Chicago trip I was able to land at Meig's okay; however, it seemed that Meig's was becoming kind of a jinx for me. After landing, ground control vectored me out into the last parking area towards the lake. The only parking spot open was in a corner near a fence. I taxied the airplane into this tight spot and all of a sudden I was stopped. It felt like the left wheel was in a hole. I gunned the engine but it still wouldn't move. Looking outside I suddenly saw why. The tip of my wing was up against a light pole. In order to get into this tight parking spot, I had extended my left wing over the fence as I pivoted around. In the early morning light with the sun shining on the fence, the light pole was virtually invisible. Because I couldn't leave the plane in this position, I called ground control. "This is Cessna Zero One Mike at the north lot. I need someone to come out and help me because I just wrapped my wing around your damn light pole!" (I did not know the conversation I was having on the ground control channel was being broadcast into the terminal waiting room.) They sent someone out to help me move the airplane. First I was mad; however, when I walked into the terminal and heard the broadcasted ground control conversations, I suddenly became very embarrassed. All of those professional pilots were having a good laugh on me. As it turned out I had twisted the main spar in the wing so the entire wing had to be replaced and I was grounded for about a month. Later I found out that I was the fourth pilot to taxi into that same light pole—now I didn't feel so bad, with some other embarrassed company.

The Cessna proved to be an easy airplane to fly but with a very poor engine. To give the aircraft more speed, they had designed it with a geared propeller, and the operating manual instructed that the engine be flown at much higher RPM's than most engines. As an example, it was recommended to cruise at 3100 RPM's; a setting that I was later to learn, the engine could not take. My engine blew up one day on a flight to St. Louis and I had to make a forced landing in Quincy, Illinois; dead stick! I was at 10,000 feet when the engine started making noises like someone waving a chain around under the hood. The prop ground to a halt and it suddenly became very quiet up there. My position was right over Kahoka, Missouri but it was a small airport so I started looking for a better one. I was navigating on Quincy radio and gave them a "may-day" call. A very helpful man came on to advise me that I had about a fifty-knot tail wind and that I should be able to glide into Quincy airport with paved runways and mechanics to help me. He was right, and I had no trouble making Quincy; in fact I had been husbanding my altitude so closely that I had to do some sideslipping to lose enough altitude to get down. Until then I had been too busy to be frightened—and what a relief to be safely on the ground. Once again, I had found that calling for help really paid off. Immediately after landing I paid a personal visit to the Quincy radio room and thanked them for their help.

Continental gave me a new engine but it started running rough after about 200 hours and that made me too apprehensive. Fearing the new engine might blow up also and this time I might not be so lucky, I landed at Midway Airport in Chicago, boarded a United Airlines flight back to Des Moines and said *sayonara* to the Cessna 175. A few months later I traded it in on a Piper Commanche 250.

During the time between abandoning the Cessna and receiving the new Commanche, I rented airplanes from Des Moines Flying Service. Renting means you are at the mercy of whatever rental planes are available and sometimes their equipment leaves a lot to be desired. On one occasion I took the family to the Kansas State Shoot in Wichita, and rented a Commanche 180, which had quite a few hours on its engine and the old one-radio routine for both navigation and communication. The 180 was underpowered, so with Ruth, the two children, and all my guns and our luggage it didn't perform too well. Additionally, I found that the old-fashioned whistle stop radio wasn't working too well either.

Everything went along okay until we were just a few miles from Wichita. Off to the west of the airport I could see a big black front approaching so I knew I needed to get in to the airport as soon as possible. Approach control had turned me over to the tower but when I tried to call the tower on that "Mickey Mouse" radio I didn't get an answer. We were on a long base leg for the airport and about this time we flew into the edge of the storm. The airplane started to bounce around in the rough air making it difficult for me to try to crank in the frequency on the radio. Picture the scene: we are still proceeding towards the airport, the plane is bouncing around like mad, Kelly in the back seat with Ruth has suddenly become air-sick and Ruth is trying to help her while she is vomiting, and then the right door, beside our little son Matt, pops open, making a loud sucking noise. I'm still fighting the radio and all hell is breaking loose around me. Still not being able to raise the tower, I cranked in approach control and happily was able to reach them. "Wichita approach this is Commanche 901 Papa with a little emergency!" Approach says, "Go ahead Commanche 901 Papa." With relief I called back, "Comanche 901 Papa, I can't raise the tower on this *Mickey Mouse* radio— I've got kids air sick, the door just popped open, we are in the edge of this storm front, and I need clearance to land NOW!" They came right back and cleared me to land immediately without calling the tower.

We were really relieved to be on the ground. Ruthie's hands had been full because Kelly, in addition to being airsick, was really scared, as was Ruthie! Although it would have been impossible for Matt to fall out of the door (it only cracked open an inch or two and the slipstream prevented the door from opening enough for someone to fall out) he was naturally terrified and crying. Once again my Irish luck came through, plus the great cooperation I received from FAA people in Approach Control. I have always been appreciative of the assistance these people are willing to give if you forget your ego and ask for help. With that in mind, I phoned the tower after our landing and thanked them with all the appreciation I could possibly show. The man I talked to said he could tell I had my hands full and was glad they could help me.

Commanche 250

My second plane, the Commanche 250, was a much more sophisticated airplane with retractable landing gear, autopilot, and more radios. It also was an easy airplane to fly and very forgiving for an amateur pilot. I flew it for another 250 hours and then, because the cost of an airplane was rather prohibitive, I sold it and stopped flying for a couple of years. When our business began to grow again, and because I missed flying so much, I invested in another slightly larger airplane, a single engine Piper Saratoga. This turned out to be a wonderful bird and I used it for business trips and family vacation. Owning airplanes is like a disease! You always want one that is bigger and faster.

One of my best friends and flying buddy is Ken Konkol. Ken was a partner in The Champion Glove Company until he retired. His factory was a few doors away from mine on Court Street in Des Moines. We were in the same boat, just starting out—our businesses each at a critical point of growth. I have many fond memories of commiserating with Ken and his partner Lee Nylen during those years of struggle. Ken was a champion handball player and designed a handball glove that became the glove for almost all players. A graduate of Drake University, Ken was instrumental in developing their handball program and recently endowed the University with the funds to build new handball courts that now bear his name. In addition to our businesses, Ken and I both shared a big interest in flying.

Ken had been flying for many years before I got the fever. On several occasions, when I was preparing for my Instrument Rating, Ken accompanied me in my new Saratoga as my instructor. I'll never forget one stormy summer night when we were enroute to Des Moines from Nashville and we had to land in Columbia, Missouri because of thunderstorms. I was hand-flying the bird on instruments as we approached the airfield. The traffic was heavy and the approach controller was vectoring us around like mad. Suddenly, I had an attack of vertigo that was so bad I asked Ken to take over—lucky thing he was there to save us!

If you asked me if I could name one person who loved flying more than life itself, it would be my friend Ken. Despite the fact that we now live 200 miles apart, we make it a point to get together on a regular basis. Ken is a fine friend, a gentleman, a fellow well met. Thanks Ken for all the devoted friendship and great flying!

Malibu 9131X

My next airplane was a Piper Malibu, one of the largest single engine airplanes on the market. It had a walk around cabin, seated six passengers, was air conditioned and pressurized to 25,000 feet. It was a very efficient airplane with all the latest electronics including autopilot, radar, Loran, DME and full instrumentation for instrument flying. Both Matt and I had to attend a special school in Vero Beach, Florida to be checked out on the Malibu before we could get any insurance. The Malibu was an exceptional plane and Matt and I certainly enjoyed our time with her for business and pleasure.

I had by-pass heart surgery in 1989 and from then on, the FAA required detailed physical exams and a yearly review. Each year it took longer to get my license renewed during which time I was not able to fly. I finally decided that because I was not flying many hours, flying a sophisticated airplane like the Malibu might become dangerous.

My last flight on Malibu 9131X was in November of 1995, for a duck-hunting trip to Peoria, Illinois. My dear friend Homer Clark had invited me to hunt with him at his duck club on the Illinois River south of Peoria. He was to pick me up at the Peoria flying service and we'd drive down to the camp. My hour and a half flight from Des Moines to Peoria in bluebird weather was pleasant and uneventful. I hadn't flown for a few weeks so I was a little nervous and still not as comfortable with the Malibu as I had been with the old Saratoga. My approach into Peoria was a little high but the Malibu had speed brakes that you could use to slow yourself down for the descent. Everything was going great but just off the end of the runway I started to feel some pressure and angina pains in my chest. I landed, turned off the active runway, and taxied slowly

With my airplane Malibu 9131X, April 1994.

over to the flying service. Once there I shut off the engine and then just sat in the airplane to see if the feeling would subside. I took a couple of Rolaids thinking it might be indigestion but they didn't help. Thinking I might be in trouble, I walked slowly into the flying service office where I told the girl at the counter that I thought she should call 911 as I was having some kind of a heart problem. Well, then all hell broke loose! To be on the safe side she also called the National Guard there at the airport and they immediately sent two ambulance loads of paramedics. In the meantime, a doctor who had just landed behind me heard the conversation and had me sit down so he could check my pulse, etc. Then the National Guard arrived; a gung-ho bunch of young guys just dying to practice their paramedic skills on somebody. Immediately they had me lying down, had loosened my clothes, were checking pulse, and had blood pressure cuffs on me. By this time I was feeling a little better but still scared.

So this was the scene my friend Homer walked in on when he came to pick me up. He turned absolutely white and I thought he was going to have a heart attack. The 911 paramedics arrived about this time and they immediately put me in an ambulance and administered nitro tablets under my tongue. Homer came along with me to the hospital. Just a few seconds after the nitro, the pressure and angina pains disappeared and I felt great. To be on the safe side however, I was admitted to the hospital and they immediately proceeded to run various tests. They could find nothing wrong and I was beginning to think it all was a false alarm and that nerves might have brought on the pressure. They kept me in the hospital for four days and God bless Homer for spending most of the time with me. I insisted that he go back to the duck camp each night so that he could get in on the early morning shooting each day. Then he'd come back to the hospital to keep me company. I really appreciated him but felt bad that I had fouled up the hunt he had planned for us.

Aviation writer Ernest Gann once said that flying is ". . . hour after hour of boredom punctuated by moments of sheer terror!" Ernest, you have summarized my flying experiences perfectly. However, all I can say is that someone who has never flown has missed one of the truly great adventures and pleasures in life and I still miss it.

Chapter 13

"Party Hunts"

One of the most interesting benefits for me in the Bob Allen Sportswear business was our involvement in hunting events, which, for lack of a better description, I've always called "Party Hunts." In a sense they are very similar to Pro-Am Golf Tournaments. Almost all of the party hunts are fundraisers for some local charity or for wildlife conservation and are usually held in the fall of the year. My company received great publicity through co-sponsoring the hunts or contributing merchandise that was auctioned off to raise money. Another wonderful fringe benefit for my son Matt and me was being able to participate in these events. The Bob Allen Bush Coat became the official uniform for attendees and is still the uniform for the One Shot Antelope Hunt, the Enid Grand National Quail Hunt and the Nebraska One Box Hunt. All of these get-togethers provided colorful embroidered emblems and it became the custom to sew the emblems all over the bush coats to demonstrate how many hunts one had attended. It warms my heart every time I see hundreds of hunters all in one place wearing my Bush Coat.

314

The One Box Grouse Hunt, Ashern, Manitoba, Canada

The earliest hunt in the year was the Ashern, Manitoba "One Box Grouse Hunt." Ashern is a town of less than one thousand population located about one hundred fifty miles northwest of Winnipeg on the west side of big Lake Manitoba. In addition to the outstanding hunting for wildfowl and sharp-tail grouse, the fall scenery is breathtaking. One year I put together a team with top shooters, including world champion Homer Clark, Johnny Broughton, as well as friends like Lex Hawkins and Herb Elliott, who flew us to Ashern in his new Beech Duke. At this hunt they auctioned off the teams in a "Calcutta." I don't know where the term Calcutta came from but each shooter was auctioned off and sold to the highest bidder. All of this money went into a pot with the winning buyer of a team receiving the largest share, the hunter (or team) getting a next largest percentage and the organizers of the hunt getting the balance. It was a great way to raise money and it gave the hunters a real incentive to shoot well. We managed to buy ourselves at this Ashern hunt and won the event by bagging 23 out of 25 sharp-tail grouse. The Calcutta purse was worth several thousand dollars.

The One Shot Antelope Hunt, Lander, Wyoming

The granddaddy of all the hunts is the One Shot Antelope Hunt held annually every September in Lander, Wyoming. It began in 1940 when the Governor of Wyoming challenged the Governor of Colorado to put together a three-man team and compete to see which team could kill their antelope with just one shot, and if the teams tied, the time of the shot would be the deciding factor. The objective was to make a clean kill with one shot; however the rules also stipulated that if the antelope was merely wounded, it immediately would be humanely dispatched with a second shot. Of course this second shot disqualified the hunter for a one shot score. Non-partisan guides accompanied each hunter and registered the time of the kills. The hunt received so much publicity that both governors thought it was an event that should be repeated every year. After WWII, the number of teams was increased to five governor teams, a celebrity team, a past shooter team, and later, when the space program was big news, an astronaut team was added. The hunt is a prestigious affair because only those invited by their Governor may attend. Thus, the list of Past Shooters reads like "Who's Who." The list of previous attendees includes movie stars like Roy Rogers, Robert Stack, Robert Fuller, John Russell, Rick Jason, and too many more to mention here. Laurence Melchior, the famous opera star, was a regular at the hunts for many years. His rendition of the National Anthem was very moving for all at the awards banquet. Chuck Yeager, WWII flying ace and the man who first broke the sound barrier also comes every year, as do many of the astronauts and sports greats. Once you have shot on a team you automatically become a member of the Past Shooter's Club and may come back each year to participate in the many special festivities that are arranged by the event committee and the town's people. Several hundred Past Shooters attend each year; however one may only be on a team once in their lifetime. The One Shot Antelope Hunt is an exciting and colorful event with great camaraderie among old friends that makes them come back year after year.

Remember I mentioned that the Governors of Colorado and Wyoming were the original founders of the One Shot Antelope Hunt so there is always a Colorado and Wyoming Governor's Team. In the thirty some years that I have attended the hunt, the two most outstanding Governors were John Love of Colorado and Ed Herschler of Wyoming. As different as two humans can be, these colorful individuals did a great deal to make the hunt a big success.

John Love served two terms as Governor and then went on to become a United States Senator. He had a great sense of humor and was a wonderful storyteller, which made him the most popular speaker at the One Shot banquets. He had developed a kind of Indian *Pidgin* English, which he used most effectively in telling stories about our government in Washington. Washington D.C. was referred to as "camp run-a-muck on the Poto-muck," the President was called "the big

My wife Ruthie with Robert Stack at One Shot Antelope Hunt, 1990.

chief" and the legislature the "council." Using these terms and others, he wove many humorous stories about our government and everyone looked forward to his time at the podium. On the banquet night with several hundred hunters in the audience and all the Governors on the stage behind him, John Love related this wonderful story.

"Last night I dreamed I had died and gone to heaven. When I reached the pearly gates St. Peter ushered me into a building with a long hallway. There were doors alphabetically marked with the names of each state— Alabama, Arizona, Arkansas, etc. We walked down the hall until we came to the door-marked Wyoming and entered. All of the walls were lined with clocks, some with pendulums swinging, others flashing electronically, all ticking away. While we were looking at one of the clocks, its hand jumped a full minute. I asked, what does that mean? And, St. Peter replied, "That means someone down in Wyoming has sinned!" A few seconds later another clock's hand jumped about ten minutes and St.

Peter said, "That means a mortal sin has been committed in Wyoming!" About that time I asked, "Where is Ed Herschler's clock?" Nonchalantly, St. Peter replied, "Oh we keep Hershler's clock down in the kitchen to use as a fan!"

It took the crowd many minutes to stop laughing because just that year 60 Minutes had featured a story about Herschler's involvement in a gambling scandal in the town of Rock Springs, Wyoming. Ed was well known as a hard partier, a gambler, and with some questionable political affiliations so Love's story really hit home. Ed just sat there on the stage with a big smile on his face. Despite his background, he was probably the most loved Governor in Wyoming's history. To demonstrate how much he was loved, Ed was a Democrat but most Republicans voted for him. He was the typical Wyoming cowboy complete with the big hat, western cut clothes, cowboy boots and a wonderful congenial smile. Everyone knew him and despite his reputation as a rascal, he had a jillion friends all over the country.

A high point for me was in 1983 when I was able to get my son Matt involved in the hunt. He was invited to shoot on an Iowa team headed by Governor Terry Branstad, with the other position filled by a friend, Gary Kirke of Des Moines. Matt also had the pleasure of being Ed's hunting partner a few years later. Matt said, "Dad, never in my life, have I ever had as much fun as today hunting with Governor Ed Herschler!" After they killed their antelope, as is the custom, they tail-gated for a while, and then after a few drinks, when they no longer felt any pain, they headed for Lander to check in at hunt headquarters. Matt was anxious to record their score but Ed insisted on stopping at every ranch along the way. They were invited in with open arms to have a drink so after quite a few stops they were both really smashed. As they pulled up to the check-in ranch to register their score, the crowd greeted them with a tremendous ovation. Things like this are what endeared Ed to the people of Wyoming; he was a down to earth human being to whom everyone could relate.

Ed and I attended a number of the same hunts for several

years, so I got to know him quite well. On two different occasions we sat together on United Airline's flights from Reno where we had both attended the Carlsberg invitational hunt. I learned that Ed's wife had a serious illness, so behind his happy countenance was a worried and empathetic husband.

Iowa Democratic Governor Harold Hughes invited me to be on his team in 1969. I was at the peak of my shooting career, and this is probably the only reason why he invited me because I wasn't a Democrat! As it turned out all three of us missed the antelope with our first shot. Had my partners both made one-shot kills and I missed, I really would have been roasted. After this hunt I became a member of the "Past Shooter Club" and active in the organization's politics. I was nominated to be a Director of the club and served several years in that capacity. In 1974 I became its Chairman. In this position I had an enjoyable role in the planning of the festivities, which included working closely with the Shoshone Indians who were and still are a big part of the ceremonies. Herman St. Clair, the Chief of the Shoshone tribe, became a good friend and I learned to admire him greatly.

For a long time, I had felt strongly that the club should be doing something for the good of the area and its wildlife. I began talking to people about a conservation thrust as the reason for our existence. One of our members, Norden Van Horne, conceived the idea to provide watering places for antelope and other wildlife. Thinking this was a wonderful program to adopt, I asked Norden to make a presentation to the Board of Directors and his plan was accepted. Water was always a problem in the west and without regular rain fall, many times the wildlife was in trouble. His plan was to draw water from previous oil well drillings which had not produced oil and which had been capped off. To accomplish this a cement pool was constructed with a hood over it to prevent evaporation and to trap condensation. This water benefited not only wildlife but also livestock. The program was titled "Water for Wildlife" and we formed a non-profit foundation to raise money. This foundation is functioning to this day and has built numerous "guzzlers" as these wells are called.

In 1974 through a friendship with astronaut Ron Evans

(who I had met on a hunt in Hawaii) I arranged for an Astronaut Team to join the One Shot competition. Ron called me one day to inquire, "Would you like to have a Russian Cosmonaut Team also?" (At that time there was a Russian Cosmonaut group training with our people in Houston.) I jumped at the opportunity. And, much to our horror, the Russians almost beat us at our own game. They killed three antelope but were defeated by our astronaut team—Joe Allen, Stuart Roosa, and David Scott, who had also killed three but at an earlier recorded time. The two things I remember most about the Russians was first their astonishment at how Americans carried firearms around so freely and casually (they observed that every Wyoming pick-up truck had a gun rack in the back window), and secondly how they drank their vodka straight and from a full 8-ounce water glass!

Activities for the Past Shooters include a day of shooting events at a special range in a canyon near town, an extraordinary luncheon at a local rancher's hacienda, and a day at Sink's Canyon, a spectacular canyon up in the mountains a few miles from Lander. Here the Shoshone Indians pitch their teepees and hold a ceremony where they bless the bullets of each team member. Additional shooting events are held and everyone relaxes in the beautiful mountain air. On Friday evening the banquet is followed by an outdoor ceremony with the Shoshone Indians. Teepees are pitched near the banquet hall and a huge fire is started. The team members are seated around the fire as the story of the hunt is recited in a ceremonial voice in the Shoshone tradition.

"The great Shoshone tribe and the white man have joined forces this fall to hunt together and make sure that there will be enough food for everyone during the long winter to come. Let us dance together and pray to the Great Spirit that we will be successful tomorrow."

With that the Shoshone Indians started a ceremonial dance to the beat of many drums. There are at least fifty Shoshone dancers ranging in age from three up, including men and women. The authentic Shoshone costumes are colorful and beautifully made with bleached antelope hides and beadwork. The team members wearing special orange scarves join in the ceremonial dance. In the cool mountain air, by the flickering light of the big fire, and to the rhythmic beat of the drums your mind takes you back to a different time and place. This is a very moving ceremony that sets the tone for the hunt the next morning.

Following the day of hunting on Saturday, a banquet is held for the presentation of awards to the winning team. Those team members who miss their one shot are required to come up on the stage, be dressed like an Indian woman and dance with the Shoshone squaws. From personal experience I can tell you that dancing with the squaws up there on the stage is very embarrassing. As part of the ceremony each losing team member is required to give a short speech explaining why he missed his one shot. The stories and excuses concocted get pretty wild and this is the fun part of the evening.

At one of the banquets they were auctioning off some art prints and other items to raise money for Water for Wildlife. When I came into the banquet hall I was wearing a brown western felt hat, which was festooned with pins and medals I have collected during my shooting travels all over the world; so many in fact that it weighed about ten pounds. This hat had become sort of a trademark for me and had been used in many of our advertising pictures. When I sat down at one of the tables near the stage, I took the hat off and set it on the table. One of my friends grabbed my hat and threw it up to the auctioneer and told him to auction it off. He thought that I would probably have to spend a couple hundred dollars to buy it back and everyone would have a good laugh. However, the first bid on the hat was for two thousand dollars and it was no longer funny to me! Magazine publisher Bob Petersen and a famous hat collector from Hollywood by the name of David Halopoff proceeded to get into a bidding war and finally Halopoff bought my old sweaty hat for $6500.00!

I really prized that hat and was a little upset about it at first. Halopoff mollified me a bit by telling me that at some point he would contribute it to the One Shot Museum in Lander. As it turned out, he passed away in 1998 and true to his promise, his widow sent me the hat so I could give it to the museum. It now resides there beside the Ruger, One Shot Rifle that had been awarded to me the year I was Chairman of the hunt. I was further consoled by the fact that several articles were written about the hat in shooting magazines so it ended up being exceptional publicity for my sportswear business, plus it raised money for the Water for Wildlife.

The Grand National Quail Hunt, Enid, Oklahoma

Another very prestigious hunt is the Grand National Quail Hunt, an invitational hunt held in Enid, Oklahoma every November. Attendance list for this hunt reads like "Who's Who" also and includes many movie, TV, and country western celebrities. A new shooter is called a "Bobby" (named after the Bob White quail) and are put on teams for the Saturday hunt. The opening event is a skeet and trap shoot at the gun club on Thursday. This is followed by a cocktail and dinner reception where the guides and teams are assigned. At this reception Roy Clark and Tennessee Ernie Ford put on an impromptu performance that lasted over an hour and was more entertaining than if it had been a feature show on a big stage in Las Vegas. They really brought the house down!

Landowners are included in all the festivities for without their lands to hunt on, there would be no hunt. Friday is the Qualifying Round Quail Hunt and points are awarded on a scoring system that allots points for birds bagged, bonus points for doubles, triples, and six birds with six shots. Added bonus points are given for using a smaller gauge gun such as a 20, 28, or 410-gauge. The same scoring system is used on Saturday's Championship Round Quail Hunt. Points are deducted for missed shots and field judges make certain rules are followed. There is another big banquet on Friday night. On Saturday one of the high points of the hunt for me is a brunch that is held out in the field, usually at one of the ranches. Saturday night is the gala presentation banquet with big name entertainment. Awards are given for the High Team, Top Gun, Past Shooter's Championship, Master's Cup, and a special award for the highest individual score by a "Bobby." In my first year at the hunt in 1987 I was fortunate to win a beautiful Winchester Model 23, 20-gauge double barrel shotgun for being the high Bobby. That year I got a big thrill out of hunting with Tennessee Ernie Ford and Roy Clark of Grand Ole Opry fame. Like the One Shot hunt, once you've been invited, you become a Past Shooter and may come back every year to participate in the special activities for the Past Shooters. The Bob Allen Bush Coat was adopted as the special uniform for this hunt and it always warms my heart.

As a side note, all of these "party" hunts have many things in common. As an example, the first day is usually some kind of a shooting event followed by a cocktail/dinner reception. The second day has special activities followed again by a cocktail/dinner party. Saturday is usually the big hunting day followed by an awards banquet. Most of the hunts are patterned after the One Shot Antelope Hunt, which is the Grand Daddy of them all.

The One Box Pheasant Hunt, Broken Bow, Nebraska

For pheasant hunters the Nebraska One Box Pheasant Hunt held each November in Broken Bow, is outstanding! The Nebraska Governor sponsors this hunt and five-man teams are made up of invited hunters. Each team is given one box of shotgun shells, hence the name of the hunt. Guides serve as referees and accompany the teams to hunt on ranches provided by landowners.

Matt and I put on our trick shooting demonstration at the gun club there one year when Matt was only twelve years old. The crowd gave us tremendous applause and it was a big thrill for Matt performing before an adult audience for the first time. Matt was put on a team with Ron Evans and three other Astronauts for the big Saturday hunt—quite a thrill for a young boy! I always enjoy coming to Broken Bow because it had been a regular stop for me prior to WWII when I was traveling Nebraska for Johnson & Johnson. I would stay at the Arrow Hotel (appropriate name for a town named Broken Bow) and it was now where most of the hunters stayed for the hunt. In the early days I always remembered the Arrow as being the hotel that, for fire emergencies, had a big rope with knots in it coiled and tied up by the window in each room. I remembered the hotel for another funny memory also. At dinner in the hotel coffee shop one night I asked for a fruit cocktail but was told by the waitress "Sorry sir, we don't serve mixed drinks here!" The hunt is a big social event for this town of about four thousand people and the Saturday night banquet is attended by great numbers who come out to meet the many celebrities participating in the hunt. The friendly hospitality of this western town's people makes this hunt an outstanding event. Here again I was proud that our bush coat had been adopted as the official uniform for all the hunters.

The Annual Two Shot Goose Hunt

The event is held in Lamar, Colorado every fall and is a unique and very enjoyable hunt. Usually the hunters gather in Denver and ride down to Lamar on chartered buses. The bus ride is part of the fun as there is a bar set up and the three-hour ride gives everyone a chance to get acquainted. Jokes reign and everyone arrives in Lamar in a great mood. My first year at the hunt, Roy Rogers was on the bus. I had known him for several years and it was indeed fun to see him again. Evidently the word had spread in Lamar that he was coming. When the bus pulled up in front of our motel half the town of Lamar, including the high school band, was waiting for him. We were all tired and anxious to get checked in to clean up and I am sure Roy felt the same way. But, God bless him, he got off the bus and spent the next hour and a half with the crowd, signing autographs and posing for pictures with the children. He said later that those children were his fans and he couldn't let them down. That is just one of the many reasons why Roy has to be the all time greatest western cowboy star!

The Lamar hunt had all the usual banquets, shooting events, and great camaraderie. Guides were provided for the Saturday hunt and prizes were awarded at the banquet that night for teams and individuals who had killed the most geese with their two shots. One year the winner had killed three geese—a single with one shot and a lucky second shot that killed two geese at once. All geese shot were cleaned and frozen for us to take home after the hunt.

The 16½ Shot Turkey Hunt

After having participated in the One Shot Antelope Hunt and the Enid Grand National Quail Hunt, Carl Langford, the mayor of Orlando, Florida started a hunt, which he called the Sixteen and ½ Shot Turkey Hunt. I'm not sure where the name came from but the ½ shot portion of it undoubtedly applied to the hunters. By invitation only, hunters gathered in Orlando for a banquet on Thursday night. Here each hunter was assigned to a team and a hunting camp. In Florida almost all hunting area is leased to hunters and clubs for yearly hunting rights—there is very little free hunting area left! After the banquet, your hunter takes you to his camp. A local dentist and some friends owned my camp. They had moved four large house trailers to the camp and had arranged them in a square around an open sided cook/dining shed in the center. The trailers were air conditioned so this was a pretty deluxe camp and that made me very happy. The owners pitched in on preparing the meals and because of their propensity to include jalapeno peppers in almost everything, I thought they were going to kill me. I ran out of Rolaids the first day! The hunting was for turkey, deer, and wild pig with points being awarded for each of them. We hunted from special vehicles—pick up trucks with seats mounted high on a special platform so you could see out over the palmettos. They used dogs to stir up the deer and placed us on stands where we stood waiting for the dogs to drive something by. The Florida deer are very small—probably only weigh about a hundred pounds! While I was standing by a tree, one of them ran up and stopped a mere twenty-five feet away from me as he listened to the baying of the dogs. He was so beautiful and so small I didn't have the heart to shoot him so I just watched him bound off as the dogs approached. The next day they put me in a tree stand where I was able to bag my first wild turkey. That same day I killed a two hundred pound boar; however I didn't have enough points to win anything and my team was in the same shape. The hunt culminated in an outing that began at noon on the Mormon Ranch headquarters that was located east of Orlando about half way to the Cape. Incidentally, I was interested to learn that this is one of the largest cattle ranches in the world—surprising to find it in Florida! A luncheon had been prepared for us and then we had some shooting competition, saw a trick-shooting exhibition by my old friend Tom Frye followed by a barbecue banquet. After the banquet the Mormon Ranch cowboys put on an authentic rodeo that was exciting. All in all it was a very enjoyable hunt with many unusual features.

I'd be remiss if I didn't make a few remarks about Carl Langford. He had been Mayor of Orlando for several terms and was very popular there despite being a real character. He almost got arrested in Lander, Wyoming for stealing street signs for his collection. Only the intervention of sheriff Pee Wee McDougall, who was also one of the hunt officials, saved him. At the Enid Grand National Quail Hunt I heard that he again almost went to jail for firing his pistol into the ceiling of his motel room. Luckily nobody was hurt.

The first year I was invited to his hunt, I flew into Orlando on Delta Air Lines. When my flight arrived at the gate, two policemen came on board and conferred with the flight attendant who then made an announcement, "Will passenger Bob Allen identify himself?" When I raised my hand, the policemen elbowed their way down the crowded aisle to me and then escorted me off the plane, down the stairs by the jet way, and in full view of all the passengers they put me in the back seat of their police car. I'm sure the passengers must have thought I was *public enemy number one*. At any rate, once in the car, the officers leaned back and said "Mayor Langford welcomes you to Orlando Mr. Allen" and they took me to my hotel. Boy was I sweating! Langford had struck again!

The Buffalo Bill Celebrity Shootout

In Cody, Wyoming they have an annual celebrity shoot that is called The Buffalo Bill Celebrity Shootout, a fund-rais-

With General Norman Schwarzkopf at Buffalo Bill Celebrity Shoot, Cody, Wyoming, 1999.

er for the Buffalo Bill Historical Center. This shoot combines skeet, trap, five stand, sporting clays, and rifle shooting. Their cocktail receptions and banquets are really outstanding and fun to attend. Former U. S. Senator Alan Simpson is usually the Master of Ceremonies and tears the crowd up with his great humor. He's the one who coined the phrase, "In Wyoming, our idea of gun control is how steady you can hold your gun!" At the 1999 shoot I had the great pleasure of shooting in the same squad with Alan Simpson and General Norman Schwarzkopf. Those two are great storytellers and kept us laughing constantly. Held during August each year, Cody is a beautiful place to visit. Yellowstone Park is only a hundred miles away and makes an interesting side trip. The Cody rodeo is a must to attend also. The Buffalo Bill Historical

Center contains the largest collection of guns in the United States and possibly the world. Several years ago Winchester donated their large collection to the center and it has since been supplemented by the addition of the Ruger collection and others. Their collection of western and Indian art and memorabilia is the most complete I've ever seen. The Historical Center is now Wyoming's largest tourist attraction.

The Carlsberg California Honker Hunt

One of the most interesting hunts I ever attended was the California Honker Hunt; a goose-hunting event sponsored by two Los Angeles brothers; Art and Dick Carlsberg. A strictly invitational hunt, I was always honored to be invited because most of the hunters were movers and shakers or big name celebrities. Roy Rogers and his son attended every year. There were always several astronauts and the California Governor often attended.

The Carlsberg boys were as avid hunters as you can find. They were both born on a ranch in Alturas, California and hunted constantly as youths. After graduating from UCLA they settled in Los Angeles and founded the Carlsberg Financial Co. One of the big buildings in Century City carried their name for many years. Both were big game hunters but Art was the more dedicated of the two when it came to big game.

Hunters would gather in Reno, Nevada for a cocktail reception. The next morning buses would take us all to the Carlsberg lodge which was located on a lake near Alturas, California. There were two days of hunting with local ranchers providing hunting areas and guides. Each night there was a delightful banquet with toasts, speeches, and presentations to the hunters. An interesting part of the banquet on Saturday night was a ceremony honoring past participants who had passed away during the year. As their names were read off, someone just outside the door would fire a twelve-gauge shotgun; sounds corny but it made for an emotional moment.

Among their guests were show biz comics. Ken and Wendell Niles, famous radio announcers and gag writers for

Me with General Chuck Yeager at Carlsberg California Honker Hunt.

the big radio/TV shows, were usually the Masters of Ceremony. They always would work in a one liner for every hunter in the room. One they directed at me got a big laugh from everyone including me. Ken pointed at me and said "and there sits Bob Allen in all his sartorial splendor, L.L. Bean's illegitimate son!" He said that he and his brother came from a town in Idaho so small that when you plugged in your electric razor, all the lights in town dimmed and that it was so small that the only prostitute in town was still a virgin. Astronaut General Joe Engle would put on an imitation of General Patton that brought down the house. Those banquets were about as entertaining as you can get plus the food was always excellent. The Carlsberg lodge could sleep about sixty hunters but you always had to double up with another hunter. I shared a room once with Monroe Lutrick from Tulsa; and he wants me to tell everyone that he really does not snore. Another time I shared a room with famed big game hunter Elgin Gates who was also a great trapshooter. Another roommate was Maurice Stans, formerly of President Nixon's staff, who wrote the book "The Terrors of Justice" which concerned the Watergate fiasco. The camaraderie at this hunt was the big attraction but the goose hunting was darn good too.

Tragedy was to strike the Carlsberg family! Art was on a safari in Afghanistan and, in a strange accident, fell off a mountain ledge and was killed. Two years later he was posthumously awarded the Weatherby Big Game Hunter of The Year award. Then to cap it off, Dick Carlsberg was grouse hunting in Scotland with some guests and died of a heart attack. This was too much for any family to bear! They were great guys! Real entrepreneurs in the business world, outstanding sportsmen, and the finest hosts I've ever encountered. They and the hunt they originated will always be remembered fondly.

The Foss, Floyd and Dean Pheasant Hunt

South Dakota was host to the Foss, Floyd and Dean Pheasant Hunt every October. It was named after the founders, Governor Joe Foss, TV stations owner Joe Floyd, and real estate entrepreneur Hoadley Dean. A strictly invitational hunt, it included hunters from all over the country and was aimed at attracting industrial growth for South Dakota. Proof of its effectiveness was the sewing factory I located in Arlington, South Dakota as a result of my being exposed to what South Dakota had to offer indirectly through the hunt.

The hunt was always held in the state capital Pierre, South Dakota and all of the participants stayed in the same hotel. There were hunt breakfasts and banquets every day. On the first night everyone would be assigned to teams and guides. Local ranchers furnish the lands to hunt on and do some of the guiding as well. The entire hunt was well organized.

Attended by many famous people, one year at the hunt I had the very great pleasure and honor of hunting with one of my heroes, General Jimmy Doolittle, the commander of the first bombers to bomb Japan in early 1942 just after Pearl Harbor. Using B-25's modified to fly off our aircraft carrier "Enterprise", these bombers terrified the Japanese and gave a great morale boost to the United States when everyone was still reeling from the Pearl Harbor fiasco. At the time of the hunt, Jimmy was 80 years old but you'd never know it the way he walked the fields and ditches always insisting on walking in the heaviest cover. He was no slouch as a shooter and regularly got his limit. At this hunt I learned to know Jimmy well and then had the pleasure of shooting with him at some of the other party hunts.

Strange and hilarious things happen! After one of the banquets we conceived the idea of going across the river to south Pierre for a nightcap. As we were getting in our car in the parking lot, a brand new Buick automobile drove up to park right beside us. One of our group, Vern Gagne, opened our car door to get in and accidentally banged it against this new car that had just parked beside us. The driver of the new car immediately jumped out and took offense over the door being banged against his new car. He was a BIG Rancher, about six feet eight, and weighing at least three hundred pounds. In his bib overalls he was a terrific sight, something for the comic books. To make the situation worse, he was blind drunk and immediately wanted to fight Gagne. Of course he didn't know that Gagne was the World Champion Professional Wrestler. Joe Foss, who was governor of South Dakota at that time, jumped out of the car and proceeded to calm the rancher down. When things had settled, Foss introduced the rancher to his would-be opponent by saying, "and I give you Vern Gagne the famous world Champion Wrestler . . . the man you wanted to pick a fight with." With this proclamation the entire scene changed because the rancher was an adamant wrestling fan and Gegne was one of his idols. He ended up falling all over Gagne and wanting to buy us all a drink. As we drove off, we all began to razz Gagne by saying that if it had been a fight, we thought that big rancher would have cleaned Gagne's plow!

These hunts were held in the years when South Dakota had a tremendous pheasant population. It was normal to get up several hundred pheasants out of one big field. When Joe Foss stepped down as Governor, his successor changed the name of the hunt to The Governor's Pheasant Hunt. The hunting isn't quite as good as it was years ago but is still the best pheasant hunting in the United States and this hunt is one of the best organized events I have attended.

The Black Hills Turkey Hunt

South Dakota's Governor also plays host to a wild turkey hunt that is held out in the spectacular Black Hills near Rapid City. I attended two of these hunts and they were great fun but really challenging. Those Black Hills give the birds great cover and the steep terrain really gets your heart pumping. You really have to be part billy-goat to run up and down those ridges. If you've never experienced the thrill of calling in and shooting a wild turkey, you have missed one of America's greatest hunting thrills.

The Big Country Celebrity Quail Hunt

In February of each year the annual Big Country Celebrity Quail Hunt is held in Abilene, Texas. This is a very efficiently organized operation that is a fundraiser for Disability Resources, an organization that trains, finds jobs, and boards disadvantaged people. Celebrities are invited and local ranches and sportsmen provide guides and places to hunt. One year at this hunt I had the greatest quail hunt of a lifetime when we got up numerous coveys of quail.

A trapshoot is held the first day of the hunt as a warm-up and there are the usual luncheons and banquets every day. The friendliness of the people of Abilene makes this one of my favorite party hunts. A good part of the hunt is getting to know the ranchers who are rugged and wonderful people. At the hunt last year I was riding in the back of a pick-up truck along with two other hunters and a bird dog. Every once in a while the truck would go under some trees with low hanging branches and each time the dog would let out a deep growl. The dog's owner said that in the past the dog would snap at branches as they went by but one time he snapped and his teeth locked into a branch and wouldn't let go. The dog was flipped about fifty feet up in the air and dropped on the road unconscious. He came around okay later but now, whenever he encounters branches, he just growls a lot.

The Kurt Russell Celebrity Elk Hunt

One year, along with several other outdoor products manufacturers, we sponsored the Kurt Russell Celebrity Elk Hunt on Colorado's western slope. About sixty celebrities from movies, TV, sports, and politics attended. A temporary camp was set up in a canyon at the eight thousand foot elevation in the mountains. This was not roughing it in any sense! A small stream was dammed up and stocked with trout, nylon tents with floors and zippered doors were pitched, four hot tubs were installed, and a big circus tent was set up to provide a dining room in which a New Orleans caterer provided gourmet meals. Several gasoline generators provided power for lights, electric blankets, and heat for the hot tubs. We were all very disappointed when, at the last moment, Goldie Hawn had to cancel and did not attend.

We hunters flew to Grand Junction, Colorado where we were picked up by hosts from the hunt and driven up to the camp. I arrived late the first year and didn't reach the camp until after dark. I was immediately shown to my sleeping tent so that I could freshen up before dinner. Gifts, donated by manufacturers, for each of the hunters were lined up on the bed and included, almost unbelievably, a Benelli 12-gauge semi-automatic shotgun, an H. & K. high power rifle, Bushnell binoculars, a duffle bag, shooting glasses, an assortment of smaller items and a hunting coat which was furnished by my company, Bob Allen Sportswear.

Going from my tent to the dining tent I was shocked to see tables with white tablecloths, china and silver service, and an extensive bar with waiters to serve us. The meal catered by this Cajun food caterer from New Orleans was outstanding. After dinner each hunter was assigned a guide and a hunting companion. The hunt was to be for both elk and deer with points given for each. Hunters were formed into teams and there were trophies for teams as well as individuals. I met my guide and was told to meet him at breakfast and be ready to leave for the day's hunt right after breakfast that was scheduled for four A. M. It was to be a short night and not much fun to roll out of that electric blanket into the freezing mountain air.

My hunting partner turned out to be the baseball great Billy Martin who I remembered as being the guy who invented the idea of kicking sand on the umpire. Kurt Russell's ten-year-old son also went with us and turned out to be a great asset as he had the sharpest eyes I've ever seen and spotted deer and elk long before the rest of us. Billy was a great story-teller and had us laughing constantly.

I didn't get a shot at an elk but did kill a buck deer. All of the game killed on the hunt was butchered and delivered to institutions in the Grand Junction area. Unfortunately the hunt got some bad publicity in the Enquirer. Somehow they heard of the hunt and that Goldie was going to attend with Kurt. They wrote it up to sound like it was going to be a bunch of big shots having a contest to see who could kill the most animals; completely the opposite of the philosophy of the hunt. We had Officers from the Colorado Department of Natural Resources in the camp to assure that we all had proper hunting licenses and legally killed our game. It was a great outing with many interesting people in a beautiful environment and it was a shame that the Enquirer besmirched it.

During the hunt I had constant problems breathing and some chest pains that I mistakenly blamed on the high elevation at which we were hunting—sometimes as high as twelve thousand feet. I was constantly out of breath and had some burning chest pains, which Rolaids did not take away. A few days after the hunt I was pheasant hunting back in Iowa and had some of the same symptoms. I was alarmed enough that I called Sean Cunningham, my doctor in Des Moines, who made me stop hunting immediately and report to him at the hospital. After a few tests he put me into the hospital and scheduled by-pass surgery for the next day even though it was Thanksgiving eve. He said I was the luckiest Irishman in the world that I didn't have a massive coronary out there in the wilds of the Colorado Mountains. I guess I'll never forget that party hunt!

The Heartland Celebrity Pheasant Hunt

In 1998 the Heartland Celebrity Pheasant Hunt was held for the first time in Osceola, Iowa. It has attracted a lot of interesting celebrities primarily because Osceola is the home of the Company that bought me out, Boyt Harness Company. Between their President Tony Caliguiri and me we were able to publicize this hunt and use our contacts from other hunts to invite celebrity hunters. Iowa is famous for its pheasant hunting so many were excited to accept an invitation to participate. As an example, last year's hunt was attended by motion picture stars Marshall and Lindy Teague, John DiSanti, Roy Rogers Jr. Anne Lockhart, Leslie Easterbrook as well as song writer T. J. Clay, artist Larry Anderson, and Iowa's Governor Terry Branstad.

Here again, hunters are put into teams and awards are made for teams and individuals. At the big Saturday night banquet, an auction is held to sell items donated by the celebrities and local businesses. As an example, I donated a .22 caliber rifle that I had used in our trick shooting act for many years; it brought in $1800.00 for a youth conservation project in Osceola. Steve Kanaly, star of TV series "Dallas", donated his white Western hat. An Osceola housewife bid two thousand dollars for it probably thinking Steve went with the hat.

The Louise Mandrell Celebrity Shoot

With the growing popularity of the new shotgun shooting sport, "sporting clays", several shoots have sprung up similar in organization and activity to the party hunts described here. Outstanding among these is the Louise Mandrell Celebrity Shoot held annually in Nashville, Tennessee as a benefit for her favorite charity, the Boy Scouts. Each year she raises over a hundred thousand dollars for that worthy organization. Through her show biz following, her shoot probably has more celebrities per square inch than any other similar event. Her shoot is set up like a Pro-Am golf tournament with shooters paying a large fee for the privilege of shooting in a squad with a celebrity. I've been involved each year because Bob Allen Sportswear has contributed clothing and shooting accessories for the event. As you might expect, the entertainment at the banquets during this shoot is outstanding. Louise puts on a show that tops anything I've ever seen! She is an extremely

With beautiful Louise Mandrell at her Celebrity Shoot in Nashville.

gracious host for the shoot and thus it has grown in attendance each year. Louise and her husband John Haywood are avid shooters as are Barbara Mandrell and her family. If I had to choose just one of these party hunts to attend, it would be a tough choice for me to decide between Louise's shoot or the One Shot Antelope Hunt in Wyoming.

The Charlton Heston Celebrity Shoot

The National Rifle Association (NRA) sponsors the Charlton Heston Celebrity Shoot each year. Held in California near the homes of show biz celebrities, it attracts many of them. Charlton Heston is a dedicated hunter and shooter and participates in the festivities. This shoot includes shotgun events like Sporting Clays and Five Stand as well as some unusual pistol and rifle events. A TV show is filmed here each year and is shown on stations all over the country for the following year providing good exposure for the shooting sports. Recently the event was renamed "The Hollywood Celebrity Shoot" and is now held in Los Angeles and promoted by an interesting guy, Sandy Abrams.

To summarize, you can see from all of this that being involved in these events has been a wonderful experience for me, and great publicity for Bob Allen Sportswear. Although I sold out and retired, I currently have a public relations agreement with my old company that involves me attending these party hunts as well as the Grand American National Championship trapshoot. It's a tough job but someone has to do it!

Chapter 14

Shooters and Shooting

Shooters in The War Effort

At the start of WWII our Armed Services desperately needed people who could train aerial gunners. Champion trap and skeet shooters were a natural for this job. All of the services quickly enlisted their aid. It was fortunate that a great pool of trained experts existed in this time of emergency.

Phil Miller—one of our champion trap shooters was given a direct commission to enlist other top shooters into the Air Corps gunnery program and was instrumental in getting me into the program. *Robert Stack* had won many California and National Skeet Shooting Championships before he went into the Navy as an instructor. *Clark Gable* also had some skeet experience and was sent to England where he became a Gunnery Officer for a B-17 Bomb. Group. He flew missions on B-17's and also made gunnery training films. I still have one in my library.

Johnny Broughton and D. Lee Braun were instructors at the Combat Gunnery Officer's School in Laredo, Texas. While I was stationed at Orlando I was sent to Laredo to get my

Gunnery Officer rating and wings. I remember vividly sitting in a hot, non air-conditioned classroom located next to the skeet ranges in Laredo and trying to concentrate on my studies with the sounds of skeet shooting right outside my window. After the classes were over I'd race for the skeet ranges to shoot a round or two. D. Lee Braun went with Remington after the war and became one of the top pro shooters. Johnny Broughton started following the trap and pigeon circuit like me and was undoubtedly one of the top shooters in the country. Billy Perdue, a skeet and pigeon champion, was also a Navy gunnery instructor. This was one instance where wartime experiences could be utilized in civilian life!

Joe Hiestand had been one of our nation's best trap-shooter before the war. He was given a direct commission as a Gunnery Officer at Fort Myers, Florida Gunnery School. In 1943 when I was assigned the job of Staff Gunnery Officer for the 9th Bomb. Group in Orlando, Florida, Joe invited me to come down and inspect his facilities at Fort Myers.

This trip precipitated a really funny situation on the flight down. I asked a pilot friend of mine, a Captain Bill Quinlan, to fly me down in a B-17. About ten miles out he called the tower at the gunnery school airport to ask for landing instructions. A feminine voice cleared us to land and gave us runway 90. We swung out over the gulf and were on final approach to land, with gear and flaps all down, when all of a sudden we see two P-47 fighter planes taking off directly towards us. Quinlan firewalled the throttles, pulled up the gear and flaps, and when he had everything under control and had missed the P-47's he got on the radio and proceeded to raise hell with the gal in the tower. She listened patiently as he ran off at the mouth and then calmly stated, "I beg your pardon SIR but there is no B-17 landing at this airport." We had been talking to the gunnery school airport tower but were mistakenly landing at Paige Field, a P-47 Fighter training school located about five miles from the gunnery school. Quinlan was so embarrassed he almost refused to continue on and land at the proper airport. When we landed, he called the WAC in the tower and apologized. It was an honest mistake as he had never flown into Ft. Myers before and didn't realize that there were two airports there—he just spotted the airport and started to land! I don't know if he ever learned his lesson.

Joe Hiestand met us, took us to lunch, and then gave us an escorted tour of the school. One of their training exercises was called "moving base." Gunnery students would sit on specially constructed seats in the back of a truck, which moved around a track similar to a racetrack. Traps to throw clay targets were mounted along the track at intervals—each presenting a different kind of trajectory to train the gunners on proper leading and the apparent motion method of shooting which was being taught then. Targets might be thrown away from the truck, back at it to catch up, high in the air, or along the ground. It was a tricky course and good training. Joe invited me to shoot the course with him and said he'd bet me five bucks and he'd shoot from the hip. I took him up real fast but regretted it later because Joe broke the 25 straight from the hip and I only broke about 20. He had shot the course so many times he had become bored with shooting in the regular fashion off the shoulder and started shooting from the hip just for fun.

Shooting Exhibitions

Shooting exhibitions, sometimes called trick shooting, began in our old west with the Buffalo Bill Western Show. Buffalo Bill and Annie Oakley were truly fine shots. Their shows were held in wide-open spaces where rifles and pistols could be fired with safety. As our population grew this type of show gradually disappeared and was replaced by trick shooting acts performed by ammunition company professionals. And, prior to WWII, ammunition companies like Winchester and Remington hired trick shooters to travel around the country to perform their skills. Their shows were in demand for county fairs, shooting tournaments and sporting events. One of the most famous trick shooters was Ad Topperwein of San

Antonio, Texas and his wife Plinky. When the war broke out the Topperweins and other professionals continued putting on their acts for the military bases throughout the country.

The Australian Shooters

Monte Carlo afforded an opportunity to meet fascinating people from all over the world. Several people spring to mind including an Australian shooter by the name of Keith Veall who I first met in 1947. We have maintained our friendship all these years. Keith first attracted my attention because of his relaxed way of shooting and his shooting ability. In order to shoot well, I have always been fussy about my clothing and equipment. As an example: my shooting coat or vest must have a gun pad with a smooth surface but a surface like leather, which will grip my gun and keep it from slipping. Before going out to shoot I always adjust my cap visor so it is in just the right position, insert my earplugs, and make sure my shooting glasses are clean. Most shooters go through a similar preparatory routine, but not Keith. He didn't own a shooting garment and always shot in a button-front cardigan sweater, which he never bothered to button. When he put the gun to his shoulder the sweater was generally wrinkled up under his gun butt—a situation that would have driven me crazy. Keith would nonchalantly walk out, put his gun up and shoot without any routine. He was very fast and generally dropped his birds very close to the trap. He quickly became a favorite of the gamblers because he placed well in most of the shoots.

Keith has constantly invited me to visit him in Melbourne, but I have never been able to take him up on his invitation. My daughter Abby went to Melbourne for a Variety Club convention and was royally greeted and entertained by Keith, his wife and family.

The Hungarian Shooters

Right after the war there were several Hungarians who were the top shooters and the ones you had to beat in order to win. One by the name of Strassburger was outstanding. Another was Dora Sandor who was shooting to win money to buy his wife out of a Russian concentration camp. Strassburger and Sandor usually placed in the prize money in every match despite the fact that they shot at long handicap yardages. They quickly became role models for me and I studied their technique every time they went out to shoot. The Secretary of the FITASC (International Shooting Federation) M. DeKiss, was also a Hungarian and we became friends.

One night at dinner he was telling stories about how rough it had been during the war when he served in the German army and when the Russians invaded Hungary. I razzed him by saying it should have been rough because he fought on the wrong side and lost. His reply was, "We had a choice of fighting for Germany or Russia and only an idiot would have fought for the barbarian Russians so I chose Germany as the lesser of two evils—but we didn't fight very hard!" He told another story which I've never forgotten. Evidently he came from a wealthy family that owned a lot of property and had a big estate with servants. Just before the Russians invaded, his parents moved out of their big house and into one of their servant's quarters so the Russians would leave them alone. Before moving out they tried to hide their wine cellar by bricking up the entrance and disguising it with cobwebs and dust. DeKiss said that the Russians who came were Siberians and just a cut above being savages. After taking over the big house it only took them a few hours to find the wine cellar. He also explained that the house was heated by fireplaces in every room and that his folks had enough firewood for the winter stacked up behind the house. The Russians were such slobs that they were too lazy to carry in the wood; instead they tore up windowsills and flooring for fuel. They were only there for a few weeks but totally trashed the beautiful estate.

The Italian Shooters

We soon found out that the Italian shooters were by far the best and dominated most of the shoots. They were very competitive and many of them were shooting for a living, in contrast to the wealthy French, Spanish, and Portuguese shooters who came primarily for sport. In the miss-and-out shoots, when it would get down to six or eight shooters, it was common for the remaining shooters to get together and agree on a split with the winner taking a little more than the others. The Italians did this constantly but when there was an American in the final group, they continued to shoot rather than split. We tried to kill them with kindness and one day the final group had six Americans and two Italians. We agreed to split with them but a few days later when the situation was reversed, they once again didn't give the Americans a chance to split. The splitting routine was foreign to us anyway so from then on we just shot it out with them.

European Gun Clubs

European gun clubs were unique to us because of the sophistication of their facilities. As an example, in each club one floor (usually just below ground level) was called the Armory and here you were issued a number for your shotgun and, when you were not shooting, your gun would always be in a rack at that number location. In return for a mandatory fee, you were provided with the gun rack and a small locker adjacent to it. The service also included wiping off your gun with oil and swabbing out the barrel after each time it was shot. Shotgun ammunition was also sold here and the number of different brands of shells offered always awed us Americans. In America the ammunition industry is a monopoly with basically only three brands of shotgun shells sold— Federal, Remington, and Winchester. In Europe it was common to see fifteen or twenty different brands offered; several each from Italy, France, Spain, and Portugal. For years the Italian shells were considered the best and dominated the market. We soon learned that there was no point in bringing shells with us, as the Italian shells were far superior.

Every gun club had a "planchon" (pattern board) where you could test fire your gun to check its point of impact and pattern. Usually there were two of these boards side by side so you could fire two shells for a comparison. The boards were made of heavy steel and a bucket of whitewash and a brush were kept beside them. Your shot left a definite impression in the wet whitewash. Shells of higher velocity made a bigger splash and you could quickly learn which brand of shells made the more desirable dense pattern required for clean pigeon kills.

Madame Guerlain

I learned about the difference in shells the hard way on one of my first European trips. Figuring that they would be superior to anything I could buy in Europe, I had brought along some of my favorite American shells. My first tournament was in Paris at the gun club in their city park, the Bois du Boulogne. I wasn't killing my pigeons cleanly and, at first, assumed it was my shooting. During the shoot I had become acquainted with Mr. and Mrs. Guerlain the world famous perfume makers in Paris. Madame Guerlain had been watching me shoot and made the comment that I should try some of her shells which were specially loaded by the Callens Company of Paris. She coaxed me into going to the "planchon" and comparing her Callens shells to my American brand. I was absolutely astounded to find that her shells not only gave a tighter and more uniform pattern but also, according to the splash their shot made on the board, were of much higher velocity. I immediately bought some of the Callens shells and there was a very noticeable improvement in my shooting. Madame Guerlain, I am very grateful for the friendly advice you gave me.

The Gunsmiths of Europe

The services of excellent gunsmiths were available in the Armory of European gun clubs. Sometimes gun makers such as Beretta or Perazzi would provide them. Collectively, they could fix just about any problem a shooter might have. One American shooter, Elmer Clemons of Port Clinton, Ohio, was shooting a Winchester Model 21 side-by-side, double barrel shotgun. The Model 21 is a fine pointing gun and is considered by many to be America's finest double gun. They did have some mechanical problems and one of them was "doubling" which means that both barrels go off at once. This is a disconcerting problem as the gun kicks like hell and, if you aren't on the pigeon, you have a loss without the second shot being there to save you. Elmer's gun was doubling and it was starting to get him down psychologically so he took it into the Armory to have it fixed.

A half dozen gunsmiths representing several countries gathered around his gun as it was taken apart. Elmer was standing by watching like an expectant father and was commencing to worry because they were doing a lot of jabbering in different languages. One of our shooters, Tony Banchero, could speak and understand French and Italian so Elmer asked him to translate what was being said. Tony listened for a few minutes and Elmer nervously asked, "What are they saying?" Tony replied that their comments didn't translate into English exactly but what it amounted to was, "Yuck, what a pile of junk!" It was obvious that the Europeans held our gun makers in disdain and probably for good reason. The Model 21 was the pet project of Spencer Olin of the Olin family that owned Winchester and Western Cartridge Company. I thought this was such a funny story that I told it to Spencer one time when I ran into him at a shoot, but he didn't think it was so funny and I think it affected our relationship for years. Despite the Model 21's problems it pointed so well that people shot them well and the guns became increasingly popular and expensive after Winchester stopped making them. A model 21 that probably originally sold for three hundred dollars now brings two or three thousand dollars regardless of condition.

Elmer Clemons

A word or two about Elmer Clemons is indicated because he was such an interesting character. He and his wife Hope attended the European shoots for several years. Elmer had lost an eye early in life and wore a black patch. He always wore a white cowboy hat so with his eye patch he was quite a distinctive-looking shooter. Although he wasn't one of our top shooters, he shot well enough so that he got into the prize money regularly. I mentioned earlier how sometimes the shooters would stop for a brief meeting and agree to a split of the prize money when one of the miss-and-out shoots got down to a half dozen shooters. In a situation like this, splitting was considered to be the courteous thing to do. Elmer had killed about eight pigeons straight and there were only a half dozen shooters out of the entry of over a hundred that were still straight. There were five Italians and Elmer. Elmer politely suggested to the group that they agree to split before proceeding. Among themselves, the Italians had decided that they could shoot Elmer out so they refused to split. Elmer was a gambler and knew immediately what was going on and it made him so angry that he was determined to out-shoot them. They shot four more birds with three of the Italians missing so it was down to Elmer and two Italians. At this point the Italians stopped and suggested a split to which Elmer gave a resounding "No!" The longer the shoot went, the better Elmer shot and he finally killed eighteen straight to win the shoot and the top prize money. This was one time the Italians misjudged and lost money because of their greed. We were really proud of Elmer and from then on he had the respect of everyone and particularly of the gamblers in the gallery.

The Lake and Shooters

There are several lakes in northwest Iowa that make up the Iowa Great Lakes. When I retired, I chose a home on West Lake Okoboji, which is a beautiful, spring-fed, blue water lake. The lake is completely surrounded by beautiful all-weather year around homes. Gone are many of the old lake "cottages." Lake frontage now sells for thousands of dollars a foot so the old cottages have been replaced by modern homes, each with dock and boats. Life here completely revolves around the lake and residents use boats for shopping and going to dinner. Although our house is on Lake Okoboji, our mailing address is Spirit Lake, Iowa. To further confuse the issue, there is a big lake named Spirit Lake and it is adjacent to our Lake Okoboji and is part of those Iowa Great Lakes.

The Okoboji Indians

With my background and interest in shooting, it is interesting to note the shooting history of Spirit Lake, Iowa. MacKinlay Kantor gave a fanciful history of the area in his best seller of 1961 titled "Spirit Lake." This area is the birthplace of the Okoboji Indians, a shooting group well known to all trap shooters. In the early nineteen hundreds the Okoboji Indian shoots were some of the largest and best known in the United States. In later years the organization moved to Ohio and exists to this day. Note the picture of the contestants in one of the early Okoboji Indian shoots. Interesting to me, as a shooting clothing designer and manufacturer, is the fact that not one of the shooters is wearing any kind of a shooting garment. It looks as though they shot in their Sunday *go to church* suits! The picture I am reproducing in my book is on display in the Iowa Maritime Museum on Lake Okoboji along with memorabilia from the Okoboji Indians. Around 1900 their traps were located on the lakeshore and they threw targets out over the lake (nobody worried about lead shot poisoning wildfowl then) and hundreds of targets, still intact, have been brought up by divers and are on display in the museum. I sent one of them to the White Flyer Company, the manufacturer of the targets, and Brian Skeuse owner of the company now, says it was manufactured around 1900 and is one of the oldest targets he has ever seen.

Three Spirit Lake Shooters in the Hall of Fame

In the early nineteen hundreds, two of the toughest trap shooters in the country both came from Spirit Lake; Fred Gilbert and Johnny Jahn. Both of them are in the Trapshooting Hall of Fame and now, with me living here, Spirit Lake becomes the only town in the country, that I know of, that can boast three shooters in the Hall of Fame. Fred Gilbert was gone by the time I began to shoot in 1938 but he

Okoboji Indians Shoot held on Lake Okoboji in August 1908.

achieved a tremendous reputation as a live pigeon champion and market hunter as well as a winning trap shooter. Back in those days it was common for shooters to challenge each other for money purses. It is said that Fred never lost one of those challenge races. In 1895 he set a world's record by killing thirty pigeons straight to win the World's Championship. In 1901 he won the British presentation cup as well as the Championship of America. His record of breaking 591 clay targets straight stood for many years and he won the high average honor for six consecutive years. In his lifetime he shot over a million targets plus, nobody knows how many shells he shot as a wildfowl market hunter. In 1919 at the age of 54 he had an average of .9753 on 6860 targets—an average almost as high as any shot now with improved guns and ammunition.

Johnny Jahn

I knew Johnny Jahn personally and he became a good friend. When I began shooting he was a Hercules Powder Company professional. Back in those days when you bought shotgun shells of any brand, you could specify the brand of powder you wanted as well as the brand of shells. As an example I could walk up to the shell stand and say I wanted Winchester shells with Hercules Red Dot powder. Shortly after WWII the shotgun shell manufacturing monopoly, consisting of Winchester, Remington, and Federal, got together and decided that they would no longer disclose what kind of powder was in their shells. This was the end for all of Hercules professionals and Johnny Jahn after having spent most of his life with Hercules, was given early retirement, which broke his heart.

I like to tell a true story about Johnny Jahn which gives you an inkling of what a tremendous shot he was. He didn't want to show favoritism to any particular brand of shells so when he went out to shoot the hundred, he'd get a box of Winchester, a box of Federal, a box of Remington, and a box of Peters; of course, all would be loaded with Red Dot Powder. He'd mix them all together and then, to prove that the powder was more important than the brand name of the shells, he'd proceed to break a hundred straight. My 1939 Trap shooter's Average Book lists him as having shot at 3625 targets for a .9825 per cent average and I'd guess that his lifetime average was around .98. He was exciting to watch because he not only broke the targets, he absolutely smashed them with all of his targets being a ball of smoke about ten yards out of the trap house. He shot a Parker single, held a high gun over the house, and shot extremely fast in an era where most shooters shot a little more deliberately. He didn't like to shoot doubles or handicap and seldom shot either. The last time I saw Johnny was in 1981. Sadly, he was in a nursing home with Alzheimer's and didn't recognize me; he was to pass away the following January. His two sons Russell and Ross and daughter Betty still live in Spirit Lake. Shortly after his death, Spirit Lake honored him by naming a City Park after him. As I now drive by the Johnny Jahn Park, almost every day, I see you Johnny in full Technicolor.

There were literally thousands of men who learned to shoot skeet and trap in the service. It really surprised me after the war that more of them didn't take up shooting, as a sport, but the cost of shooting may have been a deterrent at that time.

Duck Hunting with Sheldon Brooks

A good duck hunt is an experience one never forgets. I've had some great hunts with Jimmy Robinson in Manitoba, with Joel Campbell of Dupont in Maryland, and with Arch Ruddell on the Mississippi. However, some of the most enjoyable hunts have been with my friend Sheldon Brooks at his duck camp on Lake Christina in northwestern Minnesota. Lake Christina has the reputation of being one of the greatest bluebill duck hunting spots in the country. Sheldon has a blind out on a point about a hundred and fifty yards from his lodge that provides the sportiest shooting I've ever experienced. The wind is always blowing from the northwest at about fifteen or twenty knots. When those bluebills come downwind they are really whistling! Getting your limit from this blind is almost a mortal cinch—in fact some years you can select the kind of ducks you wish to shoot.

I first met Sheldon at Land O' Lakes, Wisconsin back in 1948 when we were both competing in a live pigeon shoot held at the King's Gateway Hotel Gun Club. Sheldon and his beautiful wife had flown in and landed on the hotel's landing strip. They caught my attention because they looked like a really classy couple and I enjoyed meeting them at the shoot. We became friends and often saw each other at various events. A few years later Sheldon invited me to be his guest at The Bohemian Grove outing held north of San Francisco on the Russian River. That was an outstanding experience I shall always remember.

Growing older has made me become kind of a softie so one of the big features at Sheldon's camp is the short walk from the blind to the lodge. When you are cold and wet that becomes a real asset, however the greatest asset of the camp is the lady that is responsible for preparing the fantastic meals. The lodge dining room has a round table that seats about eight. This wonderful lady prepares a feast of eggs, bacon, ham, pancakes, oatmeal, fruit, juices, plus rolls and toast, all placed on a big rotating Lazy Susan in the center of the table—you just turn the Lazy Susan to what you want as often as you wish, and it is all delicious. Her luncheons and dinners are equally fantastic—better meals than you can find in the best restaurants or hotels.

There is a gigantic fireplace in the living room and here we all gather to discuss the hunt and be entertained by Sheldon's incredible stories. He has the most extensive repertoire of jokes I've ever heard and specializes in Oley and Lena jokes performing the dialect to everyones amusment. Whenever I feel a little blue all I have to do is go to my e-mail and there is a joke from Sheldon.

To get to Sheldon's camp I would usually fly my airplane to Alexandria, Minnesota where Sheldon, Dave Yeager, and Tom Binger would meet me. We'd then have a leisurely lunch and head for the camp arriving in time to get in a little late afternoon shooting. I have some wonderful memories of those hunts and will always be grateful to Sheldon for hosting them.

Quail Hunting with Ed Connally

Hunting friends always occupy a special place in my heart! Ed Connally was my insurance man in Des Moines and through quail hunting we became very good friends. When the Iowa quail season opened, Ed would spend the entire season hunting with clients. He had several pointers and would bring out different ones each day. The farmers in the southern Iowa quail area all knew Ed so he always had places to hunt. I later learned that he had a mailing list of those farmers and every Christmas he sent them hams or slabs of bacon.

Ed was at least twenty years my senior and once when I was about fifty Ed literally walked me off my feet. It was early in the season and I wasn't in very good shape yet. We hunted hard all morning and went into a small town café for lunch. I stiffened up during lunch and really didn't feel like going back into the field but I didn't want to disappoint Ed. We hunted hard all afternoon and my knees and right hip were killing me—I still wouldn't say "uncle." Ed drove me home and when I tried to get out of the car I was so stiff I thought someone was going to have to carry me into the house. I soaked in a hot tub for an hour and had to have three jolts of Canadian Club before I could move. One of my knees and my right hip gave me trouble for years after that and I finally had to have a hip replaced and the knee worked on too. I hated to admit that a seventy year old could out-walk me.

Ed gave up quail hunting when he lost one dog and then another to hoop traps. The Iowa trapping laws had just outlawed the regular spring traps and made use of the new hoop trap mandatory. Their thought was that the hoop trap was more humane because it strangled or suffocated the animal quickly. There was a lot of trapping activity in the part of Iowa that Ed loved to hunt. He had dogs get caught in the old spring traps several times but in each case they would let out a yelp so he could find them and release them from the traps. In the worst case scenario the dog would have a broken leg, which could be set and would heal. With the hoop trap, the dog would just disappear with no sound. After much searching Ed found both dogs dead in the traps. He loved his dogs and said he'd never subject them to that kind of a risk again.

Ed had a farm west of Des Moines where Matt and I would go to practice our shooting act. Both Matt and I were very attached to Ed and when he contracted cancer and passed away we felt a tremendous loss. As a final gesture of friendship, Ed willed to me a complete collection of Federal duck stamps. His farm is now the location for the beautiful Glen Oaks Country Club and home development.

Pheasant Hunting with John Spence

John Spence of Des Moines is another hunting buddy whose friendship I value highly. John was associated with Roland Holden in the seed corn business and every fall the two of them would host a pheasant hunt on Roland's seed corn farms near Amana, Iowa. They worked hard to create the right conditions for a good pheasant crop each year by providing proper cover, controlling predators, and sometimes by releasing young birds in the spring. It was usually the same crowd each year but in 1981 we had the honor of hunting with wildlife artist John Ruthven who did an original pencil sketch of a pheasant which we all signed and kept as souvenirs.

Some of the other guests were Ivan Johnson, Ben Condon, Lex Hawkins, Al Glass, Bob Misalok, Ray Johnston, Arnold Fletcher, Roy Kobl. We'd take over suites of rooms at the Amana Holiday Inn and, of course, availed ourselves of the fantastic food at several of the Amana Colony's famous restaurants—known for their family style meals. I seem to be fortunate in falling in with great story-tellers and John Spence was one of the best. It was a hell of a group and we always had a big time! Sadly, Roland Holden has since passed away so the hunt no longer exists. John is a few years older than me but is in good health and now does a lot of hunting in Florida where he spends his winters.

Anti-Gun Movement

With guns, shooting, and hunting being such a big part of my life and being so close to my heart, it would be remiss of me if I didn't use this opportunity to relate to you how the growing anti-gun sentiment has affected me and how I think it affects you.

First of all I respect our Constitution and feel that the 2nd Amendment giving all American citizens the right to bear arms was important in our past history and is very important today. "The Right Arm of America" song by Country Western singer Paul Ott and written by Gregg Harbison, Paul Carruth and Fred Foster was so moving when I first heard it that I felt it was worth printing here:

*I was with the brave Columbus when he discovered this
  great land
And when the Pilgrims landed, I was ever close at hand
I fired the shot heard 'round the world that all men might
  be free
I thundered for Old Glory, I roared for Liberty*

*And I was there with Washington in Valley Forge's bloody
  snow
At the shoulders of determined men we overcame the foe
In the hands of Volunteers this time in New Orleans
We denied the Crown again—We had no need for earthly
  kings*

*When Travis called, I answered—but the Alamo was lost
Then I returned with Houston and we showed them who
  was boss
When brothers from the North and South began their bit-
  ter fray
'Twas not for me to choose a side so I was Blue and I was
  Gray*

*Then again the challenge came, a challenge deeply felt
And I went down to San Juan Hill with Teddy Roosevelt
Then in Nineteen Hundred and Seventeen the Yanks and
  I went Over There
To face the Kaisers armies, and we whipped 'em fair and
  square*

I went again in Forty Two before all Europe fell
To Hitler's rage and tyranny in the war they all called hell
I was there in the Philippines on the hip of General Mac
When the Rising Sun flew 'oer our land, I helped to win it
  back

I was there on Pork Chop Hill and once again in Viet Nam
Call me the Right Arm of America for that is what I am
I'll go again when there's a need and liberty the cause
I'll fight by any righteous man, I'll help protect his laws

I am Smith and Wesson, Colonel Colt and Remington
I'm often called Winchester, I'm how the West was won
Marlin, Sharps, and Browning, Stevens, Fox and Ruger
  too
Many are the brands I've worn and those are just a few

On the battlefield or in the home, I am your security
A tool of Peace from Freedoms Forge I'll help to keep you
  free
There are those who say I'm evil, they condemn me and
  they damn
Yet they are free to say I should be banned because of who
  I am

In the U. S. Constitution, Amendment Number Two
You were given the absolute right to own me, the choice is
  up to you
I'm only what you make of me, I'll do what you want done
Treat me with my due respect—I am your Nations Gun

From the time the early settlers came to this country guns provided food for the table, protection from the Indians, and made it possible for our Revolutionary Army to defeat the British. Unhappily, in the Civil War we used our guns against each other but in all our other wars, the fact that we had a population of hunters and outdoorsmen, already marksmen, made it possible to quickly form a trained army as no other country in the world has been able to do.

As you have read in this book, shooters like me were available to our Services to quickly train gunners and marksmen in WWII. Because of our heritage of hunting and shooting a big percentage of American recruits already had marksmanship training. This has been true every time we have had a war and needed to mobilize quickly.

The National Rifle Association (NRA) has been picked on by the media and has received a black eye that they do not deserve. NRA members are hunters and sportsmen like me throughout our country; I seriously doubt if Al Capone was ever a member! They have set up gun training programs, certified instructors, organized shooting tournaments, and constantly taught gun safety—they are the only ones providing our country these services. Their training programs have been adopted by most of our Military Services and they are in the forefront of technical development in cooperation with our Services. They have developed legislation not only to protect the rights of members but also to reduce crime. Their Board of Directors is made up of caring law-abiding citizens who are conscientious and patriotic. I have not always agreed with some of the stands they have taken but I must admit that they are the only bulwark we sportsmen have against the evils of gun registration and confiscation, which have befallen other countries like Britain and Australia. In view of what has happened in these other countries you can hardly fault them for opposing most gun legislation because the government has already shown that if they are given an inch, they take a mile! I feel that military semi-automatic weapons are unnecessary in our society but I hesitate to be for some of the legislation, which has been proposed for fear it would end up taking away my duck hunting automatic shotgun. Believe me, it could happen!

I don't understand what has happened in our country. When I was growing up they had R.O.T.C. rifle training in high schools throughout our country. The kids brought their rifles to school and the ammunition for them was often sold in the school cafeteria. Try that one today! When I was in high school my friends and I all had rifles or shotguns and we were careful of the way we used them. It strikes me that it is NOT THE

GUN that is causing the problem. Look at Switzerland a country with one of the *lowest* crime rates in the world and where every household has military weapons and ammunition stored. Their men are required to have annual military training and they keep their weapons and ammunition in their homes ready for immediate use should they be required.

Another reason why American sportsmen worry so much about gun legislation is because they have seen what has happened in other countries. Registration and then confiscation of guns occurred in Germany and made it impossible for those who opposed Hitler to do anything in the face of his armed party. In Great Britain only a privileged group were allowed to have guns prior to WWII. At the outbreak of the war when an invasion by Germany was imminent, guns were needed to supply the civilian population but there were none. A cry was sent out to America and our sportsmen and NRA members donated their high power sporting rifles to the defense of Britain. Now in England all sporting firearms must be locked up in the home in a government approved cabinet and, the *police have the right to search homes to enforce this law without a search warrant.* Transporting guns in automobiles to shoots and hunts is also subject to strict regulations. All of these laws handicap the law-abiding citizens only; the criminal disregards all laws! We certainly do not want the pendulum to swing this far so that we find ourselves in the same mess now that exists in Britain and Australia as well as some other countries. My friends in Australia tell me that they have given up on hunting because of the many restrictions.

The anti-gun group fails to recognize that guns are an art form and thousands of Americans collect guns, which they never fire and own because they admire their fine wood checkering and artistic engraving. They are displayed just like fine paintings and sculptures. I personally own many guns in this category and keep them because I enjoy seeing them and showing them to my friends.

My solution? Certainly not more legislation as most of the gun laws on the books now are not being enforced. No sportsman wants gun registration as we feel that is a prelude to confiscation. Plus, consider the cost of the bureaucracy that would be required for such registration. My solution has several points:

1. Enforce current laws to keep guns out of the hands of known felons and mentally deficient persons.
2. Require classes on gun training and safety.
3. Do not license or certify questionable people.
4. Make capital punishment mandatory in cases of assassination attempts, terrorist activities, kidnappings, bombings, mass shootings, and heinous crimes (Manson).
5. Move these crimes to the front of the docket and try them immediately.
6. Capital punishment should be by more humane lethal injection and reserved only for use in cases where there is no shadow of a doubt on guilt.
7. Televise executions.
8. Mount a massive public relations drive on the safe handling and storage of guns in the home. Now only the NRA and the National Shooting Sports Foundation sponsor such programs; the government should be paying for this type of program.

Food for thought! In a society where Sirhan, Hinckley, and Manson are still alive, what can we expect? I grew up during the time of the Lindbergh kidnapping and several others that followed shortly after. When the Lindbergh Law, which required capital punishment for kidnapping, was passed, the kidnappings stopped and didn't start again until after the repeal of that law; tell me it didn't work!

The media needs to recognize the rights and feelings of sportsmen and let the world know that not all people who like guns are nuts. The trapshooting sport is a beautiful example; has been in existence since 1872 and there has never been a fatality. Their National Championship Tournament, the Grand American, held in Dayton, Ohio each August, draws 5000 shooters and their families. They camp, fill up all the hotels in the area and spend ten days shooting and socializing. There has never been an incident. The same is true of the National Skeet Shooting Association meets, and the NRA sponsored rifle and pistol events. And, I can't back this statement up, but I seriously doubt if any of the children of these groups are shooting up their high schools.

Chapter 15

Celebrities

Getting A Kick

A fringe benefit to my sportswear manufacturing business was the opportunity I had to personally meet many famous and exciting people. I don't believe there is anyone who doesn't get a kick out of meeting famous people—celebrities, for lack of a better descriptive word. The mutual interest in the outdoors, hunting and shooting made it possible for me to associate with a number of professional stars in a way that would not have been possible under normal circumstances. With a few exceptions, I prize many memories of these famous people who were also great people.

The Paramount Insult

The paramount insult you can bestow on a show biz celebrity is to not recognize them for who they are and what they do. This lesson came to me the hard way, several years ago, when I was a guest of Mayor Carl Langford of Orlando, Florida, at the "16½ Shot Turkey Hunt" he sponsored. If you know Langford the name doesn't surprise you. Around sixty celebrities were invited to this fun event. It kicked off with a big banquet that ended with the guests being assigned a host, guide and campsite. After the banquet, each host escorted two celebrities to their camp. We had a few drinks around the fire and retired early, because the hunt at dawn would come all too soon.

As I retired, I realized that my host did not make me aware of who my hunting partner was and, unfortunately, I did not recognize him either by name or face. As we were being driven out to the hunting area, just to make conversation, I asked my celebrity-hunting partner what he did for a living. Wow! The air turned immediately fifty-degrees-below-zero and my companion didn't bother to answer me, let alone speak more than two or three words to me the entire day and those three words were almost like "Get out-of-my way!" Later that evening, while talking to my host, I was shocked to discover that my hunting partner was a famous movie star. I made a few feeble attempts to patch things up with him but the freeze continued. Of course, I shall not now, nor ever, reveal his name for fear of repeating my faux pas.

The story doesn't end there, however! A year later, I was invited to a dove hunt in Alamos, Mexico by an old friend, Jack Manning of Denver. The invitation had a double significance because my sister Anne, who was Pat Manning's closest friend, was there and my arrival was to be a surprise for a big birthday party for Anne that Pat had been planning. This same celebrity (who it turned out, also had a big-name celebrity wife) showed up at the party. It was quite evident that Mr. & Mrs. "Celeb" had recognized me and were choosing to ignore me. It was a big gathering of about seventy people, so it was easy for me to keep my distance. When I told Jack and Pat about my previous embarrassing meeting with this star, Jack said he didn't recognize the "unnamed" celebs either, and then when he discovered that his wife had not invited them, big Jack Manning went into miming how he was going after Mr. and Mrs. (Crash My Party Will You) celebs to bodily escort them out. Pat saved the day by physically restraining Jack and pleading with him to allow them to stay. The party included all the neighbors from this small community, and it turned out that this unnamed celeb and his wife were neighbors, living on the same street and just a few doors away from the Mannings. Theoretically at least, they had been invited so they stayed. Later we all had a really good laugh as Jack re-enacted how he was going to bodily throw them out of his home.

This story is in sharp contrast to the experiences I have had in meeting other celebrities. I found that generally the bigger the star, the more genuine and down to earth the person would be. The little anecdotes I write here, on each of these famous people, illustrates what I mean. (Not wishing to commit another "faux pas" and realizing that, to show-biz people, top billing is important, my vignettes are in alphabetical order.)

Bud Anderson

One of the leading Air Corps fighter-pilot aces of WWII was *Bud Anderson*. Flying P-51's over Europe in the same Group with Chuck Yeager, he shot down 16 German planes. His "tiger"reputation is belied by his quiet, gentlemanly demeanor. Bud comes to many of the "party" hunts and

My wife Sari with WWII fighter aces Bud Anderson & Joe Foss at the 2001 SHOT show in New Orleans.

through our mutual interest and my admiration for courageous men of WWII we have become friends. I've always been envious of the great friendship between Bud and Chuck Yeager. Not many of us are fortunate enough to have as close a comradeship. These two live near each other, hunt and fish together, and fly their P-51's to Air Shows.

At the 2001 SHOT Show (Shooting, Hunting, and Outdoor Trade Show) in New Orleans, Bud and another great WWII fighter-ace, Governor Joe Foss, sat at a special table in the Bob Allen Sportswear booth and autographed sketches of their WWII aircraft. There was always a line of people waiting and they thrilled immeasurable numbers of WWII buffs with their colorful stories. Once during a lull in the signing, I asked them what would have happened if Bud in his P-51 had a dogfight with Joe in his Wildcat. I thought Bud's answer was priceless as he quipped, "Joe would run out of gas before he got to the scene of the dog-fight!"

That night while in New Orleans we celebrated Bud's 79th birthday at New Orleans' top restaurant, Commander's Palace, with his lovely wife Ellie. I'm really proud to claim Bud as a friend!

Foster Brooks

Foster is tops on my list in many ways. Not only is he one of the funniest men I've ever experienced but he is also a remarkable poet, a gentleman and great fun to be around. Foster and I first met at one of the hunts and we seemed to hit it off immediately. When he found out I was from Des Moines, he related to me that he had lived in Des Moines for several years while working for the Des Moines Register. He said that some of the beer cans that he threw out of his office window might still be on the neighboring roof. Foster was disappointed when I told him that a high rise Marriott Hotel now stood in that spot so his beer cans must now be part of the foundation.

Our Iowa Governor wanted to have an invitational pheasant hunt for an economic development effort. By inviting business people and celebrities to these hunts they were introduced to new places and possibilities for commerce. (An example was Governor Joe Foss who held the Foss-Floyd-Dean Pheasant Hunt that was instrumental in Citi-Bank moving its credit card processing headquarters to South Dakota.)

Knowing of my attendance at many hunts, Gov. Branstad asked me to work with his Department of Natural Resource people in planning his hunting event. Shortly thereafter, I ran into Foster Brooks again and invited him to come to Des Moines and attend the hunt as our guest. He graciously accepted and flew in for the big event. There were banquets on Friday and Saturday nights and on both occasions Foster put on an impromptu comedic act after he was introduced. He broke the place up and made a bevy of new friends that weekend. The Friday night banquet was held in the Izaak Walton Club. Behind the podium was mounted a trophy size moose head. When Foster came up to the podium in his inimitable drunken way, he kept looking back over his shoulder and finally interrupted his bit by looking back at the moose and asking "How fast was that moose going when it hit that wall"? That opening remark broke everyone up!

Because I expressed an interest in his serious poetry, when Foster returned home to California, he prepared a cassette tape for me on which he recorded his poems. I prize that tape and listen to it often. Another way I see Foster these days is through his hilarious videotapes, which I have collected. I'm sure I have every one he has ever made, including his outstanding performances at the Dean Martin Roasts. Indeed, Foster Brooks is one of the funniest men in show biz. Thanks Foster for the joy and laughter you have given the world and me.

Governor Edmund Brown

The governor of California and I were guests of the Carlsberg brothers, Art and Dick, for the annual invitational "Three Shot Honker Hunt" held at their ranch in Alturas, California. I had never met Governor Brown before however after we were assigned as roommates, I got to know him pretty well. At that time his son was considering a run for the

Presidency and he asked me what the people of Iowa thought of him. His son was virtually unknown in Iowa and that was what I passed on. He also confided in me that he had a daughter that probably would have made the best politician in the family. I don't think that hunting was his favorite pastime but he cheerfully put up with getting up at five in the morning and going out in the snowy dawn to hunt geese.

Governor Terry Branstad

Terry Branstad was the youngest Iowa Governor in history and the Iowa people loved him enough to make sure he served two full terms. Now, Governor Ed Herschler of Wyoming and I had become good friends and I persuaded him to dispatch a challenge to Governor Terry Branstad to bring an Iowa team to the annual Lander, Wyoming, One Shot Antelope Hunt. My ulterior motives were not only to urge our Iowa Governor to get into the competition but also to make it possible for my son Matt to be invited as part of the three-man team so he could experience this extraordinary hunt. The Iowa team was made up of Governor Terry Branstad, my son Matt, and Gary Kirke of Des Moines who flew us to Wyoming in his Citation Jet.

The Iowa contingent had a great time and our Governor was very popular with the people of Wyoming. The first evening in Lander we all walked a block or two from our hotel to a popular bar to take in some of the local color. When the word spread that our Governor was there, cowboys started buying rounds of drinks and beer for everybody in our group. At one point each of us had about a dozen glasses lined up in front of our faces. I'll never forget a remark the Governor's bodyguard (a burly Iowa Highway Patrolman) made that night. He didn't see any way in this world, in that environment, that he could protect the governor. I told him he really didn't need to worry in Lander, Wyoming. The quality of these friendly western people was beyond reproach. They were proud he was there in their territory. You just don't find too many *kooks* in Lander, Wyoming—just red blooded, pioneering

Americans. The Governor had an incredible time and we are good friends to this day. Thanks Terry for being a great Governor for the state of Iowa and my friend.

My Buddy Buchwald

Remember, I said this chapter was about famous people who were also great people—with a few exceptions—well here comes another big exception. The year I won the Grand Prix of France at the shoot in the Bois du Boulogne in Paris, I had the flu and was so sick after the shoot, I spent several days hibernating in my room at the George V Hotel. At that time *Art Buchwald* was a correspondent for an English newspaper in Paris and nobody had ever heard of him. He phoned one day and wanted to know if he could interview me about the shoot. I told him that he was welcome if he didn't mind coming to my hotel room. My assumption was that he wanted to do a story about the winning American shooters, and that it would be good publicity. I could not have been more wrong! When the article appeared the next day it was a story about a bunch of rich Americans with fancy shotguns murdering innocent pigeons that had been released from traps. Here he was an American writing for an English speaking newspaper with an excellent opportunity to write something good about Americans but instead he just added to the European's view of the Ugly American. If it had been any other sport, from tiddly-winks to tennis, he would have given some praiseworthy coverage but there wasn't one good word about an American winning the Grande Prix of France, a great honor for me and our country.

It is interesting to note that cities like Paris, all over the world spend millions of dollars drowning, poisoning, and killing pigeons in other ways because they deface buildings and statues or because they carry diseases. So in those days, we pigeon shooters felt we were doing something good for the world. Plus pigeons killed in competition are always cleaned, dressed and distributed to institutions for human consumption.

The rest of the American Team was ready to kill me and

I had a tough time convincing them that what he wrote was not what we had talked about. I was furious and tried to contact him to vent my anger but, of course, could not get through to him.

Twenty-three (23) years later, I was in New York City with my attorney David Belin having breakfast in a hotel where prominent people in the financial world met. And there he sat at the next table, *my buddy,* Buchwald! He is not the most handsome guy in the world so I immediately recognized his face. By now, Buchwald had become famous in America, for what I don't know. I found my blood pressure rising, boy did I want to tell him off!

During breakfast my emotions raged and as we were leaving the dining room, I couldn't resist venting my displeasure. I turned abruptly and excused myself to the rest of the men at Buchwald's table and then reminded Buchwald that he had interviewed me after I won the Grand Prix of France in Paris . . . and how despicable his reporting was of me, the event and our fellow Americans . . and how he twisted the interview . . . and how he used me to report his own personal biases. At first he looked at me like I was crazy but then his eyes changed to reveal that he did remember the interview. I didn't give him a chance to respond to me; he just sat there with his trap wide open as I apologized once more to his table guests for the interruption and walked away. To this day I assiduously avoid reading any of his junk and tune him off if I see him on T V. There aren't too many people that can make me boil, or that I engrave on my *special* list, but Buchwald has a lifetime membership!

Pete Coors

Now on the other hand, a man like Pete Coors, the beer magnate from Colorado, is a wonderful person, sportsman and conservationist. I first met Pete at the annual mountain-men's spring rendezvous called; Foo Foo Rah sponsored by the One Shot Antelope Hunt. Later we were both guests of Winchester Arms for a hunt at their famous NILO Farms. Pete is a tall handsome man and having him wear Bob Allen products is wonderful advertising for my sportswear. He is an avid hunter, a fine shot who (you can probably tell from his beer adds) just loves the outdoors. Through his position and stature in the industry he has always been a promoter and sponsor of conservation that is so dear to my heart.

As an aside, NILO stands for Olin spelled backwards; the Winchester company, owner's name. The NILO farm is the original game farm created by Winchester to teach others how to establish and manage the propagation of wildlife. They have pioneered methods for raising game birds such as pheasants, quail, partridge and ducks, the planting of proper cover, and the control of predators. It became the number one working example for other enterprises as well as a research center where seminars are held. With our wide-open spaces shrinking, Winchester felt that the future for hunting in America would be in game farms and preserves as it has been for years in European countries. They invite people who want to start game farms, and as a result there are several hundred farms now raising game birds that, in many cases, are purchased by conservation groups and released into the wild. Many critics of hunting are not aware that both pheasants and partridge are not indigenous to our country and were imported many years ago. Were it not for American sportsmen we would not have these beautiful birds in our country for everyone, including non-hunters, to enjoy.

Astronaut Walt Cunningham

I first met Walt at the "One Box Pheasant Hunt" in Broken Bow, Nebraska. We were hunting partners there and saw each other at several other hunts over a period of years and became good friends. My business took me to Houston often and Walt and I would make it a point to get together for dinner. During the time that I was on the board of a large hospital in Des Moines, we were looking for an outstanding keynote speaker for our annual meeting. Walt graciously accepted my invitation to speak for our group. He flew himself into Des Moines in his own jet fighter. A NASA embellished, pure white jet fighter is assigned to each Astronaut as their mode of travel while not floating around in outer space. Walt landed at the Des Moines airport in the middle of a blizzard and created quite a stir as he taxied up to park at the National Guard Armory hangar.

He gave a terrific speech and my arm was sore for days from people coming up to pump it while thanking me for getting Walt to entertain our gathering. I was a hometown hero! Walt had to hole-up at our home for an extra day because of bad weather. Our kids were thrilled to be around this congenial man. The next day at school, Matt told his teacher that an astronaut had stayed at our house. The teacher patted him on the head and said, "Sure Matt." Later, at a teachers meeting, she seemed concerned that Matt was making up stories and was very embarrassed when we advised her that Walt Cunningham, had, in fact stayed with us overnight.

When I took Walt out to the airport the following day, he gave Des Moines a thrill by doing a high performance take-off. Immediately after breaking ground, with after-burners roaring, he pulled the jet's nose up and flew straight up into the sky and disappeared with one colossal reverberation. Walt, you really made an impression on my family and the city of Des Moines. Many thanks for the big thrill you gave us!

Will Clark

This baseball great, is about as devoted a hunter as you will ever find. He attends and thoroughly enjoys many of the Celebrity Hunts. He was born and grew up in Louisiana where he and his Dad were always hunting. Because of his hunting experience, I invited him to serve on my hunting and shooting clothing TEST STAFF, and he kindly accepted. His comments, along with those from other TEST STAFF members contributed greatly to help us constantly improve our products. One year we used Will as a model in our catalog. I flew my plane down to Cincinnati, where he was playing, and we spent an entire day on location for the catalogue photography. We had great fun while shooting whether it was targets or photographs and I thoroughly enjoyed watching all the attention Will got wherever we went. Many thanks Will!

John DiSanti

I first met John at the Heartland Pheasant Hunt. This is a man who is a natural born comedian. He started his career in commercials in Florida and then went out to California where he landed roles in movies like "Lenny," "Star Chamber," "Batteries Not Included," plus many TV episodes. John is a Brooklyn boy who started hunting at age eleven and loves it to this day. His presence at the celebrity hunts adds greatly to their success because he is a gregarious guy who loves people. John is also an artisan, creating beautiful wood lathe-turned bowls. He contributes his creations to the various hunt auctions to help raise funds for charitable causes. During the auctions, John has distinguished himself by the way he comedically works the crowd in raising their bids. "After all, its for the kids, or for conservation and for the animals," you'll hear him say. If someone is bidding and suddenly their bidding slows down, John stands up on a chair in front of his "bird" and performs "salaams" and bows until he embarrasses the bidder to come up with more dough. He used this treatment on me at the Abilene Big Country Quail Hunt and I ended up winning the bid on one of John's gigantic and magnificently turned, thirty inch, pecan, wide mouth bowls; she now sits proudly on my dining room table.

In June of 2001 we invited John to come to Spirit Lake and serve as celebrity auctioneer for our Art Center's annual fund raising banquet. John graciously accepted and, through his efforts, we raised a record amount of money for the Art Center and he charmed all of our attendees. I had promised John that I would take him fishing and shooting sporting clays if he would agree to come. At a sporting clays club near Lakefield, Minnesota we were shooting and having a good time until John inadvertently dropped a 20 gauge shell into the bottom barrel of his over-under followed by the proper 12 gauge shell. When he attempted to shoot the next targets, there was an explosion like a stick of dynamite, a fourteen-inch flash of flame, and John staggered backward dropping the gun. The forearm, which had rested in John's left hand, completely disintegrated and there was an eight-inch split in the bottom barrel where the explosion had caused it to rupture.

It was evident he was badly hurt so, wrapping his hand in a towel to sop up the blood, we jumped in the car and sped to the emergency room at the Spirit Lake hospital about thirty miles away. On our cellular phone we alerted them that we were coming and, God bless people in small towns, they were waiting for us in front of the emergency room door to wave us in when we arrived. Fortunately a skilled hand surgeon was there and John was immediately taken into the operating room where he spent several hours having a broken thumb set and pinned, shot taken out of his hand, and the extensive lacerations sewed up. Thankfully there was no nerve damage and the prognosis for recovery was good. He spent the night in the hospital and then a few days in our home recovering before he had to fly back to Cocoa, Florida.

This exact accident has happened to many other sportsmen and there is an inherent danger in having the smaller 20 gauge shells anywhere near the larger 12 gauge shells. John's incident has prompted both of us to adopt a policy of NEVER having 20 and 12 gauge shells in the same shooting jacket!

John brings wonderful humor and gaiety where ever he goes. I look so forward to seeing him each year at the various hunts. John is without a doubt the consummate gentleman, the fellow well met by all. And if you ask for a really good restaurant in Florida, he'll tell you Saint John's Retreat ~ that is John's house ~ home of a great Italian chef. Thanks John for all you do for others and for me!

Paul Derringer

The World Series winning pitcher for the Cincinnati Reds, Paul was a fervent hunter. After he retired from baseball he started following the live pigeon shooting circuit and we became good friends. He was a lovable big Kentucky hillbilly boy who stood about six foot six, weighed in at 260 pounds, and had hands like hams. He used to brag that if he couldn't defeat a batter any other way, his hands were strong enough that he could knead loose the cover on the ball. If the batter hit the ball, it would just flutter and couldn't go very far.

When he was shooting, his 12-gauge over-under shotgun looked like a toothpick in his big hands. Paul was an excellent shot until pressure took over. You'd think that a World Series pitcher could take any kind of pressure but in a pigeon shoot there wasn't a team backing him up. Paul could kill the first twenty straight but almost always came apart during the last five birds when the pressure was the greatest. He knew it, we, his friends all knew it;, and no matter how hard we pulled for him, he almost always got in trouble with the last five birds.

I stayed with Paul and his wife in their home in Cincinnati one weekend. It was one of those big three story houses built on a bluff over looking the river. Paul told me that shortly after they bought it, he was walking down the upstairs hall one night and his foot went through the floor. To their horror they found that the house was just about eaten up by termites. They spent a ton of money to get it repaired and rid of the termites. Paul loved to entertain and at every shoot he planned a big dinner party where all the shooters and their wives would attend. A very gracious man, he had a huge following and many friends.

Andy Devine

When I was a kid growing up, I was always thrilled to see another Andy Devine movie; he was a ponderous-sized man with that famous gravel voice that made him outstandingly funny. Like quite a few other movie stars, he liked skeet shooting and was a pretty good shot. At the National Skeet Championship Shoot, which was held in 1946 on Hoot Gibson's ranch in Las Vegas, I had the pleasure of shooting on the same five-man squad with Andy for several days. He was really fun to shoot with because he wasn't taking it as seriously as the rest of us; he was just there to have fun and not beat anyone; just entertain us!

Although I hadn't met Andy until that shoot, he had been a mail order customer for my shooting vests. When his first order came in, we were a bit perplexed because we had nothing that came close to fitting him. We ended up having to make a new special pattern to accommodate his fifty-inch waist. When I finally met him I told him that we couldn't make any money off his orders because they took too many yards of cloth. He got a big kick out of me razzing him about this every time we met. I can still see his big belly jiggling when he laughed. From time to time afterwards I'd run into Andy and had an opportunity to meet his lovely (tiny) wife. Andy Devine will always have a warm spot in my memory book.

General Jimmy Doolittle

Now we come to one of my biggest heroes and a man I respect tremendously. General Jimmy Doolittle became a hero to me during World War II when he led our first bombing raid on Japan, flying B-25 bombers off the aircraft carrier Enterprise. Surviving the raid he went on to become Commanding General of the 8th Air Force bombing Europe from England. Prior to WWII he had distinguished himself in the old Army Air Corps by pioneering instrument flying and proving that bombers could sink ships.

I had read extensively about Jimmy and knew a little about him from knowing his son who was a B-26 pilot when I was in the 9th Bomb. Group in Orlando in 1943. I first met Jimmy personally at the Carlsberg Honker Hunt in California where we were both invited guests. A year later, I had the honor of hunting in the same group with him at the Foss-Floyd-Dean Pheasant Hunt in South Dakota. Jimmy was eighty at that time and despite his age insisted on walking the fields and brush with everyone; he wouldn't allow us to shield him in any way. I really got to know him then and we ran into each other at many of the other hunts on a regular basis. It pleased me that he was a great fan of my sportswear products and wore them regularly.

Jimmy was a very soft-spoken little man but had piercing eyes and a demeanor that automatically received respect. He was always available to help on charitable causes and came to Des Moines on one occasion to assist on a fundraiser for our

Science Center. The last time we hunted together was again at the Carlsberg Honker Hunt.

The invitees to the hunt had all met in Beverly Hills and then flew to the Carlsberg ranch on a chartered Nevada Airways Martin 404 that was an airline-weary twin-engine passenger plane. The plane made it to the ranch okay but on the return trip we had problems. When it was time to leave the ranch we filled up every seat plus each of us had two or three frozen geese, our guns, and all our gear. We must have been over-loaded but the intrepid pilot prepared to take off. The ranch runway was only five thousand feet and was at an elevation of about 3500 feet and that affects the efficiency of any engine.

I was seated in a window seat in the front row and Jimmy Doolittle was beside me. Across the aisle were California Governor Edmund Brown and General Curtis LeMay. Behind us were Roy Rogers and Astronaut Joe Engle. The pilot taxied out to the head of the runway, ran up the engines full throttle with the brakes locked, and then released the brakes and started the take-off run. I anxiously watched out the window as the end of the runway (which ended at a cliff over a canyon) approached. We used every inch of the runway; the plane didn't take off, it just flew off the end and out over the canyon. The gear came up but the engines stayed on full power, as we were not climbing like we should have been. We were all sweating it out; the number one engine on our side of the airplane was spewing oil all over the wing. At one point Jimmy said to me "it sure would be a hell-of-a-note to survive all that WWII combat and get killed in a bucket of bolts like this!" We literally flew through the mountains rather than over them and when we arrived at Reno, Nevada an hour and half later the crew made an emergency landing and all of us fled the old airplane and booked flights on airlines for the balance of the trip.

I must say that Jimmy was much calmer than me during the flight. This flight ended the use of chartered aircraft for the Carlsberg Hunt. The thought occurred to me that had we crashed and all been killed, I would always be remembered for the company I was with on the occasion of my death. On later hunts we all met in Reno and used chartered buses for the trip to the ranch. In some ways the buses were more fun as we had a bar set up and everyone could stand or move around to visit. The buses made a stop at a ranch belonging to some friends of the Carlsberg brothers. Here we had a great lunch and "Clay Goose" shoot. Clay targets were thrown over a pond and each of us was allowed two shots using #2 shot goose loads. Then it was back on the buses for another two hours to reach the Carlsberg lodge near Alturas, California. It was comforting to know that when the hunt was over, we would not have to risk our lives on one of those chartered airplanes.

Leslie Easterbrook

Leslie is an accomplished motion picture actress and is most famous for her appearances in the Police Academy movies. It was a real delight to have the opportunity to shoot in the same squad with her at the Big Country Celebrity Quail Hunt in Abilene, Texas. I've had the pleasure of shooting with her at the Heartland Pheasant Hunt each year as well. Leslie is a beautiful and very talented, down-to-earth person. A graduate of Stephens College theatrical school she played in their summer theater at Lake Okoboji, Iowa, where I now reside. Finding this out gave us something more in common and Leslie is contemplating coming to Okoboji next summer to visit us and relive some of her earliest show biz experiences. Incidentally, she is a hell of a good shot both at sporting clays and in bird hunting. She has recently teamed up with shooting instructor Gil Ash to produce a shooting video that covers the entire shotgun shooting sports. I recently viewed it and think it is the best I've seen.

Astronaut, General Joe Engle

Joe loves to hunt and has attended all the Carlsberg hunts, the One Shot Antelope Hunt, the Nebraska Pheasant Hunt and I'm sure many others. We hunted together at the One Shot Antelope Hunt in Lander, Wyoming one year and I witnessed Joe perform one of the greatest stalks I've ever seen. Shortly after dawn we spotted a lone trophy antelope, grazing in a green valley, about five hundred yards from where we sat in our vehicle. With our guide we studied the animal through our binoculars and noted that it regularly lifted its head to look at us. Our guide, an experienced Wyoming rancher, said there was no point in trying for this one. Joe objected and said he'd like to try a stalk. Getting out of the vehicle he'd wait until the antelope put its head down to graze and then he'd move forward in a crouch for five or six yards. He repeated this procedure for almost an hour and, to our astonishment, got to within fifty yards of the big antelope. The suspense was almost unbearable but finally Joe kneeled, we watched his rifle come up, and then saw a little puff of smoke come out of the barrel. He was so far away it took several seconds for the sound of the shot to reach us. The antelope took off like it hadn't been hit and we were afraid he had missed but the animal only ran about fifty feet before it dropped to the ground. Joe had made a spectacular "One Shot" kill which is the whole point of the hunt.

We drove to Joe and the downed antelope and, drawing from his experience in hunting in Germany, Joe performed a "blessing of the game" ceremony, as is the custom in that country. Then, as is the custom in Wyoming, we let down the tail gate and proceeded to drink toasts to the antelope, to each other, to the guide and to just about everybody else. We arrived back at the check-in ranch in a happy state and learned that the other astronauts on the team had also accomplished their one-shot kill. So the Astronauts won the hunt and the day.

Joe has brought down the house at many of the shoots when he does his imitation of General George Patton. He dresses himself to look like Patton and has Patton's voice imitated perfectly. I've lost track of how many space and shuttle shots Joe has piloted and I prize all the photographs that he has autographed and sent to me over the years. In my home we have created an Astronauts gallery filled with their pictures and memorabilia they have given me. Joe is an outstanding example of the quality of our military and with guys like Joe our country is in good hands!

Astronaut Ron Evans

Ron was the first astronaut I had the pleasure of meeting. We were both attending an African First Shotter Hunt on the big Island of Hawaii where we, along with about twenty-five others, were hunting goats and pigs on the slopes of Mauna Kea. We hit if off at once and, with our wives, became good friends. Ron attended many of the other party hunts after Hawaii so we got to see each other often. When my son Matt was about thirteen years old he shot on an astronaut team with Ron at the Nebraska One Box Pheasant Hunt. On two occasions I leaned on Ron to come to Iowa as a keynote speaker. He met people well and gave exciting speeches. This was at the time when the astronauts and the space program were BIG news; so wherever we went, autograph seekers mobbed Ron. He was like a magnet for women! I've never seen anyone, including mega-movie stars attract women like Ron; yet he was oblivious of the attention he received.

Ron was the pilot on the first night launch at Cape Canaveral and thrilled my family by inviting us down to watch his blast-off. At that time they kept the astronauts quarantined for a few days before their mission so Ron's wife Jan met us on our arrival, had arranged our hotel reservations, invited us to some pre-mission parties in the homes of some of their friends at the cape, and had space reserved for us in the VIP area to see the launch. It was a fantastic experience for our family, one that we will never forget. I took several pictures of the launch, which I have framed at home alongside a framed letter, and American flag that Ron took with him to the moon. Ron made a video on the space program and sent me a copy that I prize. He and his wife were great hosts! I had an opportunity to visit Ron at his home in Phoenix a couple of times before he passed away of a heart attack. My family and I shall always remember Ron with great affection.

Governor Joe Foss

One of my biggest heroes is Joe Foss! I had heard much about Joe during World War II when he was a big Marine fighter ace flying out of Guadalcanal. I met Joe for the first time when he was Governor of South Dakota and host for the Foss, Floyd, Dean Pheasant Hunt. I was invited to that hunt several different years and also ran into Joe at the One Shot Hunt as well as some of the other hunts. Joe's wife Didi came from Des Moines so I had an opportunity to see Joe there also. I really learned to know Joe when we both served as Directors for the African First Shotters group. There is extensive information on Joe in another chapter of this book that I have titled "The Ten Most Interesting Characters I Have Met." I am reminded of Joe every time we fly out of the Sioux Falls, South Dakota airport (the closest international airport to our home on Lake Okoboji). In the main lobby of the airport stands a bigger than life sculpture of Joe in his Marine flying uniform. A brass plaque on the base tells the Joe Foss story. He is certainly Mr. South Dakota and much more! I'm very proud to consider him a friend.

Robert Fuller

Robert Fuller, the star of the popular TV series "Emergency" is a very thoughtful and kind man. We had met at some of the hunts and when he heard that my wife Ruthie was in the Mayo Clinic recovering from a brain hemorrhage, he phoned her in her room several times which really cheered her up and I believe hastened her recovery. This occurred at the height of the popularity of the "Emergency" show so each time when he called he had all the nurses in a tizzy. We shall always be grateful to you "Bobby"!

Clark Gable

In 1943, Clark Gable was in my Officer Training School squadron at Miami Beach. We were both there to get our commissions so we could become Gunnery Officers. Gable had been selected for this job because of his hobby as a skeet shooter in California. Never has a guy earned his commission in a more difficult way than Gable! It was downright mean the way he was picked on just because he was a big star. All of us were

given a "butch" haircut on arrival but they used a razor to
shave every bit of hair from Gable's head! Under the West
Point system, upper classmen could haze the lower classmen
at will. They over-did it with Gable just because they wanted
to get near him. We lived in the Carlton Hotel ~ one of the
many recently restored South Miami Beach hotels. One of the
Cadet rules was that nobody could haze you if you were in the
"john." Quite a bit of studying was needed in order to graduate and the only place Gable could study in peace was in the
bathroom; he must have spent at least half of his Cadet time
there!

We visited several times about shooting and some of the
west coast shooters we knew in common. On graduation Gable
was sent to the 8th Air Force in England where he became a
Gunnery Officer for a B-17 Group and made a number of
Gunnery Training films. I have one of his films and it is fun to
view it and reminisce. He was a great guy because he really
loved shooting and hunting; so much so, that I'm told he had
a clause in his studio contract that allowed him hunting time.

Curt Gowdy

African First Shotters made an award presentation to the
top four conservationists in the world at a banquet held in the
Waldorf Astoria in New York City. The nominees for this prestigious award were motion picture star Bill Holden, Gov. John
Connally of Texas, Jomo Kenyatta (the President of Kenya),
and Gen. Jimmy Doolittle. We asked Curt Gowdy, the famous
sports announcer, to be our Master of Ceremonies with no
remuneration. He graciously accepted and flew in from the
west coast, just for the night, to be our M.C. and did an outstanding job. I had admired him for the work he did on his TV
outdoor series. We had several friends in common and I
enjoyed visiting with him. Quite a hunter himself, I asked him
if he would serve on my TEST STAFF and once again he graciously accepted. Remember what I said earlier about the bigger people being more generous?

Grits Gresham

Grits Gresham is a household name with every sportsman. Everyone reads his wonderful articles in the outdoor magazines. He became even better known when he established the Sports Afield Outdoor TV series. Grits and I had rubbed elbows for years and he served on my TEST STAFF. When my son Matt was fourteen years old Grits invited us to do our trick-shooting act on his TV series. Little did he know that we would have given our eyeteeth to get the kind of publicity for our business that this show would afford.

Grits and his wife came to Des Moines with a whole production crew and we spent four days shooting the show at a rifle range located at Camp Dodge in Des Moines. They did a very professional job and Grits as the moderator made it easy for us. The show was a big success and re-runs are being shown regularly to this day on TV stations throughout the country. Grits and I have become good friends and I always look forward to seeing him wearing the weathered hat that has become his trademark.

Van Heflin

Winchester held the finals for their National Claybird Championships in West End, Bahamas at the Jack Tar Resort. To spice up the activities they invited five of us to shoot in a special Celebrity Squad. Motion picture star Van Heflin was the outstanding member of the squad and, because I had always admired his pictures, I was really excited to be included. Besides shooting trap and skeet clay target events, Winchester had scheduled other activities to entertain our squad. One whole day was spent deep-sea fishing and I had the opportunity to spend a lot of time visiting with Van. We sat together through several banquets and luncheons and by the time the weekend was over we were friends. I asked Van, as busy and popular as he was at that time, why he would accept an invitation like this from Winchester. He said the only reason he accepted was because Winchester promised a deluxe

African safari for him and his son as payment; an opportunity that was just too good to pass up.

On the fishing trip and at most of the meals we were with some of the Winchester bigwigs and their wives. One of the wives was a continual "chatty Cathy" and was so enthralled by being near Van Heflin she spent all her time carrying on a one-sided conversation with him. I could tell it was really bothering him and, at the big Saturday night banquet which was the wind-up of the shoot, it finally got to him so badly that he justifiably blew! Much to his consternation she had contrived to be sitting beside him and proceeded to carry on her one-sided, non-stop, silly conversation. Sitting on his other side, I heard her say that she and her husband often visited Los Angeles and that the next time they came out they would call Van so they all could have dinner together. This was the "straw" and Van really let her have it! He said, "NO, G__ ____t, DO NOT CALL ME, I CHOOSE MY DINNER COMPANIONS VERY CAREFULLY AND YOU ARE THE LAST PERSON IN THE WORLD I WANT TO HAVE DINNER WITH!" With those piercing eyes, as only he can do, he was looking her right in the eyes. There was a moment of stunned silence at the table and then one of the guests broke the tension by clapping! The lady's husband had been embarrassed by her for three days and I could tell he wanted to join in clapping but abstained. She never uttered another word for the entire meal as Van turned his back on her and talked to me. I reached under the table and shook his hand. After the shoot I received a nice letter from Van telling me how much he had enjoyed shooting with me and thanking me for my "support." Unhappily, he was found floating face down in his swimming pool a few months later, and presumably he had suffered a heart attack. I never did hear if he had his safari. I remain a big fan of his movies and one of my favorites is his western classic "Shane" which I have on tape and run periodically.

Ernest Hemingway

In 1947 I made my first shooting trip to Cuba and had the great honor of meeting Hemingway. In Havana, he lived not far from the Cazadores del Cerro Gun Club and attended the shoots almost every day. Most of us stayed at the Seville Biltmore hotel and hung out at Sloppy Joe's bar, which was Ernest's favorite hangout. Ernest was a great storyteller and loved to talk about his African hunting experiences. His son Bumby later became a white hunter and guided many Americans on safari including my friend Homer Clark.

A rugged individualist, Ernest caught one of his Cuban friends treating another's wife in a very ungentlemanly way. Even though he was attending a party in that Cuban's home, Ernest grabbed the man by the collar, pulled him down near the swimming pool where everyone could see and hear him, and then announced to the crowd what the man had done. He finished by punching him and telling him that every time he saw him for the next year, he was going to punch him again. The story is that when this man would see Hemingway coming, he'd cross the street, hide in an alleyway, or do anything else he could do to escape being seen.

Hemingway became a good mail order customer for our sportswear and would often phone from his home in Ketchum, Idaho to order a hunting coat or something. His calls would thrill our office staff. I wasn't aware that Ernest had cancer until I heard of his suicide. I guess it was typical of him to use his favorite shotgun to end his life rather than allow the cancer to take him slowly.

Charlton Heston

For those of us who love hunting, shooting, and guns, Heston is our hero! Nothing needs to be said about his fame in motion pictures but the dedicated work he has done for the National Rifle Association makes us all indebted to him. We've run into each other at NRA affairs, at the Charlton Heston Celebrity Shoots which I have had the pleasure of attending, and at the SHOT Show. In 1996 he and his wife came to Des Moines to support Jim Lightfoot in his bid to become Iowa's Governor. A group of about a hundred supporters were invited to spend an afternoon of shooting at Jim Cownie's ranch near Des Moines. Jim asked my son Matt and me to put on our trick shooting demonstration especially for Charlton and his wife. As part of our act, we atomize grapefruit by blasting them with a high power rifle. I'm sure Charlton's wife will never forgive us for some of the grapefruit debris was carried her way by the wind and stained her beautiful dress.

Charlton is a fine public speaker and presents the gun owner's view in a calm, dispassionate and convincing manner. The TV specials he has recorded for the NRA have shown the world the positive side of the gun issue. He has suffered much criticism from others in the entertainment industry. Not many celebrities of Charlton's caliber would be as courageous and outspoken as he is for the causes he feels are just. For his invaluable support I, along with millions of hunters and gun owners, thank him from the bottom of our hearts.

Wally Hilgenberg

Wally was an All American football star for Iowa and then went on to be a star playing for the Minnesota Vikings. A big guy with an engaging smile and extroverted personality he was tremendously popular with the fans and had a big following in Minnesota. After retiring from football he went into the insurance business and scored another success. During all of those years he never gave up his love of hunting and to this day hunts with his dogs whenever he can. He was a natural to be invited to the "party hunts" so we got together often. I was very pleased when he accepted my invitation to be a member of my TEST STAFF and am grateful for the support and input he has given me.

Bill Holden

Holden's movies are classics and everyone has enjoyed them for many years. What few people know about is the outstanding role he has played in conservation of wild life, particularly African animals. A few years ago The African First Shotters, a sportsman's conservation group for whom I was a director, hosted a black-tie banquet at the Waldorf Astoria Hotel in New York City to honor the top four conservationists of the world. Bill Holden was one of the four recipients of this honor and I had the pleasure of spending time with him during this event. Bill loved Africa and had built a hotel (which still exists) called the Mt. Kenya Safari Club. Hundreds of big game hunters made this hotel their headquarters and it has also become a must stop for all tourists. Bill rescued injured or orphan animals and nursed them back to health in the facilities he established adjacent to his hotel. Through his efforts many endangered species were rescued and his assistance in the war on poaching was invaluable. It was for this work that he received the Conservationist of the Year award at our banquet.

Another of our Directors, Fritz Kielmann the North American Manager for KLM Airlines, and I met Bill's flight at Kennedy airport and carried him to the Waldorf Astoria. I was really looking forward to meeting him and, true to his reputation, he was about half smashed when he got off the plane and thought that Fritz's secretary was a girl we had brought along just for him. It took a little while for us to get him settled down and we had some fun with him. My remarks should not be construed in any way to detract from this great man's achievements for I am one of his greatest fans. He was such a unique guy!

Senator Harold Hughes

Hughes served as Iowa's Governor for two terms and then became a United States Senator. In 1969 he received a challenge from Ed Herschler, the Governor of Wyoming, to bring an Iowa team to the One Shot Antelope Hunt. At that time I didn't know Hughes; in fact we didn't even belong to the same political party. I was at the peak of my shooting career and receiving a lot of publicity particularly in Iowa. Hughes chose me for his team purely on the basis of my shooting record. As it turned out, he had done me a tremendous favor because my involvement in the One Shot Hunt was to affect my life and my business in a very positive way.

Hughes had an interesting and unusual background for a Governor. He had operated a small trucking firm in Ida Grove,

Iowa and had been an alcoholic for many years. Alcoholics Anonymous turned his life around. He was a large man with a charismatic personality and a magnetism that was felt when you heard his speeches. At the time of the election Iowa did not have liquor by the drink. Trying to repeal that law was considered a hot issue but, despite his background, Hughes came out for liquor by the drink and won the election handily.

We flew out to Lander in his big, old, twin Beech aircraft. Hughes instantly became the most popular of the Governors attending with teams. Wherever he went people would instantly surround him. At the ranch where the teams checked in, there was a small trout stream that Hughes started to fish. He drew an immediate crowd of spectators including many TV and newspaper people.

I missed my one shot and was almost afraid to come back to the ranch. I figured that if both Hughes and our teammate killed, my name would be mud and I was scared to face Hughes. Luckily for me both Hughes and Lerlia had missed so I was off the hook.

We had become friends and went on some other duck and goose hunts together. Sitting all day in a duck blind gives you an opportunity to really learn to know someone and I became a big fan of Hughes. When he left the U. S. Senate, he established a shelter for people involved in alcohol and substance abuse; and devoted the rest of his life to this cause, becoming a great spokesperson for programs for these people. Yes, Harold Hughes qualifies as a celebrity!

Rick Jason

Rick has been in a lot of movies but will always be remembered for his role as the Officer in the "Combat" WWII series. I was his hunting partner the first year he came to the One Shot Antelope Hunt. Until then he hadn't been a hunter but he became an avid hunter and usually attends the One Shot each year. He is a great storyteller and has a great sense of humor that makes it fun to be around him. He is particularly good on "dialect" stories. If you have the occasion to phone him at his home in Los Angeles be prepared for a wild message on his answering machine.

Steve Kanaly

Of all the TV and movie stars I have met, Steve is the most dedicated hunter of them all. He is most famous as one of the stars in the TV series "Dallas" but has made many Hollywood movies and had his own African TV series. His love of hunting has prompted him to accept invitations to many of the "party" hunts and we've had an opportunity to see each other often. He generously donates something to each of the hunts for their fund raising auctions, from his famous white cowboy hat which raised over six thousand dollars to his original paintings. He is a very handsome guy with an engaging smile and friendly personality. At all of the hunts, as you can imagine, he is very popular. He has also helped my business and me by being a member of my TEST STAFF. He makes great contributions because of his hunting experiences and having him wear BOB ALLEN clothes certainly doesn't hurt! Many thanks for your friendship Steve!

General Curt LeMay

At the end of World War II, I was on the staff at 20th Air Force Hq. on Guam. My relationship with the General was pretty formal then with me usually standing in a brace reporting to him. The only time I got to know him on anything resembling an informal basis was at the skeet range at Guam where I gave him some shooting lessons. I might add that he later took up skeet in earnest and won a number of Nebraska championships when he was stationed at SAC Hq. in Omaha.

Many years later I had the honor of being his hunting partner at the One Shot Antelope Hunt. Here I found a totally different man and, over a few days we became friends. LeMay is a devoted and experienced hunter who reloads his own ammunition and has an additional hobby of bench rest shooting. In retirement he spent some time almost every day at a gun club near his home in California. While stationed in

Germany he did a lot of hunting and continued to enjoy the sport when he came home. At the One Shot Hunt he made an excellent one-shot-kill. After dressing out his antelope, we tailgated for about three hours toasting each other on the successful kill. It was one of those typical fall days you get only in Wyoming—bright sunshine in a cloudless sky, crisp but pleasant temperature in the sixties, and a gentle breeze. As we drank our toasts and ate the sandwiches the guide had provided, the conversation turned to WWII. I'll never forget some of the comments that LeMay made that day. He remarked that the accomplishments of the young men of America at that time were almost unbelievable. As an example; he brought to my attention the fact that the average airplane commander on a big B-29 Super-fortress bomber was around 21 years old, probably only had about 300 hours of flying time and now was flying the biggest and most sophisticated aircraft in the history of man, let alone being responsible for a crew of eleven other lives. What these young crews did was amazing; LeMay remarked that it was a pretty good navigational feat just to find Japan let alone find a target and bomb it successfully. He had nothing but praise for the aircrews and played down the tremendous impact his leadership had on concluding the war in the Pacific.

Later, I was to hunt with LeMay again at The Carlsberg Hunt in California and at succeeding One Shot Hunts. We corresponded by mail and phone but never did get together in California as we had planned. I was really shocked when I heard of his death a few years later. LeMay was a real tiger, like Patton and Yeager, the kind of guys who win wars. I feel really privileged to have known him.

Anne Lockhart

Anne is a beautiful and well-known motion picture actress who comes from a family that has a long line in that profession. She loves to hunt and is an accomplished shooter. We first met at the Big Country Celebrity Quail Hunt in Abilene, Texas but have shot together also at the Heartland

Pheasant Hunt in Iowa. I had the pleasure of hunting beside her several times and can attest that she doesn't ask for any special consideration, hunts hard, and is a good shot. She is a great contributor to these hunts, meets everyone well, and graciously signs autographs for all. She lives in Lake Sherwood in California with her son and daughter.

Astronaut Jack Lousma

I first met Jack at the One Shot Hunt. Later I was able to prevail upon him to fly to Des Moines on two occasions to give speeches. He's a thoroughly fine man and did a great job on the speeches. His arrival and departure from Des Moines airport in his T-30 jet fighter will long be remembered. Later he was kind enough to send me several photographs including one which shows Des Moines from space. Many thanks Jack!

Astronaut Jim Lovell

Jim became more famous than most of the astronauts because of almost being lost in space. His book "Apollo 13"and the movie made from it publicized the near tragedy in space. In 1972 as part of the African First Shotter's group, my son Matt and I had the pleasure of being on an African safari with Jim and his son who was the same age as Matt. We toured Amsterdam together enroute to Africa and got to know each other. Then as we visited Johannesburg in South Africa and Biera in Mozambique we became good friends. We didn't hunt in the same camp but spent a day together on a camera safari while the group was staying in Gorongosa Park. I can't think of anyone who would be a stronger ally to have than Jim; am sure that is why he survived his near tragedy in space a few years later. I prize all the pictures I have in my slide collection of Jim and our sons in Africa.

Lee Greenwood

The Louise Mandrell Celebrity Shoot is one of the most exciting shoots held each year. My first year I attended, I shot with this country western singer and his wife and we really had fun together. Lee's wife, I must add, is one of the prettiest ladies I've ever seen. A few months later he brought his show to Des Moines and I had the pleasure of hosting this very patriotic guy—a great American.

Billy Martin

Billy Martin, the baseball great was my hunting partner at the Kurt Russell Celebrity Elk Hunt held in Colorado. After dinner the first night of the hunt each hunter was assigned a guide and a hunting companion. I met my guide and was told to meet him at breakfast and be ready to leave for the day's hunt immediately after the four A. M. breakfast. I was told that my companion was to be Billy Martin. Not being much of a baseball fan, the name didn't ring a bell at the time.

At breakfast the guide advised me that his vehicle was parked behind the chow tent and suggested that I put my gun and gear in it and wait for him to gather the other hunter and Kurt Russell's son who was going to ride with us. Obediently I put my gun and gear in the back of the Jeep station wagon and then sat down in the front seat to await the others. As I sat there I heard a voice say, "Who in the hell is that guy sitting in the front seat and who does he think he is taking that seat?" I didn't realize it at the time that Billy Martin dearly loves to put people on and this was his way of getting to me. To make a long story short, he bugged me about the front seat all day long and we had a lot of fun out of it. The second day, I made certain that I sat in the back seat. A few weeks later I got even with Billy when, in an auto junk-yard, I located a bucket seat, had it gift wrapped, and shipped it to him at his home in New York. I enclosed a card that read, "You always wanted the front seat so here it is you S.O.B.!"

I've hunted with many celebrities but must confess that Billy was more fun than any of them! He was a great joke teller and we did nothing but tell stories for two days. I got a glimpse of why he had such a great reputation when we went into a little town to buy some supplies. The store-keeper immediately recognized him and, while we were there talking, the principal of the local high school just happened in. When he learned who Billy was he asked if Billy would be kind enough to come back to the school for a few minutes and address the students. He said he would call an immediate assembly so Billy would only have to spend a few minutes. Billy graciously accepted so off we went to the school. Several hundred students heard Billy gives a great speech on sportsmanship, school spirit, and pride in our country. He really made a big hit and hung around afterwards to sign a few autographs. Everywhere we went Billy was recognized and received more attention that some of the big name movie stars. Being with him was a great experience and I was very saddened to hear a few months later that he had been killed in an auto accident.

Albert Mitchell

You're going to have to be darn near as old as me to remember Albert Mitchell who became famous back in the fifties as the Van Dyke Cigar "Answer Man" on Radio. His radio show bits were on the air for about ten years so he was quite famous. He really missed his calling; he should have been a stand-up comedian as he was one of the funniest men I've ever met. He also wrote songs and would come up with a little musical ditty on the slightest provocation. Albert loved to attend the pigeon shoots and, because his shows were all recorded, it was easy for him to get away. He was never a factor to beat but his presence with his charming wife sure added to the enjoyment of the shoots.

Albert was a great practical joker and I must relate to you one of his stories. Seemed that when he went to work at the radio studio in Chicago's loop, he always parked his car in one of those storage buildings where they take your car, drive it into an elevator, and then move it to a higher level to park. Albert always had a new car of which he was proud and it always irked the hell out of him, the way the car jockeys would burn rubber for the few feet to the elevator, then hit the brakes so hard that the car would rock back and forth. Then Albert would have to listen to the tires screaming as his car was being driven around on the upper floors. He decided to teach these gorillas a lesson. He bought a junker car at a used car lot, had the foot brake disconnected and then gingerly drove it to the parking ramp using the emergency brake and the gears if he needed to stop or slow down. He drove it into the ramp, took his parking receipt from the car jockey and then stood back and watched him drive it into the far wall of the elevator. Luckily the driver didn't get seriously injured but it changed their way of handling cars for some time. Albert just loved to tell this story!

It was in Albert's will that when he died he wanted to be cremated and have his ashes scattered from an airplane over his lake home in northern Wisconsin. His wife honored his wish and a mutual friend, John Garber, flew her in his airplane so she could scatter Albert's ashes.

Louise Mandrell

In just a few short years, Louise with her annual Celebrity Shoot in Nashville, has given the shooting sports the greatest public relations boost that I have ever witnessed. Proceeds from the shoot are for the Boy Scouts and Louise has raised hundreds of thousands of dollars for them.

Televised widely, Louise shooting with her sister Barbara and fifty other celebrities has elevated the status of shooting, illustrated to the world that shooting is fun, and people who love guns and shooting are not the "bad guys" as the media portrays them.

Louise and her husband John Haywood are friendly and down to earth people who love shooting so much they have their own skeet range and sporting clays course on their farm outside Nashville. The whole Mandrell family shoots including Barbara, her huband Ken Dudney and their son Matthew. Each year at the shoot, Barbara and Ken open up their spectacular home for a cocktail buffet in honor of the celebrities—it is one of the outstanding events of the shoot! I value knowing Louise and John and congratulate them for what they have done for the shooting sports and the Boy Scouts. I remember my scouting years fondly so am really in accord with Louise for helping this organization.

Ted Nugent

Ted is a world famous rock singer. A little less known fact is that he is the manufacturer of archery products and is an avid bow hunter. I've run into Ted at the annual SHOT Show where all of us who manufacture products for the hunting and shooting sports show our wares to dealers each year. I've also hunted with Ted at events like the Foss, Floyd, and Dean Pheasant Hunt in South Dakota. He has a beautiful wife and family. The image of the typical rock star disappears when you see Ted in the archery or hunting environment. He is a Director of the National Rifle Association and is a vociferous spokesman for gun enthusiasts.

His show came to Des Moines and he provided special tickets for my family. I can't say I am a fan for his music (I'm more the big band type) but there was no mistaking his popularity with the mob of people who came to hear him that night. We were given a special back-stage tour that was very thoughtful of Ted. My youngest daughter Abby was in her teens then and is still talking about the experience.

Dale Robertson

Dale is as big as life and twice as natural! We first met at the Enid, Oklahoma Grand National Quail Hunt and subsequently when he came to the Grand American Trapshoot in Vandalia, Ohio. At the Grand American he spent a lot of time in our store where he visited with other shooters and graciously posed for pictures with them. He enjoys life to the fullest, is easy to know, and is very friendly. I prize having met him.

Roy Rogers

What can I say about Roy that hasn't been said? When I was a boy I didn't like Roy's movies as much as those of Ken

Maynard, Buck Jones, and a few other cowboy stars because I thought a cowboy who sang was a sissy. Once I knew Roy personally, I found out he definitely was no sissy. He came up the hard way in the rodeo circuit, was a real outdoorsman and hunter, rode motorcycles, and was one of the best trapshooters in the country. He came to the Grand American Trapshoot (the National Championship shoot) and broke 199 X 200 clay targets and almost won the event.

Roy was a fierce competitor no matter what he was doing. At the spring Foo-Foo-Rah (rendezvous) for the One Shot Hunt we do all kinds of goofy competitive games; everything from tomahawk throwing, archery, trapshooting, and water boiling contests. Roy was a consistent winner and hated to be beaten. I used to watch him in the water-boiling contest and it was interesting to see how hard he worked at it. In this competition, the contestant is given a quart bucket of water, a log six inches in diameter and twelve inches long, a hatchet, a knife and two matches. With a person with a stopwatch keeping time the contestant must build a fire, make a crib to hold the bucket in the fire, and then make the water boil. The one who has his water boil in the shortest time is the winner. It is quite an achievement just to get your fire going; many use up the two matches and have no fire. Roy had it down to a fine art and would always end up winner by a few seconds.

Roy was fortunate in having many good friends. He and Dick Dobbins had a group that they hunted and traveled with including African Safaris. Roy attended most of the One Shot Antelope hunts and that is where I first met him. He was also a regular at the Carlsberg Honker Hunts where he captivated everyone by the way he charmed the little Modoc Indian children who were part of the ceremony there. Each year at this hunt the Modoc Indian tribe does their authentic dances in full costume.

When Roy appeared at the Iowa State Fair, when my children were very small, he came to Des Moines with Dale and all their children. I felt sorry for them being cooped up in a downtown hotel so I invited the whole gang to come out to our home for an afternoon steak fry. We tried to keep it a secret but by the time Roy and his family had arrived, the board fence around our back yard was lined with little faces peeking over the top. We had a lot of fun and that night from the big stage in front of the grandstand at the State Fair, Roy told the crowd that he had just had the best steak of his life at Bob Allen's house. Needless to say, my kids were heroes in these parts for a long time.

Roy fought heart trouble just as competitively as he had everything else. He had several heart procedures but it finally took its toll and he passed away. Now Roy "Dusty" Rogers Jr. and his son are regular attendants at some of the hunts. A singer and entertainer in his own right, Dusty generously provides entertainment at the hunts. He and his son are great ambassadors for the Rogers family. At the Big Country Celebrity Quail Hunt in Abilene, Texas Dusty always brings along some bit of Roy Rogers memorabilia which he donates to the fund raising auction benefiting Disability Resources, the organization which puts on the hunt. Funds raised provide care for developmentally disabled people; a great cause!

He and I have reminisced about the time his whole family were guests in our home in Des Moines. At that time he was only about eight years old—now he is a strapping six foot five and in his boots and trademark black hat is bigger than life! Dusty's son is a very mature young gentleman and has the same great smile as his dad and grandfather. Dusty now runs the Roy Rogers Museum and his son works in the museum along side him. I always look forward to seeing them! "Happy Trails" is certainly a great way to describe Roy and his family.

John Russell

Remember the "Law Man" TV western series? Handsome John was the star of this series who appeared in many other movies as well. John was a regular attendee at the Carlsberg Honker Hunts where we hunted together. On the long bus ride to the hunt we had an opportunity to spend several hours visiting and I found him to be a very soft hearted man with a deep interest in current events, politics, and causes to assist disadvantaged people. Have you ever met someone whose company you enjoyed and you wished that you might have the opportunity to spend more time with that person? John was in that category for me.

Johnny Rutherford

I've only been to the Indianapolis race once and that was one of the years it was won by Johnny. You can imagine how thrilled I was a couple of years later to be his hunting partner at one of the party hunts. We met again at the General Schwarzkopf Sporting Clays shoot in Tampa. Johnny is a very interesting guy with a variety of talents including flying a P-51. I saw a TV show which showed Johnny in a wreck where his racing car completely disintegrated. The next time I saw him I asked him how he lived through something like that and his reply was, "Which wreck are you referring to?" Because he has done a lot of hunting I asked him and he agreed to be on my TEST STAFF. We used him as a model in our catalog one year and I flew into Indianapolis where we had a fun day together doing photography for our catalog.

Robert Stack

Robert Stack has been a tremendous ambassador for the shooting sports for over fifty years. I first met Bob at the National Skeet Shoot in Las Vegas in 1946. Prior to WWII he had already made a name for himself in the skeet shooting world by winning the National 20 gauge championship at age 17, being on the All-American team for three years, setting a world's long run record, and being a member of a record five man team. Because of his extensive shooting experience, like me, he was tapped to become a gunnery instructor for the Navy. Several other famous shooters served in the Navy with him—Alex Kerr, Rudy Etchen and Art Durando. His interest in shooting and hunting have continued and, in an era where there has been a lot of anti-gun and anti-hunting pressure, he has become a great spokesman for those of us who love our guns and shooting. Bob has hunted in Africa and throughout the North American continent. Several books have been written about him and he has appeared in many hunting TV shows. His many movies and TV series have made him world famous. Through all of this, with his calm and gentlemanly demeanor, he has been a great role model for all of us in the shooting world. I've always been proud of him for many reasons. He has never been part of the Hollywood "goofy" set, has been married to the same lady for over fifty years, and just quietly goes along being much in demand and being very good and successful in whatever role he is playing.

I've had the pleasure of shooting with Bob at several of the "party" shoots including the One Shot Antelope Hunt, the Schwarzkopf Sporting Clays Shoot, and the Charlton Heston Celebrity shoot. He always shoots well, is a great sport, and is always available for photos, autographs, and visits with shooters. I'm proud that Bob always liked my shooting clothing well enough that he agreed to serve on my TEST STAFF where he supplied some great input. Thank you Robert Stack for all you have done for those of us in the shooting and hunting world!

Frank Tallman

Frank is a great stunt flyer who became famous for flying the old World War I aircraft in movies. He was also the one who flew the twin-engine airplane through the Coca Cola sign in the crazy movie "It's a Mad, Mad, World." He was my hunting partner at the One Shot Antelope Hunt and fascinated me with the stories of some of his flying experiences. I had just started flying myself so was particularly interested. In one story he was flying a vintage World War I Spad and dog fighting with a German triplane. The film was being made in an area of foothills north of Los Angeles with few emergency landing spots. It wasn't a good place to have an engine quit but that's what happened. Frank picked out the best emergency landing spot he could find which was a dried up stream in a canyon. He set it down okay but immediately ran into a big boulder that flipped him over on his back. He hit his head on something almost scalping himself and was hanging upside down by the seat belt with blood running down covering his face when a rescue helicopter sat down to help him. They thought he was dead but he lived through this one too.

Frank had a prosthetic leg that most people assumed was the result of an airplane accident. On the contrary, he told me it was the result of a burn he received from the exhaust pipe of his son's motorbike that turned into an infection. That leg made it very difficult for him to walk during the antelope hunt; the terrain in Wyoming is covered with sagebrush that you cannot walk through without lifting your feet over each bush and this soon tired Frank. We tried to tell him to take it easy but he insisted on hunting until he finally got his shot. I'm very proud of an autographed copy of a beautifully illustrated tabletop book titled "Flying The Old Airplanes" which Frank has written and edited. You don't meet unusual people like Frank Tallman every day!

Marshall Teague

The most dedicated hunters among the celebrities I have met are, without any doubt, Marshall and his beautiful wife Lindy. Whenever they are not making movies they spend all their time hunting and their diet at home is primarily game they have shot in their travels. I get to see them each year at the Heartland Celebrity Pheasant Hunt in Osceola, Iowa. Not content with just hunting pheasants in Iowa, they went deer hunting as well. (You'd be surprised how many deer we have in Iowa—they are so numerous they are a constant driving hazard). This hunt is a fundraiser for needy children. To raise added money the public can buy tickets to the Saturday night banquet that is the high point of the event. A special table is set up for the Celebrities to sign autographs for the public. Marshall and Lindy are very popular at this hunt and most gracious signing autographs and posing for pictures.

General Paul Tibbets

One of my heroes from World War II is General Paul Tibbets, the Commanding Officer of the 509th Atomic Bombardment Group and the pilot of the Enola Gay that dropped the first atom bomb. I didn't meet Paul until after the war but, over a period of years, we have become good friends.

Paul Tibbets of Enola Gay fame visits our store at the Grand American.

He is an avid hunter as well as a trap and skeet shooter. He lived in Columbus, Ohio and would attend the Grand American Trapshoot in Dayton almost every year. We shot together a few times and he always dropped by our shooting clothing stores on the firing line. He accepted my invitation to be the keynote speaker at our 504th Bomb. Group reunion in Colorado Springs and did a terrific job. All of us in the 504th felt a close kinship to the 509th Atomic Group because it had been formed from a squadron in our Group that had been mysteriously transferred away from us in 1944 when we were training in Nebraska. All of us had friends in the 393rd Squadron that then became the 509th commanded by Tibbets. As a boy Paul had lived in Iowa and still has relatives there. He has a standing invitation to visit us at our home on Lake Okoboji and we hope to see him again in 2001.

I'd describe Paul as being little but mighty! He stands about five foot ten and I'd guess weighs about one hundred sixty pounds. He has piercing eyes and speaks with a very positive tone. He's quick to admit that he feels no guilt regarding the atom bombs, as he is positive they ended the war and saved literally millions of lives that would have been expended had we invaded Japan. Paul came to Des Moines for an air show a few years ago and I learned something new about the atom bomb as we discussed the war over dinner. A third bomb had been transported by air as far as Sacramento, California and, had the Japs not capitulated after the second bomb, this one was going to be dropped. The target had not been chosen but the bomb was on its way! Paul's book "The Enola Gay" is great reading and I prize the autographed copy I have in my library.

General Norman Schwarzkopf

In my estimation, *Stormin Norman* is the most exciting thing that has happened to America in the last fifteen years. He had already established himself as one of my heroes before I had the opportunity to meet him in person. You can therefore understand how exciting it was for me to shoot with him in the Schwarzkopf Celebrity Sporting Clays Shoot in his hometown of Tampa, Florida. I found him to be an extremely personable guy, a fine shot, and a great storyteller. It was a pleasure to also meet his wife and one of his sons at this shoot. I ran into him again at some of the other shoots and had the pleasure of shooting in his squad at the Buffalo Bill Celebrity Shoot in Cody, Wyoming. Senator Al Simpson of Wyoming was also in our squad and the story telling and kidding around began the minute we started shooting. It was really fun to be around them. The shooting included skeet, trap, five stand, sporting clays, and some rifle events. He was outstanding in all. My wife Sari and I had the honor of being at his table for two of the banquets at this event and he just charmed us. He is an absolutely tremendous guy and I only wish that one of the parties had tapped him for some kind of a cabinet or elective job in Washington.

Astronaut Wally Schirra

Another pioneer, Wally still remains one of the best known of the early space-men. He regularly attends the One Shot Antelope Hunt, The Carlsberg Honker Hunt, and the Lamar, Colorado Two Shot Goose Hunt. One year when the Lamar hunt was over Wally invited me to ride with him driving back to Denver. He had just purchased some kind of a wild Italian sports car and, although he was an excellent driver, he scared the living daylights out of me, as he would rocket into curves at a tire screeching 125 miles an hour. He got a big kick out of scaring me and reminds me of it every time I see him. The capsule that Wally rode in on his first space shot is on display in the Alabama Space and Rocket museum in Huntsville, Alabama. After seeing it I had something to razz Wally about the next time I ran into him. He had gained so much weight that I told him he would never fit into the capsule now. Wally does a lot of hunting all over the world, so I could draw upon his experience; I invited him to serve on my TEST STAFF. He loves stories and practical jokes. His live mongoose practical joke is one of the most effective I've ever seen.

Astronaut Deke Slayton

Deke headed-up the astronaut program. As you may remember he was originally denied a space shot because of some kind of a minor heart problem but was ultimately given a shot. Deke attended the One Shot Hunt, the Carlsberg Hunts, and the Nebraska One Box Hunts on a regular basis so we became friends. In 1969 Deke and his thirteen-year-old son were part of the African First Shotter's African safari along with my thirteen-year-old son Matt and myself. Also on the trip were Jim Lovell and his son who was about the same age. The three boys had a great time together and it made for a closer relationship between Deke, Jim, and myself. A year or so later when Deke was in space, I would go out in my back yard to watch his "star" pass over Des Moines. It was an eerie experience realizing that someone you knew was riding in that star. Deke left the space program to join a civilian company planning space exploration. I was saddened to learn later that he had passed away. I'll always remember him for his easy smile and his friendly, easy-going way.

Maurice Stans

Maurice, a California attorney, was a prominent fund-raiser for the Republican Party and was on Richard Nixon's cabinet. He escaped the stigma of Watergate and wrote a book called "The Terrors of Justice" which he autographed and sent to me. I had first met him when we shared a room together at the Carlsberg Honker Hunt. John Ruan was a mutual friend in Des Moines so Maurice and I always had something to talk about. I was in Japan on a business trip and ran into him at the Tokyo airport; that was the last time I saw him.

Tom Watson

Tom is one of the greatest golfers in my lifetime. We met at the One Shot Antelope Hunt and ran into each other at some of the other party hunts. An avid hunter I felt he would be a valuable asset to my TEST STAFF; and of course, his name on the staff certainly was good for Bob Allen Sportswear. He accepted the appointment and both he and his manager became great boosters. I prize highly an autographed picture of Tom which graces the wall in my Lake Okoboji home.

Charley Walker

Charley Walker of Nashville Country Music fame is one of the nicest guys I've ever met. He loves to hunt and shoot and is a regular attendee at the Louise Mandrell Celebrity Shoot and the One Shot Antelope Hunt. For years he wore one of my bush coats on his show and of course, this pleased me no end. As a member of my TEST STAFF he contributed many great ideas. Many thanks Charley.

Hank Williams Jr.

Hank, like his dad, has become a legend in the country music world. It was a real pleasure meeting him at his Tennessee headquarters and I was pleasantly surprised to learn that he is a really enthusiastic hunter and gun collector. His dad has a car museum at their headquarters and I suggested to Hank Jr. that his guns should also be a part of this museum.

General Chuck Yeager

Last but not least, by a long shot, is my admiration for Chuck Yeager. He is a tremendous guy and has been a great friend. During WWII he became famous as a P-51 fighter ace. To illustrate what a "tiger" he is, he was shot down on a mission and managed to evade the Germans by walking through France, Spain, and out through Portugal where he went back to England and lived to fight another day. Usually after a flyer had evaded capture after being shot down, he would not be allowed to fly combat again for fear of being captured and revealing the secrets of how the underground had helped him to evade capture the first time. Despite this ruling, Chuck wanted to get back in action again so he had to be cleared by the highest authority. After the war he was a test pilot and became world famous by being the first one to fly an aircraft through the sound barrier. A movie was made on this feat and was titled "The Right Stuff" which Chuck certainly has. Chuck has a little vignette part in the movie—plays the part of the bar tender in the bar where all the test pilots hung out. You have to look twice to see him. Nobody loves to hunt and shoot more than Chuck and now that he is retired he has the time. He's very fortunate that his best friend, also a P-51 fighter ace, Bud Anderson lives nearby and the two hunt together. I first met Chuck at the One Shot Antelope Hunt but in the years since we have seen each other at many of the other hunts plus he always attends the SHOT (Shooting, Hunting, and Outdoor Trade) show.

To illustrate what a great guy and fine friend Chuck has

been to me, I must tell this story. About the time that his movie "The Right Stuff" came out, Chuck was the most publicized man in America and was much in demand for advertising and speaking engagements. At a time when he was receiving thousands of dollars for the use of his name in advertising various products he allowed me to put him on our TEST STAFF. I wanted to use him in our magazine and catalog advertising but didn't figure I could afford him. When I mentioned this to him he shocked me by saying he'd be happy to do it for free. I felt guilty in accepting his offer so countered by saying that we'd give him a lifetime supply of hunting clothing or anything else from the Bob Allen line. For this Chuck posed for pictures and allowed us to use his pictures in all our magazine ads and in our catalog—advertising that we could never have afforded without his generosity. About five years ago I sold Bob Allen Sportswear to The Boyt Company, and I am happy to say that they are still honoring this agreement. Chuck never asks for anything so about once a year we put together an assortment of new items and send them to him. There is no way in which I can ever repay Chuck for his help but I tried to in a small way when I learned that his home town in West Virginia was raising money for a bronze statue of Chuck to be placed in the town square. I contributed to that cause and received a miniature of the sculpture, which I prize very highly and is on display in my home on Lake Okoboji.

Chuck is an amazing man! Although he is about the same age as me, his health is perfect, his vision is intact and, the last time I heard, he is still flying jet aircraft. He's a good hunter and an excellent shot. He gives a hell of a speech and is in much demand for banquets. My son Matt, who is also one of Chuck's greatest admirers, invited Chuck to come to Des Moines to be the keynote speaker for an YPO (Young Presidents Organization) banquet. The meeting was held at the National Guard headquarters and so was attended by many Guard members who were enthralled by Chuck's presentation. Chuck gets a big laugh when he describes the early model "G" suits that were used in the P-51's later in the war. The suits were water filled ponderous things and when the mission was over, the ground crew would help the pilot out so he could sit on the leading edge of the wing. A pair of drains on the front of the suit would then release the water. Chuck said that after such long missions, there usually would be three streams of water! Chuck, it is a real pleasure knowing you and I thank you from the bottom of my heart for what you have done for our country, our friendship, and all you've done to help Bob Allen.

Chapter 16

Characters

Viva la difference!

Thank God we are not all alike or it would be a pretty boring world. In my eighty-one years, I've run into some mighty interesting and different people. Some of them were so unusual and singular that I lovingly call them "characters." It was fun for me to select the ten most interesting and unforgettable characters of my lifetime and to present them here for your entertainment. They are all my friends and I hope they will remain so even after reading why I have classified them as the ten most unforgettable *characters* I have known.

My number one character is definitely ~ JIMMY ROBINSON.

Once I had made up my list of characters, there was no doubt that Jimmy would be the number one personality on the list. Living in Minneapolis, Jimmy was an outdoor journalist for the Minneapolis Star, plus he did a monthly column on Skeet and Trapshooting for Sports Afield Magazine. He originated the idea of a Sports Afield All-American Trap and Skeet team and personally chose the team members. Because of his close association with the shooting sports, he became an authority and historian on the subject. For many years he was the only one who submitted publicity releases to hometown newspapers on winners of the National Championship shoots. Along with some other twin city sportsmen, he established the Sports Afield Duck Camp in St. Ambroise, Manitoba, Canada. This was the finest duck hunting in North America and attracted celebrities from all over the world.

Jimmy was born in Canada, played professional hockey and baseball for Winnipeg, and served in the Canadian Army in WWI. Because of his extensive hunting and outdoor background the army made him a sniper. At the duck club he told amazing stories of his war experiences including once when he became trapped out in "no-man's-land" between the German and Allied trenches. He had hidden in a shell hole, which was a good vantage point to pick off Germans. However, they discovered where he was hiding and began shelling him with mortars. To add to his problems he also discovered that the shell hole harbored some residual poisonous phosgene gas, making his position more untenable. He ended up being trapped there for forty-eight hours until an Allied attack overran his position and rescued him. As a result of his exposure to the gas he acquired a lifetime lung disability that occasionally manifested itself in a rabbit-like wrinkling of his nose, which intensified when he was excited or was telling a story.

Jimmy loved cigars! He usually just chewed on them and was constantly spitting out bits of the tobacco. If you were standing near him while he was talking, you'd end up covered with cigar bits. The combination of the rabbit wrinkles and the cigar spitting made him a real sight.

It was a genuine honor to be invited to the duck camp, so I was thrilled the first time he invited me to join the hunt. Immediately upon arrival, I began to learn that Jimmy was indeed a lovable character!

Indian guides working for the camp rowed us out into the tall reeds along the south end of Lake Manitoba. No blinds were used; the guides just tossed out a few decoys, tied the boat to some reeds, and you waited for the ducks to come. The

Jimmy Robinson presenting me with a trophy at the 1987 Fawcett Shoot.

ducks were so plentiful that getting your limit was an cinch and you could even pick out the type duck you wanted to bag. Usually you were done in a half hour and went back to the lodge for a tremendous breakfast cooked by Jimmy's staff under the direction of his wife Clara who was also kind-of-a-character. In fact, anyone who could live with Jimmy had to be a loveable character!

Breakfast consisted of fruit, bacon, eggs, ham, oatmeal, pancakes, toast and omelets; just about anything you wanted and as much as you could eat. The hunters sat at a long table for twelve. Jimmy always sat at the head of the table and the minute he sat down the stories began. And what stories they were! He was a walking encyclopedia of information on baseball, football, hockey, plus trap and skeet shooting. He had perfect recall for all the champions and their scores and was without a doubt the premier historian for the shotgun-shooting world. He loved to tell stories and was so good at it that the meals became the high point of the hunt for everybody.

Jimmy was totally dependent upon his wife Clara for everything. A hundred times a day you would hear him holler "Clara" and she'd come running. She ran the camp and handled all of the day-to-day details of personnel and food, leaving Jimmy to socialize with all the hunters.

It was time for me to fly home, so I went to Jimmy to say my good byes. That is when I found out that I wasn't a real guest. Jimmy presented me with a bill for a sizable amount. After I was able to control the amazed look on my face, I paid the bill thinking to myself it was expensive but worth every cent because the hunting was unbelievably good and the food outstanding and the stories would make me laugh out loud for a life time, even if I was in a room all by myself!

Jimmy was a great booster for my business, my reputation, as well as a good customer. He selected me for his All-American team eleven times. He always mentioned me in his column, writing that he considered me to be one of the top two all-around shooters in the United States. By all-around he meant a shooter who could shoot trap, skeet, as well as live pigeons. Considering his knowledge of the shooting game and individual shooters, I felt this was a tremendous accolade.

Jimmy seemed to attract friends in high places and many celebrities were among his true friends. Clark Gable and Carol Lombard were regulars at the duck camp as were Ernest Hemingway and his wife. Baron Hilton entertained Jimmy whenever he was on the west coast. Jimmy always said that money didn't mean anything to him as he had rich friends. When he wanted to go to California in the winter, he'd call Baron Hilton or Bob Stack and announce that he and Clara were coming. He was such a character and so much fun to be around that he got away with it and they always welcomed him with open arms. I guess you could call him a freeloader but he never really asked for anything; he just told you what he was doing and things just seemed to come to him!

He wrote several books on hunting and shooting and his way of assuring a good market for his books was to mention as many names as he could. Then, when the book was published, he'd just send each person named a case or two of books along with a bill. (I could pull the same stunt, however, I'm a little too late ~ most of my friends are dead!) Ruthie and I had just been married and frugality was always on our minds. Much to our consternation, a carton of fifty books arrived one day by Railway Express, along with a bill for $200.00. To us it may as well have been a couple of thousand dollars. Needless to say, my new bride was really shocked and upset; but that was Jimmy!

Once I invited Jimmy to Des Moines so we could hunt ducks together at a duck camp operated by our mutual friend, Omaha beer magnate, Art Storz. I flew Jimmy down to the Storz duck camp in my new Cessna 175. Just after take-off we flew over a little town and Jimmy asked me the name of it. Without thinking of the impact of my words I simply said, "I don't know." This threw Jimmy into a panic as he thought we were lost. He finally settled down after I explain how we navigate on VOR and it really didn't matter that we didn't know the name of each little town we flew over. Later I found out that flying gave him a good reason to be nervous. The summer before, Jimmy had been fishing in a remote lake in Canada. He hired a floatplane to pick him up and they crashed into the treetops on take-off. Jimmy was lucky to get out with his life.

The night before this trip we had dinner at Des Moines' best restaurant at that time: Johnny & Kay's. On their hors d'oeuvre tray they had a lot of pickled beets, one of Jimmy's favorites. As he devoured the beets he left some red stains on the white tablecloth. I watched in amusement as he systematically covered up the spots nonchalantly by placing a saltshaker or dish to cover each spot so they wouldn't show. By the end of the meal he had all the small objects on the table clustered around him to cover his beet spots.

After he left our home the next morning, Ruthie found his deposited gum on the inside of the guest-bedroom lampshade. Yes, Jimmy was an unforgettable character, a lovable slob who was true to his friends and generous to everyone. Anyone who ever knew him loved him. He will always be in my memory as a true friend, a person who helped me immeasurably, especially when I was nobody.

All of the signboards in the twin cities honored Jimmy when he passed away in 1986.

Jimmy is the only person for whom roadside billboards were erected in his memory. His lifelong hunting friend Jimmy Naegely owned the biggest sign company in the twin cities. When Jimmy died all of the Naegely signs in the twin cities carried a *Maas* (a famous artist friend of Jimmy's) duck scene and the words:

"JIMMY ROBINSON ~ THE MEMORY LIVES ON."

My number two most unforgettable character is VIC REINDERS.

When I first started shooting in 1939, Vic Reinders was one of the top trapshooters in the country. Early on he became one of my idols but I didn't have an opportunity to meet him until after WWII. We became friends and shot in the same squad together whenever possible. He will undoubtedly go down in history as one of the world's greatest trapshooters. A member of the trapshooting Hall of Fame, Vic's lifetime average percentage may have set a record nobody will ever be able to break.

A college professor, he had many idiosyncrasies, which is why I have included him as one of my "characters." As any shooter who has shot in the same squad with him will attest, he was unique. A very meticulous person, he carried a little spiral notebook in his pocket and, after each event, he'd jot down notes on that event. He kept track of every target he ever missed and he developed statistics that covered his entire shooting career of some sixty years. I'd like to study the statistics he developed and hope that someone will publish them some day as a reference for other shooters.

Like me, Vic had been in the military gunnery program during WWII. His gun was a Remington 31TC trap gun and he shot the same gun for sixty years. I doubt if there was ever a gun that had more shells fired out of it than Vic's. For many years Vic ran the Waukesha, Wisconsin gun club and was instrumental in getting many new shooters started. An excellent instructor, you could always identify one of Vic's students by the way in which they called "Pull" when they were ready for their target. Most shooters simply say, "Pull!" some grunt, and any other audible call usually will suffice. However, Vic had the idea that if the shooter stretched out the call by saying "Puuuuulllllll" it would even out the pullers response and prevent either fast or slow pulls; both of which are responsible for a lot of misses. The only drawback to his system was that the puller really didn't know when to release the target, at the start of the word, or during it. I never agreed with the philosophy but it worked for Vic and many of his students. As you went down the trap line you could identify all of his protégées by the way they sang out *puuuulllll*. It was often said that if you put Vic and four of his students in the same squad, it would sound like a choir.

To soften the recoil of his gun Vic pinned a potholder under the gun pad on his shooting vest. Most shooters needed some extra padding as the guns kicked harder back in those days. From observing the safety pins holding the potholder under his vest, I designed and patented a feature that put all of our shooting clothing way out in front of the competition. I called it "INSERT A PAD" and it was a special foam rubber pad inserted into a pocket we created behind the gun pad. The pads were offered in varying thicknesses depending upon how much protection the shooter wanted. So, my great invention was really just a sophisticated copy of Vic's safety pinned potholder.

Vic was a real gentleman, a great squad mate, and he and his wife Tommy were superb ambassadors for the trapshooting world, and they had many friends across the country. My memory is filled with countless, and outstanding experiences shooting with Vic. My first 200 straight was broken at the Wisconsin State Shoot with Vic in the squad. As any shooter will tell you, having a squad with good timing and concentration is of ultimate importance in shooting a good score.

In 1952 Vic and I shot in the same squad at the Iowa State Shoot. In the 200-target match, we arrived to shoot the last trap and Vic was 175 straight without a miss. There was a little striped chipmunk, which we Iowans call "squintys" that had found a hole in the back of the traphouse. It had been running around all day and several shooters had remarked that watching that little creature darting about was pretty hard on one's concentration. This sets up the scene as we arrived at the last trap to shoot our last 25 targets. Vic is straight (no misses) and despite his great experience is naturally under considerable pressure. We shot a few targets and the squinty kept running around. It was bothering me a little and I knew it must have been working on Vic too. About halfway through the event Vic stopped the squad and asked if anyone would mind if he shot the squinty to get rid of it. We all agreed, so Vic very carefully aimed at the squinty (which by now was standing up at attention) and pulled the trigger. Just as he shot, the squinty moved and he missed it by about a foot as it ran into its hole. That really broke up the squad and it took several minutes for us to stop laughing. Then Vic called for his next target and missed it; his first miss in 187 targets! That really broke up the squad again and it took several more minutes before things settled down and we could continue shooting. Vic's final score was 199 out of 200 and one missed squinty! For years we razzed him by asking things like, "How far do you lead a standing ground squirrel?" I've often wondered how he wrote that one miss up in his little notebook.

My third most notable character is DAVID BELIN.

In 1957 Dave became my attorney. I inherited him when my former attorney, Ross Sidney, left the Herrick, Langdon law firm. Dave was fresh out of Michigan State Law School, graduating number one in his class.

My first need for Dave came when I decided to contest a traffic ticket for supposedly running a red light. Coasting through on the yellow, not wanting to slam on the brakes because I had the baby in the car, was more like it. Kelly was about a year old and I didn't want to throw her out of her car seat. The Officer would not listen to reason so I told him that I was going to contest this ticket in court.

Dave appeared with me at a court presided over by a Judge everyone called "Alcoholic Harrison" because he was a prominent AA member. I had never had much respect for him, as I felt his judgments were often questionable. He listened to the cop's testimony and then heard Dave who read the statute concerning stoplights. I unquestionably had not violated the statute but it was my word against the cop and the deck was stacked. After hearing the testimony, Harrison banged his gavel down hard and said, "Guilty as charged, fine $50.00," and that was it! I started to stand up to complain but Dave grabbed my sleeve and said, "Sit down, in traffic court you are not innocent until proven guilty, you are guilty until proven innocent!" For years after I ribbed Dave about being a brilliant corporate attorney but that he wasn't worth a dime in a traffic court.

As my business grew, Dave's role grew also. When we started making airline bags, he drew up a license agreement that was so good the airlines' legal departments signed it without making any changes. He successfully defended these agreements against several manufacturers who "knocked us off"~ by copying our bags and illegally using the airline names and logos, for which we had been given exclusive rights.

When President Kennedy was assassinated, President Johnson appointed Dave to the Warren Commission, which investigated the assassination. Dave was convinced that it was not a big conspiracy and that it was a "one man" operation carried out by Oswald. He wrote a book on the assassination, which was widely read and became the basis for research studies by many scholars.

A few years later Dave was appointed by President Gerald Ford, to head up a special committee to investigate the CIA. David was never able to tell me very much about this except that one project was to investigate the CIA plotting to kill Castro. Dave's assignment to these two prestigious committees just robbed me of an outstanding attorney for a couple of years.

By now Dave had developed a sort of Will Rogers look, which included bow ties, shoes that usually didn't match his suits and a time-worn black leather briefcase that was really decrepit. He had developed a nervous "tic" in his right cheek that caused him to wink at inappropriate times. The general effect was a kind of a "country boy" look that really deceived his opponents.

Dave's office was the most disorganized mess I've ever seen! His desk was always piled high with files and briefs. It drove his secretary Kathryn wild but Dave knew exactly where everything was. He had the greatest memory I have ever encountered and remembered details about my business that just amazed me. He constantly surprised me with his grasp of business details and like all good attorneys could come up with alternative approaches to any problem.

By now he had attracted a lot of attention and was asked to serve on several prestigious boards such as General Mills and Kemper. He established an office in New York City and commuted regularly between New York and Des Moines.

About 1993, when several companies showed interest in buying us out, I turned all the negotiations over to Dave. It was now that I learned of his tremendous negotiating skills. One company, Norwood Promotional Products of Austin, Texas, was really pursuing us. My son Matt, Dave, and I met with the top man and his staff at the Fairmont Hotel in Dallas for an initial meeting. They had rented a large suite with a big sitting room to impress us, with a huge bowl of fruit pleasantly sitting on the coffee table. After all the introductions were complete we all sat down, Dave on the couch and the rest of us seated around the large coffee table. There Dave sat, center stage, with his usual Will Rogers appearance. He looked more like a country judge than an attorney, with his bow tie, his rumpled suit, questionable shoes, and the crowning touch— his old-fashioned valise-type briefcase. Then, to cap it off, Dave took off his shoes and proceeded to silently consume all the fruit in the bowl. What few questions and remarks he made however were to the point and really "loaded!" When we broke for lunch, as we were walking out, I was asked, "Where did you get this guy Belin?" It didn't take long for them to gain a healthy respect for Dave.

The negotiations with Norwood went on for two years with Belin constantly reminding me to remain silent. Several times we reached figures that I thought were pretty good but each time Belin had us walk away until finally Norwood came up with an offer close to what Dave had in his mind.

In March of 1995, Matt, Dave, Quentin Boykin from Belin's firm, and I all flew to Austin for the closing. Several times I thought we had reached an acceptable deal but each time Dave had us walk out of the room for a private meeting. Each time Dave zinged them for a little more money. We finally settled for a deal that was far above what I had imagined. Dave, the supreme negotiator, was right.

My great friend and advisor Dave Belin came to an untimely and strange end in 1999. He had gone, in good health, to Rochester, Minnesota for his annual check up at the Mayo Clinic. He was found unconscious in his hotel room and never came out of the coma. They determined that somehow he had fallen and struck his head. The speculation was that possibly he had fainted after some of his tests. Thus, Dave's was a very untimely ending to a brilliant life and career. I shall always remember you Dave Belin, a man to be admired for your brillance, a man I could always depend on, a man that was . . . you are deeply missed, Dave.

The fourth most interesting character in my life is HOMER CLARK JR.

Homer Clark should go down in the shooting history books as the greatest American shotgun shooter. He is the only American to win the Championship of the World twice, has won many championships at the Grand American and is in the Amateur Trapshooting Association Hall of Fame and the Pigeon Shooting Hall of Fame. Homer shot in Europe every year from 1947 through 1994 and amassed literally hundreds of trophies. His trophy-game room in his home at Alton, Illinois has to be the greatest display of shooting trophies ever collected by any one shooter. The trophies presented at shoots in Europe are spectacular and Homer's trophy for winning the Championship of the World in Madrid is an ornate sterling cup that stands about four feet tall. It was so heavy Homer didn't know how he was going to get it home until the Captain of a U. S. Navy ship volunteered to bring it back to the US on his destroyer. Homer had a special hexagonal trophy room built on to his home to showcase this gorgeous trophy that now stands on a dais in the center of the room. Around the base beneath the trophy some of Homer's finer guns are display. Special lighting makes his trophy shine like a star and the effect is spectacular.

Additionally Homer was personally responsible for the beginning and growth of shotgun shell reloading. He foresaw the need for shotgun shooters to be able to reload their own shells just like pistol and rifle shooters had been doing for years. In 1947 Homer and I were shooting in Italy when he negotiated with Italian ammunition makers and started to import shotgun shell primers and powder. He had already started making wads in the basement of his home in Alton. Later he formed the Alcan Company which was the only independent ammunition company in America and which manufactured and sold all kinds of reloading components.

This was noteworthy because at that time the United States manufacturers of ammunition—Winchester, Remington, and Federal (with the blessing of our government, an organized monopoly)—tried their best to stop reloading. Some even went so far as to print on their shell boxes that it was illegal to reload. Despite this and other things the industry did to discourage Homer, his Alcan Company prospered and grew.

During WWII, Homer was not allowed to enlist in any of the services because of his chemical engineer job at Winchester. Ammunition being so critical to our defense, all Winchester employees were frozen in their jobs. With this experience and his chemical engineering education, Homer was uniquely equipped to found a company like Alcan. I consider him the world's top shotgun ballistician.

At the end of the war Homer went to work for Ithaca Gun Company as sales manager. For three or four years he traveled the country for Ithaca and attended shoots on weekends. He had been shooting a Browning over/under shotgun at the pigeon shoots and winning most of the events. Ithaca wanted him to shoot one of their guns and made up a special 12-gauge side-by-side double barrel shotgun with 28" barrels. It was a much heavier gun than the Browning and was difficult to swing. To reduce weight Homer had the barrels shortened to 25 inches, the forearm hollowed out and reduced in size, and the stock also hollowed out a little. He ended up with an eight and a half pound gun that was lightning fast. With it he won two World Championships and many other events. With those short barrels he was the fastest shot in the world. Most of his birds would be dead three or four feet from the traps while other shooters would be rolling theirs up against the boundary fence seventeen yards away. Shooters were always razzing Homer about his sawed-off shotgun that was just long enough to be within the Federal law.

His big break came when the steel industry asked him if it would be practical to reload the eight-gauge "kiln" shells, which, they used to shoot slag out of their blast furnaces. They were buying new shells from the ammunition companies at a premium price and were throwing away the empty shells. One of the steel company executives was a trap shooter and became aware of Homer's wad advertising and recognized that Homer was an expert ballistician. They figured out that if they could reload their kiln shells they could save at least fifty percent of the original cost.

A kiln shell contained a large lead slug instead of lead shot which, when shot into the blast furnace, would remove the slag and the lead would be filtered out with other impurities. The use of these shells saved the steel industry thousands of dollars because they no longer had to shut down the blast furnace to remove slag.

Homer knew about the tremendous volume of kiln shells used because of his past experience at Winchester. He jumped right on their inquiry, flew to Pittsburgh for a meeting, and came home with a contract to reload shells plus enough money to buy loading machines to make new ammunition. Part of his deal with the steel industry was that he could use these machines to make his own products after he had filled all their orders. This launched Alcan in a big way! Homer put up a building, imported state of the art loading machines, and soon was grinding out top quality shotgun shells.

Remember, if you will, all of this occurred at a time when the ammunition industry was trying to stop reloading. One company even went so far as to print on their shotgun shell boxes that it was illegal to reload their empty shells. They fought Homer in many dirty ways but he was able to prosper despite this tough competition.

When I began shooting after the war, in 1946, Homer was already the top pigeon shot in the country and became my idol. Subsequently, we became friends and Homer was very helpful to me. In time, several of us began traveling together to the shoots to save expenses. Homer, Earl Roth, Joe Hiestand, and myself made up a foursome that came away with most of the prize money at every shoot.

Homer's eating habits were one of the many reasons I dubbed him as a character. He loved to eat and ate prodigious quantities. I jokingly used to say that there were gourmets and then there was Homer a gourmet-glutton. He also loved good wine and imported large quantities from Europe for his wine cellar at home. One time while shooting in Rome, we all had dinner at an Alfredo's restaurant which proclaimed itself to be the "first original Afredo's." Homer had their Alfredo

Fettuccini and almost inhaled it. He said it was so good that when the time came to order dessert, he ordered another entrée of the Fettuccini.

Even when he was just starting out and poor, Homer lived like a millionaire; staying in best hotels, best restaurants, and driving fine cars. In 1957 we all shot in the Championship of the World in Rome. Homer brought over his new Cadillac convertible, the 1957 model with huge fins in the back (the same Caddy he lent me for my honeymoon). To top off the special color and tires he had a pair of 36" Buell air-horn trumpets mounted on the right front fender; it was truly sensational and the Italians loved it. The only problem was that its size made it difficult to negotiate through the narrow streets of Rome. The car barely made it into the Excelsior Hotel parking garage with only a half-inch to spare on each side.

About 1989 Homer sold the Alcan Company so that he and Mary could be free to travel to Europe for shooting and to Africa for a safari each year. Then disaster struck! Mary hadn't been feeling well so they went to the Mayo Clinic for an examination. They called me at home with the alarming news that Mary had been diagnosed with the dreaded Lou Gehrig's disease.

The disease progressed rapidly and soon Mary was confined to bed and unable to move anything but her eyes. Homer stopped everything to stay home and care for her. He and his daughter Shelley devoted their entire lives to taking care of Mary. Even though they had registered nurses around the clock, the strain on Homer was terrible; he lost weight and looked like he had been "pulled through a knot hole." After several years of illness Mary passed away but it was to be two or three years before Homer began to get his life back on track and enjoy shooting, hunting, and playing a little golf.

Homer's last act of generosity to me was in 1996 when he flew to Portugal to be my presenter into the Pigeon Shooting Hall of Fame. He didn't even bring a gun; he just flew over for a few days to be part of my induction ceremony and then flew home. My true and beloved friend, Homer!

For about fifteen years we made it a custom to shoot in the same squad at the Iowa State Shoot and the Grand

American. This ended in 1998 when Homer peacefully passed away in his sleep at his winter home in Naples, Florida. Yes, Homer was a "character" and shall always be remembered as my true friend.

The fifth most interesting character I have known is LEON MEASURES.

This is the most enthusiastic guy and the most avid quail hunter I have ever had the pleasure of knowing! I met Leon through a rather strange set of circumstances. He was a big booster for my hunting clothing but I had never met him. Leon and a friend, Mike Jones, were hunting together in south Texas on a day when the temperature was about 80 degrees. You don't want to wear heavy clothing in this kind of weather so they were hunting in shirtsleeves; however they were wearing the new BOB ALLEN snake chaps, which I had just designed and placed on the market. The dogs hit a point on a covey of quail and Mike walked up on them. As he stepped into the brush beside a ledge, a big rattlesnake hit him from behind on the calf of his leg. He let out a yell and shot the snake as Leon came running. Although Mike was struck so hard it almost knocked him over, when they took off the chaps they found that the fangs had not been able to pierce the chaps' special nylon. There were just two wet spots of venom on the inside of the chaps where the fangs had struck. The snake was so large that had the fangs pierced the chaps, they undoubtedly would have also pierced the jeans Mike was wearing underneath. With a snake this large it surely would have been a fatal attack. Leon was so pleased with the protection our chaps had given his friend, he wrote me a letter. Because the chaps were new in our line and this was our first real field test with a snake in the wild, we were thrilled with the result. We had tested the chaps with all kinds of snakes at a snake farm but this was the real thing! I was so excited that I immediately called Leon to thank him for the feedback. In his own inimitable way he charmed me into an invite to quail hunt with him in Texas. That was the start of a friendship that has endured to this day. As a thank you we sent Leon a free pair of snake chaps, which he is still wearing.

Shortly thereafter Leon phoned me to get some marketing advice on a new system for teaching instinct shooting for which he had registered the trademark "Shoot Where You Look." We had many phone conversations and letters concerning this system that involved shooting with a BB gun with the sights removed. He starts his students out by having them shoot at a spot on a piece of paper. He then has them mount the gun up to the shoulder and cheek and shoot by looking over the gun at the target without sighting. Repetitive shooting like this causes your instincts to take over and all of a sudden you are miraculously hitting the spot nine times out of ten. He then has his students graduate to throwing cans up in the air and following the same procedure until they are hitting the can every time. Next he has the shooter start shooting at smaller and smaller items until finally he has them able to hit a penny every time. Finally, and this is hard to believe, he teaches them to toss up a BB and hit it with the same size BB from the BB gun. You have to see it to believe it!

The best part of it is that Leon is an excellent instructor and loves teaching. He started by teaching Boy Scout and Girl Scout groups. As his reputation grew, adult skeet and trapshooters sought him out for help. Leon now travels around the country putting on "Shoot Where You Look " seminars. What he enjoys the most is setting up a special booth at gun shows, fairs, and similar functions where people walking by are intrigued to stop and try his system. His booth has a canvas and clear perimeter so he can actually shoot the BB gun and demonstrate in the booth. Before long he draws a crowd and they are entertained not only by his shooting but also by the line of Texan chatter that definitely adds to the show. To promote his system he has written the best book I have ever read on instinct shooting. He also has created excellent videotape. As part of his program Leon has created a kit that includes the specially altered gun, his book, some safety glasses, and the video. The video is as entertaining as his line of chatter in person.

When he first contacted me and before he had fine-tuned

his program I suggested that he copy right it and then sell it to someone like the Daisy Air Rifle Company as it would be perfect for them to use in promoting the sale of their BB guns. Daisy discussed a royalty program with him but the restrictions were such that it was difficult for Leon to make a deal. They wanted him to buy 1000 guns at a time but forbade him to sell his kits to any of their dealers. This wasn't practical because it limited him to selling only to the consumer. They also wanted to change his book and video, which I have already said are the best I've seen. It just didn't work out and the last I heard Leon was negotiating to have his own line of BB guns produced.

Leon was constantly urging me to come and hunt quail with him but my work schedule at that time made it impossible for me to carve out the necessary time. Finally, in February of 1995 I was invited to shoot in "The Big Country Celebrity Quail Hunt" at Abilene, Texas. This seemed like an excellent time to work in a hunt with Leon so we set it up however I didn't realize what I was getting into!

Leon picked me up at my hotel in Abilene and his hunting rig astounded me! It started with a Chevy Suburban that was packed to the roof with enough gear for an Alaskan expedition and a special trailer with six dogs. He had every kind of a soft drink you ever heard of, ice, plus sandwiches for our 200-mile trip to Big Spring, Texas where a motel would be our headquarters. During the drive, he regaled me with stories about his dad and hunting. When we arrived he insisted on sharing a motel room and I then learned that this meant sharing it with the dogs too as he brought them in to feed. By this time in my life I had become sort of a "hot house" hunter whose idea of roughing it was staying at a Holiday Inn. I always preferred quail hunting because you don't have to get up in the middle of the night and freeze your rear off in a blind. It was not to be that way with Leon! He had me up at the crack of dawn, and after a breakfast, which I insisted we stop for, we were on our way to the quail area he had reserved for us with a rancher friend. It seemed like we went through fifty gates, each of which had a different way of fastening. If you have hunted anywhere in the west you know what I am talking about. Every rancher has his own idea of gate fasteners and some really rugged cowboy had made those we encountered. My city muscles had a hell of a time getting some of the gates open, let alone shutting them again!

About twenty miles into this ranch backcountry following just a dirt path, it suddenly started to rain. Do you all know about Texas and rain? Well, the rain soaked up the first three inches of that Texas red topsoil which quickly became a glue-like gumbo that clogged the wheels so badly that even the Suburban's four-wheel drive couldn't move us forward. We were mired down to the running boards and even though we piled brush under the wheels, we couldn't move. I thought we were there for the summer and, this being before cell phones were so common, we couldn't just call for help. I don't know who could have come to our aid anyway.

It didn't bother Leon one bit. He said, "We're here, we're stuck, so we might just as well hunt until the sun comes out to dry up this mud," and that is just what we did. He let out a couple of dogs and it was only a few moments before they hit a point and we had our first birds. Plus, I learned very quickly that if you wanted to get in a shot, you had better be quick, as Leon is one-hell-of-a-quail-shot. To make it worse, he showed me up by shooting with a Winchester model 42, 410-gauge shotgun. For those of you who don't know about the 410, it is the smallest gauge shotgun made and has only about one third the amount of shot my 12-gauge throws. By noon the sun came out, the mud dried up just as Leon had predicted, and we were able to get the Suburban moving again.

At the time I was about seventy-five years old and Leon wasn't too far behind me but he walked me off my feet. By five o'clock I was pooped but Leon was still going strong. Finally, I had to say *uncle* and begged him to quit for the day. Back at the motel, after dinner, I got another surprise when Leon brought all the quail into the room to clean them and to flush the unwanted remains down the toilet. We slept that night with the aroma of quail, feathers, guts, and wet dog smell permeating the room.

The next day was a repeat of the first except that I was having some intense hip pains and had to quit walking shortly after noon. A few weeks later I had my hip replaced. Ever since that operation I have told people that Leon not only walked me off my feet but he wore out my hip.

A big part of the fun was hearing Leon's stories and unique Texas sayings. As an example, in describing a rather stupid guy we ran into, Leon said, "That dog won't hunt!" It was with regret that I had to leave for my flight back to Des Moines. Leon, being the perfect host, had the quail we had bagged, frozen and over-nighted to me in Des Moines. All in all, it was an outstanding and very enjoyable hunt that I will never forget and always be grateful to Leon for providing.

Leon really loves practical jokes and played one on me that is about as good as I've ever heard or experienced. To make it work he used the services of my secretary Lynn Rappold. He told her to relay to me that he had called to tell me that he was shipping me a bird dog puppy named "Spike" that was the best of the litter from his finest dog. When Lynn told me about the puppy I instructed her to immediately call Leon back, thank him for his generosity, but tell him that there was *no way* in which I could keep a bird dog in the City of Des Moines. Lynn went to her desk to call Leon and then returned to my office to inform me that it was too late; the dog had already been shipped via airfreight and it was sitting in our receiving room at that very moment! At this point one of my guys from receiving (who was also in on the joke) burst into my office carrying a huge box. I angrily opened the box thinking I really don't want or need a dog, Leon! My receiving guy lifted the puppy out and to my amazement "Spike" was indeed a pointer, but made out of steel railroad spikes welded together. He was on point with his front leg lifted in the characteristic pose, his head erect, and his tail straight out in a classic point. He is still with me and now points the way to our home's front door on Lake Okoboji.

Leon had really sucked me in and I remember the long few moments being absolutely aghast not knowing what I could say to refuse the dog without hurting Leon's feelings. I immediately phoned him to let him know that he had indeed zinged me really well. My secretary and everyone else at the factory knew about the gag and all enjoyed my befuddled moments. At the Shot Show this past year, Leon saw fit to add a friend for Spike ~ a cute little pup that we named "Spiffy."

Leon and I are in constant contact and in 1997 he and his wonderful wife Frillie were invited to our house-warming party on Lake Okoboji. They arrived the night before the party from Texas and just like Leon with his thoughtfulness, he and Frillie pitched in to help us with the last minute preparations that certainly made the party a success. We had about two hundred guests for which Leon became a star! He had brought along his BB gun and fascinated the guests with a shooting demonstration that lasted into the night.

Leon and Frillie are now traveling around the country putting on their "Shoot Where You Look" seminars and he has marketing plans which include a web site as well as nationwide distribution. Knowing Leon and his enthusiasm, I know he will get the job done and in style.

The sixth most interesting character I have known is ROY GILMAN.

My first knowledge of Roy Gilman was when he was dating the gorgeous blonde that was the cashier at the Strand Theater where I worked in my hometown of Fort Dodge, Iowa. Martha was a blue-eyed, natural Norwegian blonde with a Victoria's Secret body and, by far, the best-looking girl in town. Back in those days the theater cashiers always sat in a separate little glass-enclosed cage well in front of the theater entrance. Most theaters tried to hire pretty girls for the job, as they were an attraction on their own. Martha was so spectacular that she caused traffic accidents on the main street in front of the Strand. Men would be driving down Main Street gawking at her and when the car in front of them stopped there would be a rear-ender.

Roy and his dad operated the Gilman Drug Store, the oldest pharmacy in town. On his own, Roy had become quite an entrepreneur and, among other things, was promoting local prizefights as well as managing some fighters. He always drove a big black Buick and was dressed impeccably. Because he was fifteen years older than me, I envied the lifestyle he led and, must admit; I was secretly envious of him being able to have the affections of a girl like Martha. Because of Roy's fighting connections he and Martha traveled all over the country to see the big fighters like Joe Louis; I thought that was pretty hot stuff! My folks didn't think much of Roy because he was on such a fast track. They also knew Martha and, after I had gone into the service, they gave her my address so she could write me letters overseas; letters that I enjoyed because she outlined all of the adventures she was having with Roy who was 4F and not able to get into the Service.

When I arrived home after the war in 1946, I found that Roy had made an honest woman out of Martha and they were married and living in a home not far from my mother and dad. They were anxious to hear of my adventures so invited me over for dinner several times and we gradually became friends. Their home was pretty exciting for someone like me. One of Roy's businesses had been the ownership of the old Princess Theater in Fort Dodge; a stage theater where most of the Broadway plays appeared until the movies came along and caused it to shut down. Roy had taken many of the mirrors, furnishings, and decorations out of the theater and placed them in his home. As an example, in the bathroom just off his party room in the basement of his house he had installed the toilet from the female star's dressing room at the old Princess. He loved to tell his guests that the most famous "prats" in show biz had sat on that stool!

At that time Roy's hobby was raising and crossbreeding roses. He had some beautiful roses and had won many garden club prizes for his hybrids. He had never hunted or shot a gun but was tremendously intrigued by the shooting I was doing. He asked me if he could accompany me to a shoot and I was able to borrow a gun so he could experience a little shooting. Well, that was all it took for Roy to get hooked on shooting. The roses fell by the wayside while he literally dove into the shooting sport. He was one of those people who doesn't do anything halfway so ended up by buying a fine shotgun and going out to the local gun club to practice regularly. Our local gun club didn't amount to much so Roy bought some great property on a bluff overlooking a Des Moines River valley north of town and built his own gun club, which was immediately the finest in Iowa. He ran some big shoots and was open for practice several days and nights a week. The grounds were kept impeccably, he offered fine food and his gun club was a vast improvement over anything else in the Middle West.

Roy was a little guy about five foot eight and 155 pounds. He had a deep voice that really carried and a crooked nose, which was the result of a punch he received from another fight promoter when they were arguing over the box-office take after a fight. He had coined a lot of phrases of his own; phrases unique to him such as, "I'm going to jump up your nose and bark like a fox" which meant, I guess, that he wanted your attention. Roy loved to drink and in later years he got pretty wild sometimes. I don't think you could call him an alcoholic in the normal definition of the word but he sure couldn't hold his liquor very well. You could almost predict some of his standard stunts after a few drinks. Going into a restaurant with Roy was like throwing a skunk in to a hen house! In a fine restaurant he'd put a towel over his arm like a waiter or maitre de and go from table to table asking people if everything was all right. That was a great way to meet girls and, I forgot to mention, that was his second big vice—women! He was literally thrown out of a restaurant in Peoria, Illinois, one night. He liked to be a "big shot" and after a few drinks would start buying drinks for everyone in a bar. One time we were shooting in Chicago and staying at the old and famous Edgewater Beach Hotel. Having drinks in their Yacht Club Bar one afternoon, he told the bartender his name was Seagram. The bartender was pretty sharp so immediately announced in a loud voice so everyone in the place could hear "Hey everybody, Mr. Seagram of the Seagram Distillery is here and wants to buy everyone in the bar a drink!" Roy was pretty shocked but went ahead and bought about twenty-five people a drink. (Drinks were only about two or three bucks back in those days so he didn't get hurt too badly.) Antics like this used to embarrass me no end so when Roy started to show signs of goofiness after a few drinks, I'd desert him.

He wasn't a very good shooter but had more fun out of

shooting than just about anyone I know. Breaking 89 out of a hundred was a thrill to him and he got just as much satisfaction out of winning class "C" as he would have in winning the whole shoot.

One last story sums up what a character he was. His drug store was one of those old-fashioned stores where the chocolates, instead of being in boxes, were stacked up in trays inside a refrigerated glass showcase. One of his employees was hooked on caramels and every time he went by the case, he'd slide the door open and filch a caramel. Roy had a peephole where he could look out into the store from the prescription department and had observed this theft of expensive candy. He warned the clerk several times but it continued. So one day Roy took a hypodermic needle and inoculated the caramels with the same laxative that is used in prescriptions to initiate an immediate bowel movement. Roy tipped off his dad and the other clerk to not sell any of those caramels and then he sat back and waited. It was only a few minutes before the clerk looked about to see if anyone was watching and then slid the door open to the case and filched another caramel. Two minutes later he was standing near the front of the store, suddenly got a stunned look on his face, and then took off running for the bathroom. While the clerk was sitting on the pot, Roy stuck his head in the door saying that he'd be fired if ever caught him stealing again.

JOE FOSS is number seven on my unforgettable characters list.

You probably know Joe better than any of the other "characters" I am listing. In addition to being an unforgettable character he tops my list of heroes. You only have to talk to Joe for a few minutes and you immediately perceive that he is a unique personality and a guy who knows where he is going all the time. Born and reared in South Dakota, he was our #1 Marine fighter pilot ace flying a Wildcat out of Guadalcanal and credited with shooting down 26 Jap planes. Of this Joe once told me that there were several other "smokers" for which he didn't get credit but he knew they never got home. I've listened to a lot of his stories and they top anything I've ever heard.

I had the pleasure of attending a banquet in his honor when he retired from the South Dakota Air National Guard. Many of his old flying buddies attended and the stories ran rampant. One I like concerned one of the four times Joe got shot down off Guadalcanal. After bailing out in his parachute he paddled ashore in his one-man raft, walked about ten miles through the jungle back to Henderson Field, got into another airplane and went up to shoot down two more Jap planes. When asked afterwards if he didn't think he'd had a day's work after being shot down, Joe replied "No, damn it I was mad!" He tells of another time when his plane was out for repairs and when the field was under attack, he jumped into another plane that, unbeknownst to Joe, had been sidelined for repairs. He barely got off the ground when it conked out and he had to crash-land it in a grove of big coconut palms. He said there were barrels of gas and other supplies stored among the palms but he luckily had picked out two rows of palms to land between that were clear but with only a few feet between his wing tips and the palms. He said God was looking out for him and he walked away from that one too.

He is a patriotic American to the core! We both served as Directors on the Board of a conservation group called the African First Shotters. Once at a Board meeting in Los Angeles it was suggested that, because of the anti-hunting slant of the media, we change our name to something that didn't sound like hunting or shooting. Joe came right up out of his chair and speaking only as he could, said, "No, I'm proud that I am a hunter and sportsman just as I'm proud to be an American. Let's leave our name as it is." That was the end of that discussion and the name stayed the same. I was proud of Joe once again.

Joe served as president of the NRA and in speeches and public appearances was quick to defend the rights of Americans to own guns. To listen to a speech or story by Joe is pure entertainment as he has words and phrases you've never heard before.

In the lobby of the airport in Sioux Falls, South Dakota is a more than life-sized bronze statue of Joe with a plaque under it that outlines his war record. The lobby has a domed ceiling and looks as though it was made to have the sculpture positioned in the middle. Instead it stands off to the side in a corner. I thought this was bad so one day when I had some time between flights I went up to the airport manager's office and asked him why Joe's sculpture wasn't in the middle where it should be. I prefaced my question with the statement that there aren't many airports that are named after heroes who are still alive. And, in addition to being a war hero, Joe was a past governor and had done more to put South Dakota on the map than any other person. I didn't get a very straight answer from the manager. I still think it should be moved to the center and will continue to write letters and talk to people who might be able to right this wrong.

He has more "kudos" after his name than anyone I know. Think of it, the biggest Marine Ace of WWII, recipient of our military's highest tribute, The Medal of Honor, two terms as Governor of South Dakota (probably could have served more if he'd wanted to), Commissioner of the American Football League, and President of the National Rifle Association. I feel very fortunate that I get to see Joe several times a year and am proud to call him a friend.

My eighth character is ALBERT CHAUGGUS.

In 1958 we constructed a new factory building a few blocks south of downtown Des Moines. On the edge of the property were three little houses that had been rented out by the former owner. Two of them were empty and we planned to tear them down. A little old man by the name of Albert Chauggus and his wife lived in the third house but I had never met them. The day after our groundbreaking ceremony several of us met on the property and were talking with our contractor. I noticed this dark-complexioned little man who came up near us and stood patiently waiting to talk to us. He asked for Mr. Allen and then introduced himself to me and asked if I was planning on tearing down his house too. He went on to explain that he was a retired construction worker and knew all about projects like ours. Advising us that theft of raw materials and tools was common on construction sites, he said that he was in an ideal spot to watch over our project and see that nothing was disturbed. He added that he didn't expect to be paid for this if we were not going to tear down his house.

Figuring we had nothing to lose, I told him we'd be pleased to have him be our watchman and assured him that we would not be razing his house but at that moment I had no idea he was going to take the watchman job so seriously. He really took over and, as a result, we had absolutely no theft on the job. Once the factory was open he asked if he couldn't continue to be our watchman and we eagerly agreed. In the meantime we had decided to not charge him any rent for the little house he was living in and this pleased him. I think the rent was probably only thirty or forty dollars a month but in return we were getting a full-fledged night watchman. Did I say Albert really took over? Well, now he really took over! We gave him keys and he periodically went through the plant to make sure all was okay. On one occasion he saved the plant. A small fire had started in one of our coin food machines in the lunchroom and the flames were just about to get into the ceiling crawl space. Albert put out the fire with an extinguisher and then called the fire department. Our alarm system would go off occasionally and Albert was always there to meet the police and save me a trip from my home. He became indispensable to me and to our employees also, as he had taken it upon himself to walk the girls to their cars in our parking lot if they had worked late. When it snowed during the day he would brush off all the car windshields for our employees.

What made him such an unforgettable character was his appearance and his way of talking. He was a full-blooded Choctaw Indian and had originally come from Oklahoma. A little man, he stood only about five foot six and had deeply tanned skin with white hair. When we first met him he was retired and in his sixties. His wife ultimately passed away and his job with us became his whole life. In the meantime we had moved him into a better house on some property we owned across the street from our plant. His old house had been torn down for a plant expansion. He loved to tell stories about his past and some of them sounded as though he might have made them up although they always came out the same. I did a video interview of him a few years later when he was in a nursing home and it is a classic.

In his working days he had been a hod carrier for a construction company. The hod carrier was the guy who carried a load of cement or bricks on his shoulder up a ladder to where the bricklayers were working. It was a brute of a job and must have been tough on little Albert. During the depression he and many of his co-workers were periodically laid off. They would hang around the Union hall hoping for jobs.

I was Albert's idol and he would do anything for me. At about age 90 he started having some problems. One night during a blizzard he got lost in the blowing snow just going the sixty yards from our factory to the door of his house. He finally found his way into the house but the next morning he didn't show up to open the doors for our employees as usual. We sent someone over to his house and they found him lying on the floor beside his bed. He'd had a small stroke but after spending a few days in the hospital he wanted to come home. He was never the same after that and finally reached a point where he could no longer care for himself. He had no relatives so our company was his family. We searched around for a nice nursing home and found one not too far from our factory. We moved Albert there but he missed seeing all our employees although he had visits from all of us regularly. He was 99 years old and enjoying pretty good health but would occasionally catch cold and it would always turn into pneumonia. A couple of times I had to give him pep talks to make him want to live. He got sick one more time and sadly I was unable to talk him out of it and he finally willed himself to die, as I understand Indians were able to do. Our people turned out for his funeral and we had him buried beside his wife. He was a wonderful little man and an absolutely unforgettable character.

Number nine on my character list is HERB PARSONS.

Herb Parsons worked for Winchester as an exhibition shooter both during and after WWII. He described himself as a hillbilly boy from Somerville, Tennessee but was proud of his roots. Herb was probably the best-known exhibition shooter since Buffalo Bill. In addition to being one of the very best trick shooters, his advantage over all the others was his showmanship. He had a line of chatter to go along with his act that kept his audiences in stitches. In the sixties Winchester made a movie of his act which was titled "The Showman Shooter." It is still being shown on TV and has since been copied onto videotape and is in wide distribution. I prize the copy I have in my video library. Several times he was called to Hollywood to do some trick shooting in western pictures. In addition to being a fine trick shot, he was also an excellent trapshooter and won some National Championships at the Grand American.

One year at the Grand American Herb pulled off one of the funniest things I've ever seen. Winchester was in the habit of furnishing their salesmen new cars every year. Herb needed a station wagon to haul all his show gear so Winchester let him make his own car trades each year. The year that air-conditioning first came out, Herb traded for a Pontiac station wagon with air conditioning. When he turned in the bill, Jack Boone, the Sales Manager for Winchester, refused to pay for the air conditioning. At the Grand American National Championship Trapshoot in Vandalia, Ohio that year Herb was scheduled to put on his shooting act. He and Jack were both staying at the Dayton Biltmore Hotel in downtown Dayton, Ohio where most of the shooters stayed. The morning after Jack Boone had flown in, he and Herb were waiting for Herb's car at the parking ramp in the hotel. Jack was planning to ride to and from the shoot with Herb. Herb's new station wagon was brought down and Jack started to get into the front seat. At that point Herb stopped him and said "Just a damn minute Jack. The ride to the gun club in the company car is free but the air conditioning is going to cost you $5.00 each way." Herb was dead serious but the laughter of all of us who were standing around embarrassed Boone into paying the $5.00.

In 1995 Herb was inducted into the Trapshooting Hall of Fame and I was deeply honored when I was asked to be the "presenter" at the Hall of Fame banquet. I told this same story plus some others about Herb. He was a wonderful friend and a tremendous booster for shooting. Unfortunately he had passed away prior to his induction so I made the presentation to his brother Dr. Parsons.

The tenth most notable character is
LEON MANDEL.

Early in the fifties, through my shooting, I had the pleasure of becoming acquainted with Leon Mandel and his wife Carola. Leon owned the Mandel Bros. Department Stores of Chicago and came from a wealthy and prestigious Chicago family. Whenever I was in Chicago Leon would invite me to lunch in the executive dining room of his department store. The sumptuous surroundings and the beautifully served luncheon impressed me tremendously; I thought I was really living! In addition to his interest in shooting, Leon was an avid polo player and traveled throughout the world playing for a Chicago polo team. It was while he was playing in Havana, Cuba that he met his wife Carola. She came from a Catholic-Spanish family, and because Leon was Jewish, it came as a surprise to many when they were married.

It was 1957, Ruthie was pregnant with Matt, our second child, and we had left our one-year-old daughter Kelly with friends, Bill and Nadine Curphy, in Dallas so we could accept an invitation from Leon and Carola for a shooting cruise on their yacht. Ruthie and I were excited about the invitation and the luxury trip we were about to take as the Mandels' guests. However, we should have known with Ruthie pregnant it would turn out to be a dreadful trip for her because the slightest rolling motion of the yacht made her seasick. It all started on the first morning at breakfast when she got a whiff of some clam juice that was being served; she beat a hasty retreat to the head where she ended up spending a lot of time on this trip.

Carola moved to Chicago where she soon found that she had a lot of time on her hands. Carola had never handled a gun before but quickly became intrigued with skeet shooting. Leon hired the club manager to give her lessons and she immediately became so hooked on skeet that she started spending several hours every day shooting. I'm told that she often shot several hundred targets a day. With her intense concentration and competitive personality it was no surprise when she started winning Chicago area skeet shoots including several Illinois State Skeet Championships. She became so good that soon she was not only winning women's events but was also beating all of the men. In 1955 at the Skeet Nationals in Dallas she won all the ladies' events, broke 248 out of 250 in the 12 gauge event and almost beat all the men. I shot in the same squad with her and was witness to seeing her tear the place up with her scores. During the years 1952 through 1958 Carola dominated both the Illnoise State Shoot and the Skeet Nationals. She captured the High Average Honors four years in a row with a 99% average.

Carola's next challenge was to shoot live pigeons. She had seen a lot of live bird shooting in Cuba and felt that this was the most exciting of the shooting sports. Leon's primary interest in shooting had always been the live pigeon shoots so soon he and Carola were following the tournament circuit. He asked me if I would coach Carola and teach her the secrets and technique of this very different type of shooting. She already knew how to handle a gun and had become a good "instinct" shooter so it was not difficult to teach her. Within a short time she became the top female pigeon shooter in the U. S. and won many women's events. In 1958 at the Championship of the World shoot in Madrid she won her first world's event at live birds.

We shot together at pigeon shoots in Land O' Lakes, Wisconsin; Maysville, Kentucky; Orleans, Indiana and in Florida as well as several places in Europe. In January of 1957 they invited my wife Ruthie and me to join them on their yacht in Palm Beach, Florida and attend shoots while living on the yacht. I use the term "yacht" rather loosely because it was 135 feet long and looked like an ocean liner to me. Leon told me that it had originally been built for the Mellon family of Pittsburgh. It was sumptuous beyond my imagination with mahogany wood and gleaming brass everywhere. It had ten staterooms and a large master suite. To get to the staterooms you descended a wide staircase from the fantail of the boat and doors to the staterooms were on both sides of a long hallway. The staterooms were ample in size but because their portholes were small and just a little above the waterline, I found the room to be claustrophobic and had difficulty sleeping. Although Leon was a gourmet chef himself the crew included a chef along with a Captain and servants. The yacht had been designed for use in rivers and the inter-coastal waterways; was of shallow draft and not suitable for taking out to sea. Leon said they had once tried to go to Cuba and it almost capsized in high seas. To provide ground transportation wherever we docked, Leon's chauffeur and a station wagon kept pace with us on land and were always there to greet us when we docked at a new port.

When not cruising, Leon and Carola lived on the boat, tied up to the Palm Beach Biltmore docks and plugged into their telephone switchboard. They did a lot of entertaining on board and generally had guests living with them. Once a year they would make a trip up the inter-coastal waterway, stopping each night to invite friends on board for dinner. When we were on the boat we went to a shoot in Tallahassee, Florida making stops at three different overnight ports. We were in awe of some of the guests who came on board. On one stop Robert MacNamara (then president of GM and later Secretary of Defense) and his wife came on board. Other guests making the trip with us included Jim Simpson and his wife Beth from Wadsworth, Illinois. Leon's idea of a hard day's schedule was to get underway about ten A. M., cruise slowly up the waterway and then tie up for the night around four in the afternoon. He would arrange over night stops at places where he had friends who would come on board for dinner. The food on board was five-star and included a big breakfast, and a brunch. The evening meal was a gastronomic delight featuring one of Leon's gourmet creations.

The dining salon had a table for twelve that ran lengthwise on the boat so that guests on both sides of the table would be looking out on the scenery. High point of the evening for me would be when, after dessert and coffee, we'd all sit back and listen to Leon's stories. He was a great storyteller and had a lifetime of unusually interesting adventures to relate.

During WWII Leon and the seagoing yacht he owned at that time were conscripted by our Navy to do secret espionage work in South American ports on the Atlantic side. His mission was to try to locate the ports where German subs were being fueled and supplied. This mission was made to order for Leon because he had been visiting those ports for years and had friends in all of them to invite on board for parties. With everyone consuming many drinks, tongues would soon start divulging information that Leon would immediately code and radio to our Navy. As a result of Leon's work many of these ports were ultimately closed to the German subs, and our Navy, which lurked outside these ports, was able to sink several of them after having been tipped off by Leon. For this fine spy work, Leon received several decorations from the U. S. Navy and I'm sure he was not paid a dime.

On another occasion, this same yacht was used for a scientific expedition to the Galapagos Islands on behalf of the Chicago Museum of Science. I'd never heard anything about those islands previously so was fascinated by his stories. Modern TV has made those islands well known to everyone now but remember, there was no TV then.

When the United States got into the war, Leon enlisted in the Army Air Corps and became an Air Transport Command pilot flying all over the world. He had many exciting experiences and enjoyed telling about them. He had some particularly funny stories about experiences in Tangiers and other North African places.

The yacht was so tall that all the drawbridges on the

inter-coastal had to be lifted for us to pass. I remember being embarrassed, while we were sunbathing on the top deck, by the dirty looks we'd get from people in the traffic jam of cars held up by the drawbridges. I could almost feel the animosity those motorists must have felt towards us rich dudes holding them up with our fancy yacht!

For a "poor boy" from Iowa these were pretty heady experiences and I have always been grateful to Leon and Carola for the hospitality they extended. We were treated royally and as equals with the other guests who were generally wealthy socialites. We spent two weeks on the yacht and when the pigeon shoot at Tallahassee was over, we caught an airline back to Dallas where we had left our one-year-old daughter Kelly with our friends. We continued to see Leon and Carola at shoots everywhere including Italy and Spain. Carola was an experienced pigeon shooter by now and one to be reckoned with. Leon's vision was deteriorating and his shooting suffered to the point where he stopped entering the shoots and devoted his time to coaching Carola and entertaining all of us. Sadly, Leon passed away unexpectedly at an early age and shortly thereafter Carola dropped out of shooting. She still resides in Palm Beach and we exchange Christmas Cards each year. Leon definitely qualified as one of my favorite "characters" and they were an unforgettable pair!

Chapter 17

Pivotal Points

My success in life was often due to the kindness of people who were interested in me and who stepped forward to show me another path or a new way. Each person's intervention proved to be a turning point in my life. It took me a long time to understand why certain people extended a helping hand, but once I understood the satisfaction connected with being of help, I have tried to emulate their example.

Phil Miller

In 1940 and 1941 when I first tried my skills at shooting tournaments, Phil Miller took me under his wing, giving me shooting tips and a huge amount of encouragement. I guess he enjoyed my eagerness and enthusiasm. Most people in his position would not give me the time of day. I was just a kid from Iowa starting out at the bottom of the game, while Phil was at the top. He was one of the top three shooters in the country, traveled with his wife and pet dog in a big Buick station wagon; a man with a incredibly warm personality. He had once served as Lt. Governor of Texas and possessed a magnificent speaking voice with a Texas drawl that really intrigued me. Plus I grew up admiring impeccable dressers and Phil was one of the best.

Several times while we were shooting in the same squad, Phil would give me a little tip as we walked past each other to change posts. Most good shooters would never risk breaking their own concentration to help anybody else. Then, after the event was over, Phil would often sit me down and tell me how I might improve my shooting. In a few instances he took me to a side trap in order to coach me through a practice round.

When WWII broke out, Phil was given a direct commission in the Army Air Corps gunnery program with the specific job of recruiting top shooters across the United States in order to staff the gunnery schools. Many gunners would be needed for the amount of bombers being planned. Phil tried to recruit me but I had my heart set on becoming a pilot and had already enlisted in the Aviation Cadet program. When I washed out of that program in the fall of 1942, I called on Phil to get me transferred into his gunnery program. He came through for me like the champ that he was, even though he had to break through many obstacles that neither of us expected.

After the war when I began to try to make a living by following shooting tournaments, once again Phil was there for me with shooting tips and his friendship. Phil passed away many years ago and I don't know if I ever made him understand how he played a pivotal role in the path my life would take toward succeed. I don't know if I ever thanked him enough. Phil, I hope you are tuned into what I am writing here and know you will always be my hero.

Lt. Harold A. Bates

After washing out of pilot training I was sent to the dreaded *Unassigned Pool* at Minter Field near Bakersfield, California.

A turning point came one day when I heard shotgun shooting somewhere on the base. I walked around the airport until I discovered a skeet range. Lt. Bates, the range Officer, observed me watching with drool on my chin and asked me if I'd like to shoot. Boy, did I ever! When I luckily broke a 25 straight, something that wasn't done around there too often, he and the squad congratulated me profusely. That gave me an opportunity to relate to him my story. Could he rescue me from the Unassigned Pool until Phil Miller was able to get me transferred into the Gunnery School Program. Lt. Bates immediately suggested that a transfer to his Ordinance Department would hold me at Minter Field until my gunnery school transfer could be arranged. Besides, he told me with a smile, "I desperately need a skeet instructor!" There is absolutely no doubt in my mind that he saved me from being transferred out of the Unassigned Pool to some undesirable assignment. I shall always be indebted to this kindly man!

Harold Russell

Harold was Vice President of Sales for Federal Cartridge Company of Anoka, Minnesota. I had shot with him several times prior to the war and as I was struggling to build my business after WWII, Harold and I became better acquainted. I think he perceived at once that I was going to have a tough time getting my business started. And in 1946 shotgun shells, which had been virtually non-existent during the war, were suddenly in big demand. Knowing that I needed help to get started, Harold offered to give me some priority in buying a carload of Federal shells. I was able to sell them on the phone in just a few days and the tidy profit I made helped to launch my business. This was a tremendous boost for me and I appreciated the fact that Harold really went out-on-a-limb selling me the shells when he had many established distributors who should have been given first priority. My back will never forget unloading this carload of shells Harold. Thanks for helping me with the birth of my business.

Frank Miles

Frank was President of the huge American Uniform Co. with sewing factories all over the country. At the end of the

war the government chose him as one of our industrial ambassadors and sent him to Japan and Taiwan to facilitate their
setting up a sewing industry. Frank was one of a group of business leaders who were called "dollar-a-year-men" because that
was all they were paid for their consulting work in the Orient.

I had met Frank through shooting and he knew of my
efforts to get my shooting-clothing designs manufactured.
Like a father he took me under his wing and advised me on
every facet of the sewing industry. He invited me to tour some
of his factories in Tennessee and helped me develop patterns
by having his designers work on them, as well as being instrumental in getting me sources for cloth and other raw materials. I received advice and assistance from him that I never
could have afforded had I gone to a consulting firm. There is
no doubt that Frank also made the birth of Bob Allen
Sportswear possible. I can never thank him enough and I only
wish that he were still alive so my children and grandchildren
could also thank him.

Fred Horton

Although not a shooter, Fred was an avid hunter and
showed tremendous interest in my fledgling company. As Vice
President of Sales Promotion for National Broadcasting
Company, he handled many promotions for some of the companies that advertised on NBC. Most of these promotions
included skeet or trapshooting events and Fred would always
buy a lot of our clothing and bags for the participants in each
of these tournaments. We received a tremendous amount of
advertising from this T.V. coverage, plus Fred was always coming up with new ideas for our products. Wherever possible he
tried to get the Bob Allen name featured on NBC's shows. He
even arranged for me to be a guest on their "Good Morning"
show back in the days when Dave Garroway was the host.
When ever I traveled to New York he and his wife would
always entertain me. In his company, I went places and saw
things that I otherwise never would have experienced in my
lifetime. He was a delightful man who thoroughly enjoyed

helping others. I really missed him. His closing words to me on the phone were always, "Look out for the trolley cars!"

Paul Rodgers

As Vice President of Ozark Air Lines, Paul was the very first person in the airline industry I contacted when I wanted a license to use their name on our new line of Jr. Flight Bags. Paul shared my excitement over these little bags and recognized immediately the tremendous free advertising exposure they would give the airlines. He instantly signed our exclusive agreement and proceeded to instruct me in the proper way to contact other airline executives; he even went so far as to phone them in order to pave my way. With his help and encouragement we were able to sign up over a hundred airlines in our flight bag merchandising program.

Each year the Regional Airlines Association would hold a meeting. Only the President and top two or three executives from each airline were allowed to attend. However, Paul invited me to attend each year as his personal guest. Ozark maintained the Playboy Club's DC-9 jet, so we flew it to the convention held one year at the Greenbrier Hotel in White Sulphur Springs, West Virginia. The executives and their wives from two other regional airlines were on board. Meeting these people in this type of relaxed and privileged environment was to prove to be quite a valuable asset for my business.

Paul was an articulate and entertaining public speaker for the airline industry and was called upon to give keynote speeches at prestigious airline conventions all over the world. He had a way of inserting humor in his speeches that always captivated audiences. One of his stock jokes was about a passenger who was disgruntled over a delay on take-off, probably caused by the pilot awaiting an instrument clearance. The passenger grabbed the flight attendant as she walked the aisle and told her, "Go up to the cockpit and ask that blockhead pilot why we are waiting so long to take off!" The flight attendant took an about-face toward the cockpit, and a few minutes later she returned to the passenger to report. "The pilot told me to tell you that he is going to take off just as soon as he gets up enough courage."

Paul had many job offers from larger airlines but loved Ozark so much he turned them all down. He thoroughly enjoyed his job and was a perfect public relations ambassador for "good old Ozark." Twice Paul was passed over on a promotion to be President of Ozark. In each case he didn't get the promotion not because he wasn't capable but because in his present job, they felt he was irreplaceable. They could find a new President who would be bound to a desk easier then they could find another Paul as Executive Vice President who really was Mr. Ozark in the public's eye and therefore an irreplaceable sales promotion manager.

William H. O'Donnell

In our Airline Textile division, United Airlines was our biggest customer for many years. Bill was their Sales Promotion Manager and over a period of years we became close friends. Always receptive to new ideas, he and I put together a mail order catalog, which was placed, in the seat pockets of all United aircraft. This was a first for the entire airline industry and enabled us to form our Travel House Division, which ultimately administrated these seat-pocket catalog programs for eleven airlines. Bill was also responsible for the invention of our R.O.N., Remain Over Night, toilet kits which airlines gave out to people who had lost their luggage. Bill helped us to get to almost all the airlines to adopt the R.O.N. kits and they became an important percentage of our sales volume.

Bill had a great sense of humor and was always putting people on. When I first started working with him I had a difficult time reading him; at times he could have a poker face and would say something off the wall to see if you were paying attention or to get a rise out of you. Bill made himself a sort of unofficial salesman for my company. In his travels—to kill time between flights he would check the airport gift shops to make sure they were caring our United Flight Bags. In talking to the managers he'd tell them that Bob Allen—the owner of the company was a multi-millionaire playboy who flew around the country in his own airplane—needless to say the next time I hit that gift shop I was treated with a new kind of "respect!" It was great fun being associated with Bill and I'll never forget the advice and help he gave me.

David Belin

Dave was my first lawyer and advised me for almost fifty years, through, as they say, "thick and thin." Dave was the most intelligent man I have ever known. He had a memory like a bear trap and could recall details about my business that even I failed to remember. The advice he gave me was always right on and the agreement contracts he prepared for us stood the test of time. The only instances that I ever made a mistake in business were when I failed to heed Dave's advice. When the time came to sell my business, Dave handled the negotiations and hammered out a deal for me that was far beyond my expectations.

An unusual man, David was first violin for the Des Moines Symphony Orchestra, headed up an organization that was tracking down perpetrators of the holocaust, and yet had time to be a great family man. Dave, you are profoundly missed. You were the greatest!

Homer Clark Jr.

In 1946 when I decided to take my shooting seriously and try to make a living from my winnings, Homer was already the top live pigeon shooter in the United States and, in just a few years, proved himself to be the best in the world. The only American ever to win the Championship of the World twice, Homer was also a great trap shooter and is in the Trapshooting Hall of Fame to prove it. He quickly became my idol in the shooting world and, as we traveled around the country shooting, we became good friends.

Although we were competitors, Homer became my coach and I could count on him to pinpoint any problem I was having with my shooting. As I mentioned earlier, being able to

An interesting group at the 1988 Grand American Trapshoot. L to R: Bob Allen, Dave Yeager, Paul Tibbets, and two of the greatest shots in the world—Rudy Etchen & Homer Clark.

split shoot winnings with Homer enabled me to finance my marriage to Ruthie.

As time went on Homer and I became closer friends, hunting and shooting together for many years. I could always count on him for great advice and I don't think my business could have grown as it did without his wise input.

My father, Martin J. Allen

Although my dad's education in Ireland was probably only through the eighth grade and he had no formal business training, his example of hard work, devotion to family, and great integrity were invaluable models for me to emulate. Both he and my mother were quick to compliment me on tasks well done and they were constantly urging me to get ahead.

He taught me that my word is my bond and that there is no deviation from basic honesty. He had many original sayings and one that I remember vividly is his statement that "no matter how hard you try, you can't press your pants with a hammer!" Another time when he was remonstrating me for having stayed out too late he made the remark that "no matter what you are trying to do, if you can't get it done by midnight, you better go home and go to bed!"

His piano store was a small one-man operation but he operated it on the premise that the customer was always right and that he must give the customer proper service after the sale has been made. As a result of this dedication, this small businessman made a great reputation for himself throughout northwest Iowa. I am very proud of him and thankful for his influence. Like most kids, I really didn't appreciate what an unusual and wonderful man he was until I grew older. Many times in my life I have thought of his courage and determination and these examples have served me well in my life.

I am old enough to remember the great depression of 1929 through 1932 and I can't begin to know how dad weathered the strain of trying to support a family in those times. And then, when mother passed away, I don't know how he handled the loneliness of his life. He is my beloved dad who will always be alive in my memory.

It would be remiss of me if I didn't admit that there were many other people who also helped me through my life. The ten I have mentioned here are those who created, through their generosity, brotherhood, and love tremendous changes in my life; each a major turning point. Please forgive me if I have overlooked anyone.

Lifetime Shooting Record
Bob "Shooter" Allen

Appendix A

➤Iowa State Trapshooting Association, Hall of Fame—1970

➤Amatuer Trapshooting Association, Hall of Fame—1982

➤International Flyer (Pigeon) Shooting, Hall of Fame—1996
- (Induction – Portugal)

➤Des Moines Register - Iowa Sports, Hall of Fame—1997

➤Iowa Skeet & Trapshooting Championships—1950
- Only Iowa shooter to win
  both events in the same year

➤Iowa State Skeet Shooting Championships
- 18 Wins

➤Iowa State Trapshooting Championships
- 15 Wins - A record that stands today

➤All American Trapshooting Team
- 11 Years
➤Iowa State Trapshooting Team
- 13 Years

➤W.W. II – Staff Officer for the 20th Air Force
- Stationed on Tinian & Guam

➤Member of the Air Force Western Pacific Championship Skeet Team

Major Tournaments & Events

Appendix B

➢International Clay Target Championship—Havana, Cuba, 1949

➢World's All Around Shotgun Championship—Orleans, Indiana, —won twice—1957 & 1958

➢Match Of Nations – US Team Member—Monte Carlo, 1951

➢National Championship – Five Man Team—Grand American, 1951

➢Grand Prix de Paris—Monte Carlo—1951

➢Grand Prix de France—Paris, 1956

➢National Doubles Shooting Championship—Grand American 1957

➢World's Record – Five Man Squad—Grand American, 1957

➢Trapshooting Championships Won in 15 different States 1947-1960

Iowa	Texas
Oklahoma	Kansas
Nebraska	South Dekota
Wisconsin	Illinois
Indiana	Missouri
Michigan	Minnesota
Ohio	

➢Flash Cup – US Team Member—Poitier, France, 1991

Additional Achievements
Bob "Shooter" Allen

Appendix C

Bob Allen Sportswear Company founded, 1946

> Manufacturer of shooting and hunting clothing and accessories. Revolutionized outdoor clothing with patented original designs.

Airline Textile Manufacturing Company (Air-Tex) founded, 1956

> Manufacturer of custom bags and luggage.

Travel House – founded 1962

> Administrated Seat Pocket Mail Order Programs for Airlines.

Sold Companies and retired, 1995

> Small Business Man of the Year, 1966
> Chairman, African First Shotters, 1972
> Chairman, One Shot Antelope Association, 1974
> Chairman, Iowa Manufacturers Association, 1980
> Director, Iowa Lutheran Hospital Board, 1985

Greatest Achievement—Family

3 Children:	Kelly, Matt, Abby
8 Grandchildren:	Brook, Katie, Chip, George, Chad, Lizzy, Trey, Taylor